Crete

Victoria Kyriakopoulos

Contents

Hania p74

Rethymno p119

Iraklio p144

Lasithi p178

Destination Crete

Like no other Greek island, Crete welcomes and overwhelms visitors with its wealth of myths, legends and history, a blessed and dramatic landscape, and an abundance of choices and experiences. The legendary birthplace of Zeus, Greece's largest island continues to hold endless appeal, despite the onslaught of mass tourism.

You can escape the crowds and find tranquillity quickly enough, and the sheer diversity of the landscape makes Crete a delight to explore. Its stunning mountains ranges are dotted with caves and sliced by dramatic gorges, and its rugged interior is interspersed with fertile plains and hillsides blanketed in olive groves, wild flowers and aromatic herbs. Breathtaking drives along the rugged south coast lead to a sun-drenched paradise of long sandy beaches and isolated coves.

Crete's natural beauty is equalled only by the richness of a culture that spans millennia and provides endless fodder for history and archaeology buffs. The palace of Knossos is the most famous vestige of the glorious Minoan civilisation that once ruled the Aegean, but a profusion of evocative ruins reveal Crete's turbulent past, from Roman settlements and Byzantine chapels to Venetian ports and Ottoman mansions. In the charming old towns of Hania and Rethymno, Venetian mansions have been turned into elegant hotels, while on the north coast you'll find luxury resorts, spas, golf courses and nightlife.

While the pragmatic Cretans have succumbed to tourism on a grand scale, they still fiercely protect their traditions and maintain a profound attachment to the traditions, songs, dances and cuisine that have forged their identity. Crete's proud, friendly and hospitable people remain a major part of the island's appeal.

DIANA MAYFIELD

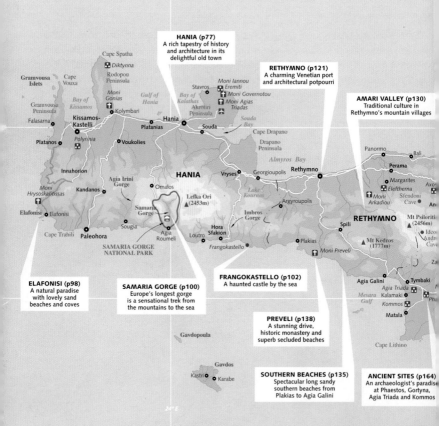

ELEVATION

2000m
1500m
1000m
500m
0

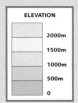

0 ———————— 20 km
0 ———————— 12 miles

SEA OF CRETE

HANIA (p77)
A rich tapestry of history
and architecture in its
delightful old town

RETHYMNO (p121)
A charming Venetian port
and architectural potpourri

AMARI VALLEY (p130)
Traditional culture in
Rethymno's mountain villages

Cape Spatha

Diktynna

Rodopou
Peninsula

Cape
Vouxa

Gramvousa
Islets

Gramvousa
Peninsula

Bay of
Kissamos

Moni
Gonias

Kolymbari

Stavros
Bay of
Kalathas

Moni Iannou
Eremiti
Moni Governotou
Moni Agias
Triadas

Akrotiri
Peninsula

Panormo   Bali

Falasarna

Kissamos-
Kastelli

Gulf of
Hania

Hania

Platanias

Souda

Perama

Margarites

Axos

Platanos

Innahorion

Polyrria

Voukolies

Souda
Bay

Cape Drapano

Drapano
Peninsula

Almyros Bay

Georgioupolis Rethymno

Eleftherna
Moni
Arkadiou   Sfendoni
Cave

An

Moni
Hrysoskalitissas

Agia Irini
Gorge

Kandanos

HANIA

Omalos

Lefka Ori
▲(2453m)

Vryses

Lake
Kournas

Argyroupolis

Spili

RETHYMNO

Mt Psiloriti
▲(2456m)

Ideo
Andr
Cave

Elafonisi   Elafonisi

Cape Trahili Paleohora

Sougia

Samaria
Gorge

Agia
Roumeli

Imbros
Gorge

Hora
Sfakion

Loutro

Frangokastello

Plakias

Moni Preveli

Mt Kedros
(1777m)

Za

SAMARIA GORGE
NATIONAL PARK

Agia Galini

Mesara
Gulf

Tymbaki

Kalamaki

Kommos

Agia Triada
Pha

ELAFONISI (p98)
A natural paradise
with lovely sand
beaches and coves

SAMARIA GORGE (p100)
Europe's longest gorge
is a sensational trek from
the mountains to the sea

FRANGOKASTELLO (p102)
A haunted castle by the sea

Matala

Cape Lithino

Gavdopoula

PREVELI (p138)
A stunning drive,
historic monastery and
superb secluded beaches

Gavdos

Kastri   Karabe

SOUTHERN BEACHES (p135)
Spectacular long sandy
southern beaches from
Plakias to Agia Galini

ANCIENT SITES (p164)
An archaeologist's paradise
at Phaestos, Gortyna,
Agia Triada and Kommos

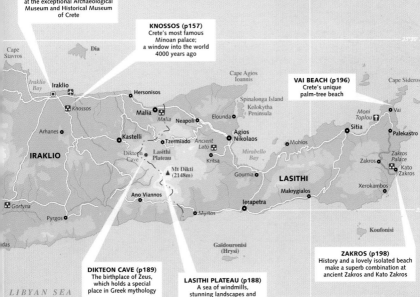

IRAKLIO (p147)
A crash course in Cretan history at the exceptional Archaeological Museum and Historical Museum of Crete

KNOSSOS (p157)
Crete's most famous Minoan palace; a window into the world 4000 years ago

VAI BEACH (p196)
Crete's unique palm-tree beach

DIKTEON CAVE (p189)
The birthplace of Zeus, which holds a special place in Greek mythology

LASITHI PLATEAU (p188)
A sea of windmills, stunning landscapes and authentic rural towns

ZAKROS (p198)
History and a lovely isolated beach make a superb combination at ancient Zakros and Kato Zakros

Crete is steeped in history and the ruins of the palaces from its unique Minoan civilisation are one of the most enthralling attractions of the island. Apart from the unmissable **Knossos** (p157), the most significant Minoan sites are the palaces of **Phaestos** (p165) in the south, **Malia** (p175) in the northeast and **Zakros** (p198) on the southeastern coast. Other significant Minoan sites include the ruins of a villa at **Agia Triada** (p167), the best-preserved Minoan town of **Gournia** (p191) and the yet-to-be unearthed palace at **Palekastro** (p197). Most of the finds from excavations are in the outstanding collection of the **Archaeological Museum of Iraklio** (p149). Important archaeological sites from later periods include the large and impressive Roman site at **Gortyna** (p164).

NEIL SETCHFIELD

Check out the island's finest relics at the Archaeological Museum of Iraklio (p149)

Explore the ruins of the Late Minoan town of Gournia (p191)

JON DAVISON

Experience the majesty of the Minoan world at the reconstructed site of Knossos (p157)

See the timeless techniques of frescoe painting at the Palace of Knossos (p157)

Marvel at the quality of artefacts unearthed at ancient Malia (p175)

Crete is renowned for its remarkable natural beauty. **Samaria Gorge** (p100) is traversed by hundreds of thousands of visitors each year, while the stunning **Imbros Gorge** (p118) is among the many other gorges than can be walked. The spectacular **Lefka Ori** (p98) mountains cut through central Crete. Inland, the windmills of the **Lasithi Plateau** (p188) are a sight to behold, while the scenic **Amari Valley** (p130) takes you through traditional villages. Crete's best beaches include the palm-fringed **Vai Beach** (p196), **Elafonisi** (p98) and and the remote beaches at **Preveli** (p138) and **Agios Pavlos** (p139). The springs of **Argyroupolis** (p128) are a delightful watery oasis.

NEIL SETCHFIELD

Take in some rays by the famous palm forest at Vai beach (p196)

Swim in the cool protected waters at Preveli Beach (p138)

STELLA HELLANDER

Release your inner hippie at the ancient caves of Matala (p169)

JON DAVISON

Drink in the vistas in the hills
around Imbros Gorge (p118)

Hike the spectacular Samaria Gorge (p100)

Plan a journey into the rugged and beautiful Lefka Ori Mountains (p98)

A glorious mix of East and West is on show across the island. **Hania** (p77) is Crete's most beautiful city, its harbour lined with well-preserved Venetian and Ottoman buildings. In **Rethymno** (p121), the massive fortress dominat the town's Venetian port. In the south you can swim in front of the castle on the beach at **Frangokastello** (p102) and in the east, a boat takes you to the island fortress at **Spinalonga** (p187). Living treasures can be found in the monasteries scattered throughout Crete, including **Moni Preveli** (p137), the fortress-like **Moni Toplou** (p196) and **Moni Arkadiou** (p130).

Hear the peals of Moni Arkadiou's triple-belled tower (p130)

JOHN ELK III

PAUL DAVID HELLANDER

Blink in the glare of the white-washed chapel at Moni Preveli (p137)

Tour the forbidding walls of the Venetian fortress at Frangokastello (p102)

NEIL SETCHFIELD

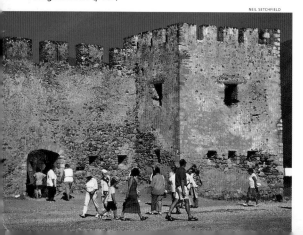

View the old city from the walls of
Iraklio's Koules Venetian fortress (p152)

NEIL SETCHFIELD

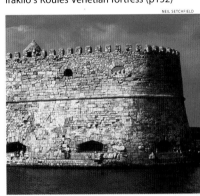

GLENN BEANLAND

Gaze up at the lighthouse that graces
Rethymno's Venetian harbour (p121)

Wander along Hania's waterfront of bars, clubs and tavernas (p85)

JOHN ELK III

Crete is renowned for its hospitable and fiery-spirited people, but it's best to get out of the big cities and tourist haunts if you want to appreciate the distinct cultural differences. You can get a sense of rural life in the villages of **Anogia** (p132) and **Spili** (p134), or the less-visited villages of the **Innahorion** (p95) region. Many formerly dying villages are being restored to offer an alternative experience for tourists, with traditional-style settlements at **Vamos** (p116) or environmentally friendly village accommodation at **Milia** (p97) and **Aspros Potamos** (p204). The northeast coastal town of **Sitia** (p193) and **Ierapetra** (p201) in the south are pleasant places that don't rely on tourism, so offer a more authentic experience.

Drink from a Venetian water spout in the village square at Spili (p134)

PAUL DAVID HELLANDER

VICTORIA KYRIAKOPOULOS

Cut the cards in a *kafeneio* in the village of Anogia (p132)

Relax at the tranquil beachside village of Kato Zakros (p199)

PAUL DAVID HELL

Getting Started

Going to Crete is almost like going to a small country and it is virtually impossible to cover the whole island, even if you have a month or two. The mountainous interior means you have to zigzag up and down the long and narrow island, although the bonus of this is seeing some spectacular landscapes, remote villages and fascinating archaeological sites on your way to that remote southern beach. The distances aren't always huge, but winding through mountains can be hard going so you need to be realistic about how far you can get in one day.

It is important that you plan ahead and decide what want to see and then choose a good base from which to explore. You will probably need to choose between the east and west – which also gives you an excuse to go again. The best way to see Crete is by car or motorbike, but an extensive part of the island is accessible by bus.

Crete is not as cheap as it used to be, but you can find good-value accommodation and food, particularly in the less-developed south. Greeks love children so travelling with kids is easier here than in many places.

WHEN TO GO
The best times to visit Crete are in late spring/early summer and in autumn when the weather is not too hot and the summer hordes of tourists have left. Conditions are perfect between Easter and mid-June, when the weather is pleasantly warm in most places; beaches and ancient sites are relatively uncrowded; public transport operates on close to full schedules; and accommodation is cheaper and easy to find. Spring and autumn are also the best time for trekking and other outdoor activities.

The first tourists start to arrive in Crete around Easter. The high season kicks in around mid-June until the end of August. In some places during August, accommodation is booked solid and is much more expensive.

In July and August the mercury can soar to 40°C (100°F) in the shade. Not surprisingly, the island's beaches get very crowded, with the heat making it tough for traipsing around archaeological sites or enjoying scenic walks. There's usually no rain at all and the sea temperature hovers at a comfortable 25°C.

DID YOU KNOW?

Crete has 300 days of sunshine every year, making it the sunniest island in the Mediterranean after Cyprus. It also stays warm off its southern coast from mid-April to November.

See Climate Chart (p209) for more information on rainfall and temperature ranges throughout the year.

DON'T LEAVE HOME WITHOUT...

Sturdy shoes are essential for clambering around ancient sites and wandering through historic towns and villages, which tend to have lots of steps and cobbled streets.

A day pack is useful for the beach and for sightseeing or trekking. A compass is essential if you are going to trek in remote areas, as is a whistle, which you can use should you become lost or disoriented. A torch (flashlight) is not only needed if you intend to explore caves, but also comes in handy during occasional power cuts. If you like to fill a washbasin or bathtub (a rarity in Crete), bring a universal plug as plugs are uncommon.

Many camping grounds in Crete have covered areas where tourists without tents can sleep in summer, so you can get by with a lightweight sleeping bag and foam bedroll.

You will need only light clothing – preferably cotton – during the summer months. During spring and autumn (and summer if you are in the mountains) you'll need a light sweater or jacket in the evening.

In summer, a broad-brimmed sunhat and sunglasses are essential. Sunscreens are relatively expensive in Crete, as are moisturising and cleansing lotions.

July and August are also the months of the *meltemi*, a strong northerly wind that sweeps along the eastern coast of mainland Greece through the Aegean Islands, the Cyclades and Crete. The wind is caused by air pressure differences between North Africa and the Balkans. The wind is a mixed blessing: it reduces humidity but plays havoc with ferry schedules. Between May and August you may encounter the sirocco wind, which blows up from Africa bringing dust and sand. The air becomes stifling, but fortunately the wind only lasts from 24 to 72 hours.

The tourist season starts to wind down in September, and conditions are ideal once more until the end of October. Most of the tourist infrastructure goes into hibernation from November until the beginning of April.

LP INDEX

Litre of petrol/gas €0.85

Litre of bottled water €0.90

Can of Amstel beer €0.90

Souvenir T-shirt €15

Souvlaki €1.80

COSTS & MONEY

Crete is cheap by northern European standards, but it is no longer dirt cheap, especially in the high season (July and August). The following budgets are for individuals; couples sharing a double room can get by on less.

A rock-bottom daily budget would be €25 to €30. This would mean hitching, staying in youth hostels or camping, staying away from bars, and only occasionally eating in restaurants or taking ferries.

TOP FIVES

FESTIVALS & EVENTS

The Cretans take their festive occasions very seriously and use any excuse to get together for a big meal, good company, music and free-flowing raki. There are festivals dedicated to snails, chestnuts and potatoes, as well as religious and cultural events. For a comprehensive list of festivals see p211.

- Feast of Agios Georgos (St George), Asi Gonia (April 23)
- Easter Festivities, mountain villages (March–April)
- Renaissance Festival, Rethymno (July–September)
- Sultana Festival, Sitia (August)
- Cretan Weddings, Anogia (any time)

TOP READS

Crete's most famous author is Nikos Kazantzakis, whose classic *Zorba the Greek* gives the definitive insight into the Greek male psyche of yore (we think), while the island has inspired many tales of love, war, drama and foreigners writing about their time on the island. See p50 for more background on Cretan literature.

- *Zorba the Greek* by Nikos Kazantzakis
- *Freedom and Death* by Nikos Kazantzakis
- *Crete* by Barry Unsworth
- *The Cretan Runner* by George Psychoundakis
- *The Life of Ismail Ferik Pasha* by Rhea Galanaki

BEACHES

Crete has some stunning beaches and the best are normally the hardest to get to, but the following are all fairly accessible, with a bit of a walk.

- Balos, Gramvousa Peninsula, Hania (p95)
- Agios Pavlos & Triopetra, Rethymno (p139)
- Vai, Lasithi (p196)
- Elafonisi, Hania (p98)
- Falasarna, Hania (p94)

Allow at least €50 per day in the summer for a simple room, meals in local tavernas, drinks at night and some sightseeing. Outside of the high season you could get by on about 25% less.

If you really want a holiday – comfortable rooms and restaurants all the way – you will need closer to €60 per day.

TRAVEL LITERATURE

Crete is the subject of numerous travelogues and books.

Crete, by Barry Unsworth, is a well-written contemporary travelogue linking past and present, written by the acclaimed author as part of National Geographic's literary travel series by prominent writers.

Still Life in Crete, by Anthony Cox, is a humorous and offbeat look at migration from Kent to Crete by an early retired British couple. It is big on food and wine and tongue-in-cheek observations of life away from the grey skies of England.

Winds of Crete, by David MacNeill Doren, is widely available on Crete. It's an amusing account of island life as experienced by an American and his Swedish wife.

The Colossus of Maroussi, by Henry Miller, is now regarded as a classic. Miller relates his travels in Crete at the outbreak of WWII with feverish enthusiasm.

Across Crete, by Richard Pokocke, Robert Pashley, Captain Spratt and Edward Lear and edited by Johan de Bakker, is the first of a three-part series that takes the traveller from Hania to Iraklio as seen through the eyes of the 18th- and 19th-century British travellers.

INTERNET RESOURCES

Lonely Planet (www.lonelyplanet.com) has information on Crete, as well as travel news, updates to our guidebooks and links to other travel resources. You may also find these sites useful:

Explore Crete (www.explorecrete.com) Good general travel site for Crete.

GNTO (www.greektourism.com) Greek National Tourism Organization, which has a page for Crete.

Greek Ferries (www.ferries.gr) Greek ferry schedules.

InfoCrete (www.infocrete.com) A site with about 100 Crete tourist-site web links.

Interkriti (www.interkriti.gr) Links to hotels, apartments, shops and restaurants, as well as an active bulletin board.

KTEL (www.ktel.org) Maps and schedules of buses around the island.

Stigmes (www.forthnet.gr/stigmes/destcret.htm) Insightful Crete magazine.

West Crete (www.west-crete.com) Comprehensive guide to western Crete.

HOW MUCH?

Packet of 20 cigarettes €2.70

An iced cappuccino €3

A Greek salad €3.50

10-minute taxi ride €11

One night at a 3-star hotel €75

Itineraries
CLASSIC ROUTES

BEST OF CRETE – THE EAST
12 to 14 Days / 480km

The eastern half of the island boasts Crete's most famous Minoan archaeological sites and the island's top resorts. Starting in **Iraklio** (p147), make the obligatory visit to **Knossos** (p157) before seeing Crete's wine country around **Arhanes** (p161). Along the north coast visit the **Palace of Malia** (p176) before cutting inland to the stunning **Lasithi Plateau** (p188), stopping at the **Dikteon Cave** (p189). Continuing east you can visit the village of **Kritsa** (p190) on the way to the resort town of **Agios Nikolaos** (p181). Head north past the exclusive resorts of **Elounda** (p185) and take a boat to the fortress of **Spinalonga Island** (p187). Heading back east consider a detour to the fish tavernas in **Mohlos** (p192). The pleasant town of **Sitia** (p193) is worth a stop, as is **Moni Toplou** (p196) on the way to the palms at **Vai Beach** (p196).

Travelling south, combine a visit to the **Palace of Zakros** (p198) with a stay at the beach at **Kato Zakros** (p199). Continue south along the driveable dirt road to **Xerokambos beach** (p200) before heading along the southern coast to **Ierapetra** (p201). Head inland via the village of **Ano Viannos** (p172) to the important archaeological sites of **Gortyna** (p164) and **Phaestos** (p165), trailing off to the southern beaches at **Kastri** and **Keratokambos** (p173) and **Lendas** (p172) on the way. Cool off near the hippie caves at **Matala** (p169) or at nearby **Kalamaki** (p171). A visit to the excellent folk museum at **Vori** (p167) is a worthwhile detour. Head north to **Zaros** (p163) a walk through the lovely **Rouvas Gorge** (p163) before driving back to Iraklio.

This route takes in the island's major archaeological sites, remote beaches and mountain villages. You could only cover this much ground in two weeks with your own transport. The distance covered is about 480km.

SEA OF CRETE

LIBYAN SEA

BEST OF CRETE – THE WEST
12 to 14 Days / 500km

This itinerary covers some of Crete's most stunning natural attractions, the unspoilt southern coast, unique villages and its two most attractive towns. Starting in **Iraklio** (p147), head inland to **Anogia** (p132) and the villages and caves at the foothills of **Mt Psiloritis** (p130), where you can link up with the **E4 trail** (p58) for an ascent to the summit. Stop past the pottery village of **Margarites** (p131) and the historic **Moni Arkadiou** (p130) before spending some time in the Venetian port of **Rethymno** (p119) with its 16th-century fortress. Heading south, the fountains at **Spili** (p134) make a good coffee stop before a visit to **Moni Preveli** (p137) and **Preveli Beach** (p138). From here you could continue east to the stunning southern beaches of **Triopetra** (p139) and **Agios Pavlos** (p139) or head west to the traveller hang-out of **Plakias** (p135) and the beachfront fortress of **Frangokastello** (p102).

Heading west through the Kourtoulioti Gorge you come to the coastal port of **Hora Sfakion** (p101). You can either take a boat trip along the southern coast to **Loutro** (p103) or **Sougia** (p106) and double back, or take the steep zigzagging road north to the Lefka Ori along the **Imbros Gorge** (p118) to the mountain village of **Askyfou** (p117). Spend at least a day in Crete's most alluring town, **Hania** (p77).

To the north, the **Akrotiri Peninsula** (p87) has some lovely monasteries and the famous beach at **Stavros** (p88) where *Zorba the Greek* was filmed. Take the circular route southwest via **Kolymbari** (p91) and **Elos** (p96), and the villages of **Innahorion** (p95), to the westernmost tip of the island at **Elafonisi** (p98).

Return to Hania via the coastal road, detouring to **Falasarna** (p94) and north to the **Gramvousa Peninsula** (p95) to the spectacular beach at **Balos** (p95). Returning east it's worth stopping at the springs of **Argyroupolis** (p128), southwest of Rethymno, and the lovely resort town of **Panormo** (p141), on the eastern coast heading to Iraklio.

This covers a pretty thorough wish list of Crete's highlights and involves lots of winding mountain drives. You should allow for plenty of stops and distractions. Total distance covered would be more than 500km.

SEA OF CRETE

LIBYAN SEA

TAILORED TRIPS

IN THE FOOTSTEPS OF THE MINOANS
Six to Seven Days / 400km

The Minoans knew how to choose their real estate so this is not a bad way to see some of the best spots on the island. Allow at least half a day at the museum in **Iraklio** (p147) to appreciate the richness of the civilisation. Start early to see the palace reconstructed by Arthur Evans at **Knossos** (p157). Take a short detour to the sanctuary of **Anemospilia** (p162) near **Arhanes** (p161), where you can stop at the excellent small museum and the **Vathypetro Villa** (p162), which was probably the house of a Minoan noble. Head east inland or along the coast to the palace of **Malia** (p176) and then to the important site of **Gournia** (p191), about 19km southeast of Agios Nikolaos. Continuing east veer off the highway to the seaside village of **Mohlos** (p192), which used to be joined to the island 200m offshore. Continue east to **Palekastro** (p197), where ongoing excavations are expected to uncover a major palace. The coastal palace of **Zakros** (p198)

is ideally located next to the lovely beach of Kato Zakros (p199) where you may want to stay on for a few days. It is a decent drive west cutting inland and along the coast to the significant sites at **Phaestos** (p165) and **Agia Triada** (p167). Further south towards the coast you come to the less significant sites of **Kamilari** (p170) and **Kommos** (p169), which are also great beaches.

GORGES & COASTAL WALKS
Three to Five Days / 120km

This itinerary combines a trek through two stunning gorges, including the famous Samaria Gorge, and a boat trip to a couple of great beaches. It is best done by bus. From **Hania** (p77) take the early bus to **Omalos** (p99) and walk through the **Samaria Gorge** (p100) leaving early to ensure you

get to **Agia Roumeli** (p105) in time to cool off with a swim and catch the 5pm boat to **Sougia** (p106). Rest your weary body at this laid-back beach community in preparation for a 7km walk down the smaller **Agia Irini Gorge** (p107) the next day. A bus or taxi from Sougia takes you to the start of the gorge and it is a reasonable walk back. The next day you can take the boat to **Paleohora** (p108), or, if you are really keen, take the stunning coastal walk from Sougia, which is part of the **E4 trail** (p57) stopping at the ruins of ancient **Lissos** (p107). Relax in Paleohora before taking the bus back to Hania.

The Author

VICTORIA KYRIAKOPOULOS

Victoria was born in Melbourne to Greek immigrant parents. She is a freelance journalist contributing to various Australian and international newspapers and magazines, and is a regular contributor to the *Age* and *Sydney Morning Herald*. She has previously worked as a columnist on the *Age*, staff writer on the *Bulletin* and reporter on the Melbourne *Herald*.

Victoria's first visit to Greece was in 1998, sparking a passion and fascination with the country that has never waned. She has been based in Athens since 2000, where she was the editor of *Odyssey* magazine, author of the first edition of Lonely Planet's *Athens Condensed* and *Best of Athens*, and reported on the 2004 Athens Olympics. Having made several trips to Crete for work and pleasure, she jumped at the chance to explore the island further for this book.

My Crete

Hania (p77) is my favourite place to start in Crete as the city's charming old quarter and port still evoke the romance and mystique of the island's rich history. Driving through the stunning mountains and along the coast of Crete in just about any direction you are constantly in awe of the island's breathtaking natural landscape and dramatic gorges, its plateaus, endless olive groves and vineyards, and the lovely mountain villages you pass along the way. It is even more rewarding when these long drives

lead to the largely unspoilt southern beaches such around **Agios Pavlos** (p139) and **Triopetra** (p139), laid-back beach communities such as **Sougia** (p106) and **Lendas** (p172), and off-the-beaten-track places like **Kato Zakros** (p199). Boat hopping along the southern coast from **Hora Sfakion** (p101) is another great way to see some fine beaches.

I love the diversity and the contrasts, and the sense of stepping in and out of a time warp as you pause to let a goat herd cross the road, or visit a centuries-old monastery. But more than anything, Crete is about a way of life, fine wholesome **food** (p64) and – most of all – its **people** (p42).

LAST EDITION

Paul Hellander wrote the previous (2nd) edition of this book.

Snapshot

As it has done for decades, Crete continues to operate virtually as an independent state rather than a Greek island – enjoying its own cultural identity and traditions, and a strong local economy based on tourism and agriculture.

Crete is a tourist destination in its own right – 15% of international arrivals in Greece come through Iraklio and many European countries run direct flights to Hania or elsewhere in Crete. Tourism constitutes two-thirds of the Gross Regional Product of Crete, providing employment to 40% of the island's workforce and relying on seasonal workers from mainland Greece, the EU and Eastern Europe to work in hotels, restaurants, shops and bars.

Crete is divided into four prefectures – Iraklio, Rethymno, Hania and Lasithi – each with its own distinctive character and economic strengths. The fertile Lasithi region depends less on tourism, while Rethymno's mountainous terrain makes tourism the prime industry. Iraklio is the commercial centre and boasts the most significant archaeological sites, while Hania, with the island's biggest natural attraction in the Samaria Gorge, enjoys a different style of tourism, attracting more independent travellers, walkers and nature lovers.

Crete suffered less than other islands from the alarming overall decline in Greek tourism in 2004, which was blamed on euro-induced inflation and tourists staying away for fear of higher prices and (ultimately unfounded) security concerns in the lead-up to the Athens Olympics. But Crete's tourism sector is being forced to rethink its tourism strategy, as price competition from Turkey, Spain and Morocco has put a major dent in Crete's package tourism market.

A trend towards all-inclusive cheap holiday packages is causing much dismay, as these tourists rarely leave the resorts to spend a cent at a taverna or shop, and even excursions usually include a picnic lunch. Overall, however, the standard of accommodation and tourist product is improving as the industry tries to offer better value for money and change its former passive 'build it and they will come' attitude.

Many towns and villages have taken advantage of EU funding programmes to restore historic buildings and preserve their traditions, folk history and identity. Agrotourism and ecotourism are on the increase, along with special-interest and activity-based tourism to venues like spas, golf courses and wineries. Crete is also experimenting with winter tourism to take advantage of its cultural and natural advantages and mild climate and continues to cultivate a healthy domestic tourism industry.

Agriculture remains the powerhouse of the island, and Crete now has one of the country's highest levels of organic farming. It is also home to many migrants who make up a significant proportion of agricultural and building labourers. Crete's population is becoming increasingly urbanised and many villages are being deserted as young people move to the cities or to Athens. Efforts are being made to reverse the trend.

With the expansion of the EU, plus many EU funding allocations drawing to a close, there is concern about the diversion of funds to the newer members.

While Iraklio received an infrastructure boost as one of four Olympic cities holding soccer preliminaries for the 2004 Athens Olympics, questions remain about the long-term viability of the massive stadium. Like

FAST FACTS

Population: 540,045

Contribution to Greek GDP: 5.3%

Unemployment: 4% (half the national average)

Annual tourists: 2 million

Package tourist percentage: 80%

Olive trees: 34 million

Inflation: 3%

most of rural Greece, Cretans are worried about price rises and the economic impact the €7 billion spent in Athens for the Olympics will have
on the rest of the country in the coming years.

On the political front, Crete's traditional left leanings held strong in the
2004 national elections, with the incoming conservative New Democracy
party polling well below the national average in Crete. In recent times the
isolated island of Gavdos, south of Crete – long a magnet for escapists and
dissidents – has gained notoriety as the retreat of November 17 terrorist
group member Dimitris Koufodinas.

History

From ancient Minoan palaces and Roman cities to spectacular Byzantine churches, Venetian fortresses and Ottoman buildings, the legacy of Crete's long and colourful history is evident everywhere.

STONE AGE

History of Crete, by Theoharis E Detorakis, is an extraordinarily complete guide to Cretan history from the Minoan times up to (but not including) the Battle of Crete.

Although the island may have been inhabited since the Palaeolithic period, the oldest evidence of human habitation was found at Knossos, and dates to what is known as the pre-pottery period (6100–5700 BC). Little is known about these early inhabitants of Crete except that they survived by hunting and fishing and engaged in ancestor worship.

Evidence is also sketchy about the people who inhabited Crete during the Neolithic period (5700–2800 BC). The earliest Neolithic people lived in caves or rough stone, mud or wooden houses, and worshipped female fertility goddesses. They were hunter–gatherers who also farmed, raised livestock and made primitive pottery.

In the late Neolithic period, trade routes developed between Crete and the Cyclades, Egypt and the Near East.

THE MINOANS

It was the Minoans more than any other civilisation in Crete that left the longest-lasting mark on the character of the island. Arriving in around 3000 BC, immigrants from the North African or Levantine mainland brought with them the skills necessary for making bronze. It was this technological quantum leap that enabled the nascent Minoan civilisation to flourish almost uninterrupted for over one-and-a-half millennia. The palaces, jewellery, art and everyday artefacts that we see in Crete and in the island's museums today all reflect the glory and brilliance of perhaps the most peaceful era in the recorded history of Crete. This period is divided into three eras: Protopalatial, Neopalatial and Postpalatial. For more information about the Minoans civilisation see p36.

MYCENAEAN CIVILISATION

For all things ancient and Greek, try the great Web portal www .ancientgreece.com.

The Mycenaean civilisation (1900–1100 BC), which reached its peak between 1500 and 1200 BC, was the first great civilisation on the Greek mainland. Named after the ancient city of Mycenae, it is also known as the Achaean civilisation after the Indo-European branch of migrants who had settled on mainland Greece and absorbed many aspects of Minoan culture.

Unlike Minoan society, where the lack of city walls seems to indicate relative peace under some form of central authority, Mycenaean civilisation was characterised by independent city–states such as Corinth, Pylos, Tiryns and, the most powerful of them all, Mycenae. These were ruled by kings who inhabited palaces enclosed within massive walls on easily defensible hilltops.

The Mycenaeans' most impressive artistic legacy is magnificent golden jewellery and ornaments, the best of which can be seen in the National

TIMELINE	5700 BC	3400–2100 BC
	Neolithic age: migration from the coast of Asia Minor and settlement of Crete by cave dwellers	Protopalatial period: first palaces built in Knossos, Phaestos, Malia and Zakros

Archaeological Museum in Athens. The Mycenaeans wrote in Linear B script (see the boxed text on p38 for details), and clay tablets inscribed with the script found at the palace of Knossos provide strong evidence of Mycenaean occupation of the island. Their colonisation of Crete lasted from 1400 to 1100 BC. Although Knossos probably retained its position as capital of the island, its rulers were now subject to the mainland Mycenaeans. The Minoan Cretans either left the island or hid in its interior while the Mycenaeans founded new cities such as Lappa (Argyroupolis), Kydonia (Hania) and Polyrrinia.

The economy of the island stayed more or less the same, still based upon the export of local products, but the fine arts fell into decline. Only the manufacture of weapons flourished, reflecting the new militaristic spirit that the Mycenaeans brought to Crete. The Mycenaeans also replaced worship of the Mother Goddess with new Greek gods such as Zeus, Hera and Athena.

Mycenaean influence stretched far and wide, but eventually weakened by internal strife they were no match for the warlike Dorians, who overran their cities around 1100 BC.

DID YOU KNOW?

The mythical Talos, a bronze giant, is believed to be the first robot invented. Hephaestus offered him as a servant to King Minos. He had one vein from neck to ankle, where a bronze nail retained the blood.

DORIAN CRETE

The origins of the Dorian civilisation remain uncertain. The Dorians are generally thought to have come from Epiros or northern Macedonia, but some historians argue that although they may have arrived from there, they had in fact been driven out of Doris, in central Greece, by the Mycenaeans.

The Dorians settled first in the Peloponnese, but soon fanned out over much of the mainland, razing the city–states and enslaving the inhabitants. Despite fierce resistance, they conquered Crete around 1100 BC causing many of the inhabitants to flee to Asia Minor. Others, known as Eteo-Cretans or true Cretans, retreated to the hills and thus preserved their culture.

The Dorians brought a traumatic break with the past. The next 400 years are often referred to as Greece's 'dark age', although it would be unfair to dismiss the Dorians completely: they brought iron with them and developed a new style of pottery, decorated with striking geometrical designs. They also worshipped male gods instead of fertility goddesses and adopted the Mycenaean gods of Poseidon, Zeus and Apollo, paving the way for the later Greek religious pantheon.

The Dorians reorganised the political system of Crete and divided the society into three classes: free citizens who owned property and enjoyed political liberty (which included land-holding peasants); merchants and seamen; and slaves. The monarchical system of government was replaced by a rudimentary democracy. Ruling committees were elected by free citizens and set policy. They were guided by a Council of Elders and answered to an assembly of free citizens.

By about 800 BC, local agriculture and animal husbandry had become sufficiently productive to trigger a resumption of maritime trading. New Greek colonies were established throughout the Mediterranean basin, and this colonial expansion provided a timely boost for Crete, which took on a prominent trade role.

2100–1580 BC	1580–1200 BC
Neopalatial period: old Minoan palaces destroyed in earthquake; new palaces built	Postpalatial period: Mycenaeans take over Knossos; Minoan palaces destroyed

The people of the various city–states were unified by the development of a Greek alphabet, the verses of Homer and the founding of the Olympic Games. The establishment of central sanctuaries, such as Delphi, for the first time gave Cretans a sense of national identity as Greeks.

Most city–states were built to a similar plan, with a fortified acropolis at the highest point. Outside the acropolis was the *agora* (market), a bustling commercial quarter, and beyond it residential areas. Rethymno, Polyrrinia, Falasarna, Gortyna, Phaestos and Lato were built according to this new defensive style.

The 6th-century-BC *Laws of Gortyna*, discovered at the end of the 19th century AD at the Gortyna archaeological site, open a window onto the societal structure of Dorian Crete. Inscribed on 12 large stone tablets, the laws covered civil and criminal matters, with clear distinctions drawn among the classes of free citizens and between citizens and slaves.

What happened after the collapse of the Cretan palaces in 1450 BC? Did Crete become a backwater or just devolve into a different civilisation? *Crete*, by WJ Cavanagh, looks at a hitherto little-known period of Cretan history.

THE CLASSICAL AGE

As the rest of Greece entered its golden age from the 6th to 4th centuries BC, Crete remained a backwater. Suffering from the constant warfare between large commercial centres and smaller traditional communities, the island became increasingly impoverished. Although Crete did not participate in the Persian wars or the Peloponnesian War, economic circumstances forced many Cretans to sign up as mercenaries in foreign armies or turn to piracy.

At the same time, Crete's role as the birthplace of Greek culture drew the attention of philosophers such as Plato and Aristotle, who wrote extensively about Crete's political institutions.

The century preceding the Roman conquest of Crete was marked by continued turmoil on the island as Knossos, Gortyna, Lyttos and Kydonia (Hania) vied for supremacy. Egypt, Rhodes and the powerful city–state of Sparta involved themselves in Cretan squabbles, and piracy flourished. Meanwhile, Rome was emerging as a great power.

ROMAN RULE

While Alexander the Great was forging his vast empire in the East, the Romans had been expanding theirs to the west and began making inroads into Greece. They had various interests in Crete, which included reducing piracy and exerting control over important sea routes. The Roman presence in Crete dated back to the 3rd century BC, but it wasn't until the second Mithridatic War (74–64 BC) that they found a pretext for intervention. Using piracy as an excuse, Marcus Antonius, father of Mark Antony, undertook an unsuccessful naval campaign against Crete. The Cretans tried to negotiate and send envoys to Rome, but they were rebuffed. Expecting a Roman invasion, the island united and assembled an army of 26,000 men. The Roman campaign began in 69 BC under the Roman consul Metellus near Kydonia, and then spread throughout the island. Although the Cretans fought valiantly, the Romans succeeded in subjugating the island two years later.

Although Crete lost power and influence under the Romans it did usher in a new era of peace, ending Crete's internal wars. Crete did not mount a major challenge to Roman rule, although they became embroiled in the

1100 BC

Dorian colonists replace Mycenaeans as Crete's new masters

67 BC

Roman Rule: Romans conquer Crete making Gortyna the new capital later rivalry between Antony and Octavian. When Antony ruled he punished the cities that supported Octavian, and when Octavian triumphed he punished the cities that supported Antony.

In the early years of Roman rule, parts of Crete were given as favours to various Roman allies. In 27 BC Crete was united with Libya to form the Roman province of Cyrene. Gortyna became the capital and most powerful city in Crete. The Romans built an amphitheatre, temples and public baths and the population increased. Knossos appeared to fall into disuse, but Kydonia (Hania) in the west became an important centre. Roman towns were linked by a network of roads, bridges and aqueducts, parts of which can still be seen. Under the Romans, the Cretans continued to worship Zeus in the Dikteon and Ideon Caves, and also incorporated Roman and Egyptian deities into their religious rituals.

CHRISTIANITY & THE BYZANTINE EMPIRE

Christianity arrived early in Crete with St Paul's visit in AD 63. He left it to his disciple, Titus, to convert the island. Little is known about the early years of Christianity in Crete, but by the 3rd century persecution of Christians began in earnest. The first Christian martyrs in Crete were the so-called Ten Saints (Agii Deka) killed in the village of the same name in AD 250.

Nonetheless, Christianity began to emerge as the country's new religion. In 324 Emperor Constantine I (also known as Constantine the Great), a Christian convert, transferred the capital of the empire from Rome to Byzantium, which was renamed Constantinople (now Istanbul). By the end of the 4th century, the Roman Empire was formally divided into western and eastern sections; Crete, along with the rest of Greece, found itself in the eastern half. While Rome went into terminal decline, the eastern capital grew in wealth and strength, long outliving its western counterpart (the Byzantine Empire lasted until the capture of Constantinople by the Turks in 1453).

Crete was a self-governing province in the Byzantine Empire with Gortyna as its administrative and religious centre. Piracy decreased and trade flourished, leaving the island wealthy enough to build many churches. Crete's attachment to the worship of icons provoked a revolt in 727 when Emperor Leo III banned their worship as part of the iconoclastic movement. The uprising was smashed and the Byzantine emperors unleashed a fierce wave of retribution.

In the early 7th century Crete was attacked by Slavs, but a more serious threat was posed by the Arabs in the mid-7th century, who finally conquered Crete around 824. The Arabs established a fortress called Chandax in what is now Iraklio. Its main function was to store the treasure they amassed by piracy. Crete was an ideal base for Arab ships to launch attacks, and as the island's criminal reputation grew its economy dwindled and its cultural life ground to a halt.

The Byzantines were in no position to help Crete despite its strategic importance. The island was far away from Constantinople and the Byzantines had enough problems defending territories closer to home. Not until the Byzantine general Nikiforas Fokas attacked Chandax in a bitter siege in 960 did the Arabs finally yield.

'The Cretan uprising was smashed and the Byzantine emperors unleashed a fierce wave of retribution.'

AD 395	960
Roman Empire splits, with Crete ruled by Byzantium (Eastern Roman Empire)	Byzantines retake Crete from its Arab rulers

The Byzantines lost no time in fortifying the Cretan coast and consolidating their power. Chandax emerged as the island's new capital and the seat of the Cretan archdiocese. The Byzantines established 12 aristocratic families on the island who eventually became powerful voices of rebellion against later Venetian rule. By the late-11th century a powerful land-holding class had emerged on Crete.

THE CRUSADES

It is one of the ironies of history that the demise of the Byzantine Empire was accelerated not by invasions of infidels from the east, nor barbarians from the north, but by fellow Christians from the west – the Frankish crusaders.

The stated mission of the crusades was to liberate the Holy Land from the Muslims, but in reality they were driven as much by greed as by religious fervour. Constantinople was sacked in 1204 in the Fourth Crusade and the crusaders installed Baldwin of Flanders as head of the short-lived Latin Empire of Constantinople. Meanwhile, to secure the throne, the Byzantine Prince Alexios promised Crete to Boniface of Montferrat. After the sacking of Constantinople, Boniface sold Crete to Venice.

VENETIAN RULE

Despite Crete's importance to Venetian control of the Mediterranean, Venice was slow to assert mastery over the island. Their rivals for naval supremacy, the Genoese, moved in on the island but after a series of campaigns the Venetians finally prevailed in 1217. Genoa made periodic efforts to recapture the island, but it remained under Venetian rule until 1669.

Venice rapidly colonised Crete with noble and military families, many of which settled in Iraklio (Candia). During the first century of Venetian rule about 10,000 settlers came to Crete, induced by the seizure of the island's best and most fertile land. The former Cretan owners now worked as serfs for their new Venetian masters, who were not only the major landholders but also held political control.

Cretan peasants were ruthlessly exploited under Venetian rule, and oppressive taxation added to the peasants' woes. Religious life also suffered. Although not particularly religious themselves, the Venetians viewed the church as a symbol of national identity. The Orthodox Church was dismantled and replaced with the Catholic Church, but despite the relentless persecution Orthodox monasteries remained hotbeds of resistance and kept the spirit of national unity alive.

Cretans rebelled regularly against Venetian rule and the frequent rebellions were followed by brutal Venetian reprisals. Eventually the rebellions forced concessions from Venice. By the 15th century the Cretan and Venetian communities reached an uneasy compromise that allowed Cretan cultural and economic life to flourish.

'Cretan peasants were ruthlessly exploited under Venetian rule, and oppressive taxation added to their woes.'

THE OTTOMAN EMPIRE

Venice was soon facing a much greater threat from the east. The Muslim Ottomans – the followers of Osman, who ruled from 1289 to 1326 – had established themselves as the dominant Turkish power. They rapidly expanded the regions under their control, and by the mid-15th century were harassing the Byzantine Empire on all sides. Western Europe was too embroiled in the Hundred Years' War to come to the rescue, and in 1453 Constantinople fell to the Turks.

The fall of Constantinople left Crete as the last remaining bastion of Hellenism. Byzantine scholars and intellectuals fled the dying empire and settled in Crete, establishing schools, libraries and printing presses. The cross-pollination between Byzantine traditions and the flourishing Italian Renaissance that was imported into Crete sparked a major cultural revival. Poetry and drama flourished and a 'Cretan School' of icon painting developed in the 16th and 17th centuries, combining Byzantine and Venetian elements. In the midst of this artistic ferment, the painter Dominikos Theotokopoulos was born in Iraklio in 1541. He studied in Italy and later moved to Spain where he became known as El Greco.

'Byzantine scholars fled the dying empire and settled in Crete, founding schools, libraries and printing presses.'

With the fall of Cyprus to the Turks in 1570 it appeared that Crete would be next, but the Turkish defeats at the Battle of Lepanto in 1571 crimped Ottoman plans for further western expansion. By the early 17th century the Ottomans were on the move again, while Venice was under severe economic pressure from the rise of Spanish, English and Dutch shipping. As a resource-rich and strategically located island, Crete was obviously attractive to the Ottomans. The island's defences had previously been strengthened against piracy, but Venice was slow to rearrange the defences in the face of the looming Ottoman threat.

The Turks found a pretext to invade the island in 1644 when pirates attacked a Turkish ship off the Cretan coast. A huge Turkish force landed in Hania in the early summer of 1645. Although the fortress was bravely defended, it fell within two months and the Turks established their first foothold on the island. Rethymno was the next town to suffer siege, bombardment and defeat. With the western part of the island secured the Turks turned their attention to Iraklio (Candia).

The siege began in May 1648 but the massive walls of the city kept the enemy at bay for 21 years. Both sides threw everything they had into the struggle, but Candia fell in 1669 leaving the entire island except for Spinalonga and Souda (which fell in 1715) in Turkish hands.

Life was not easy under the Ottomans, although they did allow the Orthodox Church to re-establish itself. Nevertheless, there were tremendous political and economic advantages to embracing Islam. Mass conversions were common; sometimes entire villages changed their faith.

Economically, the Cretans were initially no better off under the Ottomans than they were under the Venetians. The Ottomans devised ingenious taxes to wring every drop of wealth out of the island, and the economy degenerated to a subsistence level. However, trade picked up around the start of the 18th century, and living standards improved thereafter. Crete exported grain, and its abundance of olive oil launched a soap industry.

Rebellion was brewing, however, as many Cretans fled to the mountains, harassing the Turks with sporadic attacks and raids, particularly in the Sfakia region. In 1770 under their leader Daskalogiannis, 2000 Sfakians mounted an assault upon the Turks in western Crete. Although Daskalogiannis had received assurances of support from Russia, the aid never materialised and the rebellion was viciously suppressed. Daskalogiannis was skinned alive in the central square of Iraklio.

1645	1669
Hania and Rethymno fall to Turkish attack	Iraklio (Candia) finally falls to the Turks leaving Crete under Ottoman rule

THE WAR OF INDEPENDENCE

Sfakia was once again the nucleus of rebellion when the Greek War of Independence spread to Crete in 1821. The Sfakian rebels fired the first shots in the struggle that soon spread throughout the island. Unfortunately the revolutionaries were hampered by poor organisation and constant infighting. The Turks swiftly retaliated and launched a wave of massacres primarily directed at the clergy.

Bogged down fighting rebels in the Peloponnese and mainland Greece, the Turks were forced to turn to Mehmet Ali of Egypt for help in dealing with the Cretans. Chronically short of arms and undisciplined, the Cretans fought furiously but were outnumbered by the Turkish–Egyptian forces.

With the rest of Greece torn by war, Crete was left on its own, and the revolutionary movement flickered out in 1824. Fighting continued for a few more years, provoking fearsome massacres of Cretan civilians, but it was only a matter of time until the Turks prevailed. When a Greek state was finally established in 1830, Crete was given to Egypt.

Egyptian rule initially brought improvements. A general amnesty was issued that asked Cretans to lay down their arms. Muslims and Christians were to be treated equally, schools were organised and the authorities began rebuilding the island's infrastructure. Nevertheless, taxes remained high and soon new protests were under way. Meanwhile Mehmet Ali was defeated by the Turks in Syria and the Great Powers decided to give Crete back to the Ottomans in 1840.

Upon the restoration of Ottoman rule, Crete won important new privileges in the *Writ of Hatti Humayun*, allowing more religious freedom and the right to own property. A further decree granted Cretans more civil rights, but the Sultan's repeated violations of these new laws sparked yet another uprising and a demand for *enosis*, or union with free Greece. Although Russia was partial to the Cretan position, Great Britain and France wished to maintain the status quo and refused any military or economic help. Rallying around the slogan 'Union or Death', fighting broke out in western Crete. Once again the Turks joined forces with the Egyptians and attacked the civilian population. In 1866 about 900 rebels and their families took refuge in Moni Arkadiou. When 2000 Turkish soldiers attacked the building, rather than surrender, the Cretans set light to a store of gunpowder. The explosion killed almost everyone, Turks included.

With the heroic stand at Moni Arkadiou, the Cretan cause gained worldwide attention. Although demonstrations erupted throughout Europe in support of the rebels, Great Britain and France maintained a pro-Turkish stance. The Great Powers forbade Greece from aiding the Cretan rebels and the revolution petered out.

The 1877 Russo-Turkish War prompted another uprising in Crete. Sensing that Turkey might be defeated the Greek government decided to support Crete. Although the rebels seized major north-coast cities, the Berlin conference of 1878 resolving the Russo-Turkish War firmly rejected Cretan union with Greece. Turkey made new concessions in the *Haleppa Charter* of 1878 turning Crete into a semi-autonomous province, sanctioning Greek as the official language and granting a general amnesty.

In 1889 fierce political infighting within the Cretan parliament led to a new rebellion against Turkish rule, prompting Turkey to revoke the

'Rallying around the slogan 'Union or Death', fighting broke out in western Crete.'

1821	1830
Greek War of Independence spreads to Crete	Crete given to Egypt

Haleppa Charter and return to the iron-fisted policies of the past. A new figure of resistance emerged from Sfakia: Manousos Koundouros headed a secret fraternity with the goal of securing autonomy for the island, believing that it would eventually lead to unification with Greece. The rebels laid siege to the Turkish garrison at Vamos, which led to violent reprisals by the Turks and an eventual intervention by the Great Powers. The Turks were forced to agree to a new constitution for Crete.

When violence erupted again in 1896, the Greek government sent a small force to the island and declared unification between Crete and Greece. The Great Powers rejected the idea and blockaded the coast, refusing to allow either the Turks or the Greeks to reinforce their position. Greece became embroiled in a war with Turkey and recalled its forces. The Great Powers appointed Prince George, son of King George of Greece, as High Commissioner of Crete.

In 1898 a detachment of British soldiers was implementing the transfer of power in Iraklio when an enraged mob of Turks stormed through the city slaughtering hundreds of Christian civilians and 17 British soldiers as well as the British Consul. The British swiftly rounded up 17 Turkish troublemakers, hanged them and sent a squadron of ships steaming into the Iraklio harbour. The Turks were ordered out of all their island fortresses, ending Ottoman rule over Crete forever.

INDEPENDENCE

Crete was placed under international administration, but union with its cultural brethren in Greece remained an unquenchable desire. A new movement coalesced around Eleftherios Venizelos. Born near Hania, this charismatic figure was Prince George's Minister of Justice and a member of the Cretan Assembly. In the face of Prince George's stubborn refusal to consider unification, Venizelos convened a revolutionary assembly in Theriso in 1905 that raised the Greek flag and declared unity with Greece.

Venizelos then set up a rival government to administer the island. The rebellion spread, forcing the Great Powers to concede that Prince George had lost all support. They mediated a solution, allowing King George of Greece to appoint a new governor of Crete, which brought the island another step closer to union.

The populace continued to agitate for unification, however. In 1908 the Cretan assembly issued a proclamation declaring unity with Greece, but the Greek government refused to allow Cretan deputies to sit in the Greek Parliament. Even though Eleftherios Venizelos had become Prime Minister, Greece remained fearful of antagonising Turkey and the Great Powers who were adamantly opposed to the plan. Not until Greece, Serbia and Bulgaria declared war on the Ottoman Empire over Macedonia in the first Balkan War (1912) were Cretans finally allowed into the Greek Parliament. The 1913 *Treaty of Bucharest* ended the war and formally recognised Crete as part of the Greek state.

WWI & SMYRNA

King Constantine, who was married to the sister of the German emperor, understandably insisted that Greece remain neutral when WWI broke out in August 1914. As the war dragged on, the Allies (Britain, France

Richard Clogg's *Concise History of Greece* (2nd edition) is a well-written history of modern Greece from the first stirrings of the national movement in the late-18th century to 2000, punctuated with some interesting illustrations.

1840	1866
The Great Powers give Crete back to Ottomans	Outbreak of revolt against Turks; explosion at Arkadiou Monastery

and Russia) put increasing pressure on Greece to join forces with them against Germany and Turkey. They made promises that they couldn't hope to fulfil, including land in Asia Minor. Venizelos favoured the Allied cause, placing him at loggerheads with the king. Tensions between the two came to a head in 1916, and Venizelos set up a rebel government, first in Crete and then in Thessaloniki, while the pressure from the Allies eventually persuaded Constantine to leave Greece in June 1917. He was replaced by his more amenable second son, Alexander.

Greek troops served with distinction on the Allied side, but when the war ended in 1918 the promised land in Asia Minor was not forthcoming. Venizelos took matters into his own hands and, with Allied acquiescence, landed troops in Smyrna (present-day Izmir) in May 1919 under the guise of protecting the half a million Greeks living in that city. With a firm foothold in Asia Minor, Venizelos now planned to push home his advantage against a war-depleted Ottoman Empire. He ordered his troops to attack in October 1920. By September 1921, the Greeks had advanced as far as Ankara.

The Turkish forces, commanded by Mustafa Kemal (later to become Atatürk) first halted the Greek advance outside Ankara in September 1921 and then routed them with a massive offensive the following spring. The Greeks were driven out of Smyrna and many of the Greek inhabitants were massacred.

The outcome of the failed Greek invasion and the revolution in Turkey was the *Treaty of Lausanne* of July 1923. This gave eastern Thrace and the islands of Imvros and Tenedos to Turkey, while the Italians kept the Dodecanese.

The treaty also called for a population exchange between Greece and Turkey to prevent any future disputes. Almost 1.5 million Greeks left Turkey and almost 400,000 Turks left Greece. On Crete, the entire Turkish population of about 30,000 people was ordered off the island, abandoning their homes to the incoming Greek refugees.

'On Crete, the entire Turkish population of about 30,000 people was ordered off the island.'

THE REPUBLIC OF 1924–35

The arrival of the refugees coincided with, and compounded, a period of political instability unprecedented even by Greek standards. In October 1920, King Alexander had died, resulting in the restoration of his father, King Constantine. Constantine identified himself too closely with the war against Turkey, and abdicated after the fall of Smyrna. He was replaced by his first son, George II, but George was no match for the group of army officers who seized power after the war. A republic was proclaimed in March 1924 amid a series of coups and counter-coups.

A measure of stability was attained with Venizelos' return to power in 1928. He pursued a policy of economic and educational reforms, but progress was inhibited by the Great Depression. His anti-royalist Liberal Party began to face a growing challenge from the monarchist Popular Party, culminating in defeat at the polls in March 1933. The new government was preparing for the restoration of the monarchy when Venizelos and his supporters staged an unsuccessful coup in March 1935.

Venizelos was exiled to Paris, where he died a year later. In November 1935 King George II was restored to the throne by a rigged plebiscite, and he

1913	1898
Turkish rule ends; Crete ruled by Prince George of Greece	Greece and Crete officially united

installed the right-wing General Ioannis Metaxas as prime minister. Nine months later, Metaxas assumed dictatorial powers, with the king's consent, under the pretext of preventing a communist-inspired republican coup.

WWII

Metaxas' grandiose vision was to create a Third Greek Civilisation based on its glorious ancient and Byzantine past, but what he actually created was more like a Greek version of the Third Reich. He exiled or imprisoned opponents, banned trade unions and the KKE (Kommounistiko Komma Ellados – the Greek Communist Party), imposed press censorship, and created a secret police force and a fascist-style youth movement.

Metaxas is best known, however, for his reply of *ohi* (no) to Mussolini's request to allow the Italian forces to traverse Greece at the beginning of WWII, thus maintaining Greece's policy of strict neutrality. The Italians invaded Greece, but were driven back into Albania.

A prerequisite of Hitler's plan to invade the Soviet Union was a secure southern flank in the Balkans. The British, realising this, asked Metaxas if they could land troops in Greece. He gave the same reply he had given the Italians, but died suddenly in January 1941. The king replaced him with the more timid Alexandros Koryzis, who agreed to British forces landing in Greece and then committed suicide when German troops marched through Yugoslavia and invaded Greece on 6 April 1941. The country was rapidly overrun and on 23 April the leader of the Greek government, Emmanouil Tsouderos, set up a government in exile in his native Crete.

BATTLE OF CRETE

With all available Greek and Cretan troops fighting the Italians in Albania, Greece asked Britain to defend Crete. Churchill was more than willing to oblige as he was determined to block Germany's advance through south-eastern Europe. British, Australian and New Zealand troops poured on to the last remaining part of free Greece.

The Allies were in a poor position to defend the island, since commitments in the Middle East were already draining military resources. The island's defences had been seriously neglected, particularly its defence against an air assault. There were few fighter planes and military preparation was hampered by six changes of command on the island in the first six months of 1941. The terrain was also a problem. The only viable ports were on Crete's exposed northern coast, and inadequate roads precluded the use of the more protected ports on the southern coast to resupply the army.

Meanwhile Hitler was determined to seize the island and use it as an air base to attack British forces in the eastern Mediterranean. In a stunning disregard for Crete's rebellious history, Hitler actually believed that German forces would be welcomed by the native population. They were not.

After a week-long aerial bombardment, an airborne invasion began on 20 May. Aiming to capture the airport at Maleme 17km west of Hania, thousands of parachutists floated down over Hania, Rethymno and Iraklio.

Old men, women and children grabbed rifles, old shotguns, sickles and whatever else they could find to defend their homeland. German casualties were appalling, but they managed to capture the Maleme airfield. Although the Allies probably could have recaptured the airfield before

George Psychoundakis' *The Cretan Runner* is an exciting and personal account of the Cretan resistance. The author was a runner delivering messages to the Allies. It was translated by Patrick Leigh Fermor, who also wrote the introduction.

Crete: The Battle and the Resistance, by Antony Beevor, is a short and readable analysis of the Allied defeat.

1923	1941
Treaty of Lausanne: entire Turkish population of about 30,000 people leaves Crete	Battle of Crete results in German occupation

the Germans had time to secure it, confusion and a lack of wireless sets prevented the Allies from redeploying their troops around the vital air base. Although the fighting continued until 30 May, once Maleme was in German hands at the end of the first day, the battle was effectively lost.

With Hania, Rethymno, and Iraklio under German control, Allied soldiers were forced to retreat to the southern port of Hora Sfakion. About 12,000 men made their way over the eastern flank of the Lefka Ori (White Mountains) under attack by German soldiers all the way.

About three quarters of them were evacuated by ship from Hora Sfakion. Meanwhile King George and Emmanouil Tsouderos walked through the Samaria Gorge to Agia Roumeli and were then evacuated to Egypt.

The Road to Prevelly, by Geoffrey Edwards, published in 1989, is an autobiographical account of Edwards' experiences during the Battle of Crete in 1941. Under German attack, he was rescued and sheltered by the monks of the Preveli Monastery and eventually repatriated to Australia.

THE CRETAN RESISTANCE

Most of the Allied soldiers that were not evacuated were hidden by the Cretans and helped to escape. During the German occupation Allied undercover agents supplied from North Africa coordinated the guerrilla warfare waged by the Cretan fighters, known as *andartes*. Allied soldiers and Cretans alike were under constant threat from the Nazis while they lived in caves, sheltered in monasteries, trekked across peaks or unloaded cargo on the southern coast. One of the most daring feats of the resistance movement was the kidnapping of General Kreipe in 1944. The German commander was snatched outside Iraklio and spirited down to the south coast and away to Egypt.

German reprisals against the civilian population were fierce, especially after the kidnapping of General Kreipe. Cities were bombed and villages were annihilated with men, women and children lined up and shot. When the Germans finally surrendered in 1945 they insisted on surrendering to the British fearing that the Cretans would inflict upon them some of the same punishment they had suffered for four years.

POSTWAR CRETE

With the defeat of the Germans, the Allies turned their attention to the political complexion of postwar Greece. Throughout the occupation of mainland Greece, the resistance was dominated by the Greek Communists. Winston Churchill wanted the king back and was afraid of a communist takeover, especially after the two leading resistance organisations formed a coalition and declared a provisional government in the summer of 1944.

DID YOU KNOW?
Crete has been invaded and ruled by eight different foreign powers since Minoan times – Mycenaeans, Dorians, Romans, Venetians, Byzantines, Arabs, Ottomans and Germans.

An election held in March 1946, which was boycotted by the Communists, was won by the royalists with British backing. A rigged plebiscite put George II back on the throne and civil war broke out, lasting until 1949.

On Crete the situation was different. The close cooperation between the Cretans and British soldiers left the islanders with strong pro-British sentiments that left little room for communist infiltration.

The British also made sure that the scarce supplies and equipment available went to noncommunist resistance organisations. Crete was largely spared the bloodshed and bitterness that left Greece a political and economic basket case in the 1950s.

A national election was held in 1950. The system of proportional representation resulted in a series of unworkable coalitions. The electoral

1944	1946–49
Germany withdraws from Greece	Greek Civil War

system was changed to majority voting in 1952, which excluded the communists from future governments. The following election was won by the newly formed right-wing Ellinikos Synagermos (Greek Rally).

THE COLONEL'S COUP

Greece joined NATO in 1951, and in 1953 the US was granted the right to operate sovereign bases. Intent on maintaining a right-wing government, the US gave generous aid and military support. Despite improved living standards during the 1950s, Greece remained a poor country.

A succession of right-wing governments was supplanted by the centrist EK or Enosi Kendrou (Centre Union) party led by Georgos Papandreou in 1964. His government was short-lived; a group of army colonels led by Georgos Papadopoulos and Stylianos Pattakos staged a coup d'état on 21 April 1967 and established a military junta with Papadopoulos as prime minister.

The colonels imposed martial law, abolished all political parties, banned trade unions, imposed censorship, and imprisoned, tortured and exiled thousands of Greeks who opposed them. Cretan resentment towards the colonels intensified when the colonels muscled through major tourist development projects on the island that were rife with favouritism.

On 17 November 1967, tanks stormed a student sit-in at the Athens Polytechnic, killing 20 and injuring many more. (November 17 became the name of a notorious terrorist group that was finally exposed in 2002.)

Suspicions that the coup had been aided by the CIA remain conjectural, but criticism of the coup and the ensuing regime was certainly not forthcoming from the US government. The perception of US involvement in the coup has left a residue of ill feeling that has not entirely dissipated.

In July and August 1974, Turkish forces invaded Cyprus following a botched junta-sponsored attempt to depose Archbishop Makarios, the president of Cyprus. Discredited by the Turkish invasion of Cyprus, the junta was dismantled within the same month.

AFTER THE COLONELS

An election was arranged for November 1974, and the ban on communist parties was lifted. Andreas Papandreou (son of Georgos) formed PASOK (the Panhellenic Socialist Union), and a national plebiscite voted 69% against restoration of the monarchy with Cretans even more overwhelmingly in favour of a republican system.

Karamanlis was called back from Paris and his right-wing New Democracy (ND) party won the 1974 elections, but his personal popularity, which was never very high in Crete, began to decline. One of his biggest achievements before accepting the largely ceremonial post of president was to engineer Greece's entry into the European Economic Community (now the European Union). On 1 January 1981 Greece became the 10th member of the EEC.

THE SOCIALIST 1980S

Andreas Papandreou's PASOK party won the election of October 1981 with 48% of the vote, giving Greece its first socialist government. PASOK promised removal of US bases and withdrawal from NATO.

DID YOU KNOW?

Crete has produced two of independent Greece's prime ministers, Eleftherios Venizelos (several times between 1910 and 1933) and Konstantinos Mitsotakis (1990–93).

1951	1967
Greece joins NATO	Army colonels stage a coup and impose martial law across Greece

Their international stance was, and remains, particularly popular in Crete, where the US naval base at Souda Bay is a regular target for protests. Crete's history of foreign occupation has given islanders a strong antipathy to the presence of foreign troops.

After seven years in government, these promises remained unfulfilled (although the US military presence was reduced), unemployment was high and reforms in education and welfare had been limited. Women's issues had fared better: the dowry system was abolished, abortion legalised, and civil marriage and divorce were implemented.

In 1988 PASOK became embroiled in a financial scandal involving the Bank of Crete. In July 1989 an unlikely coalition of conservatives and communists began investigating the scandal, quickly ruling that Papandreou and four former ministers should be tried for embezzlement, telephone tapping and illegal grain sales. The trial of Papandreou ended in January 1992 with his acquittal on all counts.

THE 1990s & BEYOND

'The dowry system was abolished, abortion legalised, and civil marriage and divorce laws were introduced.'

An election in 1990 brought the ND back to power with a majority of only two seats, and with Konstandinos Mitsotakis, a Cretan, as prime minister. Intent on redressing the country's economic problems – high inflation and high government spending – the government imposed austerity measures. It also announced a privatisation programme aimed at 780 state-controlled enterprises and cracked down on widespread tax evasion. None of Mitsotakis' reforms were popular in Crete, although the prime minister himself retained strong personal popularity.

By late 1992 corruption allegations were being made against the government (it was claimed that Mitsotakis had a large, secret collection of Minoan art) and in mid-1993 there were allegations of government telephone tapping. Former Mitsotakis supporters began to cut their losses: in June 1993 Antonis Samaras, the ND's former foreign minister, founded the Political Spring party and called upon ND members to join him. So many of them joined that the ND lost its parliamentary majority and hence its capacity to govern. An early election was held in October 1993, which Andreas Papandreou's PASOK party won.

By early 1996, 74-year-old Papandreou's ailing health finally forced him to step down as PASOK leader, and his death on 26 June marked the end of an era in Greek politics.

Papandreou's departure produced a dramatic change of direction for PASOK, with the party abandoning his left-leaning politics and electing economic reformer Costas Simitis as prime minister. The new leader had been an outspoken critic of Papandreou and had been sacked as industry minister four times before his death. He called a snap election and campaigned hard in support of his 'Mr Clean' image, winning a comfortable majority.

Securing the 2004 Olympic Games was an enormous coup for Simitis, bringing a flood of money into Greece for improvements to the infrastructure, yet his austerity packages – designed to whip Greece into fiscal shape in order to become a full member of the European Monetary Union – have caused discontent in some quarters. However, his success in the face of constant protest earned him a mandate for another four years in April 2000.

1974	1996
Democracy is restored and the monarchy is abolished	The death of Andreas Papandreou marks the end of an era in Greek politics

Greece joined the European Monetary Union in January 2002 and the euro became the national currency. Despite Simitis' economic record, a successful presidency of the EU in 2003 and the accession of Cyprus into the EU, his tired PASOK government, which had been in power for almost 20 years, was plagued by claims of graft and corruption and looked set to lose the 2004 election. Simitis stepped down as leader in January 2004, handing the reins to Foreign Minister George Papandreou, son of Andreas. Despite Papandreou's political pedigree and personal popularity – particularly in Crete, which remained a PASOK stronghold – he was unable to save PASOK from a thumping defeat in March 2004.

Athens surprised the world by staging a successful Olympic Games in 2004, a major achievement for such a small country, and achieved its goal to show the world Greece's contemporary face.

2002	2004
Greece joins the European Monetary Union, and the euro replaces the drachma	Athens hosts the Olympic Games, with preliminary soccer games hosted by Iraklio

The Minoans

MINOAN HISTORY

The Bronze Age began around 3300 BC when Indo-European migrants introduced the processing of bronze (an alloy of copper and tin) into the Mediterranean basin. This significant event gave rise to three major civilisations within the territory of present-day Greece: the Cycladic, Minoan and the Mycenaean. The Minoan civilisation (named after King Minos) was the first advanced civilisation to emerge in Europe, drawing its inspiration from two great Middle Eastern civilisations: the Mesopotamian and Egyptian. Today, archaeologists generally use two approaches to chronologically divide Minoan civilisation. The newer approach splits the period into three phases: Protopalatial (3400–2100 BC), Neopalatial (2100–1580 BC) and Postpalatial (1580–1200 BC). These periods roughly correspond to the older archaeological divisions of Early Minoan, Middle Minoan and Late Minoan, and these terms are used interchangeably throughout this book.

Many aspects of Neolithic life endured during the Protopalatial period, but the advent of bronze, which was imported from Cyprus, allowed the Minoans to build better boats and thus expand their trade opportunities. Pottery and goldsmithing became more sophisticated, foreshadowing the subsequent great achievements of Minoan art. The island prospered from trade and the groundwork was laid for the development of the two main periods of Minoan history.

Mary Renault's novels provide an excellent feel for ancient Crete. The King Must Die and The Bull from the Sea are vivid tales of Minoan times.

Protopalatial Period

Minoan civilisation reached its peak during the Protopalatial period, also called the Old Palace or Middle period. Around 2000 BC the large palace complexes of Knossos, Phaestos, Malia and Zakros were built, marking

---

MINOS: MAN OR MYTH?

Whether King Minos existed can only ever be the subject of wishful conjecture. Homer, at least, was convinced of his existence and wrote: 'Out on the dark blue sea there lies a rich and lovely land called Crete that is densely populated and boasts 90 cities… One of the 90 cities is called Knosos and there for nine years, King Minos ruled and enjoyed the friendship of the mighty Zeus' (*Odyssey* XIX, 172–9). Either way, legend has it that Minos was the legendary ruler of Crete. He was the son of Zeus and Europa and attained the Cretan throne with the help of Poseidon.

With Knossos as his base he gained control over the whole Aegean basin, colonising many of the islands and ridding the seas of pirates. He married Pasiphae, the daughter of Helios, who bore him a number of children including Ariadne, Androgeos and Phaedra, as well as the infamous half bull–half human Minotaur.

How long King Minos actually reigned, however, is open to debate. The Homeric word *enneaoros* used to describe Minos in the original Greek of the *Odyssey* could mean 'for nine years', or 'from the age of nine years'. Was Minos able to create an empire in nine short years, or was he a long-reigning monarch who started his kingly career as a boy? Controversy aside, it is believed that he did eventually come to a sticky end in Sicily when he was killed by the daughters of King Kokalios who poured boiling water over him as he was taking a bath.

Although presented as a tyrannical ruler through post-Homeric mythology, Minos is generally thought of in a benevolent light and as a just and powerful ruler. Scholars now assume that the name Minos is used to mean a royal or dynastic title for the priestly rulers of Bronze Age, or Minoan, Crete.

a sharp break with Neolithic village life. During this period, Crete is believed to have been governed by local rulers, with the island's power and wealth concentrated at Knossos. Society was organised on hierarchical lines, with a large population of slaves.

The architectural advances were accompanied by great strides in the techniques of pottery production. Kamares vases, named after the Kamares Cave where they were first produced, manifested highly advanced artisanship. The vases were used for barter, as well as for home and ceremonial use.

You can take a virtual reality tour of Knossos via the British School at Athens website www .bsa.gla.ac.uk.

MINOAN ARCHAEOLOGICAL SITES ON CRETE

Homer referred to '90 cities' in Minoan Crete, which suggests there is a wealth of Minoan settlements scattered across the island. The majority of these are still undiscovered or have disappeared completely, but there are enough sites to keep even the amateur archaeologist occupied for a month or more. Following are some of the sites that we have looked at in this book.

Agia Triada (p167) A small Minoan site at the western edge of the Mesara Plain in south-central Crete, Agia Triada was principally a royal summer residence but nonetheless yielded a number of impressive finds that are representative of Minoan art.

Anemospilia (p41) Discovered in 1979, the Anemospilia (Wind Cave) sanctuary is a Middle Minoan site that's significant because it demonstrated that human sacrifice may well have played a part in Minoan society.

Gournia (p191) An important Late Minoan site dating from 1550 to 1450 BC, the thriving community of Gournia consisted of a town and a small palace. Ruled by an overlord rather than a king, the Gournia site is less showy than Knossos or Phaestos.

Kamares Cave (p131) It was in the Kamares Cave on the southern slopes of Mt Psiloritis that fine examples of Kamares pottery were first found. Characterised by crisp designs and produced on pottery wheels, the pottery flourished throughout the whole of the Protopalatial period.

Kamilari (p170) The site of a well-preserved Minoan tomb dating from 1900 BC, the tomb has 2m-high stone walls. It is 3km from the village of Kamilari on the western edge of the Mesara Plain in south-central Crete.

Knossos (p157) The most significant Minoan site in Crete, Knossos had been inhabited since Neolithic times, but remained undiscovered from the time of its second destruction in 1450 BC until the beginning of the 20th century.

Kommos (p169) The small site of Kommos is believed to have been the port for the major city of Phaestos 12km to the east. It contains a wealth of Minoan structures and the layout of the ancient town can still be seen.

Malia (p176) The palace at Malia was one of the four major palace sites in Crete. Built in 1900 BC and rebuilt in 1700 BC after destruction by an earthquake, what we see today is the remains of the second structure. Malia is one of the better-preserved Minoan sites.

Mohlos (p192) The site at Mohlos is one of the lesser-known Minoan sites and dates back to the Protopalatial period. Primarily a site for professional archaeologists rather than casual visitors, Mohlos is still being excavated.

Palekastro (p197) The second-largest Minoan town site, according to recent geophysical surveys, Palekastro had Neolithic origins and was a large urban centre with Egyptian contacts in the Late Minoan period. After the Bronze Age, it became the Diktaion, sacred to Diktaian Zeus, ancient Crete's most important god. The most significant find to date is the Palekastro Kouros.

Phaestos (p165) The second most-important Minoan site in Crete, Phaestos dates back to at least 4000 BC, although the first palace was built in about 2000 BC. The impressive citadel was the administrative centre of the Minoan Mesara Plain. Unlike Knossos, it yielded few frescoes and has not been partially restored.

Zakros (p198) The last of the Minoan places to be discovered, Zakros in far-eastern Crete was uncovered as late as 1962. The site was unique in that it was unplundered and revealed a vast trove of Minoan treasures.

The first Cretan script also emerged during this period. At first highly pictorial, the writing gradually changed from the representations of natural objects to more abstract figures that resembled Egyptian hieroglyphics.

Linear B and Related Scripts, by John Chadwick, is a riveting insight into the process of decipherment of the Linear B scripts that extended Greek linguistic history further than had been imagined possible.

Neopalatial Period

The Middle Minoan period came to an end with the sudden destruction of the Minoan palaces of Knossos, Phaestos, Malia and Zakros in 1700 BC. Although there is some disagreement, most archaeologists believe that the destruction was caused by the eruption of a volcano on nearby Santorini, which caused a massive earthquake. The Minoans rebuilt the palaces to a more complex design with multiple storeys, sumptuous royal apartments, reception halls, storerooms, workshops, living quarters for staff and an advanced drainage system. The complex design of the palaces later gave rise to the myth of the Cretan Labyrinth.

The excavation of Knossos initiated by Sir Arthur Evans in 1900 uncovered many remnants of Minoan Neopalatial society. Brightly coloured frescoes (now on view in the Archaeological Museum of Iraklio, p149) depict white-skinned women with elaborately coiffured glossy black locks. Proud, graceful and uninhibited, these women had hourglass figures and were dressed in stylish gowns that revealed perfectly shaped breasts. The bronze-skinned men were tall, with tiny waists, narrow hips,

LINEAR B SCRIPT

The methodical decipherment of the Linear B script by English architect and part-time linguist Michael Ventris was the first tangible evidence that the Greek language had a recorded history longer than any scholar had previously believed. It demonstrated that the language disguised by these mysterious scribblings was an archaic form of Greek 500 years older than the Ionic Greek used by Homer.

Linear B was written on clay tablets that lay undisturbed for centuries until they were unearthed at Knossos in Crete. Further clay tablets were unearthed later on the mainland at Mycenae, Tiryns and Pylos in the Peloponnese and at Thebes in Boeotia in Central Greece.

The clay tablets, found to be mainly inventories and records of commercial transactions, consist of about 90 different signs, and date from the 14th to the 13th centuries BC. Little of the social and political life of these times can be deduced from the tablets, although there is enough to give a glimpse of a fairly complex and well-organised commercial structure.

For linguists, the script did not provide a detailed image of the actual language spoken, since the symbols were employed primarily as syllabic clusters designed to give an approximation of the pronunciation of the underlying language. Typically, the syllabic cluster 'A-re-ka-sa-da-ra' is the woman's name Alexandra, but the exact pronunciation is unknown.

Importantly, what is clear is that the language is undeniably Greek, thus giving the modern-day Greek language the second-longest recorded written history, after Chinese. The language of an earlier script, Linear A, remains to this day undeciphered. It is believed to be of either Anatolian (proto-Indo-Iranian) or Semitic origin, though even this remains pure conjecture.

MARTIN HARRIS

SIR ARTHUR EVANS & KNOSSOS

Sir Arthur John Evans (1851–1941) was the curator of the Ashmolean Museum in Oxford from 1884 to 1908 and was appointed Extraordinary Professor of Prehistoric Archaeology in 1909. His interest in ancient coins and the writing on stone seals from Crete brought him to the island for the first time in 1894. As an avid amateur journalist and adventurer, he had a hunch that the mainland Mycenaean civilisation derived originally from Crete. In 1900 he bought a parcel of land near Iraklio and spent a year digging. He discovered the ruins of a lost palace that covered an area of 5½ acres (2.2 hectares). Evans named the palace civilisation Minoan after the legendary King Minos.

Evans was so enthralled by his discovery that he spent 35 years and £250,000 of his own money excavating and reconstructing sections of the palace. Some archaeologists have disparaged Evans' reconstruction, believing he sacrificed accuracy to his overly vivid imagination. Unlike other archaeological sites in Crete, however, substantial reconstruction helps the visitor to visualise what the palace might have looked like at the peak of its glory. Evans maintained that he was obliged to rebuild columns and supports in reinforced concrete or the palace would have collapsed, but many archaeologists feel that the site was irretrievably damaged. Most nonspecialists maintain that Sir Arthur did a thorough job and that Knossos is a knockout.

Over the next 25 years, Evans continued digging and unearthed the remains of a Neolithic civilisation beneath the remains of the Bronze Age Minoan palace. He also discovered some 3000 clay tablets containing Linear A and Linear B script and wrote his own definitive description of his work at Knossos in a four-volume opus called *The Palace of Minos*. Evans received many honours for his work and was knighted in 1911.

broad shoulders and muscular thighs and biceps; the children were slim and lithe.

The Minoan state developed into a powerful thalassocracy, or sea-based power. Trade with the eastern Mediterranean continued to boom and was helped by Minoan colonies in the Aegean and in Asia Minor. According to ancient Greek historians, King Minos was the head of this powerful naval empire and promoted the expansion of Minoan interests.

The Minoans were not given to building colossal temples or religious statuary. Historians have concluded that their spiritual life was organised around the worship of a Mother Goddess. Often represented with snakes or lions, the Mother Goddess was the deity-in-chief and the male gods were clearly subordinate. The double-axe symbol that appears in frescoes and on the palace walls of Knossos was a sacred symbol for the Minoans. Called *labrys*, it was the origin of the word labyrinth, which later Greeks associated with Knossos. Other religious symbols that frequently appear in Minoan art include the mythical griffin bird and figures with a human body and an animal head. It is also assumed that the Minoans worshipped the dead and believed in some form of afterlife.

Women apparently enjoyed a high degree of freedom and autonomy in Minoan society. Although the evidence for a matriarchal society is scanty, Minoan art shows women participating in games, hunting and all public and religious festivals. It was not until the later invasions by the Dorians that women were condemned to a subordinate role.

Postpalatial Period

Minoan culture came to an abrupt halt around 1450 BC for reasons that have not yet been fully explained. In a great cataclysm around 1450 BC the palaces (except Knossos) and numerous smaller settlements were smashed to bits and burned. A cataclysmic volcano that erupted on nearby Santorini in or around 1550 BC may have caused damage on

DID YOU KNOW?

After King Minos' nasty death in Sicily, the Cretans built a tomb for him there. Today there is a city called Minoa, plus several other cities in Sicily originally built by Cretans.

Minotaur: Sir Arthur Evans and the Archaeology of the Minoan Myth, by Joseph Alexander McGillivray, is a fascinating portrait of the British archaeologist who revealed the Palace of Knossos to the world as a study in relative archaeology.

Crete from the resulting tidal waves and ash fallout, but it is no longer believed by archaeologists to be the reason for the ultimate destruction of the Neopalatial Period. This was most likely caused by a second, powerful earthquake a century later. Other archaeologists believe that the damage was caused by the invading Mycenaeans eager to grab the Minoans' maritime commerce. Whether the Mycenaeans caused the catastrophe or merely profited from it, it is clear that their presence on the island closely coincided with the destruction of the palaces and Minoan civilisation that had existed for over one-and-a-half millennia.

MINOAN ART
Early Periods

Little is known about Crete's Neolithic cave dwellers, but it appears that they made crude and undecorated pottery. The potter's wheel had not yet been invented, and pots were simply baked in a fire, resulting in uneven colouring. The first figurines depicted human forms, and were usually carved from stone. A male marble figurine found at Knossos is a good example of this early style, which seems related to techniques in the Cyclades. Pottery techniques advanced in the early Minoan years. Spirals and curvilinear motifs in white were painted on dark vases and several distinct styles emerged. Pyrgos pottery was characterised by black, grey or brown colours and, later on, Vasiliki pottery (made near Ierapetra), displayed polychrome surfaces. Gold, silver and bronze jewellery and daggers were finely crafted and foreshadowed the later achievements of Minoan art.

Protopalatial Period

The founding of the first Minoan palaces on Crete in 2000 BC coincided with the production of the so-called Kamares pottery in the workshops of Knossos and Phaestos. Named after the cave at Kamares where the pottery was first found, this elegant, beautifully crafted pottery flourished during the entire Middle Minoan period. Cups, spouted jars and *pithoi* (large Minoan storage jars) could now be produced quickly with the invention of the potter's wheel. The use of the wheel also gave a new crispness to the designs. The stylised motifs were derived from plant and marine life and were balanced with curvilinear abstract patterns, usually painted in white, red, orange and yellow on black or grey backgrounds. The most striking pottery was the 'eggshell' vases characterised by extremely thin walls.

Other crafts also reached a high degree of artistry during this period. Using semiprecious stones and clay, artisans made miniature master-

DID YOU KNOW?

The Minoans knew how to enjoy themselves. They played board games, boxed and wrestled, played leapfrog over bulls and one another, and performed bold acrobatic feats. Minoan dancing, portrayed in frescoes, was famous throughout ancient Greece.

MINOAN TRADE

As the population of Crete increased and vibrant commercial centres emerged in the eastern part of the island, the Minoans became well placed to trade with their neighbours in the eastern Mediterranean. Prevailing winds from the north meant that trade followed a general circular route: from the Nile delta, up the coast of today's Levant, across to Cyprus and along the southern coast of Asia Minor to Greece and beyond. Crete initially exported its natural products such as olive oil and livestock, and imported silver from the Cyclades, gold from the North Aegean, and ivory and tin from the Near East. Minoan pottery from the Neopalatial period, plus textiles and agricultural produce, subsequently found ready markets throughout the Cyclades, as well as in Egypt, Syria and possibly Sicily. Kamares pottery in particular was exported to Cyprus, Egypt and the Levant.

MURDER IN THE TEMPLE

Human sacrifice is not commonly associated with the peace-loving Minoans, but the evidence found at the site of Anemospilia near the village of Arhanes, 18km south of Iraklio, irrefutably suggests otherwise. During excavations at a simple three-room temple in the 1980s, scientists found the remains of a young man placed on an altar and trussed, with a huge sacrificial bronze dagger incised with the shape of a boar-like beast amid the bones. The remains of two other skeletons nearby – probably those of a priestess and an assistant – seemed to indicate that the boy's death was part of a sacrificial rite. The sacrifice was probably made just as the 1700 BC earthquake began, in a desperate attempt to appease the gods.

pieces out of carved seal-stones that sometimes contained hieroglyphic letters. The exquisite bee pendant found at Malia displays extraordinary delicacy and imagination in jewellery making.

Neopalatial Period

From 1700 to 1450 BC Minoan civilisation reached its 'golden age'. Although fresco painting probably existed before 1700 BC, all remnants were destroyed in the cataclysm that destroyed Minoan palaces around that time. The palace at Knossos yielded the richest trove of frescoes from the Neopalatial period. Although only fragments survive, they were very carefully restored and the technique of using plant and mineral dyes has kept the colours relatively fresh. The subjects reflect the full variety of Minoan experience and influenced wall paintings on the Greek mainland. Landscapes rich with animals and birds; marine life teeming with fish and octopuses; and banquets, games and rituals are rendered with vivid naturalism. Griffins are repeatedly represented, indicating that they may have had a protective function. Minoan fresco painters borrowed heavily from certain Egyptian conventions – men's skin was bronze and women's was white, for example – but the figures are far less rigid than most Egyptian wall paintings.

Pottery also flourished in the Neopalatial era. In the early years there was the marine style and a floral style that reflected the same themes as the era's frescoes. Octopuses, dolphins and fish appeared on some pottery, while others showed flowers, leaves and branches, along with religious symbols. By contrast with earlier pottery, the decoration was often in dark colours such as brown and rust painted on light backgrounds. After 1500 BC, vases spouted three handles and were frequently shaped as animal heads. The stone *rhyton* (drinking vessel) in the shape of a bull's head is a particularly fine example from this period.

The art of seal-stone carving also advanced in the palace workshops. Goats, lions and griffins were rendered in minute detail on hard stones, usually in an almond shape. Minoan sculptors also created fine idols in *faïence* (quartz-glazed earthenware), gold, ivory, bronze and stone. The serpent goddess in *faïence* is one of the most outstanding surviving examples.

Postpalatial Period

The second cataclysm of 1750 BC that destroyed Minoan palaces saw the decline of Minoan culture. The lively marine pottery of previous centuries degenerated into dull rigidity. Whether because of less trade with Egypt or the loss of the palace workshops, frescoes became uninspired. The production of jewellery and seal-stones was replaced by the production of weaponry reflecting the influence of the warlike Mycenaeans.

DID YOU KNOW?

There are Minoan palaces yet to be unearthed in Crete, including what archaeologists believe is the second-largest palace after Knossos, the Palekastro site in eastern Crete, which is being excavated slowly by the British School of Archaeology.

The Culture

REGIONAL IDENTITY

With their distinctive music, cuisine and traditions, the people of Crete will normally identify as a Cretan before they say they are Greek. Even within different parts of Crete, people tend to maintain a strong regional identity.

DID YOU KNOW?

Personal questions are not considered rude in Greece, so don't be surprised if you are grilled about your age, salary, marital status etc, and to be given sympathy if you are over 25 and not married.

Proud and patriotic, Cretans uphold an undeniable connection to their culture, which is particularly apparent when you leave the commercialised major tourist centres. In rural areas, many Cretans still speak a local dialect, have a distinct accent and lead traditional lives.

Centuries of battling foreign occupiers have left the island with a stubbornly independent streak that sometimes leads to clashes with Athens. National laws that conflict with local customs are often disregarded. For example, guns are strictly regulated in Greece, but nearly every household in Crete at least one illegal firearm and many homes harbour small arsenals.

Nevertheless, the Cretan people have a well-justified reputation for hospitality and for treating strangers like honoured guests. Obviously Cretans are no longer offering free food and lodging to millions of tourists a year, but if you wander off the beaten track into mountain villages you may be invited to someone's home for a coffee or even a meal. Often in a café or taverna it is customary for people to treat another group of friends or strangers to a round of drinks (however, be mindful that it is not the done thing to treat them straight back – you do the honours another time).

Cretan society is also deeply influenced by the Greek Orthodox Church and its rituals, and the calendar year revolves around religious celebrations (see p211 for a list). There are strong family ties and a sense of family honour, although the days of the infamous vendettas are (almost) gone.

The Greeks, by James Pettifer, is a worthwhile read for a remarkably accurate look at Greek contemporary life from a historical, societal, environmental and ethnographical perspective.

Cretan weddings and baptisms are still huge affairs and while shooting pistols in the air is becoming more politically incorrect (and dangerous as people have accidentally been hit and killed), it is still common in some areas, where bullet-riddled road signs are a characteristic part of the landscape.

Employment opportunities in tourism have kept many younger people from leaving the island, although many have moved to Crete's cities and towns and the society has become increasingly urbanised. Those that have left for Athens or migrated overseas (far fewer than in other regions of Greece) maintain strong cultural and family links, returning regularly.

Rivalries between the prefectures are strong. As the island's capital until 1971, Hania considers itself the historical heart of the island while Rethymno claims to be its cultural centre.

The dominant political ideology is left-of-centre with the socialist PASOK party repeatedly outdrawing the conservative New Democracy party in local and national elections. Extremists on either the right or left have little support.

Like most of Greece, there is an undercurrent of anti-Americanism in Crete, culminating in protests over the US military base at Souda and demonstrated with subtle objections such as refusing to serve Coke in tavernas.

LIFESTYLE

The Cretan lifestyle has changed dramatically in the past 20 years, the most obvious change being that Cretans are conspicuously wealthier. Living standards have improved dramatically and the towns are full of sophisticated restaurants, bars and clubs.

Cretans pride themselves on their capacity to enjoy life. You will see them dressed up and going out en masse for their evening *volta* (stroll), hanging out drinking endless coffees, dining out and patronising the many nightclubs.

Like most households in Greece, the Cretans have felt the brunt of higher living costs since the introduction of the euro. Eating out has become much more expensive, although there are still many reasonably priced tavernas in Crete, particularly in the villages.

Cretans deal with the seasonal invasion of foreign tourists by largely operating in a different time–space continuum from their guests. They will often tell you a particular place is 'only for tourists'.

From April to around October, many live in the hurly-burly of the coastal resorts – running shops, pensions or tavernas – and then return to their traditional life in the hills for the autumn olive and grape harvest. While tourists eat early in the evening in restaurants along a harbour or beach, Cretans drive out to a village taverna for a dinner that begins around 11pm. Often these tavernas produce their own meat and vegetables, saving on business costs and at the same time providing better food. Many dance clubs play Western music until around 3am when the Greek crowd arrives and the music switches to Cretan or Greek music.

The generational divide is another feature of modern Crete, as is the rural–city divide. In rural areas many people still live traditional lives: you will see shepherds with their flock in the mountains and men congregating in the *kafeneia* (coffee house) after their siesta. Mountain villages are repositories of traditional culture and you'll find that many older women and many men are still clad in black garb. During rural weddings and festivals even young men don black boots, shirt and baggy pants, tucking a pistol into their belt to be fired into the air as the evening wears on.

People still live off the land – and provide for their families in the cities – but subsistence farming has mostly given way to commercial production. Though you will still see the odd donkey, it has been replaced by the pick-up truck and Cretans rely strongly on foreign workers to do the grunt work. Public servants and many other workers are usually given time off during the olive harvest to help them produce their family oil.

The Greeks place a lot of importance on education and the free state education is supplemented with private tuition *(frontistiria)* for languages and other subjects. Most of the younger generation speak English and often German as well.

It is uncommon for Greeks to move out of home until they are married, apart from leaving temporally to study or work. The reasons for this are practical as well as cultural – most will get a house when they get married and who wants to do their own washing and cooking anyway?

POPULATION

Crete is Greece's most populous island with 540,054 people. The populations of the island's major cities are: Iraklio (130,194), Hania (53,373), Rethymno (27,868) and Agios Nikolaos (10,080). After the exodus of the Turkish population in 1923 Crete became ethnically homogenous, consisting solely of Greek Orthodox residents.

Harvard anthropologist Michael Herzfeld makes interesting anthropological observations of Cretans in *The Poetics of Manhood: Contest and Manhood in a Cretan Village*, while *A Place in History* looks at life in and around Rethymno, including issues such as the Cretan vendetta.

SPORT

Football (soccer) is the most popular sport in Greece followed by basketball. Cretan men are avid sports fans. If you happen to be eating in a taverna on a night when a big match is being televised, expect indifferent service. Crete hosted the 2004 Olympic soccer preliminaries at Iraklio's massive Pankritio stadium.

MULTICULTURALISM

In recent years, large numbers of migrant workers from the Balkans and Eastern Europe have moved to Crete, working mostly as unskilled labourers in the agricultural and construction sectors, as well as in service industries such as tourism. The majority are Albanians, many of whom have set up businesses and bought homes. Many English and Germans have also settled and bought property on Crete.

These migrants – legal and illegal – are a relatively new phenomenon for Crete, where multiculturalism is a foreign concept. Like most of Greece, whose migrant population is now over 10%, Crete is struggling to come to terms with the new reality and the issue is sure to dominate the political agenda.

MEDIA

Greeks are great newspaper readers and avid TV watchers. Media ownership is spread around half-a-dozen major players. Crete has its own media, including several regional dailies and weeklies as well as two glossy local magazines, **Stigmes** (www.stigmes.gr), which has a good English website, and *Go Hania*, which is in Greek only.

The monthly English and German newspaper *Cretasummer* is distributed around Rethymno and the monthly magazine *Kreta* is on sale in a variety of languages. Both contain useful information and interesting articles amid the ads.

You will find most major international newspapers and magazines at foreign press stands in the major cities and in tourist resorts.

There are more than 40 radio stations in Crete, including the state-owned ET1 and ET2. The mountains that dominate the island means constantly changing reception for FM stations.

There are two local state TV stations, as well as regional commercial operators. Many hotels and bars have satellite TV where you can pick up CNN, the BBC and music and sports channels.

RELIGION

About 98% of Greeks belong to the Greek Orthodox Church. Most of the rest are Roman Catholic, Jewish or Muslim, although the recent influx of immigrants has no doubt affected this mix.

The Greek Orthodox Church is closely related to the Russian Orthodox Church and together they form the third-largest branch of Christianity. Orthodox, meaning 'right belief', was founded in the 4th century by Constantine the Great, who was converted to Christianity by a vision of the Cross.

By the 8th century, there were a number of differences of opinion between the pope in Rome and the patriarch of Constantinople, as well as increasing rivalry between the two. By the 11th century these differences had become irreconcilable, and in 1054 the pope and the patriarch excommunicated one another. Ever since, the two have gone their own ways as the (Greek/Russian) Orthodox Church and the Roman Catholic Church.

EASTER IN CRETE

Easter in Crete and throughout Greece is the most important religious festival of the year. The ceremonies take place throughout Holy Week culminating in the resurrection of Christ on the eve of Easter Sunday.

The Monday evening service is the 'Bridegroom Service' because the priest carries an icon of Christ, 'the bridegroom' through the church. Tuesday is dedicated to Mary Magdalene and Wednesday is the 'Day of Atonement'. On Thursday worshippers mourn for Christ in the evening service, and on Good Friday the symbolic body of Christ is bedecked with flowers and carried through the streets in a candle-lit procession.

The climax of the week is the Saturday-evening service. Just before midnight all lights in the churches are extinguished until the priest appears with a lit candle and spreads the holy light through the congregation who are all holding candles. At midnight the priest announces *Hristos Anesti!* 'Christ has risen' and fireworks and gunshots herald the start of feasting that lasts through Easter Sunday. The ceremony is the most significant moment in the Orthodox year, for it symbolises the Resurrection. Its poignancy and beauty are spellbinding. Worshippers make their way home, trying to keep the candle lit to bless the house.

The Lenten fast ends immediately after church. Worshippers light their candles from the blessed flame and break their fast with the ritual eating of *mayiritsa* (tripe soup) at home. Cretans also celebrate with the cracking of red-dyed Easter eggs, and the following afternoon with an outdoor feast of spit-roast lamb followed by dancing and merrymaking.

During Ottoman times membership of the Orthodox Church was one of the most important criteria in defining a Greek and the church was the principal upholder of Greek culture and traditions.

Religion is still integral to life in Greece, and the Greek year is centred on the festivals of the church calendar. Most Greeks, when they have a problem, will go into a church and light a candle to the saint they feel is most likely to help them.

The Orthodox religion held Cretan culture together during the many dark centuries of repression, despite numerous, largely futile efforts by the Venetians and Turks to turn the Cretans towards Catholicism and Islam.

The Orthodox Church of Crete is independent from the Greek Orthodox Church and answers directly to the Patriarch of Constantinople.

If you wish to look around a church or monastery, you should always dress appropriately. Women should wear skirts that reach below the knees, men should wear long trousers and arms should be covered. Regrettably, many churches are kept locked nowadays, but it's usually easy enough to locate the caretakers, who will be happy to open them for you.

WOMEN IN CRETE

While men seem to take a front seat in public life in Crete, it is the women who largely run the show at home and in business, and are often the more dynamic gender.

In the villages, men and women still tend to occupy different spheres. When not tending livestock or olive trees, Cretan men can usually be found in a kafeneio playing cards and drinking coffee or raki. Although exceptions are made for foreign women, kafeneia are off-limits to Cretan women who are usually occupied with housework and child rearing. While it's becoming rarer these days, women busy themselves in their free hours with sewing, crocheting or embroidery, often in a circle of other women.

Patricia Storace's *Dinner with Persephone* is as much a travelogue as it is a series of sociological observations seen through the eyes of an American woman living in Greece. Every woman traveller to Greece should read this book.

Rural areas are still relatively conservative and girls who do not pursue an education tend to marry young. Socially, you will often see women in black segregated from the men at special events.

Cretan woman are house-proud and spend much time cultivating their culinary skills. Most men rarely participate in domestic duties (or certainly don't own up to it).

In the cities and large towns things are much more liberal. Old attitudes towards the 'proper role' for women are changing fast as more women are educated and enter the workforce. Young Cretan women in skin-tight slacks are more likely to be found in a bar than behind a loom.

ARTS
Fine Arts
MINOAN ART
See p36 for a detailed look at the history of Minoan art in Crete.

DORIAN & ROMAN PERIODS
There was a brief artistic renaissance on Crete that lasted from the 8th to the 7th centuries BC. A new movement in sculpture emerged called the Daedalic movement after a sculptor called Daedalos. Although the existence of this sculptor is uncertain, it is clear that a group of sculptors called the Daedalids perfected a new technique of making sculptures in hammered bronze. They worked in a style that combined Eastern and Greek aesthetics and their influence spread to mainland Greece. Cretan culture went into decline at the end of the 7th century BC. There was a brief revival under the Romans, mainly notable for the richly decorated mosaic floors and marble sculptures.

BYZANTINE PERIOD
Although Byzantine icons and frescoes were created from the earliest years of Byzantine rule, much of them were destroyed in popular rebellions during the 13th and 14th centuries. In the 11th century, émigrés

DOMINIKOS THEOTOKOPOULOS (EL GRECO)
One of the geniuses of the Renaissance, El Greco (meaning 'The Greek' in Spanish; his real name was Dominikos Theotokopoulos) was born and educated on Crete but had to travel to Spain to earn recognition.

El Greco was born in the Cretan capital of Candia (present-day Iraklio) in 1541 during a time of great artistic activity in the city, following the arrival of large numbers of painters fleeing Ottoman-held Constantinople. These painters had a formative influence upon the young El Greco, giving him early grounding in the traditions of late-Byzantine fresco painting that was to give such a powerful spiritual element to his later paintings.

Because Candia was a Venetian city it was a logical step for El Greco to head to Venice to further his studies, and he set off when he was in his early 20s to join the studio of Titian. It was not, however, until he moved to Spain in 1577 that he really came into his own as a painter. His highly emotional style struck a chord with the Spanish, and the city of Toledo became his home until his death in 1614. To view the most famous of his works, like his masterpiece *The Burial of Count Orgaz* (1586), you will have to travel to Toledo. The only El Greco work on display in Crete is *View of Mt Sinai and the Monastery of St Catherine* (1570), painted during his time in Venice. It hangs in Iraklio's Historical Museum of Crete (p151).

A white marble bust of the painter stands in the city's Plateia El Greco, and there are streets named after him throughout the island.

from Constantinople brought portable icons to Crete, but the only surviving example from this period is the icon of the virgin at Mesopantitissa, now in Venice. From the 13th to the early 16th centuries, churches around Crete were decorated with frescoes – many of which can still be seen today. Byzantine art flowered under the Paleologan emperors who ruled from 1258 to 1453, and its influence spread to Crete. The great icon painter of the 14th century was Ioannis Pagomenos who worked in western Crete.

THE CRETAN SCHOOL

With the fall of Constantinople in 1453 many Byzantine artists fled to Crete. At the same time, the Italian Renaissance was in full bloom and many Cretan artists studied in Italy. The result was the 'Cretan school' of icon painting that combined technical brilliance and dramatic richness. In Iraklio alone there were over 200 painters working from the mid-16th to mid-17th centuries who were equally at ease in Venetian and Byzantine styles. The Cretan Theophanes Sterlitzas painted monasteries throughout Greece, and spread the techniques of the Cretan school.

Too few examples of the Cretan school are on display in Crete. In Iraklio, you can see some fine examples at the church and museum of Agia Ekaterini (p151) – the centrepiece of the collection being six portable icons from the great Michael Damaskinos, the finest exponent of the Cretan school. Damaskinos' long sojourn in Venice introduced him to new techniques of rendering perspective, which he brought to the Byzantine style of icon painting.

Dance

Scenes of dancing Minoans in frescoes suggest that dancing in Crete began in the ancient Greek temples. Dancing is depicted on ancient Greek vases and there are references to dances in Homer's works, who commented on the ability of Cretan dancers in particular.

Cretan dances are dynamic, fast and warlike, and many of them are danced by groups of men. Dances for women are traditionally related to wedding or courtship, and are danced in a more delicate and graceful way. Like most Greek dances they are normally performed in a circle – in ancient times, dancers formed a circle to seal themselves off from evil influences.

The most popular Cretan dances are the graceful and slow *syrto*, and the *pendozali*, which was originally danced by armed warriors and has a slow and faster version that builds into a frenzy, with the leader doing kicks, variations and fancy moves while the others follow with more mild steps. Another popular dance is the *sousta*, a bouncy courtship dance with small precise steps that is performed by couples. Other Cretan dances include the *maleviziotiko* (also known as *kastrino or pidikto*), which is a fast triumphant dance.

Dancing well is a matter of great personal pride, and most dancers will take their turn at the front to demonstrate their prowess. Be aware that cutting in on somebody's dance is absolutely bad form, as families have usually paid for the dance (this is how Cretan musicians often make their living).

The best place to see Cretan dancing is at festivals, weddings and baptisms. Folkloric shows are also put on for tourists in many areas. Although these are more contrived they still normally give you a decent show of traditional dancing.

DID YOU KNOW?

The oldest surviving folk songs in Greece, dating from the 17th century, were found at Mt Athos and were revealed to be *rizitika* from western Crete.

In addition to Crete's own traditional music and dances, you will also come across music and dance from all over Greece.

Music

In Crete, music is woven into the fabric of everyday life, and almost always accompanies weddings, births, holidays, harvesting and any other celebration.

For an insight into Cretan music go to www.cretan-music.com, which is in English and Greek.

Over the centuries, Cretan music has been influenced by many musical traditions. The main instruments are the lyra, a three-stringed instrument similar to a violin that is played resting on the knee; the eight-stringed *laouto* (lute), which is played like a guitar; and the *mandolino* (mandolin). There is also the *askomandouro* (bagpipe), *habioli* (whistle) and *daoulaki* (drum).

The *bouzouki*, the mandolin-like instrument with a long neck heard everywhere in Greece, is not part of Cretan music. While it is heard on radio in Crete and is used in live performances by visiting mainland artists, the *bouzouki* plays very much second fiddle to traditional Cretan musical instruments and is rarely played in public.

One of Crete's favourite forms of musical expression is *mandinades*, rhyming couplets of 15 syllables that express the age-old concerns of love, death and the vagaries of fate. Probably originating as love songs in 15th-century Venice, thousands of *mandinades* helped forge a sense of national identity during the long centuries of occupation. The best 'rhymers' at Cretan festivals will tailor their songs to the people present and try to outdo each other in skill and composition. These days young Cretans continue the tradition, although they have been known to cheat by storing *mandinades* on their mobile phones (and you can also find them online).

Another popular form of music is *rizitika*, which are centuries-old songs from the Lefka Ori thought to have derived from the songs of the border guards of the Byzantine Empire, though it is believed they may date further back than Byzantine times.

There are two kinds of *rizitika* – *tis tavlas* (table) songs that accompany feasts and *tis stratas* (round) songs, which accompany travellers. Many of the *rizitika* songs deal with historical or heroic themes. One of the most popular is the song of Daskalogiannis, the Sfakian hero who led the rebellion against the Turks in 1770. The song has 1034 verses.

ANOGIA'S MUSICAL HERITAGE

The village of Anogia (p132), in the foothills of Mt Psiloritis in Rethymno, has produced a disproportionate number of musically talented sons: the much-loved and now long-lamented singer and lyrist Nikos Xylouris was from Anogia and his house is maintained as a kind of musical shrine in the lower village of Anogia. His idiosyncratic brother Psarantonis has since taken up the reins and is wildly popular among Cretans nationwide. Psarantonis' son, Giorgos Xylouris, plays music both at home in Crete and in Australia where he lived for many years, while his brother Giannis Xylouris is among the most-respected musicians on the island.

Vasilis Skoulas, the latest in a long line of lyra players from the same family, now proudly plays lyra and sings on the world stage as well as to fellow Cretans. Other notable musicians from Anogia include the lyra player Manolis Manouras, Mitsos and Vasilis Stavrakakis, and Nikiforos Aerakis.

More recently, the talented but capricious Georgos Tramoundanis, who goes by the stage name of Loudovikos ton Anogion (Ludwig from Anogia), has been selling his brand of folksy, ballad-style Cretan compositions to audiences all over Greece. His concerts often start at the ungodly hour of 4am.

CRETAN MUSIC TOP 10

The following broad selection of recordings provides a good introduction to Cretan music past and present.

- **The Great Masters 1920–1955** This 10-CD set is the ultimate introduction to the greats of Cretan music such as Rodinos, Baxevanis, Skordalos and Koutsourelis, and Kalogridis. The CDs can also be bought separately. It includes an excellent 220-page booklet in Greek and English.

- **Nikos Xylouris** (1982) This eponymous album is probably the best overall introduction to the music and voice of one of Crete's late and now much-lamented musical sons.

- **Kostas Mountakis** (2002) This five-CD set is a collection of rare live recordings from the post-war master of Cretan music known as 'the teacher', including private and unreleased material, performances at weddings and concerts in Crete and the diaspora.

- **NOGO** (1998) By Psarantonis Xylouris, this is considered the idiosyncratic lyra player's best instrumental work and is a little more accessible than some of his traditional and erratic hard-core material. His extraordinary vocal style can be appreciated on *My Thoughts are like Old Wine* (1994).

- **Echo of Time** (1982) Ross Daly's first and seminal recording of Cretan music that has influenced the new generation of Cretan musicians. The two-CD set has lyrics by Mitsos Stavrakakis and Vasilis Stavrakakis on vocal.

- **Palaiina Seferia** (1997) The excellent self-titled first album of this contemporary Cretan group of artists influenced by early Cretan music and led by Zacharias Spyridakis, a student of the lyra master Mountakis.

- **Drosostalides** (1993) Arguably the best recording by the popular Vasilis Skoulas, one of Anogia's most prolific producers of traditional Cretan music.

- **Oi Dikoi Mou Filoi** (2002) Features original compositions by the well-respected new-generation artist Stelios Petrakis from Sitia, who is becoming noticed on the world music scene for his contemporary take on Cretan music. He is accompanied by Giorgos Xylouris, Vasilis Stavrakakis, Ross Daly and Iranian percussionist Bhijan Chemirani.

- **Antipodes** (2002) By the Xylouris Ensemble, this recording is notable as much for its excellent music as for the unique composition of the band. Recorded in Australia, it is the most representative work of Giorgos Xylouris, with Australian musicians playing and singing Cretan songs.

- **Agrimi kai Koraso** (2002) 'The Wild Animal and the Young Girl', by Papa Stefanis Nikas, is a fine recording of original lyrics and music deeply based in Cretan tradition, featuring musicians Manos Mountakis, Dimitris Sgouros, Vasilis Skoulas and Psarantonis.

With more than 10,000 lines, the epic romantic poem *Erotokritos*, written by Vitsentzos Kornaros, has provided ample material for performers, and continues to inspire Crete's musicians. It has been put to music countless times, with each artist presenting their own interpretation of the great work.

Crete has produced a rich tapestry of music and musicians, with a swathe of artists – including the legendary Nikos Xylouris – coming from the village of Anogia (see the boxed text opposite).

A disproportionate number of composers of contemporary Greek urban music are of Cretan origin. The contemporary composer Giannis Markopoulos from Ierapetra wrote the internationally known *Who Pays the Ferryman* composition. The excellent sextet Haïnides is one of the more popular bands to emerge from Crete in recent years, playing their own brand of music.

www.hellenicbookservice .co.uk has a useful but by no means exhaustive listing of books about Crete with reviews.

NIKOS KAZANTZAKIS – CRETE'S PRODIGAL SON

Crete's most famous contemporary literary son is Nikos Kazantzakis. Born in 1883 in Iraklio, the then Turkish-dominated capital, Kazantzakis spent his early childhood in the ferment of revolution and change that was creeping upon his homeland. In 1897 the revolution that finally broke out against Turkish rule forced him to leave Crete for studies in Naxos, Athens and later Paris. It wasn't until he was 31, in 1914, that he finally turned his hand to writing by translating philosophical books into Greek. For a number of years he travelled throughout Europe – Switzerland, Germany, Austria, Russia and Britain – thus laying the groundwork for a series of travelogues in his later literary career.

Nikos Kazantzakis was a complex writer and his early work was heavily influenced by the prevailing philosophical ideas of the time. The nihilistic philosophies of Nietzsche influenced his writings, throughout which Kazantzakis is tormented by a tangible metaphysical and existentialist anguish. His relationship with religion was always troubling – his official stance being that of a nonbeliever, yet he always seemed to toy with the idea that perhaps God did exist. His self-professed greatest work is his *Odyssey*, a modern-day epic loosely based on the trials and travels of the ancient hero Odysseus (Ulysses). A weighty and complex opus of 33,333 iambic verses, *Odyssey* never fully realised Kazantzakis' aspirations to be held in the same league as Homer, Virgil or the Renaissance Italian, Tasso.

Ironically it was only much later in his career after Kazantzakis belatedly turned to novel writing that his star finally shone. It was through works such as *Christ Recrucified* (1948), *Kapetan Mihalis* (1950; now known as *Freedom and Death*) and *The Life and Manners of Alexis Zorbas* (1946) that he became internationally known. This last work gave rise to the image of the ultimate, modern Greek male 'Zorba the Greek', which was immortalised by Anthony Quinn in the movie of the same name.

Kazantzakis died while travelling in Freiburg, Germany on 26 October 1957. Despite resistance from the Orthodox Church, he was given a religious funeral and buried in the southern Martinenga Bastion of the old walls of Iraklio.

Crete has a healthy music scene with spirited established folk artists playing weddings and festivals (Cretan music is inextricably linked to dance) and producing regular recordings. A younger generation of formally trained musicians is also experimenting with new forms of expression influenced by early Cretan music.

Falling for Icarus: A Journey Among the Cretans, by Englishman Rory MacLean, is an entertaining novel about a man's attempt to build his own flying machine and the village's reaction.

The most prominent Cretan musician today is the legendary Psarantonis, known for his unique style of playing and instantly recognisable from his wild beard and straggly mane of hair. Psarantonis' performs regularly – everywhere from the smallest Cretan village to the clubs of Athens and the international circuit.

Cretan music has become quite popular throughout the world music scene and the new musical workshop, established by Cretan resident and lyra master Ross Daly near Iraklio, is further promoting dialogue with the world's leading traditional musicians (see the boxed text on p162 for more details).

Literature

Crete has a rich literary tradition that sprang from the Cretan love of songs, verses and word play. In the late-16th or early 17th centuries, Crete had a tremendous literary flowering under Venetian rule.

The era's greatest masterpiece was undoubtedly the epic poem *Erotokritos* written by Vitsentzos Kornaros of Sitia. More than 10,000 lines long, this poem of courtly love is full of nostalgia for the dying Venetian regime that was threatened by the rise in Turkish power. The poem was recited for centuries by illiterate peasants and professional singers alike, embodying the dreams of freedom that enabled Cretans to endure their many privations. Many of the verses were incorporated into Crete's beloved *mandinades*. The poem is available in translation from The **Hellenic Bookservice** (☎ 020 7267 9499; www.hellenicbookservice.co.uk; 91 Fortress Rd, Kentish Town, London, NW5 1AG).

Greece's best-known and most widely read author since Homer is Nikos Kazantzakis, born in Crete in 1883, amid the last spasms of the island's struggle for independence from the Turks. His novels are full of drama and larger-than-life characters. His most famous works are *The Last Temptation*, *Zorba the Greek*, *Christ Recrucified* and *Freedom or Death*. The first two have been made into films. *Zorba the Greek* takes place on Crete and provides a fascinating glimpse of the harsher side of Cretan culture.

Kazantzakis had a chequered and at times troubled literary career, clashing frequently with the Orthodox Church for his professed atheism (see the boxed text opposite).

Iraklio may have Kazantzakis, but Rethymno can lay claim to Pandelis Prevelakis. Born in Rethymno in 1900, Prevelakis also studied in Athens and at the Sorbonne. Primarily known as a poet, Prevelakis also wrote plays and novels, and his best-known work is *The Tale of a Town*, which is about his home town.

Emerging contemporary Cretan writers include Rhea Galanaki, who has so far published three novels – to some critical acclaim. The prize-winning *The Life of Ismail Ferik Pasha* has been translated into six languages, and focuses on the clash of Christianity and Ottoman Islam in a story based on Crete.

David Holton's commentary Erotokritos *is the best academic study of the epic Cretan love story by Vitsentzos Kornaros.*

Film

Cretans are avid cinema-goers, although most of the films are North American or British.

The Greek film industry was for many years in the doldrums, largely due to inadequate government funding and a tendency to produce largely slow-moving esoteric films loaded with symbolism, but too avant-garde to have mass appeal, despite being well made with some outstanding cinematography.

The leader of this school is Greece's most acclaimed film director, Theodoros Angelopoulos, who won the 1988 Golden Palm award at the Cannes Film Festival for *Eternity and a Day*. His other well-known films include *Ulysses Gaze* starring Harvey Keittel, *The Beekeeper*, *Alexander the Great* and *Landscapes in the Mist*.

More recently Greek filmmakers have begun producing commercially successful films, a trend started by the box office hit *Safe Sex*, a light-hearted look at Greek sexuality by Thanasis Reppas and Mihalis Papathanasiou, who have continued in this vein.

Contemporary Greek filmmakers are also making an impact on the international film festival circuit, and things were looking up after the critically acclaimed *Touch of Spice* broke all box office records in 2004. Importantly, it was the first Greek film in decades to get an international commercial release.

Crete has no local film industry and has not been the location for the dreamier Greek island films such as *The Big Blue* or *Mediterranneo*. The most famous movie shot in Crete is *Zorba the Greek,* which was shot in Stavros on the Akrotiri Peninsula, as well as on other locations. In 1956 the American director Jules Dassin *(Never On Sunday)* chose Kritsa as the backdrop for *He Who Must Die*, the film version of Katzantzakis'

Literature and Society in Renaissance Crete, by David Holton, is a comprehensive study of the literature of the Cretan renaissance in its historical, social and cultural context, with chapters on the poetic and dramatic genres contributed by leading experts in the field.

novel *Christ Recrucified* starring Dassin's wife, Melina Mercouri. The film lovingly captured the worn faces of the villagers, many of whom acted in the film.

More recently, Greek satirist Lakis Lazopoulos and Greek–Australian actress Zoe Carides starred in *Beware of Greeks Bearing Guns* (2000), a romantic comedy about a Cretan vendetta. The Greek–Australian co-production was shot in Crete and Melbourne.

Environment

THE LAND

Crete is the largest island in the Greek archipelago with an area of 8335 sq km. It's 250km long, about 60km at its widest point and 12km at its narrowest. The island has an extraordinary environmental diversity, with mountainous regions, gorges, a vast coastline and a plethora of caves.

Three major mountain groups – the Lefka Ori (White Mountains) in the west, Mt Psiloritis (also known as Mt Idi) in the centre and the Lasithi Mountains in the east – define the island's rugged interior. The Lefka Ori are known for their spectacular gorges, such as Samaria, plus the snow that lingers on the mountains well into spring. The Omalos Plateau is in the Lefka Ori at an altitude of 1000m. The highest mountain peak is Psiloritis (p130), at 2456m. It has hundreds of caves, including the Ideon Andron Cave where Zeus allegedly grew up, and the Rouva Forest on its southern slopes.

The Lasithi Mountains harbour the famous Lasithi Plateau (p188) and Mt Dikti (2148m) whose southern slopes preserve an example of the magnificent forests that once blanketed the island.

Western Crete is the most mountainous and greenest part of the island, while eastern Crete tends to be barren and rocky. Most of the interior is mountainous and marked by olive trees, scrub and wild herbs. High upland plateaus are either cultivated (like the Lasithi Plateau) or used for pasturing goats (like the Omalos Plateau). The largest cultivable area in the south is the fertile Mesara Plain. Lake Kournas, near Hania, is the only lake on the island.

Gavdos island (p111), the most southerly point in Europe, just 300km from Africa, is also part of Crete.

WILDLIFE

Animals

Mammal life on Crete is divided between livestock and endangered species. Sheep, goats and cows are treated with the respect appropriate to any money-making endeavour, but all other mammals have been hunted ferociously. Crete's most famous animal is the *kri-kri*, a wild goat often depicted in Minoan art. Only a few survive in and around the Samaria Gorge (p100). Other local mammals include the indigenous Cretan spiny mouse and a large population of bats.

One of the more intriguing rare animals on Crete is the *fourokattos* (wild cat), about which shepherds have been telling tales for centuries. Scientists assumed it existed in legend only until a British scientist bought two strange pelts at a market in Hania in 1905. In 1996 Italian scientists studying Cretan fauna found the only other proof when they discovered the 5.5kg cat in a trap. It remains unclear whether the cat was indigenous to the island or whether it was a domesticated animal that ran wild.

BIRD LIFE

Bird life is varied on Crete and includes both resident and migratory species. Along the coast you'll find birds of passage such as egrets and herons during spring and autumn migrations. Various species of gulls nest on coastal cliffs and offshore islets. Rare hawks migrate up from Africa during the summer to nest on the offshore islets. Woodpigeons still nest in cliffs along the sea, but have been hunted to near extinction.

DID YOU KNOW?

There are more than 3000 caves in Crete, of which about only 850 have been explored. The cage of Tafkos, near Petradolakia in the Anogia region, has been declared the deepest cave in Greece, descending 475m to a subterranean riverbed.

DID YOU KNOW?

The *meltemi* is a northerly wind that affects the Aegean throughout the summer months. It can blow at gale force for days on end during August and September, wreaking havoc with boat schedules.

The mountains host a wealth of interesting birds. Look for blue rock thrushes, buzzards and the huge griffin vulture. In the Samaria Gorge (p100) you may spot a *lammergeier* (bearded vulture) – one of the rarest raptors in Europe, which is now threatened with extinction. Other birds in the mountains include Alpine swifts, stonechats, blackbirds and Sardinian warblers. The fields around Malia host tawny and red-throated pipits, stone-curlews, fan-tailed warblers and short-toed larks. On the hillsides below the Moni Preveli (p137) you may find ruppells and subalpine warblers. The Akrotiri Peninsula (p87) is good for bird-watching – around the monasteries of Agias Triadas and Gouvernetou you'll find collared and pied flycatchers, wrynecks, tawny pipits, black-eared wheatears, blue rock thrushes, stonechats, chukars and northern wheatears. Migrating species such as waders, egrets and gulls are found on Souda Bay.

Hard-core bird-watchers should come equipped with *A Birdwatching Guide to Crete* by Stefanie Coghlan, or for a comprehensive reference on Greece's birdlife, try *The Birds of Greece* by Christopher Helm.

SEA LIFE

The southern Cretan coastline and its steep underwater cliffs are home to the Mediterranean Sea's most significant population of sperm whales. Research during the 1990s has confirmed that sperm whales gather, feed, breed and possibly mate in the area year-round. The southern coast is also inhabited by large groups of striped dolphins, Risso's dolphins and Cuvier's beaked whales, while bottlenose dolphins are often spotted in the shallow waters between Gavdos and Gavdopoula, as well as off the southern coast.

For pre-trip inspiration about Crete's stunning natural environment, the coffee table book *Proud Beauty* is a lovely album of photographs by Dimitris Talianis (www.topio.gr), which captures the island's landscape.

The Cretan Sperm Whale Project, run by the Pelagos Cetacean Research Institute, monitors the whale population and has launched an eco-volunteer programme. Whale-watching excursions from Paleohora were once open to the public, but these were suspended in 2004 (check the latest situation at www.pelagosinstitute.gr).

Loggerhead sea turtles *(Caretta caretta)* have been nesting on Crete since the days of the dinosaurs. The beaches of Rethymno, Hania and the Mesara Gulf host more than 500 nests each summer. Sadly, the ribbons of hotels and tavernas on these beaches have seriously disturbed their nesting habits. Because they are so vulnerable on land, the females are frightened by objects on the beach at night and can refuse to lay eggs, while hatchlings emerging at night are disoriented by tavern and hotel lights.

LOGGERHEAD TURTLES

Since 1990, the **Sea Turtle Protection Society of Greece** (www.archelon.gr) has worked with state agencies, local authorities, hotel groups, tour operators, fishermen and local residents to reverse the decline of the sea turtle population through a management plan. About 33km of beach is patrolled through the nesting and hatching season. Signposted metal cages are put around nests to protect them from sun-beds and tourists, many hatcheries are fenced off and the problem of lights on the beach is gradually being addressed. The society has the following advice for visitors:

- Leave the beaches clear at night during the May to October nesting season.
- Remove umbrellas and lounge chairs at night.
- Don't touch baby turtles on the way to the sea; they must orient themselves and the walk strengthens them.
- Urge hotel and taverna owners to cooperate with the society and shade their lights when necessary.
- Dispose of rubbish properly; plastic bags, mistaken by the turtles as jellyfish, are lethal.

Plants

Crete is renowned for its amazing variety of plants and wild flowers. It has been estimated that there are about 2000 species of plants on the island and about 160 of those are found only on Crete.

As a rule, a visit in March or April is the surest way to see the island in full flower, but mountain plants and flowers often bloom later and late rains can also extend the growing season.

Along the coast you'll come across sea daffodils that flower in August and September, and knapweeds on the west coast that flower in April and May. The purple or violet petals of stocks provide pretty splashes of colour on sandy beaches from April to May. In eastern Crete, especially around Sitia, watch for crimson poppies on the borders of the beach in April and May. At the edge of sandy beaches that are not yet lined with a strip of hotels you'll find delicate pink bindweeds and jujube trees that flower from May to June and bear fruit in September and October. In the same habitat is the tamarisk tree that flowers in the spring.

Further away from the beach in the lowlands are junipers and holm oak trees, as well as poppies and purple lupins that flower in the spring. If you come in the summer, you won't be deprived of colour since milky white and magenta oleanders bloom from June through to August.

On the hillsides look for cistus and brooms in early summer, and fabulous yellow chrysanthemums in the fields from March to May.

Many varieties of orchids and ophrys bloom in the spring on the lower slopes of the mountains turning the hills and meadows pink, purple and violet. Dense-flowering orchids, pink-flowered butterfly orchids and Cretan cyclamens are found on the Lasithi Plateau. Purple and crimson anemones are found in the same habitat in early spring followed by yellow buttercups and crowfoots in late spring.

The Flowers of Greece & the Aegean, by William Taylor and Anthony Huxley, is the most comprehensive field guide to flowers in Greece and Crete.

NATIONAL PARKS

The only national park in Crete is the Samaria Gorge (p100), the largest and most impressive gorge in Europe. It is 18km long and has a visitor centre. The Samaria Gorge is an important sanctuary for birds and animals; no-one lives in the gorge.

ENVIRONMENTAL ISSUES

The level of environmental awareness in Crete is very slowly increasing, although environmental regulation is still lacking.

There are no recycling programmes even though the huge influx of summer visitors produces tonnes of rubbish. Most tourist areas are kept

Walks with Crete's Spring Flowers, by Jeff Coleman, is based on walks around the southwestern corner of Crete, particularly Loutro, Paleohora and the Samaria Gorge.

THE HERBS OF CRETE

The pungent smell of wild mountain herbs is one that visitors to the island will never forget. Crete has one of the richest varieties of indigenous herbs in the world and Cretans collect them for a variety of uses, ranging from cooking to curing a toothache. The native dittany *(diktamo)*, used primarily for making herbal tea, has a long history. The ancients believed it would help heal wounds, or that it would ease the pains of women in labour. The goddess Aphrodite was convinced it was an aphrodisiac. Oregano *(rigani)* grows profusely all over the island. It can be made into a tea and drunk to combat diarrhoea, but it is more commonly dried and used to flavour meat dishes. Sage *(faskomilo)* has a strong aroma and is used primarily as a medicine for colds or stomach problems; its oil is particularly good for the relief of toothache. Rosemary *(dendrolivano)* is easily spotted by its long, thin aromatic leaves and is used in flavouring dishes of fish, snails or lamb. It is also used medicinally as an antiseptic, for headache relief and even for hair loss.

relatively rubbish-free, but in the interior you will often be treated to the pungent odour of garbage decomposing in an illegal dump. There have been moves for the country to clean up its act, however, after the EU fined Greece more than €5 million for not acting on its toxic waste dump at Kouroupitos in western Crete.

Outside the major cities Crete's air and water is clean, but the flora and fauna are under pressure from deforestation. Centuries of olive cultivation, firewood gathering, shipbuilding, uncontrolled livestock breeding and arson have laid waste to the forests that had carpeted the island at one time. There is no tree-replanting programme, possibly because the 90,000 goats living on the island would chew through the saplings. The use of pesticides and herbicides in farming has eliminated many bird and plant species, and hunting has decimated the animal population.

It is along Crete's shoreline that environmental damage is most acute. Marine life has suffered from the local habit of fishing with dynamite and overdevelopment of the northern coast is chasing away migratory birds. Worldwide concern has been roused for the plight of the loggerhead sea turtles, which nest on the same sandy beaches that tourists prize (see p54).

As tourism on Crete has ballooned over the last two decades, the island has had to cope with increasing demands for electricity, but plans to build a huge solar-power plant have stalled. Domestic solar power is widely used for hot water. Huge wind generators scattered around Crete also inject much-needed power into the island's electricity grid.

Things are slowly changing. Organic farming is taking off, along with a move towards sustainable tourism. Several big hotel groups, such as Grecotel, have made some award-winning efforts to protect the environment through various eco-friendly management programmes within their resorts. Green organisations, such as WWF Greece and Greenpeace, have become increasingly active in Greece over the past 10 years, and there are local environmental groups being formed in Crete.

Crete Outdoors

While the summer heat in Crete can make you just want to hit the beach, Crete is a year-round destination for travellers interested in more active experiences. Crete's rugged terrain, soaring mountains, dramatic gorges and cobalt-blue seas are a nature-lover's dream and there are growing opportunities for active and challenging holidays. You can ski on the slopes of the Lefka Ori in winter, climb its high peaks in spring or cycle along the Lasithi Plateau in summer. Spring and autumn are also the best time for great walks and serious hikes, while there are excellent horse-riding trails and every imaginable water sport, along with more extreme pursuits such as paragliding and canyoning.

CYCLING & MOUNTAIN BIKING

Cycling has caught on in a big way in Crete over the past few years, despite the mountainous terrain. While it is possible to cycle from one end of Crete to the other and barely raise a sweat, north–south routes and southern-coast cycling will test the will and stamina of most cyclists. However, the escarpment villages and valleys of the north coast and the Mesara Plain of the south do allow for some relatively flat cycling experiences.

Many do it the easy way. Tour companies now transport you and your machine to the top of the mountains and you cycle down. Plateau tours (such as those that can be spotted easily around the Lasithi Plateau) are big business. Group tours of villages in eastern Crete are also very popular, with one company offering at least seven customised rides of varying difficulty for groups of 12 to 15 riders. In Hania, Trekking Plan (see below) offers extreme biking and also all-inclusive eight-day tours for racing cyclists that cover more than 650km.

Independent cyclists coming to Crete with their own bikes are advised to bring sturdy touring bikes with multiple gears, while riders on a short fly-in, fly-out visit can hire mountain bikes for €10 to €16 per day.

Outfits such as **Trekking Plan** (☎ /fax 28210 60861; www.cycling.gr) at Agia Marina, 10km west of Hania, or **Exception Biking** (☎ 28410 89073; www.exception-biking .de) in Havania, north of Agios Nikolaos town, rent out bikes and offer organised tours.

Equipped with a serious mountain bike and enough strength in your legs you can tackle a whole range of terrain throughout what is, in essence, a mountain-biker's paradise. There are no dedicated mountain-bike guides to Crete available yet, so you may be better off joining a guided tour. Both of the companies listed above offer alternative mountain-biking tours while Trekking Plan offers biking trips for all levels, including a level three extreme biker experience for the seriously fit and committed.

HIKING & TREKKING

Crete offers an enormous variety of options for keen hikers and trekkers. Unfortunately, excellent hiking opportunities are poorly documented – there are few detailed English-language guides in publication – and the trails themselves are generally inadequately marked. The exception to this is the E4 trail, which runs the length of Crete (see the boxed text on p58).

Add to that the generally rugged and arid nature of Crete's terrain and you'll soon see why hiking and trekking here can be both a blessing and a bane. Nonetheless, the island's generally untrodden interior is probably its attraction and, while the majority of visitors may opt for a guided trek, experienced walkers will find plenty to challenge and stimulate.

There are dozens of great hikes throughout Crete that will take you through remote villages, across plains and into gorges. Some of the most popular treks, including the Samaria Gorge (p100), are detailed throughout this book.

THE E4 ROUTE

The trans-European E4 walking trail starts in Portugal and ends in Crete. In Crete the trail picks up at the port of Kissamos-Kastelli in the west and ends – after 320km – on the pebbly shore of Kato Zakros in eastern Crete. Enthusiasts planning to tackle the Cretan leg can do it in a minimum of three weeks, allowing for 15km per day, or more comfortably in four weeks allowing for stops and/or shorter hiking legs. You can, of course, tackle only sections of it if your time is limited. However, you will need to make important decisions early on as the trail splits up into two distinct sections through western Crete: the coastal route and the alpine route. The trail is marked throughout its length with black and yellow posts and signs.

From Kissamos-Kastelli the route first takes a long dip south, following the western coast via Elafonisi to Paleohora. From Paleohora there is a pleasant hike to Sougia (see the boxed text on p107). The first decision must be made at Sougia. A little east of here, the E4 alpine route shoots north and upwards and heads across the high alpine tracts of the barren Lefka Ori, while the E4 coastal route hugs the rugged coastline as far as Kato Rodakino, between Frangokastello and Plakias. The alpine route is for serious trekkers and will involve overnighting in one of three refuges along the way (see p61 for information on Crete's refuges). The E4 coastal route, while not a picnic stroll, is easier but can be quite rough in parts, particularly between Sougia and Hora Sfakion.

Neither trail actually incorporates the Samaria Gorge as part of its route, but you can easily include it. At Sougia take the first leg of the E4 alpine route as far as Omalos and hike south down the Samaria Gorge to the coast (and the E4 coastal route) at Agia Roumeli. Alpine trekkers can, of course, head north up the gorge from Agia Roumeli and pick up the E4 alpine route at Omalos. The E4 alpine route from Omalos is perhaps the toughest section of the trail and should not be attempted in the heat and aridity of July and August. It is high and exposed and there is no water other than the odd snow bank that may have lingered from winter.

From Argyroupolis, near where the two trails cross each other, the E4 alpine route now runs south of the E4 coastal route, which itself loops northwards along the escarpment of the Psiloritis massif. The E4 alpine route runs through the Amari Valley for some way, via Spili and Fourfouras, before veering west and up to the summit of Mt Psiloritis (2456m). Both trails meet once more at the Nida Plateau on the eastern side of Crete's highest mountain (see the boxed text on p131 for hikes in this area).

Heading eastward the now-unified trail meanders through the more populated Iraklio prefecture via the villages of Profitis Ilias, Arhanes and Kastelli before climbing once more to the Lasithi Plateau.

From Lasithi the route becomes alpine with a crossing of the Mt Dikti (2148m) range to the south, then turning eastwards for the remote passage down to the narrow 'neck' of Crete between Ierapetra and the Bay of Mirabello. Mountains take over as the trail threads it way between Mt Thriptis (1476m) to the south and Mt Orno (1238m) to the north. Settlements are fewer at this end of the island, so each day's trekking leg should be planned carefully.

The final leg from Papagiannades and through the villages of Handras and Ziros is less taxing and the last village, Zakros, marks the start of the hike through the 'Valley of the Dead' to the sea at Kato Zakros (see the boxed text on p200). This is the final leg on the long walk from Portugal (if you have come all the way!).

E4 WALKING TRAIL

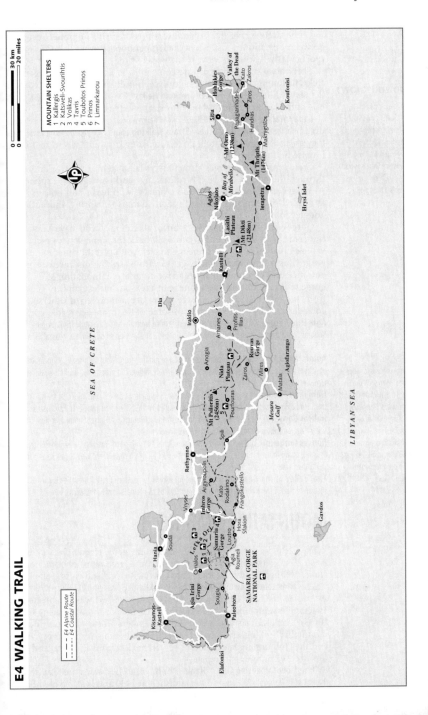

--- E4 Alpine Route
---- E4 Coastal Route

MOUNTAIN SHELTERS
1 Kallergis
2 Katsiveli-Svourihtis
3 Volikas
4 Tavris
5 Toubotos Prinos
6 Prinos
7 Limnarkarou

0   30 km
0   20 miles

SEA OF CRETE

LIBYAN SEA

While Crete is a veritable paradise for trekkers, it's not much fun at all between July and August, when the temperatures can reach 40°C. Spring (particularly April and May) is the perfect time.

There are a number of private companies in Crete running organised treks, including Trekking Plan and Exception Biking (see p57 for contact details), while Athens-based **Trekking Hellas** (☎ 210 323 4548; www.trekking.gr), one of the biggest mainland operators, runs extensive activities in Crete.

Happy Walker (☎ /fax 28310 52920; www.happywalker.com; Tobazi 56, Rethymno) can organise less-strenuous hikes. **Strata Walking Tours** (☎ 28220 24336; www.strata tours.com) in Kissamos-Kastelli do leisurely day trips and seven- to 15-day intense biking tours.

Crete's numerous gorges attract hikers from all over the world. A walk through the gorges can be a breathtaking (and hard-going) experience. Along the way you can enjoy the aroma of wild herbs and flowers, stop at shaded picnic spots, wade through streams (in spring and autumn) and get some serious exercise.

Gorge walking will involve a bit of planning if you have your own transport. You will either have to walk back the same way to pick your vehicle up, or arrange for someone to pick you up at the other end of the gorge. Bus riders can normally get to within striking distance of a gorge entrance and can often plan to arrive at an accommodation stop. Most gorge walks are doable by anyone with a reasonable level of fitness. Apart from the famous Samaria Gorge, there are a number of others worth considering. Here is a select list of some of the more accessible gorges:

Agia Irini Gorge (p107) A full-day walk best tackled from the village of Agia Irini north of Sougia. This is a challenging hike with dramatic landscape varying from alpine to coastal. It ends at Sougia.

Agiofarango A popular hike in south-central Crete running from Moni Odigitrias, 24km southwest of Mires, it ends at Agios Nikolaos beach. Alternatively, hikers can pick up the asphalt again at Kali Limenes to the east.

Hohlakies Gorge Not as well known as its near neighbour at Zakros, this short, 3km walk runs from Hohlakies village to the coast. Hikers can walk a further 7km northwards to Palekastro.

Imbros Gorge (p118) Perhaps the second-most-popular gorge walk after Samaria, it runs from the village of Imbros 8km to Komitades, near Hora Sfakion.

Rouvas Gorge (p163) This short link hike runs from the village of Zaros on the southern slopes of Psiloritis to meet up with the alpine route of the E4 trail. It's a convenient way to get to and from the trans-Crete trek.

The 'Valley of the Dead' (p200) A two-hour hike in far-eastern Crete. The valley is the last section of the E4 trekking route and runs from Zakros to the palace of Kato Zakros.

DID YOU KNOW?

Some gorges in Crete are challenging even for the fittest and most adventurous. The Ha Gorge near Mt Thriptis in eastern Crete has apparently been traversed by only 11 people.

The best maps for anyone planning to walk the E4 are the 1:100,000 *Kreta Touristikkarte* published by Harms Verlag or Iraklio-based Giorgos Petrakis' four-volume 1:100,000 maps. See p213 for more information about maps.

MOUNTAIN CLIMBING

While Crete doesn't offer the kind of stunning alpine terrain that's found in Austria or Switzerland, the island does have a large number of mountains and established mountaineering clubs catering to local and visiting climbers.

The **Mountaineering and Skiing club of Iraklio** (EOS; ☎ 2810 227 609; www.interkriti .org/orivatikos/orivat.html; Dikeosynis 53, Iraklio; ☎ 8.30pm-10.30pm) was established in 1940 and is a member of the association of Greek Mountaineering Clubs (EOS). The club has about 200 active members whose activities include mountain climbing, cross-country walking and skiing. Almost every weekend the club organises excursions to various locations in Crete, and visitors are welcome to participate.

The **Mountaineering Club of Hania** (EOS; ☎ 28210 74560; www.interkriti.org/orivatikos /hania1.htm; Tzanakaki 90, Hania) was established in 1930 and is also a member of the association of Greek Mountaineering Clubs. The club maintains the E4 trail and organises climbing, skiing, canoeing and speleology trips. The **Mountaineering Club of Rethymno** (EOS; ☎ 28310 57766; Dimokratias 12, Rethymno) likewise maintains a number of shelters (see below for a list). The **Mountaineering Club of Lasithi** (EOS; ☎ 28970 23230) looks after the Lasithi Plateau region.

Hikers tackling the E4 trail will need to do some pre-planning. While there is nearly always some accommodation within the range of a six- to seven-hour daily hikes, some of it will need to be arranged beforehand – particularly the mountain refuge huts on the alpine legs of the E4.

The mountaineering clubs (EOS) of Hania, Iraklio and Rethymno (see above) maintain the following huts:

name	location	altitude (m)	capacity (beds)	EOS
Kallergi	Near the Samaria Gorge	1680	50	Hania
Katsiveli-Svourihtis	Svourihtis foothills	1970	25	Hania
Prinos	Asites, East Psiloritis	1100	45	Iraklio
Limnarkarou	Lasithi Plateau	1350	15	Lasithi
Tavris	Plateau of Askyfou	1200	42	Hania
Toubotos Prinos	Mt Psiloritis	1500	28	Rethymno
Volikas	Volikas Keramion	1400	40	Hania

You will need to contact the clubs beforehand to organise bookings and collection of the key.

WATER SPORTS

Crete is a paradise for water sports. Parasailing, water-skiing, jet skiing, pedal boating and canoeing are available on most of the major beaches. On the northern coast, you'll find a water-sport centre attached to most luxury hotels and you don't need to stay there to avail yourself of the facilities. Elsewhere, specialist operators run snorkelling and diving courses as well as windsurfing. There are not many waves to catch in Crete so leave the board at home.

SNORKELLING & DIVING

The warm, clear waters of Crete make snorkelling and diving a pleasure. Some of the more interesting snorkelling is around the sunken city of Olous near Elounda (p187), while for clearer waters head for the generally less-populated southern coast.

There are a number of diving centres that allow you to get acquainted with diving, become a certified diver or explore the underwater wonders if you're already certified. Under Greek law, you must dive as part of a licensed diving operation and you are forbidden to disturb any antiquities you may come across. It's wise to call at least a day in advance to book a dive. Check out these companies in the following towns:

Agios Nikolaos Cretas Happy Divers (☎ 28410 82546) On the beach of the Coral Hotel.
Bali Hippocampos (☎ 28340 94193 www.ippocampos.com) Near the port.
Hania Blue Adventures Diving (☎ 28210 40608; Arholeon 11)
Iraklio Diver's Club (☎ 2810 811 755; www.diversclub-crete.gr; Agia Pelagia); Cretas Diving Centre (☎ 2821 093 616; Gefyra Klarissou 1)
Rethymno Paradise Dive Centre (☎ 28310 26317; pdcr@otenet.gr; Eleftheriou Venizelou 57)

Climb in Crete (www .climbincrete.com) has some excellent information on climbing and mountaineering on the island, including a report on the Ha Gorge.

Adventures in Crete (www.msc.gr/outdoor) has information on mountain huts, hiking trails, paragliding and rock climbing.

WINDSURFING

There's no surf in Greece, but there is good windsurfing, mostly in July and August thanks to the *meltemi* winds. The **Hellenic Windsurfing Association** (☎ 210 323 0330) can provide general information. The best windsurfing in Crete is at Kouremenos Beach (p197), the town beach of Palekastro, east of Sitia. Windsurfing is also good in Paleohora (p108) and Almyrida (p115), near Hania. Some of Crete's key water-sport centres are:

Agapi Beach Water Sports (☎ 2810 250 502) In Ammoudara, near Iraklio.

Almyrida sports centre (☎ 28250 32062) Near Hania.

Driros Beach (☎ 6944 932 760; www.spinalonga-windsurf.com) At Plaka, near Elounda.

Kouremenos Watersports Centre (☎ 28430 61116, 6979 254967; www.freak-surf.com)

Vai Watersports Centre (☎ 28430 61070) In Vai, near Sitia.

Water Sports Lefteris (☎ 28340 94102) In Bali, near Rethymno.

YACHTING

Yachting is a great way to experience Crete, but the winds make it un-reliable and its distance from other islands means it is not on the Greek island yachting loop. Some companies, however, do offer daily sailing excursions. Sailing along the southern coast also allows you to see some of Crete's finest and most isolated beaches.

Nautilus Yacht Rentals (☎ 28420 89986) in Ierapetra take private yacht tours around the south coast islands of Hrysi and Koufonisi, and can take you around the coast as far as Sitia.

Yachties can get the lowdown on sailing around Crete and Greece at www.sailing.gr or www.yachting.gr, where you'll find a huge list of links to Greek and English-language sailing-related sites.

OTHER ACTIVITIES

GOLF

While there were a few nine-hole golf courses on Crete, the island created its first 18-hole pro course in 2003. The **Crete Golf Club** (☎ 28920 26000; www.crete -golf.com; Hersonisos) is a joint venture between some of the island's top hotels and resorts, who are hoping more will follow to make Crete a more attractive golfing destination – it certainly has the weather for it. The desert-style, par 72 course near Hersonisos has been designed to blend in with the environment. The course is quite tough and also has a double-ended driving range, a golf academy and club house. It's not for

---

GOOD FOR THE SOUL

The therapeutic benefits of the sea are being exploited at a number of thalassotherapy spas that have sprung up in some of Crete's big luxury resorts. Seawater thalassotherapy pools and hydrospas, marine algae body wraps and every imaginable sea-themed pampering and rejuvenation treatment can be found.

The **Elounda Spa & Thalassotherapy Centre** (☎ 28410 65660; www.bluepalace.gr; half-day spa treatments from €140), attached to the Blue Palace Resort just outside Elounda, is the island's newest and most state-of-the-art spa. Apart from the seawater, the centre also incorporates other Cretan nutrients to provide some unique treatments, including a full-body exfoliation based on sugar and olive oil, a traditional olive-oil massage and seawater hydromassage baths using Cretan herbs. There is even a treatment using raki – not your traditional rakotherapy!

If you can't quite manage a stay at the resort for the full treatment, you can still book into the spa. There are packages and discounts at certain times for external guests.

hackers, though. An 18-hole round in summer will set you back €65, and that doesn't cover clubs or buggies.

HORSE RIDING

There are several places on Crete that offer horse riding and guided trail rides through the Cretan countryside.

Horseriding Club of Akrotiri (☎ 28210 39366; www.mjpr.com/zefiros) is located in Tersanas, on the Akrotiri Peninsula. They run pony and horse-riding lessons for children and beginners, as well as one-hour to half-day trails for experienced riders to the monasteries and beaches on the peninsula. English saddles are available.

Zoraida's Horseriding (☎ 28250 61745; www.georgioupoli.net/zoraida/index.htm), in Georgoupolis, offers beginner and advanced riding experiences on beach and nature trails, including a six-day course for advanced riders. There's also a day safari for €70 including a taverna lunch.

PARAGLIDING

Crete's climate and terrain make it an ideal location for paragliding (known as *parapente*) and it is a sensational way to see the island if you are game to fly with the birds. There are about 20 excellent paragliding take-off sites around Crete, mostly surrounding the three highest mountains, as well as coastal sites such as Falasarna and Paleohora.

Certified instructor and paragliding enthusiast Grigoris Thomakakis has chosen to base himself and the **International Centre of Natural Activities** (☎ 28970 51200; www.icna.gr) in the village of Avdou, south of Hersonisos, precisely because its special microclimate allows him to fly 187 days between April and October. The conditions are so good that on more than 180 of those days you can fly from 10am to 7pm. Grigoris also flies all over the island with groups from around the world. The company recently expanded to offer other activities such as caving (Grigoris is an expert) and mountain-bike tours, trekking, horse riding and climbing.

British nature lover Peter Thomson has created an online site (and pending CD) *Walking and Cycling Guide to Crete* at www .peter-thomson.co.uk/ crete/contents.html.

Food & Drink

Cretan cuisine is one of the highlights of a visit to Crete – you just have to make sure you avoid the bland 'tourist' establishments and choose your restaurants carefully.

Cretan food shares much of its inheritance with the cuisine of the mainland and the Mediterranean basin. It is a solid, balanced and healthy seasonal cuisine based on the wide variety of fresh produce that grows in abundance on the island. There are many specifically Cretan dishes that differ from mainland Greek food. Even within the various regions of Crete you will find local specialties and different ways of doing things; for example, in Anogia they serve spaghetti with their meat at weddings and feasts, while on most of the island they serve rice *pilafi*.

The health benefits of the Cretan diet are well documented worldwide. Many researchers, including a 1987 study by the World Health Organization, have found that the incidence of heart-related diseases was considerably lower in Crete than in many other places in the world. This is attributed to a greater reliance on pulses, fresh vegetables and fruit than on meats and processed foodstuffs. The virgin olive oil produced in vast quantities in Crete is among the world's best and is consumed as an integral part of meals in Crete. While olive oil itself has many beneficial qualities, it also makes vegetables and salads taste better and therefore ensures greater consumption. While Cretans consume more meat than they used to, it still constitutes only a small part of the traditional Cretan family meal, while fish and seafood play an important part in the diet.

Olive Oil: The Secret of Good Health, by Nikos and Maria Psilakis, gives you the complete lowdown on the golden nectar, including history, production, health benefits, correct use and 150 recipes.

Cretans are passionate about their food and eat out regularly, regardless of socioeconomic status, because eating with friends is paramount to enjoying life. They will also travel far to get to a good restaurant or eat specific food, heading to the mountains for local meat and the sea for fresh fish.

Unfortunately, restaurant food where tourists congregate can be mediocre. When you see Cretans eating out in a restaurant you can usually be certain that the food served is of a higher quality. As a general rule of thumb, the further away you move from the northern coast (where most tourists are) the better the food becomes, especially in the villages where food will predominantly be made from fresh local produce.

Most restaurants will have a combination of casseroles and bakes *(mayirefta)* and food cooked to order *(tis oras)* such as grills and special dishes. *Mayirefta* are commonly served at temperatures much lower than you might be used to. This is considered healthier by Cretans and also more practical from the restaurant's point of view, as it is hard to keep all food piping hot and they avoid using microwaves.

Jolly TV cooking show host Ilias Mamalakis explores the regional cheeses of Greece through his *Greek Cheese Map*, produced by Olive Press Publications.

Cretans will order plenty of dishes and have food left over at the end of the meal. Ordering a Greek salad or *tzatziki* as a meal – a common practice among young and budget tourists – is considered poor form and is often quietly sneered at by the restaurant staff.

By law, every eating establishment must display a written menu including prices. Restaurant staff will automatically put bread on your table and there is a cover charge.

STAPLES & SPECIALITIES

Greek and Cretan dishes often overlap, but there are many Cretan specialties worth searching out. *Dakos* or *koukouvagia* is a round barley rusk that is softened in water and soaked in oil and tomato with cheese and oregano usually sprinkled on top. *Kalitsounia* are lightly fried pastries filled with cheese or *horta* (wild greens), and the cheese variety also can be served as a dessert with honey. Cretans eat a lot of lamb and goat and are also fond of rabbit, which is made into *stifado*, or stew.

For centuries Cretans have been gathering *horta* from the hills and making them into stand-alone vegetable side dishes or using them in pies and stews. Vegetable dishes include *dolmades* (stuffed vine leaves) and *anthous* (rice-filled zucchini flowers), and okra is commonly used in stews with chicken.

Snails are gathered on hillsides after rainfall and prepared in dozens of interesting ways. Try *hohlii boubouristi*, which are snails simmered in vinegar, or snails with barley.

Crete also produces wonderful cheeses, including *myzithra*, a soft mild ricotta-like cheese that can be eaten soft or hardened for grating; the yellow *anthotiro*, a similar soft whey cheese; and *graviera* made from unpasteurised sheep's milk. Goat and cheese milk are often combined. *Staka* is a rich soft buttery cheese cooked with flour. It is often added to rice *pilafi* to make it creamier.

Sweet specialties include *Sfakianes pittes*, usually found in the Hania region, which are fine pancake-like dish with a light *myzithra* filling, served with honey.

Cretan Cooking, by Maria and Nikos Psilakis, is a well-translated version of their widely popular guide to Cretan cooking. It contains 265 mouth-watering recipes, some fascinating asides on the history of the dishes and background to the Cretan dietary phenomenon.

Snacks

Snacks include *tyropitta* (cheese pie) or *spanakopitta* (spinach pie), *loukoumades* (donut-like fritters*)*, *bougatsa* (custard-filled pastry) and *koulouria* (fresh pretzel rings). Street vendors sell bags of various nuts and dried seeds such as pumpkin.

Mezedes

Most restaurants have a wide range of mezedes (appetisers). Common mezedes include *taramosalata* (fish-roe dip), *tzatziki* (yogurt, cucumber and garlic dip), olives and feta, *ohtapodi* (octopus), *garides* (shrimps), *kalamaria* (squid), *dolmades* and *melitzanosalata* (aubergine or eggplant dip). Hot mezedes include *keftedes* (meatballs), *gigantes* (lima beans), *loukanika* (little sausages), *bourekaki* (tiny meat pies), *fava* (split pea puree), *kolokythakia* (deep-fried zucchini), *melitzana* (deep-fried aubergine), *saganaki* (fried cheese), *apaki* (a smoked meat dish) and mussel or shrimp *saganaki* (fried with tomato and cheese).

It is quite acceptable to make a full meal of these instead of a main course. Three plates of mezedes are about equivalent in price and quantity to one main course. You can also order a *pikilia* (mixed plate).

Soups

Soup is not normally eaten as a starter, but can be an economical and hearty meal in itself with bread and a salad. *Psarosoupa* is a filling fish soup with vegetables, while *kakavia* (Greek bouillabaisse) is made to order and laden with seafood so it is more expensive. *Fasolada* (bean soup) is also a meal in itself. *Avgolemono* (egg and lemon soup) is usually prepared from chicken stock. If you're into offal, don't miss *mayiritsa*, the traditional Easter tripe soup.

Feasting and Fasting in Crete, by Diana Farr Louis, is a hard-back portrait of the island and its culinary history traditions. It includes 140 recipes gathered during her travels and chapters on the island's wine, cheeses, herbs as well as special recipes for weddings and religious festivities.

Salads

The ubiquitous (and no longer inexpensive) Greek or village salad, *horiatiki salata*, is a side dish for Greeks, but many budget- and health-conscious tourists make it a main dish. It consists of tomatoes, cucumber, onions,

It's was a tough job. Gastronome Miles Lambert takes a journey through Greece via the country's tavernas in *Greek Salad: A Dionysian Travelogue*, an amusing portrayal of local characters and food culture.

olives and feta cheese, sprinkled with oregano and dressed with olive oil. Some variations include peppers or capers. Lettuce and cabbage are served seasonally and *horta* make a great warm salad. These days most good restaurants and even tavernas will have *roka* (rocket), and other varieties of salad. In spring, try *radikia salata* (dandelion salad).

Main Dishes

The most common *mayirefta* are *mousaka* (layers of eggplant or zucchini, minced meat and potatoes topped with cheese sauce and baked), *pastitsio* (baked cheese-topped macaroni with minced meat), *boureki* (a cheese, zucchini and potato bake), *yemista* (stuffed tomatoes or green peppers), *giouvetsi* (casserole of lamb or veal and pasta), *stifado* (meat stewed with onions), *soutzoukakia* (spicy meatballs in tomato sauce) and *salingaria* (snails in oil with herbs). *Ladera* is a particular type of *mayirefta* cooked in olive oil.

Charcoal-grilled meat is a common main course – mostly pork, lamb and goat or spicy *loukanika* (sausages) – and is usually shared after starters and salads. Fish is usually sold by weight in restaurants, but it's not as cheap or widely available as it used to be. Fish is mostly grilled or fried.

Desserts

Tavernas will normally serve fruit after a meal, although some places will offer *halva* (made from semolina or sesame seeds) and *pagoto* (ice cream). Greek sweets include *baklava, loukoumades* (puffs or fritters with honey or syrup), *kataïfi* (chopped nuts inside shredded wheat pastry or filo soaked in honey), *rizogalo* (rice pudding), *loukoumi* (Turkish delight) and *galaktoboureko* (custard-filled pastry with syrup). The best places to go for these delights are *galaktopoleia* (milk shops) or *zaharoplasteia* (patisseries). Preserved fruits in syrup, known as spoon sweets, are occasionally served after dinner or when you visit someone.

DID YOU KNOW?

Greek people are the world's biggest per capita consumers of olive oil – in Crete annual per person consumption is averaged out to 31L, according to a 1996 study.

Fruit

Crete grows many varieties of beautiful fruit, including *syka* (figs), *rodakina* (peaches), *stafylia* (grapes), *karpouzi* (watermelon), *mila* (apples), *portokalia* (oranges) and *kerasia* (cherries).

Many visitors are unlikely to have encountered the *frangosyko* (prickly pear, also known as the Barbary fig), which is the fruit of the opuntia

THE CRETAN DIET

The beneficial effects of the Cretan diet first gained attention in 1960 after an influential 15-year study found that Cretan men had the lowest rate of heart disease and cancer of all seven countries studied (Finland, USA, Netherlands, Italy, Yugoslavia, Japan and Crete). The mystery is attributed to a diet high in fruits, vegetables, pulses, whole grains and exclusive and plentiful use of olive oil. Another important factor may be the *horta* (wild greens) that Cretans gathered in the hills. Used in pies and salads, the greens may have protective properties that are not yet fully understood. Regular fasting may also play a role, along with the use of sheep and goat's milk instead of cow's, and many will swear by the medicinal properties of raki and wine and their role in ensuring longevity. Unfortunately the Cretan diet and lifestyle is changing as the island has prospered and become urbanised. As Cretans have included more meat and cheese in their diets, and no longer work out in the fields, heart disease and cancer rates are rising.

Crete is placing increasing emphasis on its traditional diet and its principles. Restaurants following the strict principles of Cretan cuisine can apply for recognition under Concred, a certification program introduced in 2004 to promote traditional Cretan cuisine.

cactus. They are delicious, but need to be approached with extreme caution because of the thousands of tiny prickles (invisible to the naked eye) that cover their skin. Never pick one up with your bare hands. The simplest way is peel them is to trim the ends off with a knife and then slit the skin from end to end.

Another unusual fruit is the *mousmoulo* (loquat). These small orange fruit are among the first of summer, reaching the market in mid-May. The flesh is juicy and pleasantly acidic.

DRINKS
Coffee & Tea

Greek coffee is struggling to maintain its place as the national drink with stiff competition from the ubiquitous frappe. A legacy of Ottoman rule, until the Turkish invasion of Cyprus in 1974 the Greeks called it Turkish coffee. It is traditionally brewed on hot sand in a special *briki* (pot) and served in a small cup where the grounds sink to the bottom (don't drink them). Connoisseurs claim there are at least 30 variations of Greek coffee, but most people know only three – *glykos* (sweet), *metrios* (medium) and *sketos* (without sugar).

Frappe is a frothy chilled creation made from instant coffee, usually Nescafé, which is the dominant brand in Greece. Espresso and filtered coffee are now widely available and come in chilled form – *freddo*.

Tea is not the beverage of choice in Crete but it is available, usually in bags. Herbal tea is becoming popular, especially *diktamo* or dittany tea.

Water

Tap water is safe to drink in Crete. Many tourists prefer to drink bottled spring water, which is sold widely. There are several local brands of mineral and sparkling water.

Beer

Beer lovers will find the market dominated by the major northern European breweries. The most popular beers are Amstel and Heineken, both brewed in Greece under licence. Other beers brewed locally are Henninger, Kaiser, Kronenbourg and Tuborg. Local beers include Mythos and Alfa.

Imported lagers, stouts and beers are found in tourist areas. Supermarkets are the cheapest place to buy beer, and bottles are cheaper than cans. Beer is also available in kiosks.

Wine

According to mythology, the Greeks invented or discovered wine and they have produced it in Crete on a large scale for more than 3000 years. The Minoans incorporated wine presses in their palaces.

Until the 1950s most Greek wines were sold in bulk and were seldom distributed any further afield than the nearest town. It wasn't until industrialisation (and the resulting rapid urban growth) that there was much call for bottled wine. Quality control was unheard of up until 1969, when appellation laws were introduced as a precursor to applying for membership of the then European Community.

Greek wines have improved significantly since then and Greek winemakers are making excellent wine from local and international varieties. Many boutique – and relatively expensive – wines are winning international awards and recognition in what is often referred to as a renaissance in Greek wine.

The Glorious Foods of Greece, by award-winning Greek-American food writer Diane Kochilas, is a 'must have' for any serious cook, with a regional exploration of Greek food and 60-page chapter on Crete.

The Illustrated Greek Wine Book, by Nico Manessi, is the definitive book for the wine connoisseur. He traces the history of the Greek wine and profiles leading winemakers, regions and varietals, with hundreds of reviews.

Cretan wine on the whole may not make connoisseurs tremble with delight, but it can be pleasant and even distinguished. Most of it is blended and produced in bulk by cooperatives and the quality is uneven, but the best brands tend to come from Peza, Dafnes, Sitia and Arhanes, which have appellation of origin wines.

For comprehensive information on the country's wine regions and producers, visit www.greekwine.gr or www.greekwine makers.com.

However, several boutique winemakers in Crete are now producing some excellent wines from local varieties. The best wines are labelled with the region of origin clearly stated. The most popular wine grapes are *Villana* and *Thrapsathiri*. The oldest grape variety is *Liatiko*, which has been used to make red wine for the last 4000 years. Other local red varieties include *kotsifali* and *mandelari*.

House wines served up in restaurants are usually very presentable and are a much cheaper option than bottled wine. They often have a light port taste. Ask for *kokkino* (red), *roze* (rose) or *lefko* (white). House wine is served in half-kilo or 1kg carafes, and costs around €3 per kilo (about 1L).

Spirits

Raki – often called *tsikoudia* – is the most popular drink in Crete. Distilled from grape stems and pips left over from the grapes pressed for wine, it is similar to the Middle Eastern *arak,* Italian *grappa,* Irish *pocheen* or Turkish *raki.* Each October, distilleries around Crete produce massive quantities of raki, often followed by a feast. You now need a license to make raki, although this is not always abided by.

The Greek passion for food is beautifully portrayed in the visual feast of *A Touch of Spice* (Politiki Kouzina), the hit film about the Greeks of Asia Minor.

Good raki has a smooth mellow taste with no noticeable after-burn. As long as you eat while you consume raki, don't mix it with other alcohol and accompany it with the odd glass or two of water, you can drink considerable amounts without serious after effects or hangovers. Raki is usually served in mini-carafes costing around €3.

While commonly available in Crete, ouzo has a much more limited following and is usually only drunk by mainlanders or foreigners. Clear and colourless, ouzo turns white when water is added. The most popular brands are Ouzo 12, Mini and Ploumariou. It will be served neat, with a separate glass of water to be used for dilution.

CELEBRATIONS

Food plays an integral part in Cretan life and therefore in its religious and cultural celebrations, which are normally accompanied by a feast.

Easter is preceded by the Lenten fast that involves special dishes that have no meat or dairy products – or even oil if you go strictly by the book. Come the resurrection, though, the festivities begin with a bowl of *mayiritsa*, a soup made from offal, and an Easter Sunday lunch of lamb and *kreatotourta* (meat pies). Red-dyed boiled eggs are an integral part of the Easter festivities and are also often used to decorate the *tsoureki*, a brioche-style bread flavoured with *mastic* (gum or resin made from the bark of the mastic tree) and *mahlepi* (a spice from the kernels of the Persian cherry tree).

DOS & DON'TS

▪ Do ask to look in the pots in the kitchen or select your own fish.

▪ Do ask for specific local specialties in every region.

▪ Don't insist on paying if you are invited out – it insults your host.

▪ Don't refuse a coffee or glass of raki – it's offered as a gesture of hospitality and good will.

Easter sweets include *koulouria* (fresh pretzel rings), *melomakarona* (honey biscuits) and *kourambiedes* (almond biscuits).

Rice *pilafi* is usually served at weddings and baptisms at the start of the dinner, while a *kouloura* – an intricately decorated bread – is also a tradition at weddings. Honey and walnuts, an aphrodisiac, are given to the bridal couple.

The New Year has its own cake, with a coin inserted into the mix, giving the recipient good luck for the year.

Throughout the year, there are many celebrations centred on the production of food itself, such as the festivals that occur around the various harvests – from chestnuts to sultanas (see p211 for a full list).

Andreas Staikos' novel *Les Liaisons Culinaires* is a mouth-watering erotic account of an Athens love triangle and food-inspired seduction (complete with recipes).

WHERE TO EAT & DRINK

Dining in Crete is a slow, social experience and the pace of service can accordingly be slow by normal standards. That said, restaurants are never in a rush to give you the bill and get you out of there either. The bill will always include a small 'cover' charge per person. Tipping is not mandatory but the bill is usually rounded up and around 10% added for good service.

Estiatorio (restaurant) Normally more sophisticated than a taverna or psistaria, restaurants have tablecloths, smartly attired waiters and printed menus at each table with an English translation.

Galaktopoleia Literally a 'milk shop', it sells dairy produce including milk, butter, yogurt, rice pudding, cornflour pudding, custard, eggs and bread. It may also sell home-made ice cream.

Kafeneia Regarded by some foreigners as the last bastion of male chauvinism in Europe – in rural areas, Cretan women are rarely seen inside kafeneia. When a female traveller enters one, however, she is invariably treated courteously and with friendship, especially if she manages a few Greek words of greeting.

Ouzeri/rakadiko Serves ouzo and small plates of meze or, in Crete, raki (therefore they are often called rakadika). Many ouzeris now offer menus with a large selection of mezedes and even main courses.

Psistaria These places specialise in spit roasts and charcoal-grilled food – usually lamb, pork or chicken. You can often order takeaway or dine in.

Taverna A basic eating place with a rough-and-ready ambience, although some are more upmarket, particularly in Iraklio, Hania and Rethymno.

Zaharoplasteia A patisserie that sells cakes (traditional and Western), chocolates, biscuits, sweets, coffee, soft drinks and, possibly, bottled alcoholic drinks.

Quick Eats

It's hard to beat eat-on-the-street Greek offerings. Foremost among them are the *gyros* and the *souvlaki*. The *gyros* is a giant skewer laden with slabs of seasoned meat that grills slowly as it rotates, with the meat trimmed steadily from the outside; *souvlakia* are small individual kebab sticks. Both are served wrapped in pitta bread, with tomato, onion and lashings of *tzatziki*.

VEGETARIANS & VEGANS

Crete has very few vegetarian restaurants per se, and many vegetable soups and stews are based on meat stocks. But there are normally plenty of options for vegetarians. Fried vegetables are a safe bet as olive oil is always used – never lard. The Cretans do wonderful things with *anginares* (artichokes), which can be served stuffed, as a salad, as a meze (particularly with *raki*) or used in a stew with potatoes and carrot. Vegetarians who eat eggs can rest assured that an omelette can be whipped up anywhere. Salads are cheap, fresh, substantial and nourishing and there are usually *horta* on the menu.

Lent, incidentally, is a good time for vegetarians because meat is missing from many dishes.

DID YOU KNOW?

There are at least 100 edible wild greens *(horta)* on Crete, although even the most knowledgeable would not recognise more than a dozen.

WHINING & DINING

Crete is very child-friendly and families will feel very comfortable at informal tavernas and *psistarias*, where children are welcome and treated well. You will often see families dining out late at night and packs of children playing outside tavernas while their parents indulge in a long dinner. Kids' menus are not common, but most places will make up special plates or accommodate requests (see also p108).

HABITS & CUSTOMS

Most Cretans have Greek coffee (and cigarettes) for breakfast or perhaps a cake or pastry. Budget hotels offering breakfast generally provide it continental-style (rolls or bread with jam, and tea or coffee), while more upmarket hotels serve full buffets. Some places offer a 'Cretan breakfast' consisting of a boiled egg, bread, feta, ham, olives – and raki. Otherwise, restaurants and *galaktopoleia* serve bread with butter, jam or honey, eggs and *yiaourti* (yogurt) with honey and fruit.

Lunch is eaten late – between 1pm and 3pm – and may be either a snack or the main meal, although is quite common for Cretans to have two large meals a day.

Dinner is also eaten late – after 9pm, although in tourist areas dinner is usually served earlier. A full dinner begins with appetisers and salads followed by a main course, or grilled meat or fish. *Mayirefta* are usually accompanied by bread and salad.

Dessert is commonly complimentary watermelon or fresh fruit in season, served with a shot of raki. Only very posh restaurants or those pandering to tourists include Western-style desserts on the menu.

DID YOU KNOW?

Crete has Greece's oldest olive trees, which sparked a fierce dispute between two villages (Kavourisio and Kolymbari) vying for the honour to provide the winner's wreaths for the 2004 Athens Olympics marathon. In the end, the leaves were taken from both trees.

THE GOOD OIL

The olive has been part of life in the eastern Mediterranean since the beginnings of civilisation. Olive cultivation can be traced back about 6000 years. It was the farmers of the Levant (modern Syria and Lebanon) who first spotted the potential of the wild European olive *(Olea europaea)* – a sparse, thorny tree that was common in the region. These farmers began the process of selection that led to the more compact, thornless, oil-rich varieties that now dominate the Mediterranean.

Whereas most Westerners think of olive oil as being just cooking oil, to the people of the ancient Mediterranean civilisations it was much more. It was almost inseparable from civilised life itself. As well as being an important foodstuff, it was burned in lamps to provide light, it could be used as a lubricant and it was blended with essences to produce fragrant oils.

The Minoans were among the first to grow wealthy on the olive, and western Crete remains an important olive-growing area, specialising in high-quality salad oils. The region's showpiece, the Kolymbari cooperative, markets its extra-virgin olive oil in both the USA (*Athena* brand) and Britain (*Kydonia* brand), while Biolea makes superb organic olive oil. The Sitia region in the east also produce excellent oil, including the award-winning organic oil made by the monastery at Toplou.

The oil that is prized above all others is *agoureleo* (meaning unripe), a thick green oil pressed from unripe olives.

Many families on Crete have their own olive trees, so many workers are given time off during the harvest to help with the picking.

Few trees outlive the olive. Some of the fantastically gnarled and twisted olive trees that dot the countryside of western Crete are more than 1000 years old.

Many of these older trees are being cut down to make way for improved varieties. The wood is burnt in potters' kilns and also provides wood-turners with the raw material to produce the ultimate salad bowl. The dense yellow-brown timber has a beautiful swirling grain.

COOKING COURSES

There are not many organised cooking courses on Crete, but many places hold seminars and run classes for groups.

Rodialos (☎ 28340 51340, www.rodialos.gr) regularly hosts one- to seven-day cooking seminars in a lovely villa in Panormo (see p141), near Rethymno. Participants are taken through the principles of Cretan cooking, help gather food from the garden and pick herbs and wild greens, and then cook several courses for a meal. Longer seminars can include visits to markets and fishing trips and can be tailored to individual interests. Workshops cost €50 per day and include eating what you cook. Participants can stay at the villa.

In Axos (see p132) **Enagron** (☎ 28340 61611; www.enagron.gr) also runs similar cooking workshops using local experts such as Nikos and Maria Psilakis. They also organise seasonal events around the production of cheese, wine and raki.

Crete's Culinary Sanctuaries (in the US ☎ +1 415 835 9923; www.cookingincrete.com) coordinates a comprehensive organic agrotourism programme, which focuses on Crete's culture, organic agriculture and traditional approaches to cuisine. Headed by Greek-American chef and writer Nikki Rose, the courses are conducted on a farm near Rethymno and operated by agroscientists. The three-, five- and 10-day courses include hands-on gardening lessons and cooking classes, plus cultural tours led by local farmers and chefs. The courses are approved by the American Culinary Federation, and range in price from US$550 to US$3200, including accommodation and some meals.

For updates, information and articles on Greek and Mediterranean food, check out www.gourmed.gr.

EAT YOUR WORDS

Get behind the cuisine scene by getting to know the language. For pronunciation guidelines see p234.

Useful Phrases

I want to make a reservation for this evening.
the-lo na *kli*-so e-na tra-pe-zi ya a-po-pse
Θέλω να κλείσω ένα τραπέζι για απόψε.

A table for ... please.
e-na tra-*pe*-zi ya ..., pa-ra-ka-*lo*
Ένα τραπέζι για ... παρακαλώ.

I'd like the menu, please.
to me-*nu*, pa-ra-ka-*lo*
Το μενού, παρακαλώ.

Do you have a menu in English?
e-hye-te to me-*nu* sta ang-li-ka?
Έχετε το μενού στα αγγλικά;

I'd like ...
tha *i*-the-la ...
Θα ήθελα ...

Please bring the bill.
to lo-ghar-ya-*zmo*, pa-ra-ka-*lo*
Το λογαριασμό, παρακαλώ.

I'm a vegetarian.
i-me hor-to-*fa*-ghos
Είμαι χορτοφάγος.

I don't eat meat or dairy products.
dhen *tro*-o *kre*-as i gha-la-kto-ko-mi-*ka* pro-i-*on*-da
Δε τρώω κρέας ή γαλακτοκομικά προϊόντα.

Lonely Planet's *World Food Greece* takes an in-depth look at the culture of eating and drinking in Greece.

Food Glossary

STAPLES

bread	pso-*mi*	ψωμί
butter	*vu*-ti-ro	βούτυρο
cheese	ti-*ri*	τυρί
eggs	a-*vgha*	αυγά
honey	*me*-li	μέλι
milk	*gha*-la	γάλα
olive oil	e-le-*o*-la-dho	ελαιόλαδο
olives	e-*lyes*	ελιές
pepper	pi-*pe*-ri	πιπέρι
salt	a-*la*-ti	αλάτι
sugar	*za*-ha-ri	ζάχαρη
vinegar	*ksi*-dhi	ξύδι

MEAT, FISH & SEAFOOD

beef	moschari	μοσχάρι
blackfish	ro-*fos*	ροφός
chicken	ko-*to*-pu-lo	κοτόπουλο
cuttlefish	sou-*pia*	σουπια
grey mullet	*ke*-fa-los	κέφαλος
grouper	sfi-ri-da	σφυρίδα
ham	zam-*bon*	ζαμπόν
hare	la-*ghos*	λαγός
kid (goat)	ka-tsi-*ka*-ki	κατσικάκι
lamb	ar-*ni*	αρνί
lobster	a-sta-*kos*	αστακός
mackerel	ko-li-*os*	κολιός
mussels	t*mi*-di-a	μύδια
octopus	hta-*po*-dhi	χταπόδι
pork	hyi-ri-*no*	χοιρινό
prawns	gha-*ri*-dhes	γαρίδες
rabbit	kou-*ne*-li	κουνέλι
red mullet	bar-*bu*-nya	μπαρμπούνια
sardines	sar-*dhe*-les	σαρδέλες
sea bream	fa-*ghri*/li-*thri*-ni/me-la-*nu*-ri	φαγρί/λιθρίνι/μελανούρι
squid	to ka-la-*ma*-ri	καλαμάρι
swordfish	ksi-*fi*-as	ξιφίας
veal	moschari galaktos	μοσχάρι γαλάκτος
whitebait	ma-*ri*-dhes	μαρίδες

FRUIT & VEGETABLES

apple	*mi*-lo	μήλο
artichoke	ang-gi-na-ra	αγγινάρα
asparagus	spa-*rang*-gi-a	σπαράγγια
aubergine (eggplant)	me-li-*dza*-nes	μελιτζάνες
cabbage	*la*-ha-no	λάχανο
carrot	ka-*ro*-to	καρότο
cherry	ke-*ra*-si	κεράσι
garlic	*skor*-dho	σκόρδο
grapes	sta-*fi*-li-a	σταφύλια
greens, seasonal wild	(a-ghri-a) *hor*-ta	(άγρια) χόρτα
lemon	le-*mo*-ni	λεμόνι
onions	re-*mi*-dhi-a	κρεμμύδια
orange	por-to-*ka*-li	πορτοκάλι

peach	ro-*dha*-ki-no	ροδάκινο
peas	a-ra-*kas*	αρακάς
peppers	pi-per-*yes*	πιπεριές
potatoes	pa-*ta*-tes	πατάτες
spinach	spa-*na*-ki	σπανάκι
strawberry	*fra*-u-la	φράουλα
tomato	do-*ma*-ta	ντομάτα

DRINKS

beer	*bi*-ra	μπίρα
coffee	ka-*fes*	καφές
tea	*tsa*-i	τσάι
water	*ne*-ro	νερό
wine (red/white)	kra-*si* (*ko*-ki-no/*a*-spro)	κρασί (κόκκινο/άσπρο)

Hania Χανιά

For many people, the western prefecture of Hania *is* Crete. Despite having one of the island's top tourist attractions – the Samaria Gorge – Hania hasn't surrendered itself to tourism and maintains a largely authentic feel. It is renowned for its rugged natural beauty, and its many stunning gorges and spectacular mountain ranges such as the Lefka Ori and Mt Gingilos in the rugged interior. Its capital, the port town of Hania, is the island's most romantic and alluring town, with a rich mosaic of Venetian and Ottoman architecture.

The northern coastline is highly developed, especially the stretch west of Hania, but it's possible to find more isolated spots on the Akrotiri Peninsula, which has several interesting monasteries, and further west on the barely inhabited Rodopou and Gramvousa peninsulas.

Hania's rocky southern coast is dotted with laid-back beach communities such as Paleohora and Sougia and the nearly deserted west coast has two of Crete's finest beaches – Falasarna in the northern corner and Elafonisi in the far south.

Hania's hinterland is dotted with traditional mountain villages where you'll still see shepherds tending their flocks and find family tavernas where you know their own produce and animals have been prepared for you. In Sfakia, road signs riddled with bullet holes remind you that this is the Wild West of the island.

Eastern Hania boasts the island's only natural lake, Lake Kournas, and the stunning Imbros Gorge, the very underrated rival to Samaria. Gavdos island, off the southern coast in the Libyan sea, is Greece's southernmost island – the ideal escape from it all.

Hania offers visitors a wealth of activities and experiences, from mountain climbing, gorge trekking and scuba diving to lazing on the beach and dining on the day's catch in small fishing hamlets along the coast.

HIGHLIGHTS

- Trekking the spectacular **Samaria Gorge** (p100) and **Imbros Gorge** (p118)
- Wandering through the narrow streets of the Venetian and Turkish quarters of **Hania** (p78)
- Relaxing on the remote **southern beaches** (p102)
- Chilling out on the island of **Gavdos** (p111)
- Exploring **mountain villages** (p95) and the indulging in the region's excellent cuisine.

HANIA

HANIA REGION

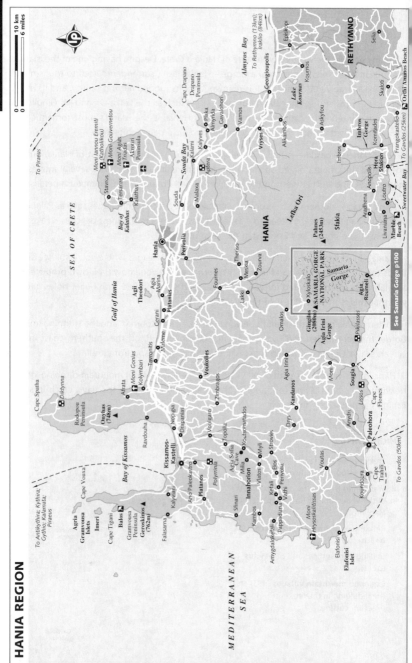

0 ____ 10 km
0 ____ 6 miles

SEA OF CRETE

To Piraeus

Rodopou Peninsula

Moni Iannou Eremiti
(Katholikou)
Moni Gouvernetou
Moni Agiás
Triadas
*Akrotiri
Peninsula*

Cape Spatha

Diktynna

Stavros
Tersanás
Kalathas
*Bay of
Kalathas*
Souda
Soúda Bay
Kalámi
Plaka
Almyrída
Gavalochori
Kalyves
Aptera
Malaxa
Vryses
Alikambos

Cape Drapano
*Drapano
Peninsula*
Georgioupolis
Almyros Bay
*Lake
Kournás*

To Rethymno (13km);
Iraklio (84km)

RETHYMNO
Episkopi
Selia

Koumos
Kournás
Askyfou
Skaloti
Orthi Amnos Beach

Gulf of Hania
Hania
Periviola
Agii
Theodori
Agia
Marina
Platanias
Gerani
Tavronitis
Maleme
Moni Gonias
Afrata
Kolymbari

Onyhus
(748m)
Ravdoúha

Theriso
Zourva
Meskla
Fournes
Lakki
Omalos

Gingilos
(2080m)
Agia Irini
Gorge
SAMARIA GORGE
NATIONAL PARK
Xyloskalo
*Samaria
Gorge*

Agia
Roumeli

Iki/lassos

Sougia
Lissos
Cape
Flomes

Leftka Ori
Sfakia
Palnes
(2453m)

Hora
Sfakion
Anopolis
Aradhena
Aradhena
Gorge
Loutro
Livaniana

Imbros
Gorge
Imbros
Komitades
Frangokastello

To Gavdos (25km)
Sweetwater Bay
Marble
Beach

See Samaria Gorge p100

HANIA

Voukolies
Zimbragos
Vatolakkos
Vlahatiana
Drapanias
Topolia
Koufos
Voutas
Kandanos
Drys

**Kissamos-
Kastelli**
Kalyviani
Agio Paleokastro
Platanos
Sfinari
Kambos
Kefali
Elos
Pappadiana
Amygdalokefali
Vathi
Strovies
Perivolia
Milia
Mili
Polyrrinia
Agia Sofia
Cave
Vatos
Innahorion

Cape Vouxa

Bay of Kissamos
Falasarna

*Agria
Gramvoúsa
Islets*
Imeri
Balos
*Gramvoúsa
Peninsula*
Geroskinos
(762m)

To Antikythira; Kythira;
Gythio; Kalamata;
Piraeus

Kalydura
Cape
Trahili
Anydri
Paleohora
To Gavdos (50km)

Moni
Hryssoskalitissas
Elafonisi
Islet
Elafonisi

*MEDITERRANEAN
SEA*

HANIA

HANIA XANIA

pop 53,373

Hania is unreservedly Crete's most evocative city. Remnants of Venetian walls still border a web of atmospheric streets in the old town that tumble onto a magnificent harbour. The Venetian townhouses along the harbour-side promenade have been restored and converted into restaurants, cafés, boutique hotels and attractive pensions. The prominent former mosque on the harbour front and Ottoman-style buildings scattered through the old town are remnants from its Turkish rulers.

Hania's war-torn history has left it with only a few impressive monuments, but the city does wear its scars proudly. Along Zambeliou, Theotokopoulou and Angelou streets in the old quarter you will come across roofless Venetian buildings that have been turned into gracious outdoor restaurants. In addition, many of the timber houses that date from Turkish rule have been restored. Even during the height of the tourist season when many of the buildings are festooned with tourist merchandise, Hania retains the exoticism of a city caught between East and West.

Hania has a lively tradition of artisanship making it a great shopping city, and the inner harbour is ideal for relaxing in a café and watching the passing promenade. Hania also has some of the islands finest restaurants.

HISTORY

Hania is the site of the Minoan settlement of Kydonia, which was centred on the hill to the east of the harbour. Excavation work has been restricted because the ruins lie under the modern city, but the finding of clay tablets with Linear B script (see the boxed text p38) has led archaeologists to believe that Kydonia was both a palace site and an important town.

Kydonia met the same fiery fate as most other Minoan settlements in 1450 BC, but soon re-emerged as a force. It was a flourishing city–state during Hellenistic times and continued to prosper under Roman and Byzantine rule.

The city came under the control of the Venetians around the beginning of the 13th century, and the name was changed to La Canea. The Venetians lost control of the city to the Genoese in 1266, but they finally wrested it back in 1290. The Venetians spent a great deal of time constructing massive fortifications to protect the city from marauding pirates and invading Turks. This did not prove very effective against the latter, who took Hania in 1645 after a two-month siege.

The Turks made Hania the seat of the Turkish Pasha until the end of Turkish rule in 1898. During this time the churches were converted into mosques and the architectural style of the town changed, becoming more Oriental, with wooden walls and latticed windows.

The Great Powers made Hania the island capital in 1898 and it remained so until 1971, when the administration was transferred to Iraklio.

The WWII Battle of Crete largely took place along the coast to the west of Hania. The town itself was heavily bombed during WWII, but enough of the old town survives for it to be regarded as Crete's most beautiful city.

ORIENTATION

Hania's bus station is on Kydonias, two blocks southwest of Plateia 1866, one of the city's main squares. From Plateia 1866, the Old Harbour is a short walk north up Halidon.

The main area for accommodation is to the left as you face the harbour, where Akti Koundourioti leads around to the old fortress on the headland. The headland separates the Venetian port from the crowded town beach in the modern quarter called Nea Hora.

Zambeliou, which crosses Halidon just before the harbour, was once Hania's main thoroughfare. It's a narrow, winding street, lined with craft shops, small hotels and tavernas.

While the old town is still popular with locals, Haniots tend to hang around Koum Kapi, a recently rejuvenated precinct in the old Turkish quarter further east. Following the port all the way around to the right you'll find the endless row of waterfront cafés, bars and restaurants.

Boats to Hania dock at Souda, about 7km southeast of town.

INFORMATION
Bookshops
NewsStand (☎ 28210 95888; Skalidi 8) A wide range of international press and magazines, as well as a reasonable selection of books, including Crete guides and maps.

Emergency
Tourist police (☎ 28210 73333; Iraklion 23; ⊙ 8am-2.30pm)

Internet Access
Notos Internet C@fe (☎ 28210 98722; Akti Koundourioti 31; per hr €3; ⊙ 9am-1am)
Vranas Studios (☎ 28210 58618; Agion Deka 10; per hr €3; ⊙ 9am-11pm)

Internet Resources
www.chania.gr The Municipality of Hania's website is worth a look for more information on the city and cultural events in happening in town.
www.chania-guide.gr Has good information on the Hania city and prefecture.

Laundry
Afroditi (Agion Deka 18; wash & dry €6)
Laundry Fidias (☎ 28210 52494; Kallinikou; wash & dry €6)
Old Town Laundromat (☎ 28210 59414; Karaoli & Dimitriou 38; wash & dry €7; ⊙ 9am-2pm & 6pm-9pm Mon-Sat) Also does dry cleaning.

Left Luggage
Bus station (☎ 28210 93053; Plateia 1866; per day €1.50)

Medical Services
Hania Hospital (Mournies) Located south of town.

Money
Most banks are concentrated around the new city, while there are some stand-alone ATMs in the old city. There are numerous places to change money outside banking hours; most are willing to negotiate their commission.
Alpha Bank (cnr Halidon & Skalidi) Has 24-hour automatic exchange machines.
Citibank ATM (Halidon)
Commercial Bank ATM (food market)
National Bank of Greece (cnr Tzanakaki & Giannari) Has 24-hour automatic exchange machines.

Post
Post Office (Tzanakaki 3; ⊙ 7.30am-8pm Mon-Fri, 7.30am-2pm Sat)

Telephone
OTE (Tzanakaki 5; ⊙ 7.30am-10pm)

Tourist Information
Tourist Information Office (EOT; ☎ 28210 36155; Plateia 1866 16-18; ⊙ 8am-2.30pm) Located in front of the Town Hall; provides helpful practical information and maps.

Travel Agencies
Diktynna Travel (☎ 28210 41458 or ☎ 28210 43930; www.diktynna-travel.gr; Sfakion 36)
Tellus Travel (☎ 28210 91500; Halidon 108; ⊙ 8am-11pm) Rents out cars, changes money, arranges air and boat tickets and sells excursions.

SIGHTS
The massive fortifications built by the Venetians to protect their city remain impressive. The best-preserved section is the western wall, running from the **Firkas Fortress** to the **Siavo Bastion**. It was part of a defensive system begun in 1538 by engineer Michele Sanmichele, who also designed Iraklio's defences. You can walk up to the top of the bastion for some good views of the old town.

The Venetian **lighthouse** at the entrance to the harbour is in need of tender loving care these days, but the 1.5km walk around the sea wall to get there is worth it.

You can escape the crowds of the Venetian quarter by taking a stroll around the Turkish **Splantzia quarter** – a delightful tangle of narrow streets and little squares.

On the eastern side of the inner harbour you will see the prominent **Mosque of Kioutsouk Hasan** (also known as the Mosque of Janissaries), which has been restored and houses regular art exhibitions.

Hania's **Archaeological Museum** (☎ 28210 90334; Halidon 30; admission €2; ⊙ 8.30am-3pm Tue-Sun) is housed in the 16th-century Venetian Church of San Francisco that became a mosque under the Turks, a movie theatre in 1913 and a munitions depot for the Germans during WWII. The Turkish fountain in the grounds is a relic from the building's days as a mosque. The museum houses a well-displayed collection of finds from western Crete dating from the Neolithic to the Roman era. Artefacts from 3400 BC to 1200 BC, to the left as you enter the museum, include tablets with Linear A script. There are vases from the Geometric era (1000–700 BC) and, among the Hellenistic and Roman exhibits, the statue of Diana is particularly impressive. Before leaving the museum, take note of the marble fountain and the courtyard decorated with lions' heads from the Venetian period.

The **Naval Museum** (☎ 28210 91875; Akti Koundourioti; admission €2; ⏰ 9am-4pm) has an interesting collection of model ships dating from the Bronze Age, naval instruments, paintings, photographs and memorabilia from the Battle of Crete. The museum is housed in the Firkas Fortress on the headland, once the old Turkish prison. An authentic replica of a Minoan ship, which sailed from Crete to Athens as part of the Athens Olympics ceremonies, is on display in one of the old shipyards on the harbour (Akti Enoseosos). The construction of the hollow rowing boat, based on ships that would have existed in the 15th century BC, was a cooperative venture between the museum and a research programme for experimental archaeology.

The **Byzantine and Post Byzantine Collection of Hania** (☎ 28210 96046; Theotokopoulou; admission €2, incl Archaeological Museum €3; ⏰ 8.30am-3pm Tue-Sun) is in the impressively restored Church of San Salvatore, on the western side of the fortress. It has a small but fascinating collection of artefacts, icons, jewellery and coins, including a fine segment of a mosaic floor for an early Christian basilica and a prized icon of St George slaying the dragon. The building has a mixed bag of interesting architectural features from its various occupiers.

Hania's interesting **Cretan House Folklore Museum** (☎ 28210 90816; Halidon 46; admission €2; ⏰ 9.30am-3pm & 6-9pm) contains a selection of crafts and implements including weavings with traditional designs.

The **Historical Museum and Archives** (☎ 28210 52606; Sfakianaki 20; admission free; ⏰ 9am-1pm Mon-Fri), southeast of the old quarter, traces Crete's war-torn history with a series of exhibits focusing on the struggle against the Turks. There are also exhibits relating to the German occupation and a folklore collection.

The **Great Arsenal** (☎ 28210 40101; www.kam-arsenali.gr; Plateia Katehaki) has been stunningly restored and is now home to the Centre for Mediterranean Architecture, a venue that hosts regular events and exhibitions.

Identified as one of the world's top 100 endangered Jewish monuments, the **Etz Hayyim Synagogue** (Parodos Kondylaki; ☎ 28210 86286;

MINOAN HANIA

The area to the east of the Old Harbour, between Akti Tombazi and Karaoli Dimitriou, is the site of **Ancient Kydonia**. The search for Minoan remains began in the early 1960s and excavation work continues. Fifty Late Minoan graves were found in 2004 in the Agios Ioannis area, which is part of the cemetery of ancient Kydonia. The site can be seen at the junction of Kanevaro and Kandanoleou, and many of the finds are on display in the Archaeological Museum (p78).

Kydonia has been remodelled by a succession of occupiers. After ejecting the Arabs, the Byzantines set about building their *kastelli* (castle) on the same site, on top of the old walls in some places and using the same materials. It was this part of town that bore the brunt of the bombing in WWII.

---

www.etz-hayyim-hania.org; ⏰ 9am-12.30pm & 6-8pm) was restored in 1999.

Hania's magnificent covered **food market** (see p84) is a worth a visit even if you don't want to shop. The excellent cheap eateries within the market offer a unique dining experience. Unfortunately, the central bastion of the city wall was demolished to make way for this fine 1911 cruciform creation, modelled after the market in Marseilles.

ACTIVITIES
Trekking & Mountain Climbing

Alpine Travel (☎ 28210 50939; www.alpine.gr; Boniali 11-19; ⏰ 9am-2pm Mon-Fri & after 7pm some evenings), in the Boniali complex, a range of many trekking programmes. The owner, George Antonakakis, who helps run Hania's chapter of the **EOS** (☎ 28210 44647; www.interkriti.org/orivatikos/hania1.htm; Tzanakaki 90), is the person to talk to for information about serious climbing in the Lefka Ori. George can provide information on Greece's mountain refuges, the E4 trail, and climbing and trekking in Crete in general.

Trekking Plan (☎ 28210 60861; www.cycling.gr), 8km west of town in Agia Marina next to the Santa Marina Hotel, offers treks to the Agia Irini Gorge, the Imbros Gorge and climbs of Mt Gingilos for about €45. They have also expanded their activities to offer canyoning, rappelling, rock-climbing and kayaking trips. See p57 for more information on adventure activities.

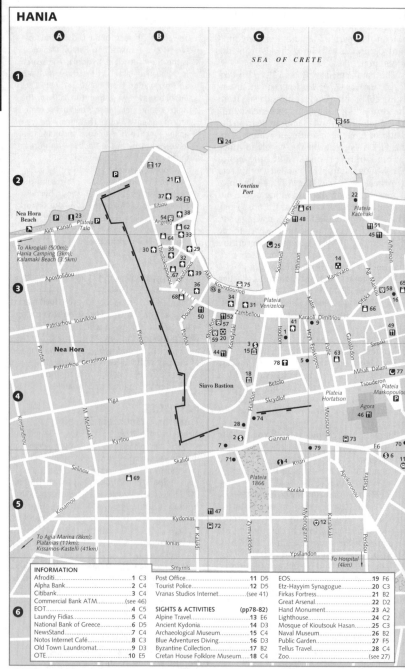

HANIA

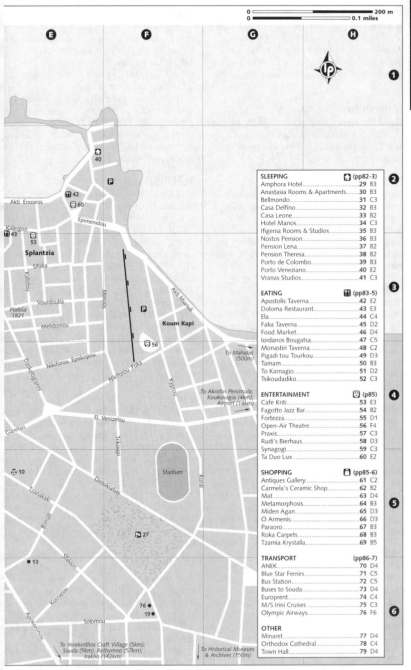

Mountain Biking

Trekking Plan (☎ /fax 28210 60861; www.cycling.gr) offers a full programme of mountain-bike tours at varying levels of difficulty, including a one-day guided tour for €50 and an all-in, eight-day racing cyclist programme for €169.

Scuba Diving

Blue Adventures Diving (☎ 28210 40608; Arholeon 11) offers a PADI certification course (€322) and dives around Hania (€70), including a beginner's dive.

Swimming

The town beach at **Nea Hora** is crowded, but generally clean if you need to cool off and get some rays but the better beaches are a long the west to Platanias; there are regular buses heading there. For better swimming, keep heading west and you'll come to **Kalamaki Beach** after about 3.5km.

HANIA FOR CHILDREN

If your five year old has lost interest in Venetian architecture before the end of the first street, head to the **public garden** between Tzanakaki and Dimokratias. There you'll find a playground, a small **zoo** with a resident kri-kri and a children's resource centre that has a small selection of books in English.

TOURS

Historian **Tony Fennymore** (☎ 28210 87139; ☎ 69725 37055; www.fennyscrete.ws; 2hr walking tour €12; ☽ Apr-Jul & Sep-Oct) can provide a wealth of information about Hania's history and culture. The walking tours head off from the 'Hand' monument on Plateia Talo at the northern end of Theotokopoulou. His witty and indispensable walking guide *Fenny's Hania* (€7.50) is available at Roka Carpets (see p86).

The Sheffield-born photographer **Steve Outram** (☎ 28210 32201; www.steveoutram.com) runs photography tours in Crete twice a year for both amateur shutterbugs and more practised photographers.

There are a number of boat excursions from Hania that take you to the nearby islands of Agii and Theodori and the Gulf of Hania. The **M/S Irini** (☎ 28210 52001; €15) runs daily cruises taking off from outside the Remezzo bar.

FESTIVALS & EVENTS

In addition to the religious and historical events that are celebrated throughout the island, the town of Hania commemorates the **Battle of Crete anniversary** with athletics competitions, folk dancing and ceremonial events during the last week of May.

In summer, the municipality hosts cultural events around the city, including the public gardens and the **open-air theatre** (www .chania.gr) on the outskirts of the city walls (on Kyprou), which has regular music and theatrical performances.

SLEEPING

Hania's Venetian quarter is brimming with chic boutique hotels and family-run hotels and pensions housed in restored Venetian buildings.

The western end of the harbour and along Zambeliou is a good place to look, but it can be noisy at night, especially along the harbour, so be warned if you want a view. Most hotels in town are open all year. Many of the older and boutique hotels have no lift and charming but daunting spiral staircases. Hotel complexes with pools can be found at Nea Hora, along the strip of beach that runs west of the town centre with resorts spreading all the way towards Platanias and beyond.

Budget

Pension Theresa (☎ /fax 28210 92798; Angelou 2; d €35-45; ☼) Three storeys of antique-furnished rooms in a creaky old house with a steep spiral staircase make this the most atmospheric pension in Hania. Even if you don't snag a room with a view, there's always the stunning vista from the rooftop terrace where you can use the communal kitchen. The rooms are spotless and all have TV, aircon and lofts with an extra bed, making it ideal for small families. It attracts many artists and writers.

Pension Lena (☎ 28210 86860; lenachania@hotmail .com; Ritsou 5; s/d €32/50; ☼) Lena's is a friendly, cosy pension in an old Turkish building where you can help yourself to a room if the owner, Lena, is not there. It has an old-world feel and a scattering of antiques. Originally from Hamburg, Lena makes all guests feel welcome.

Hotel Manos (☎ 28210 94156; www.manoshotel.gr; Zambeliou 24; d with view €25; ☼ ☐) This is one of

HANIA

the oldest small waterfront hotels in Hania and it's certainly showing its age. But despite the dated and basic décor it is clean and spacious, with fridge and air-con. The front rooms have a small balcony and harbour views.

Anastasia Rooms & Apartments (☎ 28210 88001; anastasia_ap@acn.gr; Theotokopoulou 21; studio €38/50; 😵) These stylish, spotless well-equipped studios have been freshly painted and up-dated with new beds and furnishings. They are all two level with lounge/sofa bed. The bathrooms are basic and the upstairs rooms have balconies.

Ifigenia Rooms & Studios (☎ 28210 94357; www .ifigeniastudios.gr; Gamba & Parodos Agelou; studio €30-70; 😵) This network of five different refurbished houses around the Venetian port offers a range of accommodation options. All rooms have air-con and some deluxe apartments have kitchenettes, Jacuzzis and views. Some bathrooms are very basic and the faux old-world décor in some rooms is a little contrived.

Hania Camping (☎ 28210 31138; camhania@otenet .gr; Agii Apostoli; per person/tent/caravan €5/3.50/6; 🚐) This is the nearest camping ground to Hania, 3km west of town on the beach. The site is shaded and has a restaurant, bar and mini-market. Take a Kalamaki Beach bus (every 15 minutes) from the southeast corner of Plateia 1866 and ask to be let off at the camping ground.

Mid-Range

Nostos Hotel (☎ 28210 94740; fax 28210 94743; Zambeliou 42-46; s/d incl breakfast €40/80; 😵) Mixing Venetian style and modern fixtures, this 600-year-old building has been remodelled into classy split-level rooms/units, all with kitchen, fridge phone and TV. Try to get a room in front for the view of the harbour.

Vranas Studios (☎ 28210 58618; www.vranas.gr; Agion Deka 10; studio €40-55; 😵) This place is on a lively pedestrian street and has spacious, immaculately maintained studios with kitchenettes. All rooms have polished wooden floors, balconies, TVs and telephones. Air-con is also available.

Amphora Hotel (☎ 28210 93224; www.amphora.gr; Parodos Theotokopoulou 20; s/d €75/90, breakfast €10; 😵) This is Hania's most historically evocative hotel. It is located in an immaculately restored and kept Venetian mansion with rooms around a courtyard. The rooms are

elegantly decorated, most with double beds, and the top rooms have air-con and views of the harbour. The front rooms can be noisy in the summer.

Porto de Colombo (☎ 28210 70945; colombo@ote net.gr; Theofanous & Moschon; d/ste incl breakfast €74/94; 😵) The Venetian mansion that was once the French embassy and office of Eleftherios Venizelos is now a charming boutique hotel with 10 lovely, well-appointed rooms; the top suites have fine harbour views. Prices are lower if you opt for no air-con.

Bellmondo (☎ 28210 36216; Zambeliou 10; d/ste incl breakfast €75/95; 😵) This relative newcomer has harbour views and a formal feel, with iron beds and traditional furnishings. The restored house has Turkish and Venetian features, including part of an old hammam in one room. Children up to 12 stay free.

Top End

Casa Leone (☎ 28210 76762; www.casa-leone.com; Parodos Theotokopoulou 18; s & d incl breakfast €80-130; 😵) This residence was recently converted into a classy and romantic boutique hotel. The rooms are spacious and well appointed, with balconies overlooking the harbour. There are honeymoon suites and extras like hairdryers.

Porto Veneziano (☎ 28210 27100; www.porto -veneziano.gr; Akti Enoseos; s/d/ste incl buffet breakfast €90/125/200; 😵) At the harbour's eastern edge, this is a stylish and comfortable hotel offering large rooms with TV, telephone and air-con. The decoration is light and cheerful, and there's an interior garden for relaxing.

Casa Delfino (☎ 28210 93098; www.casadelfino.com; Theofanous 7; d/apt incl buffet breakfast €140/295; 😵) This modernised 17th-century mansion has a splendid courtyard of traditionally patterned cobblestones, plus 22 individually decorated suites. The palatial, split-level apartment sleeps up to four people, and the main bathroom has a Jacuzzi.

EATING

Hania has some of the finest restaurants in Crete, so be discerning about where you go. Unfortunately, most of the prime-position waterfront tavernas are generally mediocre, often over-priced and fronted by annoying touts. Head for the back streets, where some of the best tavernas are housed in roofless Venetian ruins scattered in the streets of Splantzia and the old town.

Budget

The two tavernas in the food market are good places to seek out cheap traditional cuisine. Their prices are almost identical and the quality is excellent. There are plenty of snack food places on Halidon.

Iordanis Bougatsa (☎ 28210 90026; Kydonias 96; 150g bougatsa slice €2.10) Continuing the business started by his great grandfather in 1924, Iordanis churns out endless trays of his famous delicious creamy *bougatsa* (filo pastry filled with myzithra cheese sprinkled with a little icing sugar). It's opposite the bus station.

Doloma Restaurant (☎ 28210 51196; Kalergon 8; mayirefta €3.50-5.80; ☺ Mon-Sat) This unpretentious restaurant is half-hidden amid the vines and foliage that surround the outdoor terrace. It's a relaxed spot to escape the crowds, and the traditional cooking is faultless.

Mid-Range

To Karnagio (☎ 28210 53366; Plateia Katehaki 8; Cretan specialities €5-10.50) This place is on every Haniot's short list of favourite restaurants. Its sprawling outdoor tables near the harbour make it appealing to tourists but it has not sacrificed one whit of authenticity. There is a good range of seafood (try the grilled cuttlefish) and classic Cretan dishes, plus a fine wine list.

Tamam (☎ 28210 58639; Zambeliou 49; veg specials €3-6.50; ☺ 1pm-12.30am) Tamam has deservedly inspired a loyal following. Housed in old Turkish baths, this atmospheric place presents a superb selection of vegetarian specialities (try the spicy avocado dip on potato) and inspired dishes such as a divine pastrami, feta and tomato concoction and the excellent Beyendi chicken with creamy aubergine puree.

Pigadi tou Tourkou (☎ 28210 54547; Sarpaki 1-3; mains €8.50-14.50; ☺ dinner only) Features from this former 19th-century steam bath, including the well it is named after (Well of the Turk), are incorporated into the cosy design of this excellent restaurant. British owner Jenny Payavia offers a tantalising menu of dishes inspired by Crete, Morocco and the Middle East, including specialties such as aubergine (eggplant) meatballs with yogurt.

Monastiri Taverna (☎ 28210 55527; Akti Tombazi; mezedes €2.50-8.80) One of the few waterfront restaurants that gets the general thumbs up from discerning local and international diners, Monastiri, on the eastern side of the harbour, dishes up fish and excellent Cretan fare.

Ela (☎ 28210 74128; Kondylaki 47; specials €5-15; ☺ noon-1am) Dating from the 14th century, the building of Ela was first a soap factory, then a school, distillery and cheese-processing plant. Now Ela serves up a well-executed array of Cretan specialties, while local musicians create a lively ambience on summer evenings when the awnings are drawn for open-air dining. The rather tacky board outside tells you it's in every guidebook but the accolades are not undeserved.

Tsikoudadiko (☎ 28210 72873; Zambeliou 31; Cretan specials €4-7.50) Despite the friendly tout outside, this restaurant turns out honest Cretan cooking in a delightful roofless plant-filled shell of a Venetian building. Their special creamy baked potato with ham and cheese is excellent. There is live acoustic music most nights.

Mahalas (☎ 28210 55492; Akti Miaouli & Sparti; meze platter for 2-3 €15) This fine *mezedopoleio* (meze restaurant) on the Haniot side of the harbour has a wide range of meze and an excellent range of ouzos. Try the house special of mixed seafood and meat meze platters. There are tables outside overlooking the sea, plus a cosy stone interior.

Faka Taverna (☎ 28210 42341; Plateia Katehaki; mains €5.30-8.50) This is another of those quiet unassuming places that doesn't dish up bland tourist fare. The cuisine is solid and genuine. Good local choices include Cretan rice or artichokes and broad beans. There's a children's menu and small playpen.

Top End

Akrogiali (☎ 28210 71110; Akti Papanikoli 20, Nea Hora; ☺ dinner only) Most people consider Akrogiali the best seafood restaurant in Hania. The fish is so fresh it's practically wiggling on the plate and the accompaniments are superb. The airy restaurant opens onto the seafront giving you a great view of the sunset.

Apostolis Taverna (☎ 28210 43470; Akti Enoseos 6; seafood platter for 2 incl salad €26) In the quieter eastern harbour, this is a well-respected place for fish and Cretan dishes. Service is friendly and efficient, and there's a good wine list and a view over the harbour.

Nykterida (☎ 28210 64215; Korakies, on airport road; mains €8-15). If you want to lash out, this established restaurant is reputedly the best in Hania, graced over the years by the likes of Churchill, Anthony Quinn, Melina Mercouri and Andreas Papandreou. It has been around since 1933 and was converted to the German club during WWII. The sweets are excellent and there's an extensive wine list.

ENTERTAINMENT

Funky rock-and-roll joints play the dominant role in Hania's nightlife scene, but there are also some cosy spots for jazz, light rock and Cretan music. The harbour's lively waterfront bars and clubs are mostly patronised by tourists, while the row of clubs along Sourmeli are frequented by American soldiers from the nearby bases. When Haniots want to party the night away, they are likely to head out to Platanias, a coastal resort about 11km west of Hania. Drinks can be expensive.

Ta Duo Lux (☎ 28210 52519; Sarpidona 8; ☽ 10am-late) The imaginative changing décor at this arty café make for a refreshing change (the tea room upstairs is a nice touch). This is a long-established Haniot hangout for a younger alternative crowds and is popular day and night. The music is eclectic and there is a small but excellent selection of sandwiches.

Fagotto Jazz Bar (☎ 28210 71877; Angelou 16 ☽ 7pm-2am Jul-May) A Hania institution housed in a restored Venetian building, Fagotto offers the smooth sounds of jazz and light rock and blues. There's regular live jazz year-round, including some notable international acts. Jazz paraphernalia includes a saxophone beer tap.

Fortezza (☎ 28210 46546) This café, bar and restaurant, installed in the old Venetian ramparts across the harbour, is the best place in town for a sunset drink. A free barge takes you across the water from the bottom of Sarpidona to the sea wall wrapping around the harbour. There's a splendid view of the Venetian harbour from the rooftop bar.

Cafe Kriti (☎ 28210 58661; Kalergon 22; ☽ 8pm-late) Also known as Lyrakia, this is a rough-and-ready joint with a decorative scheme that relies on saws, pots, ancient sewing machines and animal heads, but it's the best place in Hania to hear live Cretan music.

Synagogi (☎ 28210 96797; Skoufou 15) Housed in a roofless Venetian building that was once a synagogue, Synagogi serves up fresh fruit juices, coffee, drinks and snacks by day and

is a popular lounge bar at night, frequented by trendy locals. The stone and wooden interior is stunning.

Praxis (☎ 28210 57157; Skoufon 5; ☽ midnight-late) This popular bar attracts a trendy younger crowd of locals and the odd tourist looking for an authentic night out. It has a great atmosphere and funky décor.

Rudi's Bierhaus (☎ 28210 50824; Sifaka 26; ☽ 6pm-late, Tue-Sun) Austrian Rudi Riegler packs this tiny bar with fine Belgian *guezes* and *krieks* as well as other excellent beers. He also serves some of the best mezedes in town.

Koukouvagia (☎ 28210 27449; Venizelos Graves) If you have wheels then take a 10-minute drive up to hill where the great statesman Eleftherios Venizelos is buried. This owl-themed café and bar (with an extraordinary owl décor collection) enjoys panoramic views of Hania and is a cool place to hand on summer's nights. The pita creations are excellent, as are the home-made cakes.

SHOPPING

Hania offers the best combination of souvenir hunting and shopping for crafts on the island. The main street is Halidon, which is impossible to avoid since it connects the inner town with the harbour, but the best shops are scattered through the back streets of the old town. Skrydlof is 'leather lane' with good-quality handmade boots, sandals and bags. There's also an outdoor *laïki* market Saturday mornings from 7am to 2pm on Minoos where you can pick up fruits, vegetables, local products and cheap clothes.

The Antiques Gallery (☎ 6994 427070; Akti Tombazi 1) Near the Mosque of Kioutsouk Hasan, most of the stuff here is too bulky to tuck into your suitcase, but in addition to framed paintings and old furniture there are more unusual odds and ends dating from the Turkish occupation.

O Armenis (☎ 28210 54434; Sifaka 29, workshop at No 14) Owner Apostolos Pahtikos has been making traditional Cretan knives since he was 13 and has passed on the trade to his son. You can watch them work as they match the blades to carefully carved handles. A finely honed kitchen knife costs €15.

Carmela's (☎ 28210 40487; Angelou 7) Carmela produces unique ceramics using ancient techniques her original jewellery designs, as well as unusual pieces handcrafted by young Greek artisans.

Mat (☎ 28210 42217; Potie 51) A hobby that turned into an obsession for the late national chess champion Athanasios Diamantopoulos has put this tiny shop on the world map for chess enthusiasts. His wife continues to sell a large range of his original designs include chess pieces in bronze, wood and stone. Sets range from €60 to €1000 according to weight and design, with the most popular being the 'Athenians'.

Metamorphosis (☎ 28210 70545; Theotokopoulou 50) Most of the jewellery in this shop is the work of local young jeweller Lefteris Drakakis. His original designs include some unusual pieces, with a range of themes using flowers, people and even knife-and-fork motifs.

Miden Agan (☎ 28210 27068; Daskalogianni 70) Foodies and wine lovers will be delighted with the range of products at this excellent shop that sells its own wine and liquors, along with over 400 of the most interesting wines produced in Greece. There is also a wide variety of beautifully packaged local traditional gourmet deli foods, including oil and honey.

Paraoro (☎ 28210 88990; Theotokopoulou 16) Artist Stamatis Fasoularis creates a distinctive series of decorative metal boats that all have a functional use, including candles and light fittings and a steamship oil burner. There's also jewellery and crafts from local and Athens-based artists, plus a workshop.

Roka Carpets (☎ 28210 74736; Zambeliou 61) You can watch Mihalis Manousakis weave his wondrous rugs on a 400-year-old loom using methods that have remained essentially unchanged since Minoan times. This is one of the few places in Crete where you can buy genuine, hand-woven goods. Prices begin at €30 for a small rug.

Verekinthos Craft Village (☎ 28210 81261; Verekinthos-Viopa on road to Souda) Artists demonstrate their craft at this innovative complex of workshops in the Chania Industrial Park on the outskirts of town. There are 16 pottery workshops along with artisans working on jewellery, weaving, embroidery, leather and glass.

Tzamia-Krystalla (☎ 28210 71172; Skalidi 35; ⊙ 9.30am-2pm & 6-9pm Mon-Sat) This converted old glass workshop is now a fine art gallery and café where you can find small and large pieces from local artisans, including ceramics and well-priced original creations.

GETTING THERE & AWAY
Air
Hania's airport (CHQ) is 14km east of town on the Akrotiri Peninsula.

Olympic Airlines (☎ 28210 58005; www.olympicairlines.com; Tzanakaki 88) operates at least five daily flights to/from Athens (€86.50). There are also four flights a week to/from Thessaloniki (€109.50).

Aegean Airlines (☎ 28210 63366; www.aegeanair.com) has four daily flights to Athens (€83 plus tax).

Boat
Hania's main port is at Souda, about 7km southeast of town. There are frequent buses to Hania (€0.90), as well as taxis (€8).

ANEK (☎ 28210 27500; www.anek.gr; Plateia Sofokli Venizelos) has a daily boat at 9pm from Piraeus to Hania (€21.70, nine hours) and at 8pm from Hania to Piraeus. In July and August there is also a morning ferry at 9am from Piraeus (€16.60).

Blue Star Ferries (☎ 28210 75444; www.bluestar ferries.com; Plateia 1826 14) has a faster daily service

---

CRETAN KNIVES

Given the island's unruly history, it's not surprising that Cretans have a highly developed tradition of knife making. Traditional Cretan dress for men always includes a knife, often white-handled, as an accessory to the standard black shirt, trousers and boots outfit. Knives have acquired a power that borders on the mystical. Older Cretans believe that knives made during Holy Week offer protection from evil spirits. In eastern Crete, it's considered bad luck to give a knife as a present, while in western Crete, it's considered good luck for the best man or godfather at a wedding to be presented with a knife.

Although the Minoans certainly produced knives, the current method probably developed under Turkish rule. At that time, the handles were made from buffalo horn or mountain goat antlers, but since horns have become rarer, cutlers sometimes use cattle bones. Unfortunately, customers are also becoming more scarce and the cutlers' craft is slowly disappearing.

on newer ships that take only six hours
(€23.50), although the seating is airplane style.
There are also cabins. They leave Piraeus at
4pm and Hania at 11.30pm.

The **Port Police** (☎ 28210 89240) can also be
contacted for ferry information.

Bus

In summer, buses depart from Hania's
bus station (☎ 28210 93052) for the following
destinations:

Destination	Duration	Fare	Frequency
Elafonisi	2¼ hr	€8	2 daily
Falasarna	1½ hr	€5.50	3 daily
Hora Sfakion	2 hr	€5.40	3 daily
Iraklio	2½ hr	€10.50	half-hourly
Kissamos-Kastelli	1 hr	€3.40	hourly
Kolymbari	45 min	€2.30	half-hourly
Lakki	1¾ hr	€2.30	6 daily
Moni Agias Triadas	30 min	€1.70	2 daily
Omalos (for Samaria Gorge)	1 hr	€5	4 daily
Paleohora	2 hr	€5.40	5 daily
Rethymno	1 hr	€5.55	half-hourly
Sougia	2 hr	€5.40	1 daily
Stavros	30 min	€1.50	6 daily

Check with the bus station for off-peak
services.

GETTING AROUND
To/From the Airport
There is no airport bus. A taxi ride to the
airport from the centre of town will cost
about €13.

Bus
Local blue buses (☎ 28210 27044) meet the ferries
at the port of Souda, just near the dock. In
Hania, the bus to Souda (€0.90) leaves from
outside the food market, and buses for the
western beaches leave from the main bus
station on Plateia 1866.

Local buses also go as far as Panormo,
stopping at all the beaches.

Car, Motorcycle & Bicycle
Most motorcycle-hire outlets are on Ha-
lidon, but the companies at Agia Marina
can bring cars to Hania.
Auto Papas (☎ 28210 68124; Agia Marina)
Europrent (☎ 28210 40810, 28210 27810; Halidon 87)
National (☎ 28210 38185; Agia Marina)

AKROTIRI PENINSULA & SOUDA BAY

AKROTIRI PENINSULA
ΧΕΡΣΟΝΗΣΟΣ ΑΚΡΩΤΗΡΙ
The Akrotiri (ak-roh-*tee*-ree) Peninsula, to
the east of Hania, is a barren, hilly stretch
of rock covered with scrub. It has a few
coastal resorts, Hania's airport and a naval
base on Souda Bay. There are few buses and
the poorly signposted roads make it a difficult region to explore. However, it's a good
place to escape the crowds and the peninsula has a few interesting monasteries.

Monasteries
There are three Cretan monasteries on the
Akrotiri Peninsula. The impressive 17th-
century **Moni Agias Triadas** (☎ 28210 63310; admission €1.50; ☘ 8am-7pm) was founded by the
Venetian monks Jeremiah and Laurentio
Giancarolo. The brothers were converts to
the Orthodox faith. There was a religious
school here in the 19th century and it is
still an active monastery with an excellent
library. The church is worth visiting for its
altarpiece as well as its Venetian-influenced
domed façade. The monastery is known for
its excellent *Agiotriaditiko* wine.

The 16th-century **Moni Gouvernetou** (Our Lady
of the Angels; ☎ 28210 63319; museum admission €1.50;
☘ 8am-2pm & 4-8pm) is 4km north of Moni
Agias Triadas. The monastery may date as far
back as the 11th century from a time when
an inland sanctuary was an attractive refuge
from coastal pirates. The building itself is
disappointingly plain, but the church inside
has an ornate sculptured Venetian façade.
This monastery has a small museum.

From Moni Gouvernetou, it's a 20-minute
walk (about 30 minutes on the uphill walk
back) to the path leading down to the coast
to the ruins of **Moni Ioannou Erimiti** (also known
as Moni Katholikou). In disuse for many
centuries, the monastery is dedicated to St
John the Hermit who lived in the cave behind the ruins. Near the entrance to the cave,
there's a small pond whose water is believed
to be holy. On the feast day of St John (7
October), there's a festival here that begins
with a vigil the previous evening. St John's
grave is at the end of a cave at the bottom of
a rock staircase.

There are two buses Monday to Saturday at 6.30am and 1pm to Moni Agias Triadas from Hania's bus station (€1.70, 40 minutes).

Kalathas Καλαθάς
pop 329

Kalathas is a tiny beach resort 10km north of Hania that closes down completely in the winter. In the summer the two sandy beaches lined by pine trees can fill up, but Kalathas remains a pretty place to take a day trip from Hania or spend a couple of days. It is the preferred weekend haunt of Haniots, many of whom own summer and weekend houses nearby.

Buses running from Hania to Stavros stop at Kalathas.

Esplanade Apartments (☎ 28210 64253; espland@otenet.gr; studio €55; 🖳 🎾 🏊) This is an attractive two-storey structure with a swimming pool. Studios are roomy, light and breezy and have phone, TV and kitchenette.

Georgi's Blue Apartments (☎ 28210 64080; www.blueapts.gr; studio/apt €75/105; 🎾 🏊) Signposted to the left off the main road from Hania, Georgi's is a tasteful, rather upmarket complex of rooms and apartments. All are very well furnished and have phone, satellite TV, fridge and kitchenette, plus a swimming pool.

Three kilometres north of Kalathas is the small beach settlement of Tersanas, signposted off the main Kalathas–Stavros road. You could also try looking here for a cheaper place to stay.

Tersanas Lodges (☎ 28210 39684; www.tblodges.com; studio €42; 🎾) The studios are a little on the small size, but this neat accommodation block a 10-minute walk from Tersanas and 10m from the beach is a good option. They have the usual kitchenette and bathroom facilities, TV and balconies, and are in a very quiet location.

Stavros Σταυός
pop 323

The village of Stavros, 6km north of Kalathas, is little more than a scattering of houses and a few hotels located behind Stavros Cove. It's the kind of place you go in order to really unwind and relax. There is no village 'scene' to speak of as most houses, restaurants and accommodation are spread over a fairly wide area. The main cove is a narrow strip of sandy beach dominated by a mammoth rock shelf that served as a backdrop for a scene in the movie *Zorba the Greek*.

There is some accommodation near the beach, but it is shared with a few package travellers who prefer Stavros' quiet lifestyle to the frenetic scene further west of Hania. There are quite a few more hotels and domatia on the rocky outpost about a kilometre west of the beach. Most cater to both packaged and independent travellers.

Villa Eleana Apartments (☎ /fax 28210 39480; eleana@chania.forthnet.gr; studio/apt €45-80; 🏊) Hidden away somewhat, but prominently signposted, Villa Eleana has very roomy, clean studios and apartments with microwave, TV and telephone. Most rooms have a sea view.

Blue Beach (☎ 28210 39404; vepe@cha.forthnet.gr; d €50; 🎾 🏊) Right on the beach, Blue Beach is a low-key resort hotel that welcomes independent travellers. The rooms are comfortable and self-contained with fridge and kitchenette and there is a pool for guests. Air-con is an extra €8.

There are six buses a day from Hania (€1.50, 30 minutes). If you're coming by car from Hania follow signs to the airport and then signs to Stavros.

SOUDA ΣΟΥΔΑ
pop 6425

The harbour of Souda is one of Crete's largest, and is the port of entry if you come to Hania by ferry. The Venetians built a castle at the entrance of Souda Bay, which they held until 1715, even though the Turks had already seized the rest of the island. Souda is now the site of the Greek navy's main refitting station, which sees a sizeable military presence in the area.

About 1km west of Souda, there is an immaculate Commonwealth **military cemetery**, where about 1500 British, Australian and New Zealand soldiers who lost their lives in the Battle of Crete are buried. Beautifully situated at the water's edge, the rows of white headstones make a moving tribute to the heroic defenders of Crete. The buses to Souda port that depart from outside the Hania food market on Giannari can drop you off at the cemetery.

The town of Souda, about 2km from the port, sprang up 130 years ago under Turkish rule, but little remains from that period. Today most of the activity and services – including travel agencies, banks and shops – are all clustered in the port close to the main square near the ferry quay. Accommodation and dining opportunities are limited and you are much better off in Hania.

Orientation & Information

The main street of Souda port is 3 Septemvriou, which runs parallel to the harbour. The harbour opens onto a large square with travel agencies and cafés. The National Bank of Greece is on the square and has an ATM. There is a 24-hour exchange machine at the port, while the post office and OTE are on 3 Septemvriou, right from the square.

Gelasakis Travel/Blue Star Ferries (☎ 28210 89065; ⊗ 8am-11pm), on the main square, changes money, handles air and boat tickets, and rents out cars.

Sleeping & Eating

Hotel Parthenon (☎ 28210 89245; El Venizelou 29; d €35; ☒) Right across from the main square above a taverna serving souvlaki, the rooms at this small hotel have been upgraded and have fridge, TV and air-con if you need to spend a night in the port.

Vlachakis Brothers (☎ 28210 89219; 16 Ellis St) Over in Souda town, this well-regarded simple fish taverna has had a recent facelift. Its specialty, the prawn omelette (€7), is washed down nicely with a selection of barrel wine.

Paloma (☎ 28210 89081; fish dishes €6-8, top fish per kg €45) Further along old Souda on the coastal road leading to the airport, this is one of the two pleasant fish tavernas with classic blue chairs and chequered tablecloths right on the sea overlooking the port. It is a pleasant walk past the cemetery.

Getting There & Away

Souda is about 9km east of Hania. There are frequent buses to Hania (€0.90) that meet the ferries. There are also taxis (€7 to Hania).

GULF OF HANIA

The coastline west of Hania between the Akrotiri and Rodopou Peninsulas, which forms the Gulf of Hania, is an endless 13km strip of hotels, domatia, souvenir shops, travel agencies, mini-markets and restaurants. The former villages along this coast

have become little more than entertainment strip malls. It's not the place to come if you're looking for a quiet, relaxing holiday, but the nightlife is good and it has all the services to cater to your needs.

The first tourist town is **Agia Marina**, 9km from Hania. While it caters primarily to package tourists, you will find a clutch of undistinguished domatia along the main road. The beach tends to be packed with lines of identical lounges and umbrellas, and the water is rather murky and uninspiring. Nonetheless, Agia Marina is the first port of call for Hania nightclubbers looking for action.

Next along is **Platanias**, 12km from Hania and almost indistinguishable from Agia Marina. It's also a community of mid-range accommodation, fast-food grills, bars, clubs and shops. Platanias is made up of a busy main strip and an old town that sprawls over a steep hill on the south side of the road. The streets of the old town are picturesque but touristy; there are great views from the top though. The beach, as at Agia Marina, is crowded and mediocre.

Marginally better is the more open **Gerani** at the far end of the strip. The western end beach is less crowded, but like much of the area's beach scene it's no great shakes and is better for sunbathing than for enjoyable swimming.

Further along, **Maleme** is a quiet, relatively undeveloped coastal resort. There are a few hotels and apartments near the fine pebble beach. Up on the hill, there is a moving, well-tended **military cemetery** overlooking the airfield where more than 3000 German paratroopers killed in the Battle of Crete are buried. The previous long-term caretaker was paradoxically George Psychoundakis, the former shepherd boy whose story about being a runner during the German occupation is told in *The Cretan Runner*.

SLEEPING

Many rooms and hotels line the beach road, some of which have been given over to tour operators or function as private clubs.

Ilianthos Village Apartments (☎ 28210 60667; www.ilianthosvillage.gr; Agia Marina; d incl breakfast from €160; ☒ ☒) This large resort on a wide stretch of beach is one of the more upmarket options in Agia Marina. It has a swimming pool, children's facilities, wheelchair access and all the mod cons.

Haris Hotel (☎ 28210 68816; www.hotel-haris.com; Agia Marina; s/d incl breakfast €42/60; ⬛ ⬛) This small hotel on Agia Marina beach is dated, but has family-size rooms and a swimming pool.

Tassos Cottages (☎ 28210 61352; tassosgerani@ hotmail.com; Gerani; apt €40-60) These well-equipped one and two-bedroom apartments sur-rounded by pleasant gardens are halfway between the beach and the main drag. They have a TV and fans. Call in at Tasso's taverna on the main street.

Hotel Theodori (☎ 28210 68342; Agia Marina; d €45; ⬛) This clean, modest hotel in central Agia Marina has twin bed accommodation with balconies overlooking the garden and sea. Air-con is available in most rooms.

Indigo Mare (☎ 28210 68156; www.indigomare.gr; Platanias; studio/apt incl breakfast €78/100; ⬛ ⬛) This upmarket apartment complex has well-fitted-out studios and apartments sleeping up to four people, and a lovely pool overlooking the beach.

Eria Hotel (☎ 28210 62790; www.eria-resort.gr; Maleme; d €120; ⬛) One of the few purpose-built, wheelchair-accessible hotels in all of Greece, it has larger bathrooms in the rooms, modified equipment in the gym and a special shuttle to pick up guests.

Coco Beach Camping (☎ 28240 23220; www.euro camps.net/cocobeach; Tavronitis; per person/tent €4/3.50; ⬛) This camp site just outside Hania has a bar, restaurant, Internet access, playground and mini-market.

EATING

Mylos tou Kerata (☎ 28210 68578; Platanias; grilled fillets €11.50-15) Regarded as the best restaurant in the area, this place is located in an old water mill. The ambience is pleasant, the menu and wine list extensive and the food a few notches above the generally bland establish-ments nearby. It has a huge range of grilled chicken, lamb and beef fillets.

Drakiana (☎ 28210 61677; Cretan specials €1.80-5) It is worth the lovely trek through three kilometres of olive and orange groves to get to this superbly located taverna under huge plane trees on a river bank. Manolis Mav-romatis serves excellent Cretan cuisine in-cluding a fennel pitta, meatballs in tomato sauce and special meat dishes like suckling pig on the spit. There is also a picnic area and public barbecues nearby.

Maria's Restaurant (☎ 28210 68888; Kato Stalos; mains €5-8) For a good feed try Maria's, on the eastern edge of Agia Marina, which serves Cretan and Mediterranean food on a plant-filled terrace. Try the local meat pie.

ENTERTAINMENT

Platanias and Agia Marina are lined with summer clubs whose popularity changes year to year as they constantly reinvent them-selves. In Platanias, you could start with a more sedate drink in To Milo, next to the restaurant, and then head for the popular clubs Utopia and Mylos Club, or Neromylos, the trendy beach bar next door. You might have trouble getting through the face control at the upscale Privilege club. In Agia Marina, the 'in' places were Ammos & Ilios, new-comer Costa Costa and Okeanos.

GETTING THERE & AWAY

Buses running between Hania and Kissa-mos-Kastelli (€3.40, one hour, hourly) stop in Platanias, Gerani and Agia Marina.

WESTERN HANIA

Western Crete is less affected by tourism than the rest of Hania. The northern coast is defined by the virtually uninhabited Gram-vousa and Rodopou Peninsulas. The resort of Kolymbari at the foot of the Rodopou Pe-ninsula is the most developed tourist town. The Kissamos province is a rugged region of scattered villages and towns that attracts few tourists. Its capital, Kissamos-Kastelli, is the port for boats from the Peloponnese. The nearly deserted west coast has two of Crete's finest (and surprisingly underdevel-oped) beaches: Falasarna in the northern corner and Elafonisi in the southern corner. The Selino Province includes the Innahorion region of small mountain villages.

RODOPOU PENINSULA

The barren, rocky Rodopou Peninsula has a few small villages clustered at the base of the peninsula but the rest is uninhabited. A paved road goes as far as Afrata, but then becomes a dirt track that meanders through the peninsula. If you are travelling by foot, jeep or motorcycle you can reach the Dik-tynna sanctuary at the end of the peninsula, but make sure you are well supplied since there is not a drop of petrol or water, nor a morsel of food beyond Afrata. From afrata a road winds down to the small, gravelly pebbly **Afrata Beach**, which also supports a small seasonal snack bar.

Kolymbari Κολυμπάρι
pop 952

Kolymbari, 23km west of Hania, is at the base of the Rodopou Peninsula, and appeals to those seeking a quiet, relaxing holiday. Development of the fishing hamlet is in its embryonic stage, but that is changing fast as hotels and domatia arise to take advantage of the long pebbly beach. Kolymbari is a good base for a walk to Moni Gonias and an excellent place to sample local fish at one of the well-regarded fish tavernas in the centre of town.

ORIENTATION & INFORMATION
The bus from Hania drops you off on the main road, from which it is a 500m walk down to the settlement. At the bottom of the road you'll see a post office on the left; turn left and the OTE is about 100m further. There is an ATM on the main street and a post office in the centre of the village. See www.inkmonitor.com for a wacky expatriate view of life in the Rodopou Peninsula.

SLEEPING & EATING
Rooms Lefka (☎ 28240 22211; fax 28240 22211; s/d €22/30; breakfast €5) On the way into town from the bus stop you will see this place on the right. Rooms are very comfortable and have a fridge. The taverna downstairs serves up good, honest Cretan food.

Hotel Minerva (☎ 28240 22485; s/d/apt €35/45/70; 🐱) This is the best choice along the beach for larger groups or families; it has large rooms with kitchenettes and balconies and there is also a two-bedroom apartment.

Argentina (☎ 28240 22243; fish per kg €15-44) Argentina has now spread across the road, with tables overlooking the sea. It has a similar menu of seafood-inspired cuisine and the usual grills. It is considered one of the best fish tavernas in the area.

Diktina (☎ 28240 22611; fish per kg €15-44) This fish taverna has sea views and a range of dishes as well as the predictable and usually good fish dishes.

Palio Arhondiko (☎ 28240 22124; mezedes €2-6) Right on the beach, this smart restaurant serves a range of excellent mezedes and special seafood dishes. It has good service.

DETOUR: RAVDOUHA

On the western side of the Rodopou Peninsula, the unassuming small fishing hamlet of **Ravdouha Beach** has become a popular destination for fresh fish. Follow the signs until you reach a fork in the road. To the left, a rough dirt road leads 700m to the **Waves on the Rock** (☎ 28240 23133; top fish per kg €35) run by fisherman Theodoris Falelakis, who serves excellent fresh fish. If you really feel like getting away from it all there are also five **rooms** (€25-30) upstairs with kitchenette and air-con.

Turning right at the fork will lead you to a small pebbly beach with a pier and couple of tavernas. The impressive newcomer here is **Don Rosario** (☎ 28240 23781; spaghetti marinara €8) run by a retired Italian chef, who dishes up scrumptious pans of seafood spaghetti and sophisticated Mediterranean cuisine on his shady terrace.

Milos tou Tzerani (☎ 28240 22210) This café/bar right on the sea is a great place for a coffee or an evening drink and it also has light snacks and mezedes.

GETTING THERE & AWAY
Buses from Hania to Kissamos-Kastelli stop at Kolymbari (€2.30, 40 minutes, hourly).

Moni Gonias
Founded in 1618, **Moni Gonias** (☎ 28240 22313; Kolymbari; admission free; ☷ 8am-12.30pm & 4-8pm Mon-Fri, 4-8pm Sat) was damaged by the Turks in 1645, but rebuilt in 1662 and extended in the 19th century. The monastery houses a unique collection of icons dating from the 17th and 18th centuries. Some are in the church while others are in the monastery museum. The most valuable icon is that of *Agios Nikolaos*, painted in 1637 by Palaiokapas. It perfectly exemplifies the Cretan school of icon painting that flourished in the 17th century under Venetian rule. The monastery, which also incorporates Crete's Theological College, is easy to reach from Kolymbari. Take the beach road north from the town centre for about 500m.

Diktynna
On the tip of the Rodopou Peninsula is the remains of a temple to the Cretan goddess

Diktynna, which was the most important religious sanctuary in the region under the Romans. Diktynna was the goddess of hunting and she was worshipped fervently in western Crete.

Legend has it that her name derives from the word *diktyon*, which means 'net'. It was a fisherman's net that saved her when she leapt into the sea to avoid the amorous desires of King Minos. The temple dates from the 2nd century AD but it was probably built on the site of an earlier temple.

After the collapse of the Roman Empire the temple was desecrated but you can see the temple's foundations and a sacrificial altar as well as Roman cisterns. If you are 'templed out' you can relax on a lovely sandy beach. Diktynna is only accessible by dirt road from Kolymbari, but many travel agencies in Hania offer boat excursions.

KISSAMOS-KASTELLI ΚΙΣΣΑΜΟΣ-ΚΑΣΤΕΛΛΙ
pop 3821

The largest town and capital of the Kissamos province is Kissamos-Kastelli, usually referred to simply as Kissamos. The north coast port town is where the ferries arrive from the Peloponnese or Kythira. It's a quiet town of mostly elderly residents that neither expects nor attracts much tourism, but is worth more than a passing glance. There are some fine pebble beaches on Kissamos Bay and it is a good base for walking and touring the area, with the beautiful and deserted Gramvousa Peninsula to the west and the Rodopou Peninsula to the east.

History

In antiquity its name was Kissamos, but when the Venetians came along and built a castle the place became known as Kastelli. The name persisted until 1966 when authorities decided that too many people were confusing this Kastelli with Crete's other Kastelli, southeast of Iraklio. The official name reverted to Kissamos, but locals still prefer Kastelli (and many books and maps agree) and it is now common to combine the two into Kissamos-Kastelli, which leaves no room for misunderstanding.

Ancient Kissamos was a harbour for the important city–state of Polyrrinia 7km inland. Vestiges of Roman buildings have been unearthed, but most of the ancient city lies beneath the modern town of Kissamos and cannot be excavated. Kissamos gained independence in the third century AD and then became a bishopric under the Byzantines. It was occupied by the Saracens in the 9th century and flourished under the Venetians.

Orientation & Information

The port is 3km west of town. In summer a bus meets the boats, otherwise a taxi costs around €3.50. The bus station is just below Plateia Kissamou, and the main street, Skalidi, runs east from Plateia Kissamou.

Kissamos has no tourist office, but has a reasonably informative website (www.kissamos.net). **Horeftakis Tours** (☎ 28220 23250; Skalidi) is a good source of information.

The post office is on the main through road while there are a number of banks with ATMs along Skalidi. The beach annex is separated (still) by open fields through which it is a 200m walk to reach the foreshore promenade.

Strata Walking Tours (☎ 28220 24336; www.stratatours.com) is run by Stelios Milonakis and his British wife Angela, who offer a range of walking tours for small groups, from leisurely day trips including taverna lunch for €40 in the surrounding countryside to full-on 15-day round trips (€895) reaching as far as the south coast.

Sleeping

Bikakis Family (☎ 28220 24257; www.familybikakis.gr; Iroön Polemiston 1941; s/d/ste €20/25/30; 🖾) This would have to be the best budget option in town. The 15 rooms and five studios sparkle and most have garden and sea views. Owner Giannis not only makes guests feel very welcome but he's also an expert in herbal teas and local knowledge.

Thalassa (☎ 28220 31231; www.thalassa-apts.gr; Paralia Drapanias; studio €40-55; 🖾 🖳) One of the best accommodation choices along the whole Kissamos coast, it's an ideal spot to retreat to with a stack of books. All studios are immaculate and airy. They are no more than 30m from the beach and just a 100m walk east from Camping Mithymna.

Christina Beach Hotel (☎ 28220 83333; studio €65-75; P 🖾 🖳) New in 2002 this very smart studio complex on the west side of Kissamos represents the upper end of accommodation in town. Right on the foreshore, the modern studios are large and airy and all have ISDN Internet connection.

Camping Mithymna (☎ 28220 31444; fax 28220 31000; Paralia Drapania; per person/tent €6/4) About 6km east of town, Camping Mithymna is an excellent shady site near the best stretch of beach with a restaurant, bar and shop. It also has rooms and apartments nearby (€35 to €55). Take a bus to the village of Drapanias, from where it's a pleasant 15-minute walk through olive groves to the camping ground (or walk 4km along the beach).

Also recommended is the shaded **Camping Nopigia** (☎ 28220 31111; www.campingnopigia.gr; Nopigia; per person/tent €4.80/3.50; 🏊), 2km east of Mithymna, although the beach is not good for swimming.

Eating

Restaurant Makedonas (☎ 28220 22844; ladera €3-5) For some local colour, head to this no-frills place just to the west of Plateia Kissamou, where you can dine on authentic home-cooked food. The *biftekia stifado* (beef patties in tomato sauce) are recommended by the owner.

Papadakis Taverna (☎ 28220 22340; top fish per kg €44) Opposite the Argo Rooms for Rent, this reputable and traditional fish taverna is in a good setting right on the beach and is well patronised by locals. Try the oven-baked fish or *kakavia* (fish soup).

O Stimadoris (☎ 28220 22057; mains €4-7) The best-respected fish taverna is about 2km west of town, just before the small fishing harbour. The owners are fishermen and therefore the fish is always fresh. Try an unusual salad made of seaweed in vinegar – *salata tou yialou*.

Restaurant Kastell (☎ 28220 22144; mains €4-6) The second of two oldest and popular tavernas in Kissamos, the Kastell is not flash-looking, but is reliable and of good quality and repute. Opposite the bus station on the square, you'll find dishes like satisfying *hirino kapamas* (pork stew)and other *mayirefta* (casseroles) to tempt you.

Kellari Taverna (☎ 28220 23883; Cretan specials €4-6) This well-regarded taverna is right on the beach and has an extensive range of home-cooked Cretan dishes and fresh fish. It is owned by the same family that runs Strata Walking Tours.

Also recommended for tasty gyros, souvlaki and Cypriot-style *kondosouvli* is **Taverna Petra** (☎ 28220 24387; grills €4-5) on the main square.

Getting There & Away

BOAT

ANEN Ferries operates the *F/B Myrtidiotissa* on a route that takes in Antikythira (€8.80, two hours), Kythira (€15.20, four hours), Gythio (€20.50, six hours), Kalamata (€21.80, seven hours) and Piraeus (€22, 19 hours). It leaves Kissamos five times a week between 9am and 10.30am. You can buy tickets from **Horeftakis Tours** (☎ 28220 23250) and the **ANEN Office** (☎ 28220 22009; Skalidi).

BUS

From Kissamos' **bus station** (☎ 28220 22035), there are 16 buses a day to Hania (€3.40, one hour), where you can change for Rethymno and Iraklio; three buses a day for Falasarna (€2.40, 20 minutes) and one bus a day to Paleohora (€5.40, 1½ hours).

Getting Around

Hermes (☎ 28220 23678; Skalidi) rents cars, while you can pick up a bike at **Moto Fun** (☎ 28220 23440; www.motofun.info; Plateia Tzanakaki).

AROUND KISSAMOS-KASTELLI

The ancient city ruins of **Polyrrinia** (pol-ee-ren-*ee*-a) lie about 7km south of Kissamos-Kastelli, above the village of Ano Paleokastro (sometimes also called Polyrrinia). It's a steep climb to the ruins, but the views are stunning and the region is blanketed with wild flowers in spring. The city was founded by the Dorians in the 6th century BC and was constantly at war with the Kydonians from Hania. Coins from the period depict the warrior–goddess Athena who was evidently revered by the warlike Polyrrinians.

Unlike their rivals the Kydonians, the Polyrrinians did not resist the Roman invasion and thus the city was spared destruction. It was the best-fortified town in Crete and the administrative centre of western Crete from the Roman through to the Byzantine period. It was reoccupied by the Venetians who used it as a fortress. Many of the ruined structures, including an aqueduct built by Hadrian, date from the Roman period.

The most impressive feature of the site is the **acropolis** built by the Byzantines and Venetians. There's also a church built on the foundations of a **Hellenistic temple** from the 4th century BC. Notice also, near the **aqueduct**, a **cave** dedicated to the Nymphs that still contains the niches for Nymph statuettes.

It's a scenic walk from Kissamos-Kastelli to Polyrrinia. To reach the Polyrrinia road, walk east along the Kissamos-Kastelli main road, and turn right after the OTE. There are no buses to the site.

FALASARNA ΦΑΛΑΣΑΡΝΑ
pop 21
Falasarna, 16km west of Kissamos-Kastelli, attracts a mixed bunch of travellers due to its long, wide stretch of sandy beach, which is considered one of the best in Crete. It is split up into several coves by rocky spits and is known for its stunning sunsets.

This is as far west in Crete as you can get; beyond Falasarna the next landfall is Malta. There is no village, just a scattering of widely spaced rooms and tavernas among the greenhouses that somewhat mar the approach to the beach. There is no organised 'beach scene', although there is a beach bar in the centre and the omnipresent beach umbrellas and loungers at different locations. If you like solitude, Falasarna is your kind of place – apart from the rush of activity from mid-July to mid-August.

History
Falasarna has been occupied at least since the 6th century BC, but reached the height of its power in the 4th century BC. Although it was built next to the sea, the town's ruins are about 400m away from the water because the western coast of Crete has risen over the centuries. The town owed its wealth to the agricultural produce from the fertile valley to the south. It was the west-coast harbour for Polyrrinia but later became Polyrrinia's chief rival for dominance over western Crete. By the time of the Roman invasion of Crete in 67 BC, Falasarna had become a haven for pirates. Stone blocks excavated around the entrance to the old harbour indicate that the Romans may have tried to block off the harbour to prevent it from being used by pirates.

Orientation & Information
Approaching Falasarna, the main road from Platanos forks to the north and south. The northern road takes you to the beaches that continue on for several kilometres. The big beach to the south is the livelier spot, with the middle rocky cove frequented by nudists, and there's a quieter smaller beach to

the north. Most of the hotels and domatia are at the northern end. There is no post office, bank, OTE, tourist office or travel agency, but your mobile phone will work and there are card phones.

Sights
The remains of the ancient city of Falasarna are the area's main attraction, although not much is visible. Signs direct you to the ancient city from the main road, following a dirt road at the end of the asphalt.

First you'll come to a large stone throne, the purpose of which is unknown. Further on there are the remains of the wall that once fortified the town and a small harbour. Notice the holes carved into the wall, which were used to tie up boats. At the top of the hill there are the remains of the acropolis wall and a temple as well as four clay baths.

Sleeping & Eating
There are numerous places for wild camping on Falasarna's beaches, although like elsewhere in Crete it is officially frowned upon. There is a good choice of accommodation aimed at the independent traveller.

Rooms Anastasia-Stathis (☎ 28220 41480; fax 28220 41069; d/apt €35/40; 🖳) Owner Anastasia makes her home the friendliest place to stay. The airy, beautifully furnished rooms with fridges and large balconies are perfect for stress relief, as Anastasia puts it. Her enormous breakfasts (€6) are open to all comers and are a sight to be savoured. Look for the prominent sign.

Petalida Rooms (☎ 28220 41449; r €35) A mix of older-style and new rooms in two separate blocks, Petalida is another good option, just off the main road. The attached restaurant is friendly and honest, serving up fresh fish (up to €38 per kg) and other local specialties.

Rooms for Rent Panorama (☎ 28220 41336; panorama@chania-cci.gr; d/tr €46/50 🖳) This is one of the first places you will come across, signposted to the left along a gravel track. The studios are spotless and comfortable, and have a fridge. Downstairs, the well-run and friendly restaurant with a great view of the beach serves up good Cretan cooking. Order the *pilafi* (chicken and rice special) the day before (€16 for two).

Galasia Thea (☎ 28220 41421; mayirefta €4.50-6) On the cliff overlooking the great expanse of beach, this café has spectacular views from its huge terrace. There's a big range of baked dishes and *mayirefta* such as the Sfakiano lemon lamb.

Also recommended is **Sun Set** (☎ 28220 41204), a taverna for fish and classic Cretan food. It's after the long beach.

Getting There & Away

From June through August there are three buses daily from Kissamos to Falasarna (€2.40, 20 minutes), as well as buses from Hania (€5.50, 1½ hours).

GRAMVOUSA PENINSULA
ΧΕΡΣΟΝΗΣΟΣ ΓΡΑΜΒΟΥΣΑ

North of Falasarna is the wild and remote Gramvousa Peninsula. The dirt road to the sandy beach of **Balos** (a lagoon of turquoise water that's out of this world) on **Cape Tigani** begins at the far end of the main street of Kalyviani and follows the eastern slope of Mt Geroskinos. From here, the views over the shoreline and the Rodopou Peninsula are spectacular. About 2km before the beach the dirt road becomes a path. One fork takes you to the beach while the other fork runs along the side of the mountain and eventually joins the beach path. The shadeless walk takes around three hours – wear a hat and take plenty of water. Offshore are two deserted islands: Agria (wild) and Imeri (tame) Gramvousa.

To save you the walk, from June through August there are daily cruises from Kissamos-Kastelli. The **Gramvousa Express** (☎ 28220 24344; www.gramvousa-balos.com.gr) goes to Imeri Gramvousa and Balos beach (€10) departing at 10.15am and returning at 5.30pm. The *Balos Express* departs at 11.30am for Balos only (€15) returning at 6pm. Tickets and can be bought on the day at Kissamos port.

A good base for touring this region is the village of **Kalyviani**, 7km west of Kissamos.

History

The offshore island of Imeri Gramvousa was an important vantage point for the Venetians who built a fortress here to protect ships passing in front of the island on the way to and from Venice. It was considered an impregnable fort with a large cache of armaments. The Turks did not conquer Imeri Gramvousa along with the rest of Crete in 1645; the fort remained in Venetian hands along with their other forts, Souda and

Spinalonga. Eventually the Venetians left and the fort fell into disuse until it was taken over in 1821 by Cretan revolutionaries as a base for their operations. It later became a notorious base for piracy before the Turks took it again and used it to blockade the coast during the War of Independence. Local legend has it that the pirates amassed a fabulous fortune that they reportedly hid in caves around the island.

On 10 January 1981 a Lebanese-registered ship struck engine trouble on its way from Libya towards Crete. It managed to reach the Bay of Kissamos but foundered in a storm and beached itself on the shore near Kalyviani. No lives were lost. It is now the infamous **Kalyviani shipwreck** and can be spotted lying rotting and rusty on the west side of Kalyviani beach.

Sleeping & Eating

There's one exceptionally good place to stay and eat in the village of Kalyviani.

Kalyviani (☎ /fax 28220 23204; d/tr €45/55; 🔀) is an ecotourism-oriented hostel with comfortable, tastefully furnished rooms with fridge and balconies. The excellent **restaurant** (Cretan dishes €2.50-5) serves up the genuine article wherever possible using organic produce. The *bourekia* (€4.80) are recommended, as is the *gramvousiano yiahni* – a tasty local stew (€6). Their home-made wine is excellent.

Getting There & Away

To reach Kalyviani, take a west-bound bus from Kissamos-Kastelli and ask to be let off at the turn-off to the village of Kalyviani (5km from Kissamos-Kastelli). Kalyviani is a 2km walk from the main road.

INNAHORION ΙΝΝΑΧΟΡΙΟΝ

Innahorion is the highly scenic mountainous region south of Kissamos-Kastelli, which is renowned for its chestnut trees. Locals often refer to it as 'Ennia Horia' meaning nine villages, but there are actually more than nine villages dotting the region.

If you have your own transport you can drive through the region en route to Moni Hrysoskalitissas and Elafonisi or, with a little backtracking, to Paleohora. Alternatively, you can take a circular route, returning via the coast road. Heading south from Kissamos you'll pass through some of the lushest and most fertile parts of the island.

You'll first come to the village of **Voulgaro**, which has two Byzantine churches. Three kilometres further south is the lovely village of **Topolia** with a cluster of whitewashed houses overhung with plants and vines.

After Topolia the road skirts the edge of the **Koutsomatados Ravine** bending and twisting and affording dramatic views. Just before a narrow road tunnel there is a **snack bar** on the left, which is a good place to stop and take a photo of the ravine. Shortly, you will come to the **Agia Sofia cave**, which contains evidence of settlement from as far back as the Neolithic era. The cave is often used for baptisms and celebrates the patron saint's day on 13 April. A third of the way up the 250 rock-cut steps to the cave, the **taverna Romantza** has great views over the ravine and is run by the colourful Manolis, who wears traditional Cretan dress. It's a lovely drive to tiny **Koutsomatados**, followed by the village of **Vlatos**.

Just south of Milia (see boxed the text on p97) and back on the main highway there is a turn-off for Paleohora via **Strovles** and **Drys**. While most maps suggest it is not a good road, it is actually paved and affords much quicker access to Paleohora than the more obvious route via Tavronitis.

The road south from Elia passes through extensive stands of chestnut trees, which are the major crop of the region. **Elos**, the largest town and centre of the chestnut trade, stages a chestnut festival on the third Sunday of October. The plane, eucalyptus and chestnut trees around the main square make Elos a cool and relaxing place to stop. Behind the taverna on the main square you'll see the remains of the aqueduct that once brought water down from the mountains to power the mill.

Continuing south you'll pass the atmospheric village of **Perivolia** and then come to **Kefali** with its 14th-century frescoed church. From Kefali you can take either the road to Elafonisi or make a right turn and start the loop back along the picturesque western coast to your starting point. The coastal road from Kefali winds around cliffs with magnificent coastal views unfolding after every bend in the road. This is one of the most scenic drives in Crete.

You will first pass the little hamlet of **Pappadiana** driving along the gorge and climbing into the mountains before coming to **Amygdalokefali**, which has beautiful sweeping sea views from a bluff outside town. About 50 minutes from Kefali you'll come to **Kambos** a tiny village on the edge of a gorge. It makes a good overnight stop since you can hike down the gorge to the beach, or alternatively take a hike back to Kissamos via a rough dirt track from Kambos. The trail, touted as an alternative to the better-known **E4 trail**, is known as the **F1 trail**. Call in to Hartzoulakis Rent Rooms (see p97) for a rough trail map produced by Dutch hiker **John Filos** (afto_odiki@planet.nl), which outlines the F1 trail, as well as its southerly extension to Moni Hrysoskalitissas and Elafonisi.

Continuing northwards from Kambos, the road now circles around the other side of the gorge eventually winding down to **Sfinari** after a further 9km. The languid, laid-back agricultural village stretches down to a sizeable beach, which is backed by phalanxes of greenhouses at the northern end but has a small gravely cove, a basic camping ground and a few fine fish tavernas on the southern end of the beach.

After Sfinari you'll get more coastal views before the road drops down to **Platanos**, a quiet, tree-lined and rather scattered village of whitewashed houses. From here you can detour left to **Falasarna** or keep to the right for the downhill run back to Kissamos. If you need cash there's a prominently signposted ATM on the right as you leave the village of Platanos.

Sleeping & Eating

Accommodation throughout the region consists of rather scattered domatia. There are no large tourist hotel complexes.

Topolia Rooms (☎ 28220 51273; Topolia; d €30-35; ✿) These functional domatia on the main road at the southern end of the village have air-con and baths. There are plans to open a taverna downstairs.

Panorama Taverna and Rooms (☎ 28220 51163; Koutsomadatos; d €25) With a balcony overlooking the gorge, these simple, clean rooms make a great base for walks. There's no air-con but they are cool at night. Run by Manolis and his Dutch wife, Antonia, the taverna has a range of *mageirefta* and can make meals to order for guest on longer stays.

Taverna and Rooms Kokolakis (☎ 28220 61258; Elos; d €25) The only accommodation in Elos is above the Kastanofolia taverna, right on the

MILIA VILLAGE

A few years ago, the two families who owned the abandoned farmhouses in the isolated settlement of **Milia** (☎ 28220 51569; www.milia.gr; cottages incl breakfast €50-56) managed to persuade the EU to help them reconstruct the village in its original style using traditional materials, sound ecological principles and a 'back to nature' philosophy. They bought out the rest of the ruins and the unique result is now one of the most atmospheric and peaceful places to stay in Crete. The 16 meticulously restored stone cottages have wood heating for winter, thick stone walls for insulation in summer and no electricity, so leave the laptop and hairdryer at home (there is basic lighting at night). The cottages have antique beds and rustic furnishing and there is solar energy for basic needs.

A fine **restaurant** (mains €5.50-8) has been built in the same style to service the rooms and the visitors, who come from all over to sample honest, traditional seasonal cooking using only organic produce from Milia's extensive gardens, including their own oil, wine, milk and cheese. They also have their own free-range chickens, goats and sheep. Try their own special *bourekia*, or their winter favourite – potatoes, chestnuts and baby onions in red wine sauce, the stuffed rabbit with *myzithra* or yogurt, or pork with lemon leaves baked slowly overnight. There is no Coke or anything processed.

There is a signposted turn-off on the right for the 'Traditional Village' of Milia after the village of Vlatos. The rather narrow access road is paved for the first 2km before becoming a driveable 3km dirt road. Park outside the village at the designated parking area and reach the village along the short Halepa walking track (to the left) through a shady stream gorge, or follow the vehicle access road down to the main complex.

main road by the stream that runs through the village. The rooms are very basic and the bathrooms are shared.

Taverna Polakis (☎ 28220 61260; Kefali; r €30) The only to stay and eat in Kefali is here. Rooms are simple and have great views and ceiling fans.

Sunset Rooms (☎ 28220 41128; Kambos; s/d €15/25) Great views over the valley are a big plus for these otherwise simple but pleasant enough rooms, which are very light and have a fan. The attached Sunset Taverna serves up grills (€2 to €5) and large salads for around €3.

Hartzoulakis Rent Rooms (☎ 28220 41445; manolis _hartzoulakis@yahoo.gr; Kambos; s/d €20/25) Rooms are small and basic but very clean, with large verandas. They make a good base for walkers. The taverna on the terrace serves up good Cretan fare and excellent raki.

Rooms Nerida (☎ 28220 41621; Sfinari; d/tr €40/45) This two-storey building on the road to the beach has lovely views and rooms with kitchenette and fridge, although there is no air-con.

Rooms for Rent Georgia (☎ 28220 41668; Sfinari; d €30) Opposite Nerida is this equally reasonable roomy place with kitchenettes.

Captain Fidias (☎ 23220 41107; Sfinari Beach) One of three fish tavernas on Sfinari beach, this popular one is operated by the amiable Fidias

and his four strapping fishermen sons. When they run out they have been known to go home and get the fish destined for their dinner out of the fridge.

Andonis Theodorakis (☎ 28220 41125; Sfinari; mayirefta €4-7) Up on the main road to Platanos is Andonis' little taverna and adjacent rooms. Food is all home-cooked, village style, and they serve local fresh fish. The chicken with okra is recommended. The simple homy **rooms** (s/d €15/24) have lovely sea views.

The Castle (☎ 28220 41372; Platanos; d €30; 🖵) On the main through road, the Castle has smallish but very neat and clean rooms with a fridge. All rooms enjoy a balcony views.

O Zaharias (☎ 28220 41285; Platanos; mayirefta €4-6) 'Food like grandma cooked' is the motto at this very pleasant eatery just off the main highway. All dishes are made according to closely guarded traditional recipes. Ask for *avgokolokytho* – a kind of omelette dish made with zucchini, egg, tomato and olive oil – or the *boureki* (cheese, zucchini and potato bake).

MONI HRYSOSKALITISSAS
ΜΟΝΗ ΧΡΥΣΟΣΚΑΛΙΤΙΣΣΑΣ

Moni Hrysoskalitissas (mo-*nee* hris-os-ka-*lee*-tiss-as), 5km north of Elafonisi, is a beautiful monastery perched on a rock high above the sea. Hrysoskalitissa means 'golden staircase'. Some accounts suggest the top step was gold, but could only be seen by the faithful. According to the monks living there now, one of the 90 steps leading to the monastery was hollow and used to hide the church's treasury, hence the name. During the Turkish occupation the gold, along with the sale of the monastery's estate, was used to pay hefty taxes imposed by the Ottoman rulers.

The church is recent but the monastery is allegedly a thousand years old and may have been built on the site of a Minoan temple. There are tavernas and domatia in the vicinity. Buses to Elafonisi drop passengers here.

ELAFONISI ΕΛΑΦΟΝΉΣΙ
pop 12

As one of the loveliest sand beaches in Crete, it's easy to understand why people enthuse so much about Elafonisi. At the southern extremity of Crete's west coast, the beach is long, wide and is separated from the Elafonisi Islet by about 50m of knee-deep water. The clear, shallow water and fine white sand create a tropical paradise. There are a few snack bars on the beach and stalls to rent umbrellas and lounge chairs. The islet is marked by low dunes and a string of semi-secluded coves that attract a sprinkling of naturists. The beaches are usually crowded with day-trippers. There are two small hotels and a pension on a bluff overlooking the main beach for those who want to luxuriate in the quiet that descends in late afternoon. There is a mini-market nearby.

Sleeping & Eating
Rooms Panorama (☎ 28220 61548; s/d studio €20/25) This place has a taverna overlooking the sea from its commanding position on a bluff. Rooms have a kitchenette and fridge, but many are rented by the month to itinerant workers.

Rooms Elafonisi (☎ 28250 61274; fax 28250 97907; s/d €30/35; 🕄) The 21 spacious rooms here have fridges, and there are nicely furnished bigger rooms out the back among the olive groves, as well as apartments with kitchens. The outdoor patio has views and there's an attached restaurant.

Innahorion (☎ 28250 61111; d/tr €30/35; 🕄) About 2.5km before the coast at Elafonisi, this is perhaps the least attractive of the three

options. The 15 rooms each have a fridge and kitchenette, but are set back a fair way from the beach. However, the restaurant is the best in the area, serving good Cretan food on the terrace.

Getting There & Away
There is one boat daily from Paleohora to Elafonisi (€4.50, one hour) from mid-June through September that leaves at 10am and returns at 4pm. There's also two buses daily from Hania (€8, 2¼ hours) and Kissamos (€3.40, 1½ hours) that return in the afternoon.

SFAKIA & LEFKA ORI

This region has some of the island's most spectacular sights, including the Samaria (sa-ma-*ria*) Gorge, the Lefka Ori Mountains and Mt Gingilos in the rugged interior. The province of Sfakia extends from the Omalos Plateau down to the southern coast and is Crete's most mountainous region and the most culturally interesting.

Sfakia was the centre of resistance during the island's long centuries of domination by foreign powers, its steep ravines and hills making effective hideaways for Cretan revolutionaries. The Sfakian people are renowned for their proud fighting spirit, which even in the recent past has turned family against family in the form of murderous vendettas that have depopulated many of the region's villages.

Check out the website www.sfakia-crete .com for more information on the region.

HANIA TO OMALOS
The road from Hania to the beginning of the Samaria Gorge is one of the most spectacular routes in Crete. After heading through orange groves to the village of **Fournes**, a left fork leads to **Meskla**, twisting and turning along a gorge offering beautiful views. Although the bottom part of the town is not particularly attractive with boarded-up buildings, the road becomes more scenic as it winds uphill to the modern, multicoloured **Church of the Panagia**. Next to it is a 14th-century chapel built on the foundations of a 6th-century basilica that might have been built on an even earlier Temple of Aphrodite. At the entrance to the town a

sign directs you to the **Chapel of Metamorfosis Sotiros** (Transfiguration of the Saviour) that contains 14th-century frescoes. The fresco of the Transfiguration on the south wall is particularly impressive.

The main road continues to the unspoilt village of **Lakki** (*la*-kee), 24km from Hania, which affords stunning views wherever you look. The village was a centre of resistance during both the uprising against the Turks and WWII.

Rooms for Rent Nikolas (☎ 28210 67232; Lakki; d with shared bath €25) has comfortable, simple rooms above a taverna, with magnificent views over the valley.

OMALOS ΟΜΑΛΌΣ
pop 28

Most tourists only hurry through Omalos, 36km south of Hania, on their way to the Samaria Gorge, but this plateau settlement deserves more of your time. During summer, the air is bracingly cool here compared with the steamy coast and there are some great mountain walks in the area. After the morning Samaria rush, there's hardly anyone on the plateau except goats and shepherds.

Omalos is little more than a few hotels on either side of the main road cutting through the plateau. There is no bank, post office, OTE or travel agency and the village is practically deserted in the winter. The town is about 4km before the entrance to the Samaria Gorge.

Sleeping & Eating

Generally, Omalos hotels are open when the Samaria Gorge is open, although winter tourism is evolving. Most hotels have restaurants that do a bustling trade serving breakfast to hikers and are open at meal times the rest of the day.

Hotel Neos Omalos (☎ 28210 67269; www.neos-omalos.gr; s/d €20/30) This is the poshest hotel with comfortable, modern, nicely decorated rooms that include phone, baths with shower curtains, and satellite TV. There's a pleasant lounge in the reception area.

Elliniko (☎ 28210 67169; s/d/tr €20/25/30) This is the nearest to the Samaria Gorge and has simple double rooms with TV, although they are a little cramped. There is also an attached restaurant that is often busy with tour buses during lunch.

Hotel Exari (☎ 28210 67180; fax 28250 67124; s/d €20/25) The big stone-built Exari has pleasant, well-furnished rooms with TV, bathtub and balconies. The owner Yiorgos will give walkers lifts to the start of the Samaria Gorge and for groups can deliver their luggage to Sougia. There is an attached taverna.

Hotel Gingilos (☎ 28250 67181; s/d/tr €17/25/30) Rooms at this friendly establishment are rather sparse, but are large (the triples are huge), very clean and have tasteful timber furniture and TV. There is a communal balcony and a taverna downstairs.

Kallergi Hut (☎ 28250 33199; dm for members/nonmembers €8/12) The EOS (Greek Mountaineering Club) maintains this hut located in the hills between Omalos and the Samaria Gorge. It boasts 43 beds, electricity, hot water, and makes a good base for exploring Mt Gingilos and surrounding peaks.

Getting There & Away

There are four daily buses to Omalos from Hania (one hour, €5). If want to trek the gorge and return to your room (and luggage) in Omalos, you can take the afternoon boat from Agia Roumeli to Sougia and get a taxi back to Omalos for about €35.

SAMARIA GORGE ΦΑΡΑΓΓΙ ΤΗΣ ΣΑΜΑΡΙΑΣ

Trekking through the **Samaria Gorge** (☎ 28250 67179; admission €5; 6am-3pm 1 May–mid-Oct) is one of the 'must-dos' of Crete and attracts both serious trekkers and people for whom it is clearly a one-off experience. Despite the crowds, a trek through this stupendous gorge is still an experience to remember.

At 18km, the Samaria (sah-mah-rih-*ah*) Gorge is supposedly the longest in Europe. It begins just below the Omalos Plateau, carved out by the river that flows between the peaks of Avlimaniko (1858m) and Volakias (2147m). Its width varies from 150m to 3m and its vertical walls reach 500m at their highest points. The gorge has an incredible number of wild flowers, which are at their best in April and May.

It is also home to a large number of endangered species. They include the Cretan wild goat, the kri-kri, which survives in the wild only here and on the islet of Kri-Kri, off the coast of Agios Nikolaos. The gorge was made a national park in 1962 to save the kri-kri from extinction. You are unlikely to see too many of these shy animals, which show a marked aversion to trekkers.

An early start (before 8am) helps to avoid the worst of the crowds, but during July and August even the early bus from Hania to the top of the gorge can be packed. There's no spending the night in the gorge so you are going to have to complete the hike in the time allocated.

The trek from **Xyloskalo** (the name of the steep stone pathway with wooden rails that gives access to the gorge), to Agia Roumeli (p105) on the coast takes from about four hours for the sprinters to six hours for the strollers. Early in the season it's sometimes necessary to wade through the stream.

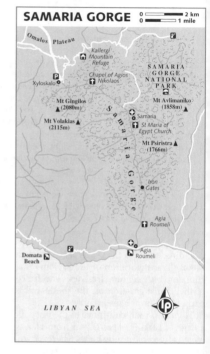

Later, as the flow drops, it's possible to use rocks as stepping stones.

The gorge is wide and open for the first 6km, until you reach the abandoned settlement of **Samaria**. The inhabitants were relocated when the gorge became a national park. Just south of the village is a small church dedicated to **Saint Maria of Egypt**, after whom the gorge is named.

The gorge then narrows and becomes more dramatic until, at the 11km mark, the walls are only 3.5m apart – the famous **Iron Gates** (Sidiroportes). Here, a rickety wooden pathway leads trekkers the 20m or so over the water and through to the other side.

The gorge ends at the 12.5km mark just north of the almost abandoned village of Old Agia Roumeli. From here it's a further uninteresting 2km hike to the welcoming seaside resort of Agia Roumeli, with its much-appreciated fine pebble beach and sparkling sea, where most hikers can be seen between 1pm and 3pm taking a refreshing dip or at least bathing sore and aching feet.

There are excursions to the Samaria Gorge from every sizable town and resort on Crete.

Most travel agents have two excursions: 'Samaria Gorge Long Way' and 'Samaria Gorge Easy Way'. The first comprises the regular trek from the Omalos Plateau to Agia Roumeli; the second starts at Agia Roumeli and takes you as far as the Iron Gates.

Obviously it's cheaper to trek the Samaria Gorge under your own steam, and Hania is the most convenient base. There are buses to Xyloskalo (Omalos; €5, one hour) at 6.15am, 7.30am, 8.30am and 4.30pm. There's also a direct bus to Xyloskalo from Paleohora (€8.10, 1½ hours) at 6am.

HORA SFAKION ΧΟΡΑ ΣΦΑΚΙΩΝ
pop 351

Hora Sfakion (ho-ra sfa-ki-on) is the small coastal port where the hordes of walkers from the Samaria Gorge spill off the boat and onto the bus. Most people pause only long enough to catch the next bus out, but the town can be relaxing stay for a few days. Under Venetian and Turkish rule Hora Sfakion was an important maritime centre and, as capital of the Sfakia region, the nucleus of the Cretan struggle for independence. The Turks inflicted severe reprisals on the town's inhabitants for their rebelliousness in the 19th century, after which the town fell into an economic slump that lasted until the arrival of tourism a couple of decades ago. Hora Sfakion played a prominent role during WWII when thousands of Allied troops were evacuated by sea from the town after the Battle of Crete.

Orientation & Information

The ferry quay is at the eastern side of the harbour. Buses leave from the square up the hill on the northeastern side. There is one ATM. The post office and OTE are on the square, and the police station overlooks it. There is no tourist office and no tourist police. You can change money at many places advertising their services. **Sfakia Tours** (☎ 28250 91130) next to the post office can change money, rent cars and find accommodation. There is a large car park near the bus stop, as well as an extra one nearer the ferry terminal. There is a useful website about the village at www.sfakia-crete.com.

Sights & Activities

There is not a lot to do here, other than sit around, eat and drink, and watch passengers boarding and disembarking from the ferries that run along the south coast. There are two beaches in town, one in front of the promenade and another less crowded beach at the town's western end. A third beach called **Ilingas** is about 2km west of Hora Sfakion, just off the road up to Anopolis.

Sleeping & Eating

Accommodation in the village is of reasonable quality and value.

Hotel Samaria (☎ 28250 91261; fax 28250 91161; s/d €25/35; ❄) This decent waterfront hotel has clean pleasantly furnished rooms with balconies.

Livikon (☎ 28250 91211; r €45; ❄) Adjoining Hotel Samaria, it has similar prices but bigger colourful rooms that are ideal for families or larger groups.

Rooms Stavris (☎ 28250 91220; stavris@sfakia-crete.com; s/d €21/24; ❄) Up the steps at the western end of the port, it has clean rooms – some with and kitchenettes and fridges.

Sofia Rooms (☎ 28250 91259; fax 28250 91259; s/d €20) The cheapest place to stay, one block back from the harbour. There is a communal fridge for guests' use.

A SHORT SURVIVAL GUIDE TO THE GORGE

The Samaria Gorge hike is not a Sunday stroll; it is long and, at times, hard. Do not attempt it if you are not used to walking. If you find that the going is too tough within the first hour, there are park wardens with donkeys who will take you back to the beginning. They will be on the look out for stragglers.

Rugged footwear is essential for walking on the uneven ground, which is covered by sharp stones. Don't attempt the walk in unsuitable footwear – you will regret it. The track from Xyloskalo to Agia Roumeli is downhill all the way and the ground makes for generally uneven walking. Take a hat and sunscreen, plus a small bottle of water that can be refilled along the way in the many springs spurting delicious cool water (it's inadvisable to drink water from the main stream). There is nowhere to buy food, so bring energy food to snack on.

Ileana Apartments (r €40-50) Run by the same family as Sofia Rooms, this is a spacious, fully equipped, air-conditioned two-room place that can house up to four people.

Samaria taverna (☎ 28250 91320; mayirefta €4-6) Has a good selection of *mayirefta* and vegetarian dishes on display, as well as the usual grills.

Getting There & Away

BOAT

Boat tickets are sold in the **booth** (☎ 28250 91221) in the car park. From June through August there is one daily boat from Hora Sfakion to Paleohora (€8.50, three hours) via Loutro, Agia Roumeli and Sougia. The boat leaves at 1pm. There are also an additional three boats a day to Agia Roumeli (€4.60, one hour) via Loutro (€1.80, 15 minutes). From 1 June there are boats (€9.50, 1½ hours) to Gavdos island (see p111) on Friday, Saturday and Sunday leaving at 10.30am and returning at 5pm.

BUS

There are three buses a day from Hora Sfakion to Hania (€5.40, two hours) – the last one leaves at 7pm. In summer there are only two daily buses to Rethymno via Plakias (€3.30, 1¼ hours) Frangokastello (€1.50, 25 minutes).

VENDETTAS

Cretans are a distinct breed, formed from the various races that have occupied the island over the millennia. However, ethnic and religious homogeneity has not brought harmony. Cretans are notorious throughout Greece for murderous vendettas that have lasted for generations and caused hundreds of Cretans to flee the island.

Particularly prevalent in Sfakia, a vendetta can start over the theft of some sheep, an errant bullet at a wedding or anything deemed an insult to family honour. The insult is avenged with a murder, which must be avenged with another murder and so on. Modernity has somewhat stemmed the carnage but, ironically, prosperity and increased mobility have allowed would-be avengers to pursue their targets across Greece and across the globe (as portrayed in the movie *Beware of Greeks Bearing Guns*).

SOUTHERN COAST

The rocky southern coast is dotted with laid-back beach communities such as Paleohora, Sougia, Frangokastello and Loutro, and these are some of the best places in Crete to relax. The Samaria Gorge ends at the village of Agia Roumeli. This region has some stunning walks and lovely beaches.

FRANGOKASTELLO ΦΡΑΝΚΟΚΑΣΤΕΛΛΟ

pop 153

Frangokastello, 82km southeast of Hania, boasts one of the finest stretches of beach on the southern coast and a well-preserved fort, a scattered settlement, an eventful history and legendary ghosts. The wide, white-sand beach beneath the 14th-century fortress slopes gradually into shallow warm water, making it ideal for kids. Development has been kept to a minimum with most accommodation set back from the shore leaving the natural beauty untouched. Frangokastello is popular with day-trippers, but is an ideal retreat for those who wish to get away from it all for a while.

To the east of the castle is the stunning **Orthi Ammos** beach, with a long stretch of steep sand dunes (not pleasant on a windy day).

History

The striking sand-coloured fortress was built by the Venetians to protect the coast from pirates and to deal with chronically rebellious Hora Sfakion 14km to the west. The Sfakia region continued to pose problems for the Turkish occupiers several centuries later. The legendary Sfakian patriot Ioannis Daskalogiannis led a disastrous rebellion against the Turks in 1770 and was persuaded to surrender at the Frangokastello Fortress. He was flayed alive. On May 17 1828, 385 Cretan rebels, led by Hadzi Mihalis Dalanis, made a heroic last stand at the fortress in one of the bloodiest battles of the Cretan struggle for independence. About 800 Turks were killed along with Dalanis and the Cretan rebels.

Orientation & Information

There's no actual village centre in Frangokastello, just a series of domatia, tavernas and residences that stretch either side of the main road from Hora Sfakion to the

THE SPIRITS OF FRANGOKASTELLO

The bloodshed of 17 May 1828 gave rise to the legend of the *Drosoulites*. The name comes from the Greek word *drosia* meaning 'moisture', which in itself could refer to the dawn moisture that is around when the ghosts are said to appear, or the misty content of the spirits themselves. It's said that around dawn on the anniversary of the decisive battle, or in late-May, a procession of ghostly figures materialises around the fort and marches to the sea. The phenomenon has been verified by a number of independent observers.

Although locals believe the figures are the ghosts of slaughtered rebels, others theorise that it may be an optical illusion created by certain atmospheric conditions and that the figures may be a reflection of camels or soldiers in the Libyan Desert. When questioned about the ghostly phenomenon, locals are understandably a little shy, but remain convinced that something does in fact happen. Most claim that the older residents of Frangokastello have seen the apparitions. Whether you will depends on your luck – or belief in ghosts.

fortress. There's no bank, post office or OTE, but there are card phones and a couple of mini-markets for supplies. The bus stops at several spots along the main road.

Sleeping & Eating

Fata Morgana (☎ 28250 92077; mains €3.20-5.80) This beachside taverna right next to the fortress is also the only place you can step out of the water and into your lunch plate. It does simple but tasty omelettes for breakfast. They also rent new fully equipped apartments and studios in the **Paradisos complex** (www.paradisos -kreta.com; r €40-80; ⊠) further east near the Faros taverna at Orthi Ammos, including two cosy mock castles.

Artemis Rooms (☎ /fax 28250 92096; d/tr €30/35; ☎) These spacious, simple rooms have a fridge and small balcony overlooking the sea. They are over a taverna on the beach near the castle.

Stavris Rooms (☎ 28250 92250; stavris@sfakia-crete .com; studio €28; ⊠) This place is on the right as you enter the town from Hora Sfakion. The rooms have balconies and sea views and there is a handy mini-market across the road.

Castello Apartments & Studios (☎ 28250 92333; fax 28250 92334; studio & apt €45-65; ⊠) These spacious and well-appointed studios and one- to two-bedroom apartments have microwaves, full-size fridges, washing machines, hairdryers and anything else you would need for a longer stay. They are on the main road but they do have an attractive garden and minimarket and are a great option for families.

Flisvos (☎ 28250 92069; fax 28250 92042; r €35 ⊠) Right on the beach east of the castle, these pleasant rooms have a fridge and balcony

and nice touches like mosquito screens on the windows. There is also a decent fish taverna downstairs.

Milos (☎ 28250 92161; www.milos-sfakia.com; studio €28-40; ⊠) This old windmill right on the beach has been turned into an apartment and the four stone cottages are now pleasant studios with air-con and fridges.

Kriti (☎ 28250 92214; grills €6-7) This is a well-designed structure across from the fortress that's elaborately outfitted with a number of terraces and a forest of potted plants. It is a little bit touristy, but the food is better than average.

Getting There & Away

In July and August only, there are two daily buses from Hora Sfakion to Plakias that stop at Frangokastello (€1.50, 25 minutes). From Hania there's a daily afternoon bus (€6.50, 2½ hours) and there are two daily buses from Rethymno (€5.50, 1¼ hours). A **taxi** (☎ 28250 92109) to/from Hora Sfakion costs about €15.

LOUTRO ΛΟΥΤΡΟ
pop 81

The small but rapidly expanding fishing village of Loutro (loo-*tro*) lies between Agia Roumeli and Hora Sfakion. The town is little more than a crescent of white-and-blue domatia around a narrow beach. It's a pleasant, lazy resort that is never overwhelmed with visitors, although it can get busy in July and August.

Loutro is the only natural harbour on the south coast of Crete and is only accessible by boat or on foot. The absence of cars and bikes make it quiet and peaceful.

HANIA

WALKS AROUND LOUTRO

A booklet called *Walks Around Loutro* is also available from shops in Loutro priced €5.

Loutro to Marble Beach via Livaniana
Distance: 6.5km
Duration: 3½ hours
Take the path beside the Hotel Daskalogiannis and follow the yellow/black E4 markers over the headland to Phoenix. As you descend there is a sign to Phoenix: take the right-hand path that goes around the houses. Cross the dirt road and head directly up the hill towards Livaniana in the distance. At the top of the hill take the path signposted to Livaniana and follow the blue-paint markers. Cross the road again and follow the obvious path that traverses up to the road on the outskirts of the village; 200m on is a taverna that sells cold drinks.

Walk on up the hill aiming for the church. Past the church, follow the blue markers to a sign pointing to **Marble Beach**. The markers take you around the field and along the edge of the old olive terrace. After 100m you come to a gap in a fence, where you look down into the Aradhena Gorge. Look out for Bonelli's eagles riding the thermals. Turn left and follow the blue-paint markers, which lead you down towards the floor of the gorge. At the bottom turn left towards the sea and Marble Beach. The route is not always obvious with the faded red paint being the most reliable waymarking. Marble Beach has a taverna that serves simple meals.

To return to Loutro, follow the E4 path that starts behind the beach and the yellow/black paint spots. After half an hour you reach the hamlet of Likkos. Walk through the tavernas then follow the path (blue paint), which leads over the headland where you meet the path to Livaniana.

Loutro to Anopolis & the Aradhena Gorge
Distance: 7km (9km if walking back to Loutro on the E4)
Duration: 5–6 hours
This is a strenuous, full-day's walk, which takes in an authentic country village, and spectacular gorge with a beach at the end of it.

Make an early start as all the hard effort is at the beginning – a 680m climb from the sea up to the plain of Anopoli. The path starts behind the Kri Kri taverna: go through the new metal gate, turn left and follow the path up the hillside. After an hour you reach a dirt road, cross it and keep going until you meet it again. Turn right and walk 100m until you reach a cistern on your left where you pick up the path again. After 200m the path forks: turn left and continue up the hill. You are aiming for the point below the walled compound you can see above you. At the top, enjoy the view, then follow the tarmac road to the town square where there are a couple of tavernas.

Follow the road sign to Aradhena and follow it for 1.5km. Just as the ruins of Aradhena come into view look for a small cairn and path on the right side of the road marked with faded blue spots. Walk along it pointing directly at Aradhena, before descending into the gorge. At the bottom turn left. After 20 minutes you reach a staircase cut into the side of the gorge, follow it with care for 300m. In the past the Aradhena Gorge was a tough proposition as getting around this section meant scrambling using fixed ropes and ladders.

Follow the cairns and faded red-paint spots until you reach the junction with the Livaniana path and continue as for the Loutro to Marble Beach via Livaniana walk above.

Hora Sfakion to Sweetwater Bay & Loutro
Distance: 5.5km
Duration: 2 hours
Follow the road west from Sfakion, signposted to Omolos. After 20 minutes you cross a culvert then ascend to the first switchback where there is an E4 sign to **Sweetwater Bay**. Follow the path marked with yellow-/black-paint marks and poles, which passes through a rock fall where the progress is slower, and arrives at Sweetwater after one hour. Across the bay the trail continues up beside the taverna to the top of the headland. Loutro is one hour further on, an easy if shadeless path.

Graham Williams
Graham Williams works for Lonely Planet and is based in the London office. He has been walking in Crete annually since 1988.

Its advantageous geographical position was appreciated in ancient times when it was the port for Phoenix and Anopolis. According to legend, St Paul was on his way to Loutro when he encountered a storm that blew him off course past Gavdos Island and on to eventual shipwreck in Malta.

Orientation & Information

There's no bank, post office or OTE, but there are many places to change money at the western end of the beach. The boat from Hora Sfakion docks in the centre of the beach but the boat from Agia Roumeli docks at the far western end in front of the Sifis Hotel. You can buy boat tickets at a stall on the beach, which opens an hour before each departure. There is **Internet access** (☎ 28250 91514; www.loutro.com; per hour €4, minimum charge €2.50) at Daskalogiannis Hotel.

Activities

Loutro is a good base for boat excursions along the southern coast. **Hotel Porto Loutro** (☎ 28250 91433) can advise on boat schedules and there's a stall in front where you can rent **canoes** (per hr/day €2/7).

Sleeping & Eating

Loutro has generally excellent accommodation options, with most places overlooking the harbour.

The Blue House (☎ 28250 91127; bluehouseloutro@ chania-cci.gr; d €35) Brothers Vangelis and George run these fine rooms above their excellent taverna. The rooms are spacious and well appointed with extras such as coffee-making facilities. They have big verandas overlooking the port. It has excellent *mayirefta* (€4 to €5), including delicious garlicky spinach and a great *boureki* bake with zucchini, potato and goat's cheese.

Apartments Niki (☎ /fax 28250 91259; www.loutro -accommodation.com; studio/apt €40-65; ✵) These beautifully furnished four-person studios with beamed ceilings and stone floors are just above the village. They have great views, ceiling fans and air-con for an extra €5. There is also a three-bedroom villa (€110).

Restaurant and Rent Rooms Ilios (☎ 28250 91460; d/tr/q €25/35/50; ✵) At the eastern end of the beach, Ilios has simple pleasant rooms with a fridge and small balconies.

Sifis Hotel (☎ 28250 91346; fax 28250 91447; s/d incl breakfast €26/40; ✵) This small hotel has pretty, well-kept rooms with air-con, fridge and sea views.

Faros (☎ /fax 28250 91334; d/tr €38/45; ✵) These relatively new, spacious and airy rooms are a stone's throw from the beach, and have air-con, fridges and balconies.

Rooms Sofia (☎ 28250 91354; d/tr €20/25) Above the Sofia mini-market, one street back from the beach, these are probably the cheapest rooms in town. They're plain and clean, but there's no air-con.

Given the captive market, the tavernas that line the waterfront in Loutro are surprisingly good. Most prominently display a wide range of *mayirefta* and you can't miss the dazzling range of cakes and sweets. Also recommended are Notos for excellent meze and Pavlos for the best grills.

Getting There & Away

Loutro is on the main Paleohora–Hora Sfakion boat route. From April to October there are four boats a day from Hora Sfakion (€1.80, 50 minutes), three boats from Agia Roumeli (€2.80, 45 minutes), and one boat a day from Paleohora (€7.50, 2½ hours). Taxi boats leave from in front of Hotel Porto Loutro, charging €12 to Sweetwater Beach and €25 to Hora Sfakion.

AGIA ROUMELI ΑΓΙΑ ΡΟΥΜΕΛΗ
pop 121

These days most travellers just pass through Agia Roumeli waiting to catch the boat to Hora Sfakion, but it's a pleasant enough for stopover, although the surrounding mountains can make it very hot and stifling. The pebble beach gets exceptionally hot and thus impossible to sit on for long unless you hire a beach umbrella and sun lounge (€3).

There are quite a few places to stay in the village and lots of decent places to eat.

The boat ticket office is a small concrete structure near the beach. There's no post office or OTE and no travel agencies.

Sleeping & Eating

Farangi Restaurant & Rooms (☎ 28250 91225; specials €4-6) This taverna has excellent Cretan specials. Sample the lightly battered zucchini flowers stuffed with *myzithra* cheese. If you're too bushed to move far after your trek and lunch, there are some tidy **rooms** (s/d/tr €18/30/35; ✵) above the restaurant where you can crash for the night.

Hotel-Restaurant Kri-Kri (☎ 28250 91089; fax 28250 91489; s/d/tr €25/35/45; ✿) This is one of the larger hotels in town, with clean, simple rooms with a fridge and small balcony. There is a very good restaurant downstairs.

Samaria Rooms & Taverna (☎ 28250 91215; specials €4-6; ✿) These modern rooms are clean and well furnished with fridge, dressing table and pleasant bathrooms. Some of them have sea views.

Oasis (☎ 28250 91391; s/d/tr €20/25/30; ✿) The family who run these rooms live downstairs, giving this place a friendly and homy feel. The rooms are simply furnished but do have air-con.

Getting There & Away

There are three boats daily from Agia Roumeli to Hora Sfakion (€4.60, one hour) via Loutro (€2.80, 45 minutes). They connect with the bus back to Hania. There's also a boat from Agia Roumeli to Paleohora (€6.80, two hours) at 4.45pm, calling in at Sougia (€3.20, 50 minutes).

SOUGIA ΣΟΥΓΙΑ

pop 109

Sougia was once a popular remote hippy hangout and many nostalgic ex-hippies return religiously each year. It has a lovely wide curve of sand-and-pebble beach and a shady tree-lined coastal road. Sougia's tranquillity has been largely preserved because it lies at the foot of a narrow, twisting route that deters most tour buses. This is another of the languid south-coast villages that offers the visitor little to do other than relax and recharge depleted batteries for a few days. It is also great trekking territory, close to the Samaria and Agia Irini Gorges.

The ancient town was on the western side of the existing village. It flourished under the Romans and Byzantines when it was the port for Elyros, an important inland city (now disappeared). A 6th-century basilica that stood at the western end of the village contained a fine mosaic floor that is now in the Hania Archaeological Museum (p78).

Orientation & Information

If you arrive by boat, walk 150m east along the coast to the village centre. The bus drops you on the coastal road in front of the Santa Irene hotel. The only other road intersects the coastal road by the Santa Irene Hotel

and runs north to the Agia Irini Gorge and Hania.

Sougia doesn't have a post office, OTE or bank. Check out www.sougia.info for information about the town.

Roxana's snack store (☎ 28230 51668; ⏰ 5am-late) can direct you to locals, who offer boat trips to nearby beaches and sells bus tickets.

Internet Lotos (☎ 28230 51191; per hr €3; ⏰ 7am-late) can get you online.

Sleeping

There's no camping ground, but the eastern end of the long, pebbled beach is popular with freelance campers and nudists. There are quite a few options for room/studio accommodation, most of it clustered towards the east end of the promenade or on the Hania road.

Idemeneas Apartments (☎ /fax 28230 51540; s/d €46/58; ✿) These spacious new studios and apartments are ideal for longer stays or families. They have marble floors and are nicely furnished and well equipped with phone, music and nice verandas. The top rooms have a sea view.

Aretousa Rooms to Rent (☎ 28230 51178; fax 28230 51178; s/d €25/35; ✿) Inland, on the road to Hania, Aretousa has very pleasant spacious and spotless rooms with wood-panelled ceilings, new bathrooms and balconies. Some larger family rooms have fully equipped kitchens (€55).

Pension Galini (☎ /fax 28230 51488; d €35; ✿) Next to Aretousa, this lovely place has well-appointed rooms with ceiling fans, air-con and small kitchens, and there are excellent barbecue facilities in the garden.

Santa Irene Hotel (☎ 28230 51342; www.sougia .info/hotels/santairene; s/d €36/45; ✿) This is the smartest accommodation on the beach, with marble floors, TV and kitchenettes. There are also two family rooms with baby cots available.

Lotos (☎ 28230 51178; fax 28230 51178; d/tr €30/35; ✿ 🖳) Right over the café (which has great music and excellent breakfasts), these rooms are light and pleasant (although some are overly furnished) and they have a fridge.

Also recommended are the homy **Rooms Ririka** (☎ 28230 51167; s/d €35/40; ✿) on the east side of the beach, and next door, **Rooms Maria** (☎ 28230 51337; s/d €30/35; ✿), which has clean, plain decent rooms, including some with air-con.

Eating

Restaurants line the waterfront and there are more on the main street.

Polyfimos (☎ 28230 51343; mains €5.50-6; ☿ dinner only) Tucked off the Hania road behind the police station, this taverna is run by Yianni, the infamous ex-hippy who is an institution in Sougia. He makes his own oil, wine and raki and makes *dolmadakia* from the vines that cover the shady courtyard restaurant. The food is excellent.

Taverna Rembetiko (☎ 28230 51510; starters €2-3) On the road to Hania, this popular taverna has an extensive menu including such Cretan dishes as *boureki* and stuffed zucchini flowers. It has a great atmosphere and is known for its good Greek music.

Kyma (☎ 28230 51670; mixed fish per kg €18) On the waterfront as you enter town, Kyma has a good selection of *mayirefta*, their own meat and fresh local fish. Try the *tsigariasto* (goat in wine) or the rabbit.

Getting There & Away

There's a daily bus travelling from Hania to Sougia (€5.40, 2½ hours) at 1.30pm. Buses going from Sougia to Hania leave at 7am and 6pm. There's a 7am bus to Agia Irini (€2.50) and Samaria Gorges (€4).

Sougia is on the Paleohora–Hora Sfakion boat route. Boats leave at 10.30am for Agia Roumeli (€3.20, 50 minutes), Loutro (€5, 1½ hours) and Hora Sfakion (€6.10, two hours). For Paleohora (€4.30, one hour) to the west there is a departure at 5.30pm. There is also a boat on Tuesdays at 9am for the island of Gavdos (€8.20, two hours).

There are two taxis in town that can take you to the Samaria Gorge.

AROUND SOUGIA

Twelve kilometres north of Sougia is the mouth of the pretty **Agia Irini Gorge**, which may not be as fashionable as the Samaria Gorge walk but is less crowded and less gruelling. The gorge is 7km long and is carpeted with oleander and chestnut trees and is fragrant with rosemary, sage and thyme. You'll see the entrance to the gorge on the right side if you're travelling from Sougia. You'll cross a streambed before coming to olive groves, but many trees were destroyed in a fire in 1994. The path follows a dried-out riverbed bordered by caves carved into the large rocks. There are a number of rest stops along the way and many tranquil places to sit and admire the scenery.

Paleohora travel agents offer **guided walks** through the gorge. It's easy enough to organise independently – just catch the Omalos bus from Paleohora or the Hania bus from Sougia, and get off at Agia Irini.

The ruins of ancient **Lissos** are 1½ hours away on the coastal path to Paleohora (see the boxed text on p107). Lissos arose under the Dorians, flourished under the Byzantines and was destroyed by the Saracens in the 9th century. It was part of a league of city–states, led by ancient Gortyna, which minted its own gold coins inscribed with the word 'Lission'. At one time there was a reservoir, a theatre and hot springs, but these have not yet been excavated. Most of what you see dates from the 1st through 3rd centuries BC when Lissos was known for its curative springs. The 3rd-century-BC **Temple of Asklepion** was built next to one of the springs and named after the Greek god of healing, Asklipios.

PALEOHORA–SOUGIA COASTAL WALK

From the town centre of Paleohora, follow signs to the camping grounds to the northeast. Turn right at the intersection with the road to Anydri and soon you'll be following the coastal path marked as the E4 European Footpath. After a couple of kilometres, the path climbs steeply for a beautiful view back to Paleohora. You'll pass **Anydri Beach** and several inviting **coves** where people may be getting an all-over tan. Take a dip because the path soon turns inland to pass over **Cape Flomes**. You'll walk along a plateau carpeted with brush that leads towards the coast and some breathtaking views over the Libyan Sea. Soon you'll reach the Minoan site of **Lissos**. After Lissos the path takes you through a pine forest and then **Agia Irini Gorge** (see p107) bedecked with oleander and outfitted with some perfect picnic spots. The road ends at Sougia Harbour. Since the walk is nearly shadeless it's important to take several litres of water, and sunscreen. If you come June through August, it's best to start at sunrise in order to get to Sougia before the heat of the day clamps down.

Excavations here uncovered a headless statue of **Asclepius** along with 20 other statue fragments now in the Hania Archaeological Museum (p78). You can still see the marble altar base that supported the statue next to the pit in which sacrifices were placed. The other notable feature is the **mosaic floor** of multicoloured stones intricately arranged in beautiful geometric shapes and images of birds. On the way down to the sea there are traces of Roman ruins and on the western slopes of the valley are unusual barrel-vaulted tombs.

Nearby are the ruins of two early Christian basilicas – **Agios Kirkos** and the **Panagia** – dating from the 13th century.

PALEOHORA ΠΑΛΑΙΟΧΩΡΑ
pop 2213

Paleohora (pal-ee-o-*hor*-a) was discovered by hippies back in the '60s and from then on its days as a tranquil fishing village were numbered. But the resort operators have not gone way over the top and the place retains a certain laid-back feel. It is also the only beach resort on Crete that does not go into total hibernation in winter.

The little town lies on a narrow peninsula with a long, curving sandy beach exposed to the wind on one side and a sheltered pebbly beach on the other. On summer evenings the main street is closed to traffic and the tavernas move onto the road. The most picturesque part of Paleohora is the maze of narrow streets around the castle.

Orientation & Information

Paleohora's main street, Eletheriou Venizelou, runs north–south. There are two ATMs, an OTE and laundry on the main drag. Walking south along El Venizelou from the bus stop, several streets lead off left to the Halikia Beach (Pebble Beach). There's an attractive seafront promenade that is the centre of activity in the early evening. Boats leave from the old harbour at the southern end of this beach. Kondekaki leads from the old harbour to the tamarisk-shaded Pahia Ammos (Sandy Beach).

The following services are available:

Municipal tourist office (☎ 28230 41507; Eleftheriou Venizelou; ☺ 10am-1pm & 6-9pm Wed-Mon May-Oct)

Notos Internet (☎ 28230 42110; notos@grecian.net; Eleftheriou Venizelou; per hr €4.40; ☺ 8am-10pm)

Post office At the northern end of Pahia Ammos beach.

Sights & Activities

It's worth clambering up the ruins of the 13th-century **Venetian castle** for the splendid view of the sea and mountains. The castle was built so the Venetians could keep an eye on the southwestern coast from this commanding position on the hill-top. There's not much left of the fortress, however, as it was destroyed by the Venetians, the Turks, the pirate Barbarossa in the 16th century and later the Germans during WWII.

From Paleohora, a six-hour walk along a scenic **coastal path** leads to Sougia, passing the ancient site of Lissos (see the boxed text on p107).

Paleohora is known for its excellent **windsurfing**. The strongest winds blow on the Sandy Beach and usually peak in the late morning and early afternoon.

Aqua Creta Diving & Adventures (☎ 28230 41393; www.aquacreta.gr; Kondekaki 4) runs a range of diving courses from beginner dives (€50) to seven- to 10-day master courses (€580). They also run one-day beach-hopping excursions to remote beaches along the southern coast and as far as Gavdos (80 minutes).

Tours

Various travel agents around town offer excursions to ancient Lissos (€29) and dolphin-watching trips (€6). Try **Tsiskakis Travel** (☎ 28230 42110; notosgr@yahoo.gr; Eleftheriou Venizelou) or **Selino Travel** (☎ 28230 42272), which also sells boat tickets.

Sleeping

Homestay Anonymous (☎ 28230 41509; d/tr with shared bathroom €22/25) This is a great place for backpackers, with clean, simply furnished rooms set around a small garden. There is also a communal kitchen. The owner, Manolis, speaks good English and is full of useful information for travellers.

Kostas Rooms (☎ /fax 28230 41248; d €30) Kostas offers attractive rooms with ceiling fans, kitchenette, fridge and sea views. The rooms have big balconies.

Spamandos Rooms (☎ 28230 41197; d/tr €40/45; ✵) In the old quarter, Spamandos has spotless, nicely furnished rooms right on the waterfront. They have a fridge and air-con.

Poseidon Hotel (☎ 28230 41374; www.interkriti .net/hotel/paleohora/poseidon; d/tr €30/35; ✵) The studios at this friendly, breezy place right on Pahia Ammos beach come equipped with

HANIA

ridges and kitchenettes and all have a little balcony.

Oriental Bay Rooms (☎ 28230 41076; d €35; ⌘) This place occupies the large modern building at the northern end of Pebble Beach. The owner keeps the rooms immaculate. There's also a shaded terrace-restaurant overlooking the sea (see p110).

Niki House (☎ 28230 41374; www.interkriti.net/hotel/paleohora/niki-houses; apt €35; ⌘) In the shade of the castle walls are these two large and fully equipped apartments, sleeping up to six people. They are ideal for self-caterers on extended stays.

Sandy Beach Hotel (☎ 28230 42138; fax 28230 42139; d incl breakfast €45; ⌘ P) This relatively new 12-room hotel, at the end of the sandy beach near the ruins of the castle, is run by the friendly Nektarios and his brother. It has spotless, pleasant rooms with balconies and sea views. They also own the more basic **Castello Rooms** (☎ 28230 41143; d €25-30) further along.

Camping Paleohora (☎ 28230 41120; tent/person €2/3.50) This large camping ground is 1.5km northeast of the town, about 50m from the Pebble Beach near the disco. There is a taverna but no mini-market.

Eating

The whole eastern seafront is full of eating choices. There are some good eateries in the village, while there are a few other options further inland.

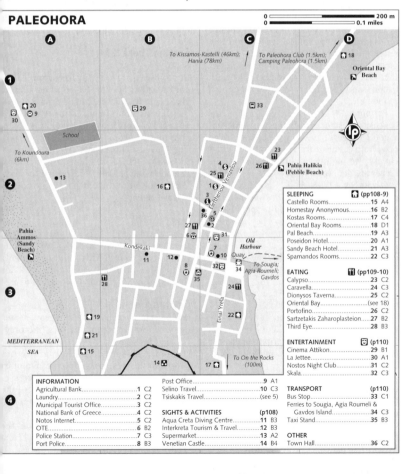

PALEOHORA

Dionysos Taverna (☎ 28230 41243; mains €4-6)
One of the oldest tavernas in town, the popular Dionysos is known for top-grade food, particularly its excellent *mayirefta*. There is a good range of vegetarian dishes and grills. It has a roomy interior and a few tables outside under the trees.

Third Eye (☎ 28230 41234; mains €4) Vegetarians flock to the Third Eye, just inland from Pahia Ammos. The fully vegetarian menu includes curries and a tempting range of Greek–Asian fusion dishes.

Caravella (☎ 28230 41131; mains €5-7) This place has a prime position overlooking the old harbour and offers an array of fresh and competitively priced Greek dishes, as well as fresh seafood.

Oriental Bay (☎ 28230 41322; mains €6.50-9) Part of Oriental Bay Rooms (p108), this beachside taverna is one of the best options on this side of the village. In addition to a range of cheap vegetarian choices, such as green beans and potatoes, there are dishes such as 'rooster's kiss' (chicken fillet with bacon) and 'drunk cutlet' (pork chop in red wine).

Portofino (☎ 28230 41114; pasta €5-8) This beachside restaurant on the port side has a good range of pasta dishes, wood-oven pizza and crepes in a menu that includes Greek, international and Italian dishes. The serves are generous.

Calypso (☎ 28230 83019; 🖳) Run by a British couple, this place has a 'quality fusion' menu with daily soup, salad and pasta specials and a range of vegetarian dishes. They also have alternative cuisine themes nights for Indian, Mexican and other ethnic cuisines. There is a children's menu and **Internet access** (per 30 min €1.50).

Also recommended are the excellent sweets and home made ice cream at **Sartzetakis Zaharoplasteion** (☎ 28230 41231).

There are also some good options in the village district. For excellent traditional Cretan food it is worth the trip to **Grammeno** (☎ 28230 41505) in the village of Koundoura, 2km west of Paleohora.

Right on Krios Beach – at the eastern end of Koundoura about 4km from Paleohora – there is a kantina among the bamboo and pine trees that serves excellent and cheap Cretan food; try the *kalitsounia* (pastries filled with cheese or wild greens) or *Sfakianes pittes* (pancakes) with honey.

Entertainment

The annual Paleohora Music Festival from 1 to 10 August presents concerts, exhibitions and song contests.

Cinema Attikon (tickets €5) Most visitors to Paleohora spend at least one evening at this well-signposted outdoor cinema. Screenings start at 10pm.

Nostos Night Club (☎ 28230 42145; btwn El Venizelou & the Old Harbour ☺ 6pm-2am) Has an outdoor terrace bar and a small indoor club playing Greek and Western music. La Jettee, behind the Elman hotel, is right on the beach and has a nice garden, while Skala by the port is an old-time classic bar.

Paleohora Club (☎ 28230 42230; ☺ 11pm-late) Next to Camping Paleohora 1.5km northeast of the village on Keratidies Beach, this used to be popular for all-night, full-moon parties but is now a less-appealing indoor club.

Getting There & Away
BOAT
In summer there is a daily ferry from Paleohora to Hora Sfakion (€8.50, three hours) via Sougia (€4.30, one hour), Agia Roumeli (€6.80, two hours) and Loutro (€7.50, 2½ hours). The ferry leaves Paleohora at 9.45am and returns from Hora Sfakion at 1pm. There are also three boats a week in summer to Gavdos (€9.70, 2½ hours), which leave Paleohora at 8.30am and return at 3pm. Tickets for all of these boats can be bought at travel agents.

BUS
In summer there are five buses a day from the small **bus station** (☎ 28230 41914) to Hania (€5.40, two hours). There is also one daily service to Omalos (€8.10, 1½ hours) – for the Samaria Gorge – that departs at 6am.

Getting Around
Notos Rentals (☎ 28230 42110; notosgr@yahoo.gr Eleftheriou Venizelou) Rents out cars, motorcycles and bicycles.

From mid-April M/B *Elafonisos* ferries people to the west-coast beach of Elafonisi (€4.50, one hour). The service increases from three times a week to daily in June through September. It departs at 10am and returns at 4pm.

The **taxi office** (☎ 28230 41128) is near the port. Sample fares are Kissamos (€35), Hania (€50; airport €55) and Elafonisi (€50).

TOPS OR BOTTOMS?

Cretans have a long tradition of welcoming foreigners, which has made them tolerant of different customs. In most places topless sunbathing is allowed. The few south coast beaches where it is frowned upon post signs to that effect. Although naturism is not widely practised and officially is not allowed, you'll find a sprinkling of naturists on the far ends of remote beaches or in secluded coves. Nude beaches change from year to year. Sometimes a taverna suddenly springs up on a popular naturist beach and the naturists disappear only to turn up on another distant cove. Beaches that are currently popular with naturists include Kommos near Matala, Sweetwater Beach, the south end of the sandy beach in Paleohora and the east end of the pebbly beach at Sougia. Glyka Nera, close to Loutro is an old standby as is Orthi Ammos 1km east of Frangokastello. Diktikos, west of Lendas, is the most reliable of Crete's nude beaches.

AROUND PALEOHORA

The village of **Anydri** is 5km northeast of Paleohora and contains the **Church of Agios Georgios** with 14th-century frescoes by the local master, Pagomenos. The founding fathers of the village were two brothers from Hora Sfakion fleeing a murderous vendetta, which is why most villagers have the same surname.

The village is accessible by foot from Paleohora. Take the road that goes past the camping ground and follow the paved road that forks off to the left, which is bordered by steep rocks. As you enter the village you'll see a sign directing you to the Anydri Gorge.

After a few hundred metres on a footpath you'll see an overgrown path on the left. Red markers direct you to the gorge. After walking along the dried-out riverbed, signs direct you to the wide, deserted Anydri Beach at the end of the gorge. You can take a different path back to Paleohora following the E4 European footpath markers that take you along the coastal cliffs.

GAVDOS ΓΑΥΔΟΣ
pop 98

Many people will tell you Gavdos (*gav*-dos) is as much a state of mind as it is an island. If you want to get away from it all, there is no better place for peace and isolation. Gavdos attracts a loyal following of campers, nudists and free spirits seeking natural beaches, long walks and laid-back holidays. This is the place for chilling out, letting your beard grow, rolling cigarettes and spending the nights looking at the starry skies.

Located under Crete in the Libyan sea, 65km from Paleohora, it is the most southerly place in Europe. Geographically it's more akin to Africa than Europe and enjoys a very mild climate. You can swim as early as February. Gavdos is surprisingly green, with almost 65% of the island covered in low-lying pine and cedar trees and vegetation, although it has a rugged natural landscape. There are several stunning beaches, some of which are accessible only by foot or boat. Most of the beaches are on the northeastern coast, as the southern coastline is all cliffs.

Gavdos has three main 'villages', which are virtually abandoned and full of ruins, and one beach settlement that gets relatively lively in July and August. At its tourist peak, the permanent population of about 55 residents may swell to 1000.

Archaeological excavations indicate the island was inhabited as far back as the Neolithic period. In the Greco-Roman era Gavdos Island, then known as Clauda, belonged to the city of Gortyna. There was a Roman settlement on the northwestern corner of the island. On his way from Kali Limenes to Rome, St Paul encountered a fierce storm that blew him off course past Gavdos Island and shipwrecked him on Malta, instead of a landing on Phoenix (or Finix). Under the Byzantines, Gavdos Island was the seat of a bishopric, but when the Arabs conquered Crete in the 9th century the island became a pirates' nest.

Until the late 1960s Gavdos had little water, electricity or phone lines and most residents moved to Paleohora or other parts of Crete or Athens. While water is now plentiful, there can still be the odd electricity shortages and blackouts in summer as only part of the island has power – the rest use generators which are often turned off at night and in the middle of the day. A new port was under construction in 2004.

While a day trip to Gavdos is possible, you won't appreciate its appeal unless you take the time to chill out and get into the spirit of the place.

Orientation & Information

The island's port is Karabe on the east side of the island, while the capital of the island is Kastri in the centre of Gavdos. There are only two families living here, plus there's the island's medical clinic. Card phones are available on the island. There's no bank or exchange facilities, and no OTE or post office, although you can send mail via Babis the postman in Sarakiniko. There's a mini-market for basic supplies at Sarakiniko.

Make sure you bring a torch (flashlight) for getting around at night as you only have the stars to guide you. Gavdos has a short season, as most tavernas and rooms shut by early September when schools start.

Sights & Activities

There is not much to see on Gavdos other than the beaches. The biggest beach community is at **Sarakinikos**, in the northeastern corner, which has a wide swathe of sand and several tavernas, as well as a new **amphitheatre** for occasional performances. The stunning **Agios Ioannis** beach, on the northern tip, has a scraggly summer settlement of nudists and campers. There are some wonderful beaches on the northern coast such as **Potamos** and **Pyrgos**, which you can reach by foot (about an hour) from Kastri if you follow the footpath leading north to Ambelos and beyond. Three giant arches carved into the rocky headland at **Tripiti** – the southernmost tip of Europe – are the island's best-known natural feature. The beach is reached by boat or on foot (a 1¼-hour walk from Vatsiana).

The restored 1880 **lighthouse** on the road to the village of Ambelos was being turned into a museum and café. Before it was bombed by the Germans in 1941, it was the world's second-brightest lighthouse after Tierra del Fuego.

In the village of **Vatsiana**, the island's priest has created a small private **museum** (☎ 28230 42167; 10am-6pm Jul-Aug, knock next door at other times) in an old stone house with items collected from the island, including agricultural and domestic tools, a loom and weavings. There is a small working traditional wood oven next door and the priest's wife Maria, runs the quaint attached *kafeneio* (coffee house), where you can try her ouzo and coconut cake.

A small open-air **cinema** (☎ 28230 42167; 10am-6pm Jul-Aug) at Metohi taverna screens movies most nights in summer. Despite the meagre population, there are 16 small churches dotted around the island. Most boat owners offer full- and half-day cruises including trips to the remote, uninhabited island of Gavdopoula, although there are no good beaches there. Ask at the tavernas.

Sleeping & Eating

There isn't much accommodation in Gavdos, where it is pretty much considered upmarket if you have a fridge and basic cooking facilities. Free camping is popular. The tavernas all offer fairly good value.

Sarakiniko Studios (☎ 28230 42182; www.gavdostudios.gr; s/d studio €30/50, small apt €60, all incl breakfast) Located above Sarakiniko beach, these studios are perhaps the best place to stay on the island. You can be picked up at the port or they are a 20-minute walk north of the port. You can camp for €5 per person nearby under the trees and have access to bathroom facilities.

Nychterida Taverna & Rooms (☎ 28230 42120; d/studio €35/50) There are basic but comfortable rooms here, right on Sarakinikos beach and roomier studios just behind with basic cooking facilities.

Taverna Sarakiniko (☎ /fax 28230 41103; d €35) operated by Manolis the fisherman, has new stone studios nearby with pine furniture and basic kitchen facilities. He also serves his fresh catch daily.

Akrogiali Taverna & Rooms (☎ 28230 42384; s/d €20/30) On Korfos beach, this fish taverna offers fresh local fish and their own goat for hearty Cretan cooking. The rooms are simple and overlook the beach.

Theophilos taverna (☎ 28230 41311) Above Agios Ioannis beach, this taverna has excellent trays of *mayirefta* each day catering to all the campers coming up from the beach.

Getting There & Around

In summer there are boats from Paleohora on Monday, Tuesday and Thursday (€9.70, 2½ hours). The boats turn around from Gavdos almost immediately but the Tuesday morning boat is the fastest and leaves

Gavdos at 3pm, which makes it feasible to do it as a day trip. In summer, there are boats from Hora Sfakion to Gavdos on Thursday, Friday, Saturday and Sunday (€9.50, 1½ hours) and a weekly boat from Sougia (€8.20, two hours) on Tuesdays. The only ferry that takes cars is on Monday night at 7pm from Hora Sfakion (2½ hours) and returns on Tuesday at 7am.

You can rent a bike or car at the port or in Sarakiniko.

EASTERN HANIA

The northeastern corner of Hania prefecture contains some interesting sights, including the island's only freshwater lake, Lake Kournas, and beach resorts such as Kalyves, Almyrida and Georgioupolis, which are more intimate villages than the resorts that spread along the coast west of Hania. There's also the restored village of Vamos and the ancient site of Aptera as well as off the beaten track villages such as Plaka and Gavalohori.

GEORGIOUPOLIS ΓΕΩΓΙΟΎΠΟΛΗ
pop 513

Although it is no longer the secret getaway that it once was, Georgioupolis retains the ambience of a languid seaside tourist town. Popular with families and nature lovers, the town's most distinctive feature is the eucalyptus trees lining the residential streets that fan out from the main square.

Located at the junction of the Almyros River and the sea, Georgioupolis is a nesting area for the endangered loggerhead sea turtle as well as hordes of mosquitoes in the summer. Georgioupolis was named after Prince George, High Commissioner of Crete from 1898 to 1906, who had a hunting lodge here. During classical times it was known as Amphimalla and was the port of ancient Lappa.

Orientation & Information
The main street leads from the highway to the town centre, where there are a number of travel agencies, tavernas and services. **Ballos Travel** (☎ 28250 83088; ballos@hol.gr), off the main square, can organise boat tickets, excursions and accommodation, and also changes money, rents out cars and is the

town's postal agency. There's a Hania Exchange Bank on the main road into the village before the main central square, and a number of ATMs off the square. **Planet Internet Cafe** (☎ 28250 61732; www.alchemist.gr; per hr €4; �9am-late) is near the main square.

There are two beaches, a long narrow stretch of hard-packed sand east of town and a smaller beach to the north of the port where the river spills its icy water into the sea.

Sights & Activities
The **marshes** surrounding the riverbed are known for their birdlife, especially the egrets and kingfishers that migrate into the area in April. At the foot of the main street in Georgioupolis, **Yellowboat** (per person per hr €6) rents out pedalboats and canoes to go up the river where you can see turtles, fish, birds and ducks.

The northern beach is marked by two small **chapels** – the church Agios Nikolaos that's splashed by waves on a narrow rocky jetty and the Agios Kyriakos to the north. If you don't have wheels, a **tourist train** runs trips to nearby Kournas Lake and Argiroupolis. **Zoraida's Horseriding** (☎ 28250 61745; www.georgioupoli .net/zoraida) runs trails around the area.

Sleeping
Egeon (☎ 28250 61161; fax 28250 61171; studio €40; ☼) To the left of the main road, these pleasant rooms are run by friendly Greek-American Polly and her fisherman husband, whose nets are often laid out in the foyer. They've upgraded the furniture and installed screens on the windows in the rooms, while some have kitchenettes, shower curtains and TV.

Andy's Rooms (☎ 28250 61394; d €29.50; studio €35-60; ☼) To the right of the main road opposite the church is Andy's Rooms, which has large rooms with mosquito screens, kitchenettes and TV. There are larger apartments for families.

Nicolas Hotel (☎ 28250 61375; fax 28250 61011; d incl breakfast €55; ☼) On the main road entering the village, this place has doubles attractively furnished in pine with a safe and home-cooked breakfast.

Apartments Sofia (☎ 28250 61325; www.river-side .gr; studios d/q €35/40; ☼) This salmon-coloured building has balconies overlooking the sea and well-equipped rooms with kitchenettes and hairdryers.

Hotel Gorgona (☎ 28250 61341; d €25) South of the village centre along the beach, this dated hotel is about the cheapest seafront option in town. Rooms are very basic and the bathrooms are cramped.

Eating
Poseidon Taverna (☎ 28250 61026; fish per kg €20-40) The best fresh meal can be had at the Poseidon fish taverna, which is signposted down a narrow alley to the left as you come into the village. You choose your dinner from the fish and seafood that's laid out on the counter and enjoy an excellent meal under the mulberry trees in the lovely courtyard.

Taverna Plateia (☎ 28250 61567; grills €5-7) Just south off the main square, Plateia is unassuming and pretty reasonable with a range of Cretan dishes as well as grills.

Fanis (☎ 28250 61374; Greek specials €4.50-6.50) On the riverbank, Fanis serves reasonable Cretan cuisine and is known for fresh local fish and meat.

You could also try **Arolithos** (☎ 28250 61406), near Andy's Rooms, which has an extensive selection of appetisers.

Entertainment
There's not much of a bar scene in Georgioupolis. Georgoupolis Bar on the main square is probably the liveliest place. Edem Cocktail Bar and Restaurant is along the beach and has a large swimming pool open to the public. It presents live Cretan music once a week in the summer, as do many of the hotels and tavernas in town.

Getting There & Away
Buses between Hania and Rethymno stop on the highway outside Georgioupolis.

LAKE KOURNAS ΛΊΜΝΗ ΚΟΥΡΝΆΣ
Lake Kournas, 4km inland from Georgioupolis, is a lovely, restful place to pass an afternoon. It's the island's only natural lake, it is about 1.5km in diameter, 45m deep and is fed by underground springs. There's a narrow sandy strip around the lake, but no beaches as such, and you can only walk two-thirds of the way around the lake. The crystal-clear water is great for swimming and changes colour according to the season and time of day. You can rent **pedalboats** and **canoes** and view the turtles, crabs, fish and snakes that make the lake their home,

although tourist buses can crowd the lake in the peak of summer.

There are a number of tavernas around the lake and a few simple places to stay.

Omorfi Limni (☎ 28250 61665; www.pinelopi-hotel.gr; d/tr €35/45; 🕾 🖵) These studios have a fridge and TV, and there's a two-room apartment (€60), plus a decent taverna attached.

Limni (☎ 28250 61674; d €18) Limni is at the turn-off for the lake. The double rooms are fine for the price, but have no fridge.

Nice View Apartments & Studio (☎ 28250 61315 d €30) On a hill overlooking the lake, this place has spectacular views. Rooms are well equipped with kitchenettes and there are bathtubs.

To Mati tis Limnis (☎ 28250 61695; mains €5-5.50 The 'Eye of the Lake' taverna on the shore of the lake is cool and shady and makes good Cretan dishes such as rabbit casserole with onions or filling *mizythropittes* (cheese pies).

The lake is below **Kournas Village**, which is a steep 5km up a hill overlooking the lake. It's a traditional village of white-washed houses, a few stone homes and a couple of kafeneia. You can get a delicious meal at the **Kali Kardia Taverna** (☎ 28250 96278; grills €5) on the main street. Kostas Agapinakis is known for his award-winning sausages (voted third in all of Greece), excellent *apaki* (smoked pork) and meats cooked on the grill outside the taverna. If you are lucky you might get to try the excellent *galaktoboureko* (custard pastry) while it is still warm.

As you enter the village there is an excellent **ceramics shop** (☎ 28250 96434; 🕑 9am-8.30pm) run by friendly Kostas Tsakalakis, who uses local clay and special lead-free glazes. There is a huge range and the prices are very reasonable.

There's a tourist train that runs from Georgioupolis to Lake Kournas in the summer, but no other public transport.

KALYVES ΚΑΛΎΒΕΣ
pop 1419
Originally a farming village, Kalyves has now become a good-sized resort. Located 18km east of Hania on Souda Bay, Kalyves is popular with Greeks on holiday as well as international guests. The town is spread out along both sides of the main road and boasts a long sandy beach as well as an appealingly low-key village ambience.

Orientation & Information

All services are located along the main road, including the post office and an Agricultural Bank with an ATM. The sandy beach stretches from the centre of Kalyves east to Kalyves Beach Hotel. West of the centre the coast is rockier and most of the domatia are located at this end.

Flisvos Tours (☎ 28250 31337; www.flisvos.com; 8.30am-1.30pm & 5.30-10pm) changes money, rents out cars, scooters and bikes, and is a good source of information.

Digiland (☎ 28250 32376; dland@otenet.gr) has Internet access for €4 per hour.

Sleeping & Eating

Most of the private domatia are clustered at the western end of the village.

Thamiris (☎ 28250 31637; www.thamiris.georgiou poli.net; d studio €20-60;) This place has a range of well-maintained comfortable rooms and fully equipped studios in two complexes, as well as two more secluded studios right on the beach next to Piperia taverna. There's a daily cleaning service.

Maria (☎ 28250 31748; r €30) Maria has small rooms with kitchenette and sea views. Look out for the giant swan opposite the supermarket as you head into town.

Piperia (☎ 28250 31245; mains €6.50-7) Right on the beach just before town, this is one of the best restaurants in Kalyves, with a great selection of Cretan specials and seafood. The menu includes dishes made from organic produce and oil, including an exceptional organic Greek salad.

You could also try the well-regarded Koumandros on the main street or Provlita

---

DETOUR: KOUMOS

One of the more quirky attractions of the area is **Koumos** (☎ 28250 32256; 10am-late) the huge stone fantasy of local builder Yiorgos Havaledakis. He has spent years collecting a hotchpotch of stones, pebbles and rocks of every shape colour and size from the surrounding mountains to create this bizarre sprawling open-air taverna and kafeneio. The church, bridges, arches, sculptures, light poles, and even the toilet block are a unique work in progress. Koumos holds Cretan music nights every Wednesday.

---

on the seaside. In the centre of Kalyves visit the Old Bakery on for scrumptious cakes and home-made breads and biscuits.

Getting There & Away

There are seven buses daily to Kalyves from Hania (€1.80, 45 minutes).

ALMYRIDA ΑΛΜΥΡΊΔΑ
pop 133

The village of Almyrida, 14km east of Kalyves is considerably less developed, although it's getting more so. Still, it's a reasonable spot to hang out for a few days and is probably a better option for independent travellers than the more tourist-oriented Kalyves. Almyrida is a popular spot for windsurfing because of its long, exposed beach and there are a couple of outfits catering to the bands of itinerant windsurfers who pass through. History buffs might note that there are the remains of an early Christian basilica at the western end of the village.

There's only one road through the village that runs along the beach. There's no post office but there is an ATM. **Flisvos Tours** (☎ /fax 28250 31100; 8am-1.30pm & 5-9.30pm), on the main road, changes money, rents out cars, scooters and mountain bikes, and is a good source of information.

Rooms Marilena (☎ 28250 32202; d €25), popular with the windsurfing fraternity, is a neat set of smallish but spotless rooms all with ceiling fan, fridge and cooking ring upon request. It's at the far end off the beach down a side alley.

Almyrida Beach Hotel & Studios (☎ 28250 32138; www.almyridabeach.com; s & d incl breakfast €80-110;), the newest hotel in Almyrida, has one main hotel complex across from the beach with a pool, and another set of comfortable self-contained studios right on the beach with interconnecting rooms for families or groups.

The beach road is lined with tavernas. **Psaros** (☎ 28250 31401; mixed seafood platter for two €25), right on the far end of the beach, has fresh fish and friendly staff.

PLAKA ΠΛΆΚΑ
pop 302

The village of Plaka, a pretty drive up from Almyrida, is unfortunately being swamped by a frenzy of development that is turning it into a British holiday settlement. The winding lanes and low-rise white buildings are still a world away from the tourist bustle along the coast, but the main square shaded by eucalyptus trees seems swamped by the look-alike holiday houses. It does have a few tavernas with lovely views down to the sea.

Eva Papadomanolakos, the owner of **Studios Koukourou** (☎ 28250 31145; fax 28250 31879; studio €35; 🛒), has gone to a lot of trouble to create a homy Cretan atmosphere for her guests and has decorated her place with tropical plants and flowers. There's also a roof garden with panoramic views over the coast. The rooms are very clean and have kitchenettes. It's well signposted as you enter town.

APTERA ΑΠΤΕΡΑ

The ruins of the ancient city of **Aptera** (admission €1.50; 🕑 8am-2.30pm Tue-Sun), about 3km west of Kalyves, are spread out over two hills that loom over Souda Bay. Founded in the 7th century BC, Aptera was one of the most important city–states of western Crete and was continuously inhabited until an earthquake destroyed it in the 7th century AD.

It came back to life with the Byzantine reconquest of Crete in the 10th century and became a bishopric. In the 12th century, the monastery of St John the Theologian was established; the reconstructed monastery is the centre of the site.

The site is still being excavated, but you can see Roman cisterns, a 2nd-century-BC Greek temple and some massive defensive walls. At the western end there's a Turkish fortress, which was built in 1872 and enjoys a panoramic view of Souda Bay. The fortress was built as part of a large Turkish fortress-building programme during a period when the Cretans were in an almost constant state of insurrection. Notice the 'Wall of the Inscriptions' – this was probably part of an important public building and was excavated in 1862 by French archaeologists. The Greek Ministry of Culture is continuing to restore the site, installing signs and paths.

There are no cafés or snack bars at the site, but a few tavernas on the way up, such as **Ta Aptera** (☎ 28250 31313; mains €5-6), serve standard Cretan cuisine.

There's no public transport to Aptera.

VAMOS ΒΆΜΟΣ
pop 665

The 12th-century village of Vamos, 26km southeast of Hania, was the capital of the Sfakia province from 1867 to 1913 and was the scene of a revolt against Turkish rule in 1896. It is now the capital of the Apokoronas province. In 1995 a group of villagers banded together to preserve the traditional way of life of Vamos. They persuaded the EU to fund a renovation project to showcase the crafts and products of the region and develop a new kind of tourism in Crete. They restored the old stone buildings of the village using traditional materials and crafts and turned them into guesthouses. They opened shops and cafés where visitors could taste regional products, and staged periodic exhibitions and musical evenings.

Vamos is a pleasant stop, although the authentic village theme is a little overrated. The guesthouse accommodation, while undoubtedly very tasteful, is rather expensive and seems pitched at well-heeled Cretans on 'country weekends' rather than travellers on more modest budgets.

There is a **tourist office** (☎ /fax 28250 23233; 🕑 8am-9pm in summer) close to the Bloumosifi taverna where you can change money, rent cars and book excursions.

In late March or early April, Vamos celebrates **Hohliovradia** (Snail Night) with a festival of cooked snails, washed down with wine and *tsikoudia* (a grape distilled spirit).

Sleeping & Eating

Traditional Guesthouses (☎ 28250 22932; cottage €88-110) The lovely stone cottages contain kitchens, fireplaces and TVs and are decorated with traditional furniture and fabrics. Most can accommodate up to four people, but there's one two-bedroom cottage that accommodates up to seven.

Parthenagogio (☎ 28250 23398; d/tr cottage €40/50) This tastefully decorated former girl's school (the name means Virgin's School) run by the municipality has eight double rooms that retain a boarding-house feel.

I Sterna tou Bloumosifi (☎ 28250 22932; mains €5-9.80) This old stone taverna is well known for its excellent Cretan cuisine. For starters try the *gavro* (mild anchovy) wrapped in vine leaves or the garlic and herb mushrooms and then move on to the *hilopita* (tagliatelle) with rooster.

Liakoto (☎ 28250 23251) This is an understated café-bar-cum-art-gallery serving light snacks. Its lovely terrace overlooking the mountains and sea is a great place to watch the sunset.

Myrovolo Wine Store & General Store (☎ 28250 22996) Next door to Liakoto, you can buy local raki, herbs, organic oil and other Cretan products.

Getting There & Away
There are four daily buses to Vamos from Hania (€2.30, 45 minutes).

AROUND VAMOS
The village of **Gavalohori**, 25km southeast of Hania, makes a pleasant stop if you're exploring the region. The main attraction is the **Folklore Museum** (☎ 28250 23222; admission €1.50; 9am-8pm Mon-Fri, to 7pm Sat, 10am-1.30pm & 5-8pm Sun), which is located in a renovated building that was constructed during Venetian rule and then extended by the Turks. The main architectural feature is the stone arches that divide the ground floor of the house into bedrooms, a kitchen, a room for a wine press and a storage room. The exhibits are well labelled in English and include examples of pottery, weaving, woodcarving, stonecutting and other Cretan crafts, including the fine *kapaneli* – intricately worked silk lace. A historical section of the museum documents Cretan struggles for independence.

Signs direct you to the **Byzantine wells**, **Venetian arches** and **Roman tombs** about 1.5km above the village.

The **Women's Cooperative** (☎ /fax 28250 22038, 9am-10pm), on the main square, sells a few rare pieces of unique *kapaneli* made by local women. You can normally see women hard at work on this painstakingly long process. Prices for quality lacework items range from €15 to €1500 depending on the size of the piece.

VRYSES ΒΡΎΣΕΣ
pop 848
Most travellers just pass through Vryses, 30km southeast of Hania, on their way to or from the south coast but this cool, pleasant and sizeable village deserves more time. There's not much to do here but the rivers Voutakas and Vrysanos run through the centre of the village watering the giant plane trees along the banks. When the coast is sweltering you can cool off in the shade in one of the riverside tavernas under the trees. Vryses is a market centre for the region's agricultural products and is a relatively new settlement, dating from 1925.

Orientation & Information
Buses stop at the crossroads in the village centre, which is marked by a monument commemorating Cretan independence. Following the main street right across the river takes you to tavernas, shops, a supermarket and the National Bank of Greece, which has an ATM. Following the main street left, you'll come to the post office and OTE about 100m up the road.

Sleeping & Eating
Spyridakis (☎ 28250 51206; studio/tr €30/40;) These rooms in the centre of Vryses have simple, large, comfortable-enough studios with a fridge and kitchenette and TV. Some have air-con but you don't really need it.

Taverna Progoulis (☎ 28250 51086; grills €4.50-6) This taverna has average food, but its tables under the river trees make for a pleasant lunchtime interlude. There's usually a lamb and other meat cooking on the spit.

Vryses Way (☎ 28250 51705; gyros €1.80) At the crossroads in the town centre, this modest establishment serves excellent gyros, *Sfakianes pittes* and yogurt with honey, which is a speciality of the town as the microclimate is perfect for yogurt.

Getting There & Away
There are three buses daily from Hania to Hora Sfakion, which also stop at Vryses (€3, 30 minutes).

ASKYFOU ΑΣΚΎΦΟΥ
pop 444
The road south from Vryses takes you across the war-torn plain of Askyfou, which was the scene of one of the most furious battles of the Cretan revolt of 1821. The Sfakiot forces triumphed over the Turks in a bloody battle here, which is still recounted in local songs. More than a century later the plain was the scene of more strife as Allied troops retreated across the plateau towards their evacuation point in Hora Sfakion. The central town of the region is Askyfou, which stretches out on either side of a hill. The post office is at the

top of the hill with a mini-market and several tavernas with fairly cheap rooms to rent.

As you enter Askyfou from Hania, one sign after another directs you to the **military museum** (☎ 28250 95289; admission free; ☎ 8am-7pm Mon-Sat), which displays the gun and military odds-and-ends collection of Georgios Hatzidakis. The Sfakian is eager to show you around his collection, which includes various artefacts from wars of the 20th century.

O Barba Geronymos (☎ 28250 95211), a traditional taverna next to the bakery, has mainly local specialties such as wild goat *tsigariasto, sfakiano vrasto* (boiled lamb or goat), *pilafi* and the area's obligatory *Sfakianes pittes* and *kalitsounia* (pastries). You can probably eat and drink their own wine till you are full and pay less than €10 per head.

IMBROS GORGE ΦΑΡΑΓΓΙ ΙΜΠΡΟΥ

The **Imbros Gorge** (admission €2; ☒ year-round), 57km southeast of Hania, is less hiked than its illustrious sister at Samaria but is just as beautiful. Cypresses, holm oaks, and fig and almond trees gradually thin to just cypresses and Jerusalem sage deep within the gorge. The narrowest point of the ravine is 2m wide while the walls of rock reach 300m.

At only 8km the Imbros walk is also much easier on the feet. You can begin from the southern end of the gorge at the village of **Komitades**, but most people begin in the little mountain village of **Imbros**. Both places are used by gorge-hikers and have plenty of mini-markets and tavernas to fuel up. There's nowhere to stay in Imbros village.

You'll find the well-marked entrance to the gorge next to Porofarango taverna (see below) just outside Imbros village on the road to Hora Sfakion. The track is easy to follow as it traces the streambed past rock-slides and caves. The gorge path ends at the village of Komitades, from where you can walk 5km or take a taxi to Hora Sfakion (€17 to €20).

At the start of the gorge, the friendly family taverna **Porofarango** (☎ 28250 95450; mains €6-7) has a big balcony with great panoramic views of the gorge and serves good-value Cretan cuisine and generous raki. The meat is usually their own and they often have wild goat. Try the special *tsigariasto* pork.

There are three daily buses from Hania to Hora Sfakion (€5.40, two hours) that stop at Imbros village. Buses from Hora Sfakion to Hania stop at Komitades.

Rethymno
Ρεθυμνο

RETHYMNO

With Crete's longest stretch of sandy beach and a charming Venetian port town as its capital, Rethymno has its fair share of attractions and visitors, even if it lacks the big draw cards of neighbouring Hania and Iraklio. Rethymno also prides itself on being the cultural capital of the island, with a rich musical tradition and its historic importance during the Renaissance. And it's close enough to both Hania and Iraklio to be a good central base for seeing the island's key sites and to give you a broad taste of what Crete has to offer.

Rethymno town itself is one of the island's architectural treasures, due to its stunning fortress and mix of Venetian and Turkish houses in the labyrinth of the old quarter. The long beach running east towards Iraklio is home to a string of big hotel complexes, while further along are the pleasant smaller-scale coastal resorts of Panormo and Bali.

Rethymno is Crete's most mountainous prefecture, boasting the island's highest peak, Mt Psiloritis, in the east and bordering the Lefka Ori in the west. Mt Psiloritis has two famous caves – Zoniana and the Ideon cave, where Zeus was allegedly reared.

Inland, you can explore diverse traditional villages such as Anogia, known for its fiery spirit, fine musicians and famous huge weddings, and Margarites, renowned for its pottery tradition. Most tourists on their way south stop at Spili to drink from its lion-head Venetian fountain, while the springs of Argyroupolis are a delightful respite from the summer heat.

On the south coast, the resorts of Agia Galini and Plakias have their loyal following, while further west the rugged cliffs are interspersed with some of the island's finest unspoilt beaches.

Rethymno also has two of Crete's most historically significant monasteries – Moni Arkadiou in the north and the Moni Preveli overlooking the Libyan sea in the south.

As most of the prefecture is composed of barren mountains and hills, only a third of the land is cultivated.

HIGHLIGHTS

- Strolling the maze of narrow streets in **Rethymno's Venetian quarter** (p122)
- Cooling off by the springs of **Argyroupolis** (p128)
- Exploring the unspoilt **southern beaches** (p137 & p139)
- Hitting the northern coastal resorts of **Bali** (p130) and **Panormo** (p141)
- Visiting the **Preveli monastery** (p137)
- Listening to *mandinades* (rhyming couplets) by moonlight in **Anogia** (p132)

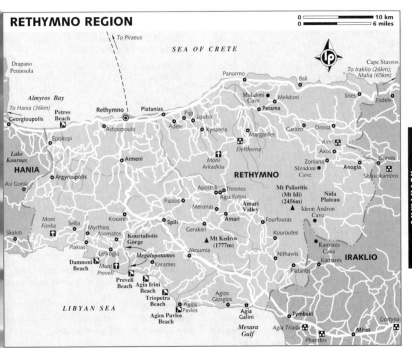

RETHYMNO REGION

0 — 10 km
0 — 6 miles

SEA OF CRETE

To Piraeus

Drapano Peninsula

Cape Stavros
To Iraklio (26km);
Malia (65km)

Panormo

Bali

Sises

Fodele

Almyros Bay

To Hania (36km)

Petres Beach

Rethymno

Platanias

Pigi

Loutrá

Melidoni Cave

Melidoni

Perama

Georgioupolis

Astipopoulo

Adele

Kyrianna

Margarites

Garazo

Drosia

Episkopi

Eleftherna

Axos

Axos

Lake Kournas

HANIA

Armeni

Moni Arkadiou

RETHYMNO

Zoniana

Sfendoni Cave

Anogia

Gonies

Asi Gonia

Argyroupolis

Apostoli

Thronos

Agia Fotini

Mt Psiloritis (Mt Idi) (2456m)

Nida Plateau

Sklavokambos

Patsos

Meronas

Amari Valley

Ideon Andron Cave

Moni Finika

Sellia

Koxare

Spili

Gerakari

Amari

Fourfouras

Kouroutes

Kamares Cave

Skaloti

Myrthios

Asomatos

Kourtaliotis Gorge

Mt Kedros (1777m)

Nithavris

Kamares

IRAKLIO

Plakias

Letkogia

Megalopotamos

Akoumia

Platanos

Damnoni Beach

Moni Preveli

Kerames

Preveli Beach

Agia Irini Beach

Triopetra Beach

Agios Giorgios

LIBYAN SEA

Agios Pavlos

Agia Galini

Tymbaki

Gortyna

Agios Pavlos Beach

Mesara Gulf

Agia Triada

Phaestos

Mires

RETHYMNO

RETHYMNO ΡΕΘΥΜΝΟ

pop 27,868

Rethymno (*reth*-im-no) is the island's third-largest town and one of the most picturesque, with a charming harbour and delightful old Venetian–Ottoman quarter.

The old quarter is a maze of narrow streets, graceful wood-balconied houses and ornate Venetian monuments, with minarets adding a touch of the Orient. While architectural similarities invite comparison with Hania, Rethymno has a character all of its own.

HISTORY

The name Rethymno means 'stream of water' and evidence now found in the city's archaeological museum indicates that the site of modern Rethymno has been occupied since Late Minoan times. In the 3rd and 4th centuries BC, 'Rithymna' emerged as an autonomous state of sufficient stature to issue its own coinage. Ancient Rithymna probably lay under Palekastro Hill, but its remains have never been excavated, although later Roman mosaics have been found underneath the modern town.

The town prospered once more under the Venetians, who ruled from 1210 until 1645, and turned Rethymno into an important commercial centre exporting wine and oil from the region. The town flourished artistically under the Venetians and became the seat of a Venetian Prefect. The Venetians built the Venetian harbour and began fortifying the town in the 16th century against the growing threat from the Turks. Sammicheli, the best military architect of the era, designed thick outer walls of which only the Porto Guora survives. The walls did not stop the city from being sacked by the pirate Barbarossa in 1538.

The Venetians then built the massive fortress on the hill, which nevertheless was unable to withstand the Turkish assault of 1646 and collapsed after a 22-day siege. Rethymno was an important seat of government under the Turks but it was also a centre of resistance to Turkish rule. The Turks inflicted severe reprisals upon the town for its role in the uprising of 1821, but the resistance continued.

Turkish forces held the town until 1897, when it was taken by Russia as part of the occupation of Crete by the Great Powers. Rethymno became an artistic and intellectual centre after the arrival of a large number of refugees from Smyrna in 1923.

These days, the city has a campus of the University of Crete, attracting a student population that keeps the town lively outside the tourist season.

ORIENTATION

Rethymno is a fairly compact town with most of the major sights and places to stay and eat within a small central area off the old Venetian harbour. The city's old quarter occupies the headland north of Dimakopoulou, which runs from Plateia Vardinogianni on the western side to Plateia Iroön on the east (becoming Gerakari en route). This is where you'll find the most atmospheric hotels and eateries. Banks and government services are to the south on the edge of the new part of town.

The beach is on the eastern side of town, around from the Venetian harbour. Coming from the south, the best way to approach the old town is through the Porto Guora onto Ethnikis Andistasis, the main drag in central Rethymno. Curving parallel one block back from the beachside Eleftheriou Venizelou is Arkadiou, the main commercial and shopping street.

Both streets lead towards the Rimondi Fountain, the old quarter's best-known landmark, which is surrounded by cafés, restaurants and souvenir shops. The maze of streets makes it an easy place to get lost, especially since street signs are a rarity.

If you arrive in Rethymno by bus, you will be dropped at the rather inconveniently located bus terminal at the western end of Igoumenou Gavriil, about 600m west of the Porto Guora (although this was due to relocate).

If you arrive by ferry, the old quarter is the end of the quay. If you are driving into town from the expressway, there are three possible exit points.

INFORMATION
Bookshops

Book Store Mediterraneo (☎ 28310 23417; Mavrokordatou 2) Stocks English books, travel guides and foreign press.

PANDELIS PREVELAKIS – RETHYMNO'S SON

Iraklio has Kazantzakis but Rethymno has Prevelakis. The writer and poet Pandelis Prevelakis was born in Rethymno in 1908. He painted an exquisite portrait of his birthplace in the book *The Tale of a Town*. One of the most moving passages of the book deals with the expulsion of the Turkish community of Rethymno in 1923 after the failed Greek invasion of Smyrna. Riots broke out as Greek refugees from Smyrna waited to move into homes that anguished Turks were destroying. Prevelakis is also known as a poet and for his critical writings on Kazantzakis.

Ilias Spondidakis bookshop (☎ 28310 54307; Souliou 43) Stocks novels in English, books about Greece, tapes of Greek music and has a small second-hand section.

Emergency
Tourist police (☎ 28310 28156; ☼ 7am-10pm) In the same building as the municipal tourist office.

Internet Access
Galero (☎ 28310 54345; Plateia Rimini; per hr €3; ☼ 6am-late)
Internet Café (☎ 28310 21324; Arkadiou 186; per hr €4.50; ☼ 9am-midnight)

Laundry
Laundry Mat self-service laundry (☎ 28310 28316; Tombazi 45) Next door to the youth hostel; charges €8.50 for a wash and dry.

Left Luggage
KTEL (☎ 28310 22659; cnr Kefalogiannidon & Igoumenou Gavriil) The bus station stores luggage for €1.50 per day.

Medical Services
Rethymno Hospital (☎ 28210 27491; Triandalydou 17; ☼ 24hrs)

Money
Banks are concentrated around the junction of Dimokratias and Pavlou Koundouriotou.
Alpha Bank (Pavlou Koundouriotou 29) Has a 24-hour automatic exchange machine and ATM.
National Bank of Greece (Dimokratias) On the far side of the square opposite the town hall.
National Mortgage Bank Next to the town hall, has a 24-hour automatic exchange machine and ATM.

Post

Mobile post office (Eleftheriou Venizelou; ☒ May-Sep) About 200m southeast of the tourist office.

Post office (☎ 28310 22302; Moatsou 21; ☒ 7am-7pm)

Telephone

OTE (☎ 28310 35000; Pavlou Koundouriotou 28)

Toilets

There is a reasonable public toilet in the centre of Rethymno in a side street just off Arkadiou.

Tourist Information

Municipal tourist office (☎ 28310 29148; Eleftheriou Venizelou; ☒ 9am-2pm Mon-Fri) Very convenient and helpful.

Travel Agencies

Ellotia Tours (☎ 28310 24533; elotia@ ret.forthnet.gr; Arkadiou 161; ☒ 9am-9pm Mar-Nov) Helpful office that handles boat and plane tickets, changes money, rents cars and motorcycles, and books excursions.

SIGHTS

Rethymno's 16th-century **fortress** (fortezza; ☎ 28310 28101; Paleokastro Hill; admission €3; ☒ 8am-8pm) is the site of the city's ancient acropolis. Within its massive walls a great number of buildings once stood, of which only a church and a mosque survive intact. The ramparts offer good views, while the site has lots of ruins to explore. The main gate is opposite the Archaeological Museum on the eastern side of the fortress, but there were once two other gates on the western and northern sides for the delivery of supplies and ammunition.

The **Archaeological Museum** (☎ 28310 54668; Fortezza; admission €1.50; ☒ 8.30am-3pm Tue-Sun), near the entrance to the fortress, was once a prison. The exhibits are well labelled in English and contain Neolithic tools, Minoan pottery excavated from nearby tombs, Mycenaean figurines and a 1st-century-AD relief of Aphrodite, as well as an important coin collection.

There are also some excellent examples of blown glass from the classical period. Various displays outline the history of archaeological excavations in the region.

Rethymno's **Historical & Folk Art Museum** (☎ 28310 23398; Vernardou 28-30; admission €3; ☒ 9.30am-2pm Mon-Sat) gives an excellent overview of the area's rural lifestyle, with its collection of old clothes, baskets, weavings and farm tools whose purpose would remain obscure without the useful explanatory labels on the exhibits.

Pride of place among the many vestiges of Venetian rule in the old quarter goes to the **Rimondi Fountain** with its spouting lion heads and Corinthian capitals, built first in 1588 and rebuilt in 1626 by Rimondi. Another major landmark is the 16th-century **Loggia**, once a meeting house for Venetian nobility, now a museum shop selling good-quality reproductions.

At the southern end of Ethnikis Andistasis is the well-preserved **Porto Guora** (Great Gate), a remnant of the defensive wall that was once topped with the symbol of Venice: the Lion of St Mark, now in the Archaeological Museum. Around the Porto Guora lies a network of old streets built by the Venetians and rebuilt by the Turks. **The Centre for Byzantine Art** (☎ 28210 50120; Ethnikis Antistaseos) is a great example of a restored Venetian/Turkish mansion and has exhibitions, workshops and a terrace café with great views of the old town.

Other Turkish legacies in the old quarter include the **Kara Musa Pasha Mosque**, which has a vaulted fountain, and the **Nerantzes Mosque**, which was converted from a Franciscan church in 1657. The building's minaret was built in 1890.

Just outside the old quarter, the pleasant **municipal park** offers a respite from the heat and crowds.

ACTIVITIES
Trekking

Rethymno's chapter of the **Ellinikos Orivatikos Syllogos** (EOS – Greek Association of Mountaineers; ☎ 28310 57766; http://rethymnon.com/clients/mountain /bindexgr.html; Dimokratias 12) can give good advice on mountain climbing in the region.

The Happy Walker (☎ /fax 28310 52920; www.happy walker.com; Tombazi 56) runs a varied programme of country walks in the region. Most walks start in the early morning and finish with lunch; they cost from about €25 upwards. Complete walking holidays are also organised for the really enthusiastic walker.

Diving

The **Paradise Dive Centre** (☎ 28310 26317; pdcr@ otenet.gr; Eleftheriou Venizelou 57) runs diving activities and PADI courses for all grades of

RETHYMNO

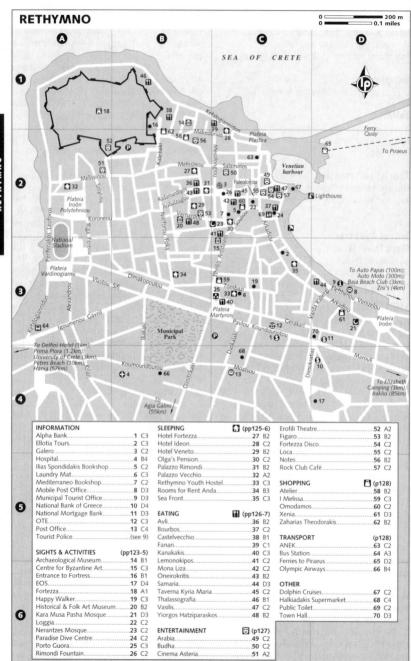

SEA OF CRETE

divers. Divers are normally taken to nearby Petres beach. Experienced divers can dive off the boat (€32) or shore (€25), while novice dives cost €65 and snorkelling costs €36. There is a €5 discount if you have your own transport.

TOURS

Rethymno is well placed for boat excursions. Along the harbour front there are several companies that offer boat trips.

Dolphin Cruises (☎ 28310 57666) offers three-hour trips on the pirate ship to nearby caves and Panormo (adult/child under 12 €20/10), and all-day trips with lunch to Marathi beach (€34/17), as well as trips on a speedboat.

FESTIVALS & EVENTS

Rethymno's main cultural event is the annual **Renaissance Festival** (☎ 28310 51199; www .cultureguide.gr), which runs from July to September. Held primarily in the Erofili Theatre at the fortezza, it features performances by Greece's leading theatre companies, as well as dance, music and acts from around Europe. It promotes the Cretan and European renaissance so you will get anything from Shakespeare to Molière to Cretan playwrights. Get tickets at the town hall or from the theatre one hour before performances.

Most years there's a **Wine Festival** in mid-July, which is held in the municipal park and offers a good opportunity to sample local wine and cuisine. Ask the tourist office for details.

SLEEPING

Rethymno's accommodation scene has something for everyone. Many hotels are open all year. For resorts, head east to the endless stretch of hotels. In the town, there's an ample supply of lovely restored mansions and friendly pensions.

Budget

Sea Front (☎ 28310 51981; www.forthnet.gr/elotia; Arkadiou 159; s/d €30/35; 🔀) This is a delightful pension with six fresh and cheerful studio apartments with sea views and ceiling fans. They can be noisy at night, however.

Olga's Pension (☎ 28310 28665; Souliou 57; s/d €25/35; 🔀) Friendly Olga's is tucked away on touristy but colourful Souliou. A quirky network of terraces, all bursting with flowers and greenery, connects a wide range of basic but colourful rooms, some with bath and sea views and others without. Most have a fridge, TV, fan and basic bathrooms.

Rooms for Rent Anda (☎ 28310 23479; Nikiforou Foka 33; d/tr €30/40; 🔀) A great choice if you have kids, these rooms are a short walk from the municipal park. The prettily furnished rooms have private bathrooms but no other amenities. Some rooms have air-con.

Rethymno Youth Hostel (☎ 28310 22848; www .yhrethymno.com; Tombazi 41; dm €8) The hostel is friendly and well run with free hot showers. Breakfast is available (€2) and there's a bar in the evening. There is no curfew and the place is open all year.

Elizabeth Camping (☎ 28310 28694; camp site per adult/tent €6.50/4.35) The nearest camping ground is near Mysiria beach, 3km east of Rethymno. There's a taverna, snack bar and mini-market, plus a communal fridge, iced drinking water, free beach umbrellas and sun lounges, and a weekly beach BBQ. An Iraklio-bound bus can drop you here.

Mid-Range

Hotel Fortezza (☎ 28310 55551; www.fortezza.gr; Melissinou 16; s/d incl breakfast €57/69; 🔀 P 🛋) This is an isle of calm in a busy neighbourhood. Housed in a refurbished old building in the heart of the old town, the tastefully furnished rooms have TVs, telephones and air-con on demand. After a day of roaming through Rethymno, it's pleasant to relax by the swimming pool.

Hotel Ideon (☎ 28310 28667; ideon@otenet.gr; Plastira 10; s/d €55/78, studio/ste incl breakfast €92/108; 🛋) This polished central establishment is one of the oldest hotels in town, spread over two restored old buildings and a modern wing. The rooms are nicely decorated and well appointed and there are balconies with sea views. The pool in the courtyard spares you the long walk to Rethymno's beach.

Hotel Veneto (☎ 28310 56634; www.veneto.gr; Epimenidou 4; studio/ste incl breakfast €100/120; 🔀) The oldest part of Hotel Veneto dates from the 14th century and it has preserved many of its traditional features without sacrificing modern comforts. The eye-catching rooms of polished wood floors and ceilings also have air-con, satellite TV, telephones, safes and kitchenettes. Rates drop significantly out of high season.

Delfini Hotel (☎ 28310 35245; www.delfinibeach.gr; Stamathioudaki 89; ste incl breakfast €80; 🔀 🛋) If you want a quaint historic building but can't bear to be away from the beach, this beautifully restored 19th-century stone building on the western beach side is a good option. It's a 15-minute walk from the old town and has lovely maisonettes and a renowned Pastopoieion restaurant on the beach.

Palazzo Rimondi (☎ 28310 51289; fax 28310 51013; Xanthoulidou 21 & Trikoupi 16; ste €80-110; 🗷) In the heart of the old city these exquisite studios, each individually decorated, have kitchenettes. A large continental breakfast is included in the room rate.

Top End

Palazzo Vecchio (☎ 28310 35352; fax 28310 25479; www.palazzovecchio.gr; Plateia Iroon Polytehniou & Melissinou; studio/apt incl breakfast €121/140; 🗷 🗷) Located in a quiet neighbourhood near the Fortezza, Palazzo is a small exclusive boutique hotel. You can take breakfast by the pool.

Palazzini di Corina (☎ 28310 21205; www.corina.gr; Damvergi 9; s/d incl breakfast €170/212, ste incl breakfast €255-306; 🗷 🗷) This regal Venetian mansion right near the harbour is one of the classiest boutique hotels in town. It has been beautifully restored, with exposed stone walls, timber vaulted ceiling and lovely internal mosaic courtyard, and is superbly decorated with antique furniture.

EATING

The waterfront along Eleftheriou Venizelou is lined with similar tourist restaurants staffed by fast-talking touts. It's much the same around the Venetian harbour, except that the setting is better and the prices higher. Rethymno does have some excellent restaurants though. The best places in town are in found the web of side streets inland from the harbour, while a couple warrant a trip outside the tourist zone.

Budget

Taverna Kyria Maria (☎ 28310 29078; Moshovitou 20; Cretan dishes €2.40-6.50) For authentic atmosphere head inland down the little side streets to Kyria Maria, behind the Rimondi Fountain. This, traditional taverna has outdoor seating under a leafy trellis, and meals end with a complimentary dessert and shot of raki.

Zisi's (☎ 28310 28814; Old Rethymno-Irakion Rd Mysiria; grills €4-6) Every local seems to recommend Zisi's for cheap, quality Cretan food, particularly the charcoal-grilled meats. It's a

---

---

little out of town along the stretch of beachfront hotels and resorts (on right just before the Creta Palace), but is worth the trek. Dessert and raki is on the house.

Samaria (☎ 28310 24681; Eleftheriou Venizelou) Of the waterfront tavernas, this is one of the few where you'll see locals families eating. There's a large range of *mayirefta* (casseroles), the soups and grills are excellent and the fruit and raki are complimentary.

Mid-Range

Oneirokritis (☎ 28310 58440; Radamanthyos 16; mains €4-7) The menu is innovative, the interior is delightful and the alfresco dining is on one of the prettiest streets in the old town. The house salad is based on avocado, plus you will find sun-dried tomatoes and roast eggplant (aubergine) for vegetarians.

Thalassografia (☎ 28310 52569; Kefalogiannidon 33; mezedes €2-8) This excellent *mezedopoleio* is the place to watch the sunset and try some fine Cretan mezedes, as well as more hearty meals. The setting is breathtaking, with views over the sea and the imposing *fortezza* (fortress), and the service is friendly.

Bourbos (☎ 28310 52214; Eleftheriou Venizelou 75; mezedes €2.70-4.50) It's easy to miss this small waterfront ouzeri, a little gem among the mayhem of the beach road. Its mezedes are first rate and served in tasteful clay dishes. Nothing is precooked and there are daily specials cooked in a clay pot. Try the exquisite creamy mushroom *saganaki* and tangy red pepper fritters.

Fanari (☎ 28310 54849; Kefalogiannidon 15; mezedes €2.50-4.90) West of the Venetian harbour, this welcoming waterfront taverna serves good mezedes, fresh fish and Cretan cuisine. The Bekri meze (pork with wine and peppers) is excellent or try the local specialty, *apakia* (smoked pork). The home-made wine is decent, too.

Castelvecchio (☎ 28310 50886; Himaras 29; grills €6-10.30) The affable Valantis will make you really feel at home in the garden terrace of this family taverna located on the edge of the *fortezza*. Try the *kleftiko* baked lamb or their variation on mousaka with yogurt.

Lemonokipos (☎ 28310 57087; Ethnikis Antistaseos 100; mains €5.50-8) Dine among the lemon trees in the lovely courtyard of this well-respected taverna in the old quarter. It's good typical Cretan fare, with a good range of vegetarian dishes and lots of tasty appetisers.

Top End

Avli (☎ 28310 26213; www.avli.com; cnr Xanthoudidou 22 & Radamanthyos; mains €11-16). This former Venetian villa is the place for a romantic evening out or at least one with maximum ambience. The food is superb and there's an idyllic enclosed garden for alfresco dining, with artful displays and décor. The wine bar in the adjacent old stables boasts more than 300 Greek wines.

Prima Plora (☎ 28310 24925; Akrotiriou 2; seafood meze €5.50-16) This stunning contemporary restaurant on the developing beachfront strip on the western side of town is worth the hike. All white and light inside, there are tables right on the water near an old Venetian water pump. Beyond the cool décor, chef Michalis offers sophisticated seafood dishes such as prawns with ouzo on rice and a great mixed salad with rocket, wild greens and pistachios.

Vasilis (☎ 28310 22967; Nearhou 10; fish per kg €45) The enticing display of fish in the showcase is no mere show. It's top-quality stuff and of the harbour-side fish tavernas, local foodies consider it the best. Fish mezedes are also a good option, as is *kakavia* (a kind of Cretan bouillabaisse).

ENTERTAINMENT
Bars & Discos

The bars and cafés along El Venizelou fill up on summer evenings with pink-skinned tourists, dazed from the sun and nursing tropical drinks.

Rethymno's livelier nightlife is concentrated in the cluster of bars, clubs and discos around Nearhou in the Venetian harbour area as well as the waterfront bars off Plastira Square, which are popular with younger locals.

The trendy new lounge bars tend to be more expensive and a loud place for a drink rather than for serious partying, for which you need to go to full-on clubs or wait till very late.

Fortezza Disco (Nearhou 20; ⏱ 11pm-dawn) This is the town's showpiece disco. It's big and flashy with three bars, a laser show and a well-groomed international crowd that starts drifting in around midnight.

Rock Club Cafe (☎ 28310 31047; Petihaki 8; ⏱ 9pm-dawn) RCC has been one of Rethymno's trendiest hang-outs for a while and still kicks on. A crowd of young professionals and tourists fills the club nightly.

Notes (☎ 28310 29785; Himaras 27; ⏱ 10pm-late) Notes is a classic little bar with a polished wood bar, and was opened by a musician who has an excellent selection of Greek music and encourages art.

Figaro (☎ 28310 29431; Vernardou 21; ☎ noon-late) Housed in an ingeniously restored old building, Figaro is an atmospheric 'art and music' all-day bar that attracts a subdued crowd for drinks, snacks and its excellent mix of music.

Baja Beach Club (☎ 28310 20333; Platanias) On the old highway east of the town, this is probably the biggest beach bar on the island, partying day and night. During the day it is packed with people of all ages enjoying the beach and huge pool.

Of the clubs around the Venetian port, the popular places were **Arabia** (☎ 28310 20375; Nearhou 26) and **Loca** (Nearhou 24), which play mainstream music in summer for tourists, and **Budha** (Salaminos 30), a huge dance club in a former cinema.

Cinemas

Cinema Asteria (☎ 28310 22830; Melissinou 21; tickets €6; ⏱ 9pm) is a small open-air cinema showing late-release movies.

RETHYMNO

SHOPPING

Rethymno's shopping strip is relatively compact and you will find an assortment of shops selling everything from souvenirs to high-end jewellery. The waterfront has mostly souvenir shops, but you'll find better-quality mainstream merchandise on Arkadiou. Souliou is crammed with shops of every kind and fun to wander through. Don't miss the Thursday market on Dimitrakaki for fresh produce, clothing and odds and ends.

Omodamos (☎ 28310 58763; www.omodamos.com; Souliou 3) The original ceramic designs in this shop are made by leading ceramicists from around Greece. Look out for Vangelis Patseas' unique stoneware dolls.

Xenia (☎ 28310 27411; Arkadiou 32) A Cretan summer may make it difficult to think about leather outer wear, but the suede and leather here is buttery soft and is made into elegant ladies' suits, jackets and coats.

Zaharias Theodorakis (☎ 28310 22738; Katehaki 4) Zaharias Theodorakis turns out onyx bowls and goblets on the lathe at his small workshop.

I Melissa (☎ 28310 29601; Ethnikis Andistasis 23) In addition to handmade icons, Melissa sells candles, incense, oil lamps and other fragrant substances.

Atelier (☎ 28310 24440; Himaras 27) Frosso Bora's pottery workshop has a wide selection of original ceramic creations as well as icons. There are also good-value rooms above the workshop.

GETTING THERE & AWAY
Boat

ANEK (☎ 28310 29221; www.anek.gr; Arkadiou 250) operates a daily ferry between Rethymno and Piraeus (€24, nine hours) leaving both Rethymno and Piraeus at 8pm.

Bus

From the **bus station** (☎ 28310 22212; Igoumenou Gavriil) there are hourly services to both Hania (€5.55, one hour) and Iraklio (€5.90, 1½ hours). There's a bus in each direction every half-hour in summer, and every hour in winter. In summer there are also eight buses a day to Plakias (€3.30, one hour), four to Agia Galini (€4.40, 1½ hours), three to Moni Arkadiou (€2, 40 minutes), one to Omalos (€10.20, two hours) and two to Preveli (€3.30). The morning bus to Plakias contin-

ues to Hora Sfakion (€6.30, two hours). Services to these destinations are greatly reduced in low season.

GETTING AROUND

Auto Pappas (☎ 28310 58324; Sofokli Venizelou 21) has reasonable rates on car rentals.

Auto Motor Sports (☎ 28310 24858; www.automoto sport.com.gr; Sofokli Venizelou 48) rents cars and has 300 motorbikes, from mopeds and 50cc bikes to a Harley 1200cc.

AROUND RETHYMNO

The hinterland villages of Rethymno make for pleasant scooter or motorbike excursions. The hills are not too taxing, the roads not too busy and the scenery is pleasantly verdant. There are at least a couple of villages to the southwest of Rethymno that make for an ideal afternoon jaunt.

The village of **Atsipopoulo**, just west of Rethymno, is worth a visit just for its renowned souvlaki made from fresh local meat – look for the fullest taverna on the square.

Episkopi, 23km west of Rethymno, is a pretty, traditional town of winding lanes and tiny houses, overlooking the valley. The springs and waterfalls of Argyroupolis are a delightfully cool surprise while the lovely village of **Asi Gonia** will give you some insight into traditional life in Crete. Every year around St George's day (April 23), Asi Gonia holds a stock-breeder's festival during which thousands of goats and sheep are gathered around the church. After the church service, the flock is milked and the milk given out to the crowd. The festival continues into the evening.

ARGYROUPOLIS ΑΡΓΥΡΟΎΠΟΛΗ
pop 402

When the summer heat becomes too intense for the beach, you'll find a natural, outdoor air-conditioning system at Argyroupolis, 25km southwest from Rethymno. At the bottom of this village is a watery oasis formed by mountain springs that keeps the temperature markedly cooler than on the coast. Running through aqueducts, washing down walls, seeping from stones and pouring from spigots, the gushing spring water supplies the entire city of Rethymno.

DETOUR: ADELE

For a glimpse of rural life past and present it's worth a visit to **Agreco** (☎ 28310 72129; www .grecotel.gr; admission free but call in advance), which has recreated a 17th-century farm and mini village on a huge estate near the village of Adele, about 13km from Rethymno. The working farm prides itself on being a showcase of organic, environment-friendly traditional farming methods and has modern equipment as well as old machinery, including an old donkey-driven olive press, watermill and wine press. You can observe the various activities of the farm – including the making of cheese, bread, raki and wine – as well as wander around the stockyard and garden. The estate is owned by the Daskalantonakis family, who have the Grecotel hotel chain. There is also a *kafeneio* (coffee house) and shop selling traditional products from the farm and the region. You can end your visit with a meal at the excellent taverna overlooking the vineyard, which serves authentic Cretan cuisine using the farm's produce.

RETHYMNO

Towering chestnut and plane trees and luxuriant vegetation create a shady, restful spot for lunch among the waterfalls and fountains that have been incorporated into all the tavernas.

Argyroupolis is built on the ruins of the ancient city of Lappa, so there's plenty to see in and around the village. The villagers maintain a traditional lifestyle, largely undisturbed by tourism, but are proud of their heritage and eager to show you around.

Information

There is no post office, OTE, tourist office or travel agency, but the innovative Stelios Marousakas at the **Lappa Avocado Shop** (☎ 28310 81070), just off the main square, is a good source of information and provides visitors with town maps. While you are there, pick up a supply of their excellent avocado-based creams and soaps, which are made from the family's avocado plantation and exported to Athens and France.

Sights

The main square is recogniseable by the 17th-century Venetian **Church of Agios Ioannis**. There is a quaint private **museum of village life** on the main street above a mini-market run by the Zografakis family next door (see p130). Over 40 years, the dynamic Kyria Eleftheria has amassed an eclectic collection of family heirlooms and historic items from nearby villages, including an old flint lighter and a leather horseshoe repair kit. If it is closed, call in at the taverna or shop and they will give you a private tour.

The old town is entered through the stone archway opposite the church with the Lappa Avocado shop on the left. Roman remnants are scattered amid the Venetian and Turkish structures.

The main stone street will take you past a **Roman gate** on the left with the inscription *Omnia Mundi Fumus et Umbra* (All Things in This World are Smoke and Shadow). In a few metres a narrow street to the right leads down to a 3rd-century-BC **marble water reservoir** with seven interior arches.

Returning to the main road and continuing in the same direction you will see on the left a **Roman mosaic floor**, dating from the 1st century BC. With 7000 pieces in six colours, the well-preserved floor is a good example of design from the Geometric Period.

There are a couple of signposted roads leading to the tavernas clustered around the tumbling springs below the town, but it's best to get a map from Lappa Avocado. A path from the bottom leads you to a **Roman bath** and a water-driven **fulling machine**, which was used to thicken cloth by moistening and beating it. Nearby is **St Mary's Church**, built on a temple devoted to Neptune.

North of the town, a footpath on the right takes you about 50m to a **Roman necropolis** with hundreds of tombs cut into the cliffs. The shady path leads on to a **plane tree** that is supposed to be 2000 years old and is so large that the path runs right through it.

Sleeping & Eating

Lappa Apartments (☎ 28310 81204; d €20-25; ⊠) Right in the village, these homy new apartments set around a courtyard and lovely garden enjoy great views of the mountains. They are fully equipped with good-sized fridges, decent bathrooms and there are barbecue facilities. It is perfect for longer stays or families.

Mikedakis (☎ 28310 81225; r €20) This charming place, half-buried behind trees and flowering bushes, offers spectacular views of the area from its balconies.

In town, you can get some home-style cooking at the **Zografakis** (☎ 28310 81269) taverna. The family also rents decent clean and cheap rooms upstairs and will happily take longer-stay guests on a tour of their farm and orchards.

The tavernas at the springs are a little touristy and overpriced, but you can't go too wrong. Right next to the quaint little chapel in a grotto after which it is named, **Agia Dynamis** (☎ 28310 81210; grills €6.50) serves reasonable Cretan fare, although the house wine was a bit rough. Further along on the left **Athivoles** (☎ 28310 81101; trout per kg €20) has excellent fresh trout, local meat and fine Cretan cuisine.

Getting There & Away
There are three buses from Rethymno (€2.30, 40 minutes) to Argyroupolis from Monday to Friday.

THE HINTERLAND

AMARI VALLEY ΚΟΙΛΆΔΑ ΑΜΑΡΊΟΥ
You'll need your own transport to explore the Amari Valley, southeast of Rethymno, between Mts Psiloritis and Kedros. This region harbours around 40 well-watered, unspoilt villages set amid olive groves, almond and cherry trees and many lovely Byzantine churches. The valley begins in the picturesque village of **Apostoli**, 25km southeast of Rethymno, reached via a scenic drive through a wild and deserted gorge bordered by high cliffs. The turn-off for Apostoli is on the coast 3km east of Rethymno. The road forks at Apostoli and then joins up again 38km to the south, making it possible to do a circular drive around the valley; alternatively, you can continue south to Agia Galini.

Taking the left fork from Apostoli you'll come to the village of **Thronos** with its Church of the Panagia constructed on the remains of an early Christian basilica. The 14th-century frescoes are faded but extraordinarily well executed; the oldest are in the choir stalls. Ask at the *kafeneio* (coffeehouse) next door for the key.

Returning to Apostoli continue south along the main road. The next town is **Agia Fotini**, which is a larger town with a supermarket. The road twists and turns along the scenic valley before it comes to **Meronas**, a little village with big plane trees, and a fine Church of the Panagia. The oldest part of the church is the nave, which was built in the 14th century. The southern side of the church with its elegant portal was added under the Venetians. The highlight of the church is the beautifully restored 14th-century frescoes.

The road continues south to **Gerakari**, an area known for its delicious cherries. From Gerakari a new road continues on to Spili.

MT PSILORITIS ΟΡΟΣ ΨΕΙΛΟΡΙΤΗΣ
The imposing Mt Psiloritis, also known as Mt Idi, is the highest mountain in Crete at 2456m. The eastern base of Mt Psiloritis is the **Nida Plateau**, a wide expanse used for sheep grazing, lying between a circle of imposing mountains. The winding, 22km paved road leading up to the plateau from Anogia is carpeted with wild flowers in the early spring and you'll notice many *mitata* (round stone shepherd's huts) along the way. The mountain's historically important feature is the **Ideon Andron Cave** – the place where, according to legend, the god Zeus was reared. The cave may have been inhabited in the early Neolithic period. It is accessible to visitors but its attraction is more historical.

MONI ARKADIOU ΜΟΝΉ ΑΡΚΑΔΊΟΥ
This 16th-century **monastery** (☎ 28310 83076; museum admission €2; ⏰ 8am-1pm & 3.30-8pm) stands in attractive hill country 23km southeast of Rethymno. The most impressive building of the complex is the Venetian baroque church. Its striking façade has eight slender Corinthian columns and is topped by an ornate triple-belled tower. This façade used to feature on the old 100 drachma note.

In November 1866 the Turks sent massive forces to quell insurrections that were gathering momentum throughout the island. Hundreds of men, women and children who had fled their villages used the monastery as a safe haven. When 2000 Turkish soldiers staged an attack on the building, the Cretans, rather than surrender, set light to a store of gun powder. The explosion killed everyone, Turks included, except one small girl. This

HIKING ON MT PSILORITIS

From the Nida Plateau you can join the east–west E4 trail for the ascent to the summit of Psiloritis known as **Timios Stavros** (Holy Cross). The return trek to the summit can be done in about seven hours from Nida. While you don't need to be an alpine mountaineer to complete the trek, it is a long slog and the views from the summit may be marred by heat haze or cloud cover. Shortly after leaving Nida a spur track leads to **Ideon Andron Cave**, with an altitude of 1495m. Along the way to the summit a number of *mitata* (round stone shepherd's huts) provide occasional sheltering opportunities, should the weather turn inclement, while at the summit of Psiloritis itself is a twin-domed, small dry-stone chapel.

An alternative access or exit route begins (or ends) at **Fourfouras** on the edge of the Amari Valley and a further 3½-hour trek to the west from the summit. There is a prominent mountain refuge run by the EOS (Greek Association of Mountaineers) about halfway along this trail. From Fourfouras you can find onward transport, or continue to follow the E4 to **Spili**. A third access/exit route from the mountain runs to the south and meets the village of **Kamares** (five hours). Halfway along this track you will pass the **Kamares cave** in which a large collection of painted Minoan urns was found and which is a popular day trek in its own right for visitors to the southern side of Psiloritis.

The best maps for anyone planning to walk in this region are the 1:100,000 *Kreta Touristikkarte* or Petrakis' *Rethymno* map (see p213).

sole survivor lived to a ripe old age in a village nearby. A bust of this woman, and the abbot who lit the gun powder, stand outside the monastery.

The exterior of Moni Arkadiou (which is still a working monastery) is coldly impressive but the Venetian church inside dates from 1587 and has a richly decorated Renaissance façade. On the right of the church there is a stairway that leads to a small **museum** commemorating the history of the monastery.

There are buses every day from Rethymno to Moni Arkadiou (€2, 40 minutes) at 6am, 10.30am and 2.30pm, returning at 7am, noon and 4pm.

MARGARITES ΜΑΡΓΑΡΙΤΕΣ
pop 331

Known for its fine pottery, this tiny town is invaded by tour buses in the morning but it's a brief interlude. By the afternoon all is calm and you can enjoy wonderful views over the valley from the taverna terraces on the main square, dominated by giant eucalyptus trees.

There is only one road that runs through town to the town square, where the bus stops. There is no bank, post office or travel agency, but you'll find more than 20 ceramic studios on and around the main street. The pottery is of mixed quality and taste, but if you skip the garish pieces that line the main street, there are some authentic local designs and quality pieces at a few places. You could visit the traditional workshop of septuagenarian potter **Manolis Syragopoulos** (☎ 28340 92363) who comes from a long line of potters and is the only one left that uses manual wheels and a wood-fired kiln to make pottery the way his great grandfather did. It's about 1km outside the town on your left.

The finer pieces in town can be found at Konstantinos Gallios' excellent studio **Ceramic Art** (☎ 28340 92304), in a lane at the far end of town, and the slick **Kerameion** (☎ 28340 92135) on the main street, where George Dalamvelas is happy to explain the techniques and history of the town. Dalamvelas uses largely local clay and has many pieces based on Minoan designs. The traditional potters use local clay, collected from about 4km away at the foot of Psiloritis, which is of such fine quality it needs only one firing and no glazing – the outside smoothed with a pebble. You will see many pieces bearing the special flower motif of the area.

From Margarites, you can visit **Ancient Eleftherna** and other Minoan settlements and Byzantine monasteries in the area.

Sleeping & Eating
Kouriton House (☎ 28340 55828; d incl breakfast €85) Just outside Margarites in Tzanakiana, this beautifully restored 1750 mansion has been classed as a protected historic monument

RETHYMNO

and is one of the Crete's newest cultural and agro-tourism ventures. Philologist Anastasia Friganaki is keen to show guests around the area's natural and historic attractions, and demonstrate traditional methods of making honey, picking herbs and greens and cooking Cretan and Minoan cuisine.

Irini Apartments (☎ 28340 92494; piterm@hotmail.com; d €25) The only accommodation in town is Irini Apartments, which has well-equipped rooms with kitchenettes and TV. It is on the southern side of the village, on the left as you come from Rethymno.

Mandalos (☎ 28340 92294) On the shady main square with lovely views is this well-regarded taverna and kafeneio.

Dionysios (☎ 28340 92100) Just off the main street in a little alley, this is a good shop to buy ham, sausage and blackberry pies. Across the street is a cheese shop with big wheels of local cheese.

Getting There & Away
There are two buses daily from Rethymno (€2, 30 minutes) Monday to Friday.

PERAMA TO ANOGIA
The roads leading southeast from the small commercial centre of **Perama** to Anogia are stunning and pass through a series of cosy villages and bustling market towns along the foothills of Mt Psiloritis.

From Perama, take the northeast turn-off to the fascinating **Melidoni cave**. Over 300 villagers took refuge from the Turkish army in the cave in 1824. When the villagers refused to emerge, the Turks threw burning materials through a hole in the top of the cave and asphyxiated everyone. After paying your respects at the martyrs at a monument, you can wander through chambers filled with several stalactites and stalagmites.

Continuing east turn left towards the pretty village of **Garazo**, which has a couple of tavernas and a post office. On the way, there is a turn-off at the village of Moutzana for **Episkopi**, a charming tiny village that was once the bishopric under Venetian rule. The town has many stone houses, including several well-preserved Venetian mansions that are being restored and turned into museums. There are some frescoes still evident in the ruins of the 15th-century **Church of Episkopi** and a Venetian **water fountain** at the end of the town next to the bridge.

BACK TO THE FARM

Agrotourism is picking up in Crete and **Enagron** (☎ 28340 61611; www.enagron.gr; studios up to 4 people €58-75) at Axos is a fine example of classy rural developments. This farm and accommodation complex hosts occasional cooking seminars based on Cretan cuisine and local produce, and allows guests to participate in any aspect of its agricultural and productive life, from raki- or cheesemaking by the local shepherd to picking wild greens. It's hardly roughing it – there is a pool in the middle overlooking the mountains, comfortable traditionally furnished stone-built studios with fireplaces, a lovely taverna serving their own fresh organic produce, and a main communal area with antiques and a country estate feel. Enagron is part of the trend towards year-round tourism. They also run guided walks and horse or donkey rides in the surrounding countryside. You can visit the farm and eat at the restaurant by booking ahead.

From Episkopi you can continue southeast on a scenic route that takes you past the area's largest town, **Zoniana**. In this region everyone seems to be dressed in black and drive a pick-up truck.

Look for signs to the **Sfendoni Cave**. According to legend, Sfendoni is named after a rebel or a robber, and it's the most spectacular cave on the island. Stalactites, stalagmites and strange rock formations make for an eerie experience. The front of the cave was a hideout for Greek fighters against the Turks, but most of the large cave was undisturbed. Walkways make exploration easier, but it's still important to watch your step.

The northern road from Garazo takes you to the village of **Axos**, which has the kind of lazy Cretan ambience that has made it a popular stop for tour buses from Iraklio and Rethymno. During the day the village is quiet, but at night the few tavernas with open-air terraces host 'Cretan folklore evenings' for the tourists.

ANOGIA ΑΝΏΓΕΙΑ
pop 2454
If ever there was a village in Crete that embodies the quintessential elements that make up the 'real' Crete, it is Anogia, a bucolic

village perched on the flanks of Mt Psiloritis 37km southwest of Iraklio. Enjoying a more temperate climate than you'll find on the coasts, Anogia is well known for its rebellious spirit and its determination to hang on to its undiluted Cretan character. It's also known for its stirring music and has spawned a disproportionate number of Crete's best-known musicians (see p48).

Anogia is a macho town where the kafeneia on the main square is frequented by moustachioed men, the older ones often wearing traditional dress. The women stay behind the scenes or flog traditional crafts that hang all over the shops in town.

During WWII Anogia was a centre of resistance to the Germans, who massacred all the men in the village in retaliation for their role in sheltering Allied troops and aiding in the kidnap of General Kreipe. Today, Anogia is the centre of a prosperous sheep husbandry industry and a burgeoning tourist trade, bolstered as much by curious Greeks as by foreign travellers seeking a Crete away from the hype of the coastal resorts. If you come to Anogia, plan to stay a few days; you never know what might happen.

Orientation & Information
The town is spread out on a hillside with the textile shops in the lower half and most accommodation and businesses in the upper half. There's an Agricultural Bank with an ATM, a post office and an OTE in the upper village. Moving between the upper and lower villages often involves some steep climbing.

Infocost (☎ 28340 31808; per hr €3; ⏲ 5pm-late) in the upper village has Internet access.

Festivals & Events
At any given time there is likely to be some event (official or not) taking place in Anogia. Spontaneous, lively *mandinades* sessions take place at any time, but particularly during the sheep-shearing season in July, accompanied by copious amounts of raki. Pistol shots often ring into the night air.

A **wedding** in Anogia is a very special event involving the entire village. Everyone gets dressed up, parades through the village to the accompaniment of live music and dances all night in the square (see the boxed text on p134) or at one of the huge tavernas on the outskirts of town. Follow the pick-up trucks carting huge chunks of meat.

In late July each year the **Yakinthia Festival** (www.yakinthia.com) is held in and around Anogia. This musical, cultural and theatrical festival includes open-air concerts – usually on makeshift stages in sheep paddocks on the slopes of Mt Psiloritis. Look around for posters in Anogia from mid-July onwards, or check the Internet for details.

Sleeping
Most domatia are in the upper village, enjoying the view to the north and the cool breezes.

Hotel Aristea (☎ 28340 31459; d incl breakfast €40) In the upper village, the friendly Aristea also enjoys good views from these simple but well-outfitted rooms with TV, private bathrooms and balconies. A new set of studios is being built next door.

Rooms Aris (☎ 28340 31460; d €30) Next door to Aristea, Rooms Aris enjoys perhaps the best views in Anogia. Rooms are clean and cosy and all have new bathrooms.

Rent Rooms Arkadi (☎ 28340 31055; d/tr €30/40) On the busy main street in the upper village, Arkadi offers comfortable accommodation with fridges but shared bathrooms.

Rent Rooms Kitros (☎ 28340 31429; d €25) This is the only accommodation in the lower village. Rooms are reasonably priced and are close to the much more atmospheric lower village. They have TV but share a bathroom between two rooms.

Eating
Eating in Anogia can be a bit of a hit-and-miss affair, with meat the dominant food. Some of the attractive restaurants in the lower village square offer little more than the local spaghetti-and-cheese specialty and chunks of char-grilled lamb.

Aetos (☎ 28340 31262; grills €4-7.50) This popular taverna has a giant charcoal grill cooking meat out the front and fantastic views out the back. It is traditionally furnished and has good Cretan cooking. A local special is *ofto*, a flame-cooked lamb or goat.

Ta Skalomata (☎ 28340 31316; grills €3.50-6.80) The oldest restaurant in town, Ta Skalomata provides a wide variety of grills and Cretan dishes at very reasonable prices. Zucchini with cheese and aubergine (€3.20) is very tasty, as is their home-baked bread. It is on the eastern side of the upper village and enjoys great views.

Taverna Kitros (☎ 28340 31429; grills €5-6.50) In the lower village, this eatery does a presentable job of dishes like *gigandes* (lima beans) in oil, or lamb and potatoes. The homemade wine and raki is very good, too.

Delina (☎ 28340 31701) The queen of tavernas in Anogia, the capacious Delina is owned and occasionally patronised by internationally renowned Cretan lyra player Vasilis Skoulas. The mezedes are high class, as are the grills and salads. The huge taverna, which hosts many functions, is about 2km outside of Anogia on the road to the Nida Plateau.

If the square in the lower village is a bit intimidating for a coffee stop, head further up to the lovely square next to Agios Yiorgos church, where you must try the divine *galaktoboureko* (custard pastries) made from sheep's milk at **Skandali Zaharoplasteio** (☎ 28340 31236), along with their home-made ice cream.

Getting There & Away

There are five buses daily from Iraklio (€2.30, one hour), and two buses daily Monday to Friday from Rethymno (€3.90, 1¼ hours).

A CRETAN AFFAIR

Cretans from all over Crete will come to Anogia if they know a wedding is in the air. It is truly an unforgettable experience and all the village joins in – 2000 guests are common. On the day of the wedding, family and friends gather to accompany the groom with a musical procession through the village to the bride's house. The staccato rattle of a machine gun, or the crack of pistols fired into the air signal the start of the groom's walk. At the bride's house, the groom's party is met with more machine gun fusillades, as well as wine, lamb and chunks of watermelon. The combined parties then make their way to the church for the actual ceremony. After the ceremony the parties retire for food and drink and then the music and dancing begins in the village square. It doesn't end until the sun comes up the following day. Ask around if you are in Anogia on the weekend; you might just score an invite to a most memorable event.

ARMENI ΑΡΜΕΝΟΙ

Heading south from Rethymno, there is a turn-off to the right to the Late Minoan **Cemetery of Armeni**, 2km before the modern village of Armeni. Some 200 tombs were carved into the rock between 1300 and 1150 BC in the midst of an oak forest. The curious feature of this cemetery is that there does not seem to have been any sizable town nearby that would have accounted for so many tombs. Pottery, weapons and jewellery excavated from the tombs are now on display at the Archaeological Museum (p123) in Rethymno. At Armeni a good place to stop for lunch is the simple **Alekos Taverna** (☎ 28320 41185), which has a small but good selection of traditional dishes (the rabbit is recommended).

SPILI ΣΠΗΛΙ

pop 642

Spili (*spee*-lee) is a pretty mountain village with cobbled streets, rustic houses and plane trees. Its centrepiece is a unique Venetian fountain, which spurts water from 19 lion heads. Bring along your own water containers and fill up with the best water on the island.

Spili is no longer an undiscovered hideaway. Tourist buses on their way to the southern coast regularly stop in the town during the day, but in the evening Spili belongs to the locals. It is a great base for exploring the region or at least a good spot for lunch.

Orientation & Information

The post office and bank are on the main street. The OTE is up a side street, north of the central square. The bus stop is just south of the square. There are two ATMs on the main street and you can check mail at Café Babis near the fountain.

Sleeping & Eating

Heracles Rooms (☎ /fax 28320 22411; d €30) Signposted from the main road are these clean and nicely furnished rooms with great mountain views. Each room has large insect screens on the door. A hearty breakfast is available for €8.50 per person.

Costas Inn (☎ 28320 22040; fax 28320 22043; d/tr incl breakfast €35/45) This is the only pension encountered with bathrobes, which are part of the homy atmosphere at these well-kept,

DETOUR: PATSOS

Near the alluring little village of **Patsos** is the **Church of Agios Antonios** in a cave above a picturesque gorge. The cave was an important sanctuary for the Minoans and the Romans, and is still a pilgrimage destination on 17 January. You can drive from Rethymno, or walk from Spili along a scenic 10km dirt track.

To reach the track from Spili walk along 28 October, passing the lion fountain on your right. Turn right onto Thermopylon and ascend to the Spili–Gerakari road. Turn right here and eventually you will come to a sign for Gerakari. Take the dirt track to the left, and at the fork bear right. At the cross-roads turn right, and continue on the main track for about one hour to a T-junction on the outskirts of Patsos. Turn left to get to the cave.

pleasant rooms. They also have satellite TV, radio, ceiling fans, fridge and use of a washing machine and, for those on longer stays, the pool at a nearby estate. Breakfast (their own fresh eggs) is downstairs at **Taverna Costas** (Cretan specials €2.50-5), which has good home cooking and organic wine and raki. Try the traditional sweets for dessert.

Maria and Costas (☎ 28320 22436; grills €4-6) Easily recognisable from the gourds hanging in the vine- and wisteria-covered courtyard on the main road, they offer good Cretan fare (try the rabbit or stuffed zucchini flowers), as well as charcoal-grilled meats.

You could also try **Yianni's** (☎ 28320 22707; specials €4-5) past the fountain for excellent *mayirefta*, such as lamb in wine, or **Taverna Stratidakis** (☎ 28320 22006; mains €4.50-5), which has the specials of the day in pots at the back of the taverna and a lovely balcony.

Getting There & Away

Spili is on the Rethymno–Agia Galini bus route, which has four daily services.

THE SOUTH COAST

As you near the coast from Spili the scenery becomes more dramatic and takes in marvellous views of the Libyan sea. Heading west then south towards the coast at Plakias you will pass through the dramatic **Kourtaliotis Gorge** through which the river Megalopotamos rumbles on its way to the sea at **Preveli Beach**.

PLAKIAS ΠΛΑΚΙΑΣ
pop 177

The south coast town of Plakias was once a tranquil fishing village before it became a retreat for backpackers. The package-tour operators have not yet totally destroyed the ambience and relaxed outlook of what is now quite a developed but pleasant resort town, which is still popular with backpackers and independent travellers. Off-season it attracts many families and an older crowd.

Plakias offers a good range of independent accommodation, some pretty decent eating options, good regional walks, a large sandy beach and enough nightlife to keep you entertained.

Orientation & Information

It's easy to find your way around Plakias. One street skirts the beach and another runs parallel to it one block back. The bus stop is at the middle of the waterfront.

Plakias has two ATMs, while **Monza Travel Agency** (☎ 28320 31882), near the bus stop, offers currency exchange and can help with accommodation, car hire and excursions. The post office is on the street off Monza Travel.

You can check mail at **Ostraco Bar** (☎ 28320 31710; per hr €4.50; ◷ 9am-late) on the main street or at the **Youth Hostel Plakias** (☎ 28320 32118; per hr €4.50).

Activities

Plakias is an excellent base to explore the surrounding region. There are well-worn **walking paths** uphill to Myrthios overlooking the sea and to the scenic village of Sellia, the Moni Finika, Lefkogia, and a lovely walk along the spectacular Kourtaliotis Gorge to Moni Preveli. An easy 30-minute path to Myrthios village above Plakias begins just before the youth hostel. A booklet and map of walks around Plakias is on sale at the mini-market by the bus stop.

Phoenix Diving Club (☎ 28320 31206; pheondiv@ otenet.gr), near the Ostraco Bar, offers day-long scuba-diving programmes and a certification course, as well as snorkelling trips.

RETHYMNO

DETOUR: ASOMATOS

On the road south to Plakias and Preveli you will pass the village of **Asomatos**, where it is worth stopping at the fascinating private **Museum of Papa Mihalis Georgoulakis** (☎ 28320 31674; www.plakias.net; admission €2.50; ☉ 10am-3pm). The octogenarian priest has amassed an extraordinary collection of ecclesiastical and historical artefacts, memorabilia, weapons, letters and posters from the Cretan resistance, icons and household items. It is displayed in a quirky, cluttered house in the middle of the village, which has a charming internal courtyard and a small café where you can buy the family's raki and oil.

There's also open-water diving courses (€300), discover scuba diving (€65), shore dive (€47) and snorkelling courses (€27).

Sleeping

There is a wide range of independent domatia on offer and they can fill up in peak season. Most are signposted on a communal wooden sign board next to Monza Travel.

Pension Thetis (☎ 28320 31430; fax 28320 31987; studio €35; ⚡) Thetis is a very pleasant, family oriented set of studios. Upgraded in 2004, the rooms have fridge, cooking facilities, coffee maker and TV. Relax in the cool and shady garden where there is a small play park for kids.

Castello (☎ /fax 28320 31112; studio €28-33; ⚡ P) It is the relaxed owner Christos and his leafy and shady garden that makes this place a happy haven. All rooms are cool, clean and fridge-equipped and have cooking facilities. There are also big two-bedroom apartments ideal for families (€45 to €55).

Pension Afrodite (☎ 28320 31266; s/d30/40; ⚡) This upmarket pension is in a lovely garden and the cheery spotless rooms have more mod cons than some hotels, including a kettle, safe and hairdryer. The breakfast is excellent but you can get a lower rate without it.

Morfeas Rent Rooms (☎ /fax 28320 31583; www.morpheas-apartments-plakias-crete-greece.com; s/d €25/38, studio €43-63; ⚡) Close to the bus stop and above a supermarket, Morfeas has light, airy and attractively furnished rooms with fridge and phone. It has, in addition, studios and apartments with self-catering facilities for two to four persons.

Neos Alianthos Garden (☎ 28320 31280; www.alianthos.gr; d incl breakfast €55; ⚡ ⚡) This small hotel is at the entrance to town next to the road overlooking the sea. It's comfortably furnished in traditional Cretan style and has two pools.

Hotel Livykon (☎ 28320 31216; fax 28320 31420; s/c €20/25) This fairly ordinary hotel on the seafront has basic, small and relatively cheap rooms. The room rate does at least include air-conditioning and there is a fridge.

Youth Hostel Plakias (☎ 28320 32118; www.yhplakias.com; dm €7.50; ⚡) For independent travellers this is *the* place to stay in Plakias. Manager Chris from the UK has created a very friendly place with spotless dorms, green lawns, volleyball court and Internet access. He also recently upgraded the toilets and showers and built a shady new porch. Partying is much in evidence here helped along by Chris's eclectic music collection. Many guests stay for up to a month. It's a 10-minute signposted walk from the bus stop.

Camping Apollonia (☎ 28320 31318; per adult/tent €5/3; ⚡) On the right of the main approach road to Plakias, this place has a restaurant, mini-market, bar and swimming pool. While the site is shaded, it all looks rather scruffy and run down.

Eating

With a few exceptions, the waterfront restaurants that tout picture menus are mediocre and bland. Choose assiduously.

O Tasomanolis (☎ 28320 31129; fish €33-38) This traditional fish taverna on the western end of the beach is run by a keen fisherman. You can sample his catch on a pleasant terrace overlooking the beach, grilled and accompanied with wild greens and wine. Look for the colourful fishing boat across the road.

Kri Kri (☎ 28320 32223; pizzas €4.50-7.10) Kri Kri, near the bus stop, makes excellent pizzas in the wood-fired oven. The vegetarian 'rustic' pizza is a predictable and wise choice from its long list of pizza combos, but the more adventurous could try the banana pizza.

Taverna Sofia (☎ 28320 31333; mains €3.90-6.50) In business since 1969, Sofia's is a solid choice, with daily specials. Choose from the trays in the window. Try the lamb in yogurt or lamb fricassee. The same family runs the other Sofia on the waterfront near the bus stop.

Siroko (☎ 28320 32055; grills €4.20-6.50) Further along from O Tasomanolis, Siroko is a popular family-run taverna. Try the lamb in egg and lemon sauce or a mixed seafood grill. Vegetarians will appreciate the range of enticing daily ladera dishes.

Taverna Christos (☎ 28320 31472; mains €4.10-9.50) One of the best waterfront tavernas, Christos has a romantic terrace overlooking the sea. It has a good choice of main Cretan dishes and fresh fish.

Nikos Souvlaki (☎ 28320 31921; grills €4-5) Popular with backpackers and just inland from Monza Travel Agency, this cheap souvlaki place with an edge has a monster mixed grill of gyros, souvlaki, sausage, hamburger and chips.

Also recommended is **Apanemo** (☎ 28320 31144; grills €3-5) for its excellent grills. It's on the western side of town.

Entertainment

Plakias has a good nightlife scene in the summer. Travellers tend to gravitate to a couple of key hang-outs. The younger and young-at-heart congregate at Nufaro, next to the Kri Kri where the youth hostel crew DJs at night, while Meltemi on the beach at the eastern side of town kicks in at around 2am and is the most popular club in town. Be prepared for a long night!

Getting There & Away

Plakias has good bus connections in summer, but virtually none in winter. A timetable is displayed at the bus stop. In summer there are eight buses a day to Rethymno (€3.30, one hour) and a seasonal bus to Hora Sfakion. It's possible to get to Agia Galini from Plakias by catching a Rethymno bus to the Koxare junction (referred to as Bale on timetables) and waiting for a bus to Agia Galini.

Getting Around

Cars Allianthos (☎ 28320 31851) is a reliable car-hire outlet.

Easy Ride (☎ 28320 20052; www.easyride.reth.gr), close to the post office, rents out mountain bikes and bicycles (€7 to €10 per day) with baby seats and kids bikes available, as well as scooters and motorbikes (€16 to €36 per day). Longer rentals are cheaper.

AROUND PLAKIAS
Myrthios Μύρθιος
pop 235

This pleasant village, perched on a hillside overlooking Plakias, used to be popular as a cheaper alternative to Plakias within easy reach of the beach. There's little difference these days (the popular hostel has closed down), but it is still a reasonable option for staying in the area. Apart from taking in the views, the main activity is walking, which you'll be doing a lot of unless you have your own transport. It's about 20 minutes from Plakias on foot.

Niki's Studios & Rooms (☎ 28320 31593; r/studio/tr €18/20/25; 🛏) is comfortable and has basic rooms, plus studios with kitchenette, fridge and air-con. It's just below the popular taverna **Panorama** (☎ 28320 32077; mains €4-6.50) run by one of the many Germans who have fallen in love with Crete.

Plateia (☎ 28320 31560; mains €4.40-6.50), a friendly place preferred by Greeks, has good views from the stone-built courtyard and food that appeals to a more discerning local palate. Pork fricassee served with potatoes (€5.80) is a good bet, along with a drop of the house wine.

Moni Preveli Μονή Πρέβελη

The well-maintained **Moni Preveli** (☎ 28320 31246; www.preveli.org; admission €2.50; 🕐 8am-5pm mid-Mar–May, 9am-1.30pm & 3.30-8pm Jun-Oct) stands in splendid isolation high above the Libyan sea. On the way to the monastery there is a prominent war memorial on the cliffs with statues of a gun-toting priest and Commonwealth soldier. From the car park outside the monastery, there's a lookout with a stunning panoramic view over the southern coast.

The origins of the monastery are unclear because most historical documents were lost in the many attacks inflicted upon it over the centuries. The year '1701' is carved on the monastery fountain but it may have been founded much earlier. Like most of Crete's monasteries, it played a significant role in the islanders' rebellion against Turkish rule. It became a centre of resistance during 1866, causing the Turks to set fire to it and destroy surrounding crops. After the Battle of Crete in WWII, many Allied soldiers were sheltered here by Abbot Agathangelos before their evacuation to Egypt. In retaliation, the Germans plundered the monastery.

RETHYMNO

The monastery's **museum** contains a candelabra presented by grateful British soldiers after the war. Built in 1836, the church is worth a visit for its excellent collection of more than 100 icons, some dating back to the early 17th century. There are several fine works by the monk Mihail Prevelis, including a wonderful icon screen containing a gaily painted *Adam and Eve in Paradise* in the middle of the altar.

Plans are afoot for a new purpose-built museum to house the precious icons and artefacts from the current museum.

From the road to the monastery, a road leads downhill to a large car park from where a steep foot track leads down to Preveli Beach.

From June through August there are two buses daily from Rethymno to Moni Preveli (€3.30).

Preveli Beach Παραλία Πρέβελη

Known officially as Paralia Finikodasous (Palm Beach), Preveli Beach, at the mouth of the Kourtaliotis Gorge, is one of Crete's most photographed and popular beaches. The river Megalopotamos meets the back end of the beach before it conveniently loops around its assorted bathers and empties into the Libyan sea. It's fringed with oleander bushes and palm trees and used to be popular with freelance campers before even that simple pleasure was officially outlawed. The beach is mainly sand, has some natural shade at either end – although umbrellas and loungers can be hired – and

enjoys cool and clean protected water that is ideal for swimming and diving. There are a couple of seasonal snack bars.

Walk up the palm-lined banks of the river and you'll come to cold, freshwater pools ideal for a swim. There are also pedal boats for hire. A steep path leads down to the beach from a car park below Moni Preveli, or you can drive to within several hundred metres of the beach by following a signposted 5km drivable dirt road from a stone bridge to the left just off the Moni Preveli main road. From the end of the dirt road walk west along a 500m access track over the headland and you're home.

You can get to Preveli from Plakias by boat in summer for €8 return or by taxi boat from Agia Galini for about €15 return.

Beaches between Plakias & Preveli

Between Plakias and Preveli Beach there are several secluded coves popular with freelance campers and nudists. Some are within walking distance of Plakias, via **Damnoni Beach**. To reach them ascend the path behind the Plakias Bay Hotel. Just before the track starts to descend, turn right into an olive grove.

At the first T-junction turn left and at the second turn right. Where six tracks meet, take the one signposted to the beach. Walk to the end of Damnoni Beach and take the track to the right, which passes above the coves. Damnoni Beach itself is pleasant out of high season, despite being dominated by the giant Hapimag tourist complex.

THE PREVELLY WAY

In August 1941 Australian soldier Geoff Edwards was caught up in the Battle of Crete and cornered by invading German troops. Rescued by a shepherd in the harsh mountains of southern Crete he was delivered to the safety and protection of the monks of the Preveli monastery. He was eventually evacuated on the HMS *Thresher* and found his way back to Western Australia after the war.

In gratitude for his rescue by the monks at Preveli he built and dedicated a chapel at a settlement in the south of Western Australia that he called Prevelly. St John the Theologian Chapel of Prevelly was consecrated and given to the monks and villagers surrounding the Preveli Monastery while various units from the Australian Army contributed funds and material for the furnishing of the chapel. The opening ceremony took place in 1979.

Over the years Mr Edwards contributed various memorial gifts to the monastery including an annual student scholarship for a university student from the prefectures of Hania, Rethymno and Iraklio, and a Memorial Water Fountain that was built in the grounds of the Preveli Monastery. His book *The Road to Prevelly* documents his experiences and is on display in the monastery's museum.

AGIOS PAVLOS & TRIOPETRA
ΑΓΙΟΣ ΠΑΥΛΟΣ & ΤΡΙΟΠΕΤΡΑ

It's not surprising that the fabulous remote sandy beaches of Agios Pavlos and Triopetra have been chosen by yoga retreats (see p209). These unspoilt and peaceful beaches surrounded by sand dunes and rugged cliffs are arguably one of the most beautiful stretches of unspoilt coastline in Crete.

Agios Pavlos makes a strong claim to being the location from where Icarus and Daedalus took their historic flight in ancient mythology, although this is disputed by nearby Agia Galini, which makes the same claim.

Agios Pavlos is little more than a few rooms and tavernas around a small cove with a sandy beach, but the best beaches are just over the cliffs. There are some stunning rock formations in the cliffs leading to the first of three sandy coves below (about a 10-minute walk, then it gets tougher). The sand dunes reach all the way to the top, which is stunning but can get a bit nasty on very windy days. The furthest coves are the least busy, although there are a few thatched umbrellas and lounges scattered around for your comfort once you get there.

Triopetra, named after the three giant rocks the stick out of the sea just off the coast, can be reached from Agios Pavlos (about 300m is drivable dirt road) or via a 12km windy asphalt road from the village of **Akoumia**, on the Rethymno–Agia Galini road. Just past Akoumia there is the Byzantine church of **Metamorphosis tou Sotira**, which has fine frescoes dating from 1389.

There is also an asphalt road leading to **Agia Irini beach**, via the village of **Kerames**.

While the roads to these beaches were sealed a few years ago – and were being extended to Ligdes in 2005, with plans to go as far as Preveli in future – they have so far not been spoilt by overdevelopment. It's a great part of Crete to unwind.

There is no public transport to any of these beaches.

Agios Pavlos Hotel & Taverna (☎ 28320 71104; www.agiospavloshotel.gr; d €30) is a family-run place that first opened when there was no power or water in the area and access was via a rough dirt road. They have simple rooms in the main building with small balconies overlooking the sea, or more spacious rooms under the shady terrace below the taverna.

The **Kavos Melissa complex** (r €40) further up on the cliff has large self-contained studios. The **taverna** (specials/mayirefta €3.50-6) has good Cretan food while the café-bar next door is the place for breakfast and drink, and has Internet facilities. There is a mini-market attached to the taverna.

Yirogiali Taverna & Rooms (☎ 28320 71122; d/tr/q €25/30/35; Triopetra; ✷), right on the big beach, is run by two brothers, with their mother cooking in the kitchen. The rooms are a recent addition, with marble floors and bathrooms, attractive timber furniture, fridge, TV and balconies.

For real isolation, **Pavlos Taverna Pension** (☎ /fax 28310 25189; www.triopetra.com.gr; d/tr/q €26/28/30) on the smaller eastern beach has decent rooms with small kitchens and great sea views behind the taverna, which serves local meat and fresh fish and lobster (€36).

AGIA GALINI ΑΓΙΑ ΓΑΛΗΝΗ
pop 1260

Agia Galini (a-ya ga-lee-nee) is another erstwhile picturesque fishing village that has been overdeveloped due to package tourism and consequently lost much of its original charm.

Hemmed in against the sea by large sandstone cliffs and phalanxes of hotels and domatia, Agia Galini can be rather claustrophobic – an ambience that is made worse by the ugly cement blocks in the harbour.

It is probably the most touristy southern beach resort, and is popular with British and German tourists. While it still gets lively during peak season, it has become a more sedate resort attracting a middle-aged crowd and families.

Before the advent of mass tourism Agia Galini was a port of the ancient settlement of Sybritos. At the turn of the century it was populated by families from nearby mountain villages who built a cluster of white houses around the harbour.

The late-19th-century village is the core of Agia Galini's appeal even though the crowds at the height of the season obscure the village's undeniable charm and character. Still, it does boast 340 days of sunshine a year, and some places remain open out of season, which is probably the best time to go.

It's a convenient base to visit Phaestos and Agia Triada, and although the town beach is crowded there are boats to better

RETHYMNO

beaches. It has a friendly and lively atmosphere but unless you are after nightlife, you might ultimately be better off elsewhere.

Orientation & Information

The bus station is at the top of Eleftheriou Venizelou, which is a continuation of the approach road. The central square, overlooking the harbour, is downhill from the bus station. You'll walk past the post office on the way. There are four ATMs and travel agencies with currency exchange, while the OTE is on the square, and there's a **laundry** (☺ 10am-2pm & 5-10pm) just off the square. You can go online at **Cosmos Internet** (☎ 28320 91262; per hr €5; ☺ 9am-late).

Tours

Monza Travel (☎ 2832 091 278) offers bus tours around the region, and rents out cars and bikes.

Cretan Holidays (☎ 28320 91241), near the port, can assist with accommodation and offers minibus tours to Knossos for €35.50, a tour of southern Crete that includes Zaros and Phaestos for €32 and a tour of western Crete that includes Moni Arkadiou, Lake Kournas and Rethymno for €32.50. Samaria Gorge is €35.50.

Boats at the port offer day trips to local beaches (see p226).

Sleeping

There is no shortage of places to stay in Agia Galini, but you may have trouble finding a room at the height of peak season as a large percentage of the accommodation is pre-booked by tour operators.

Stohos Rooms & Taverna (☎ 28320 91433; d incl breakfast €50; ☒) This is the only accommodation on the main beach, with apartments upstairs with kitchenettes and big balconies, and huge studios downstairs ideal for families or groups. They are all run by the friendly Fanourios, who presides over the excellent taverna downstairs (try the clay oven dishes).

Erofili Hotel (☎ 28320 91319; hotelerofili@hotmail .com; d incl breakfast €35-45; ☒) This pleasant brightly coloured 10-room hotel has loads of character and a traditional feel. There are plain rooms and also some with air-con, fridge and TV, while all have great sea views. It's signposted to the right off the main road.

Areti Hotel (☎ 28320 91240; s/d incl breakfast €30/40; ☒ **P**) The pool makes this the stand-out option among the hotels on the hill as you enter town. The rooms are standard and have balconies with sea views. They charge an extra €6 for air-con.

El Greco (☎ 28320 91187; fax 28320 91491; s/d incl breakfast €40/50; ☒) At the hilltop leading into town, this family-run old-style hotel offers comfortable rooms with balconies and sea views.

Hotel Rea (☎ /fax 28320 91390; hoter-rea@gmx.net; s/d €20.50/23.50; ☒) On the main road near the port, this budget hotel is dated, but has clean, reasonably sized twin and double rooms with pine furniture.

Agapitos Rooms (☎ 28320 91164; d/tr/q €30/35/40; ☒) They don't have a view but these homy studios halfway down the hill are reasonable value, with balconies and back porches and some have new bathrooms.

Agia Galini Camping (☎ 28320 91386; per adult/ tent €5/3) Next to the beach, 2.5km east of the town, this camping ground is signposted off the Iraklio–Agia Galini road. It's well shaded and has a restaurant and mini-market.

Eating

The restaurants in Agia Galini generally have a decent reputation.

Kostas (☎ 28320 91323; fish per kg from €4.70) Right on the beach at the eastern end, this established fish taverna is known for its excellent fresh fish and seafood. The sardines and the fish soup are recommended.

Madame Hortense (☎ 28320 91215; Mediterranean specials €6-12) The most atmospheric and elaborate restaurant/bar in town is on the top floor of the three-level Zorbas complex on the harbour. Cuisine is Greek Mediterranean, with a touch of the East.

Faros (☎ 28320 91346; fish per kg to €40) Inland from the harbour, this no-frills place is one of the oldest fish tavernas in town, dishing up reasonably priced fresh fish as well as a range of grills and *mayirefta*.

La Strada (☎ 28320 91053; pizza €5-7.50; pasta €4.50-6) This pizzeria is on the first street left of the bus station and has excellent pizzas, pastas and risottos.

On the harbour front, Bozos and Zefyros are well established and have extensive menus that include traditional Cretan food, while the *rakadiko* Petrino has an authentic atmosphere and fine mezedes.

Getting There & Away

BUS

In peak season there are nine buses each day to Iraklio (€5.50, two hours), seven to Rethymno (€4.40, 1½ hours), nine to Phaestos (€1.50, 40 minutes) and five to Matala (€2.50, 45 minutes).

TAXI BOAT

In summer there are daily boats from the harbour to the beaches of Agios Giorgios, Agiofarango and Preveli (Palm Beach), but they are expensive (€15 to €20). The beaches, which are west of Agia Galini, are difficult to get to by land and therefore less crowded than the Agia Galini beach. Departures are between 9.30am and 10.30am.

Getting Around

Mano's Bike (☎ 28320 91551), opposite the post office, rents out scooters and motorcycles, while **Monza Travel** (☎ 28320 91278) rents out cars and organises bus excursions.

THE NORTH COAST

The Mylopotamos Province has some of the more dramatic scenery in northern Crete. The coastline east of Rethymno is indented and pockmarked with watery caves and isolated coves that are only accessible by boat. The chief resorts along the north coast are Bali and Panormo. The hilly interior contains a scattering of villages and farming towns that are just beginning to attract some tourism. Within this region you will find some of Crete's most outstanding crafts, including the pottery at Margarites and the textiles at Anogia.

PANORMO ΠΑΝΟΡΜΟ

pop 887

Panormo is one of the lesser-known and relatively unspoilt beach towns on the northern coast. It has a couple of good sandy beaches and is easy to get to from Rethymno. While the beaches are not the always most pristine, the village does have a relaxed folksy atmosphere and makes for a quieter alternative to the occasionally claustrophobic scene immediately east of Rethymno and at nearby Bali. There are a couple of big hotel complexes to the west of the town, but Panormo itself retains an authentic village feel.

The village was built on the site of an ancient settlement of which little is known. Coins found here indicate that the village flourished from the 1st to the 9th centuries AD when it was destroyed by the Saracens. There was once an early Christian basilica, probably built around the 6th century, and there are the ruins of a Genoese castle on the harbour. Panormo was once a busy commercial port for citrus and carob exports.

Orientation & Information

The bus stop is on the main road outside of town. The post office is one block behind the remains of the castle. There is no OTE or bank, but there is an ATM in one of the hotels just outside Panormo. A new cultural centre in the old carob factory behind the bus stop has been classified an industrial monument as it still has the old machinery for processing carob. Information about the concerts, cultural events and the town itself can be found at www.panormo.com. A tourist mini-train leaves from the main street for the nearby Melidoni Cave (p132) and the pottery village of Margarites (p131). A well-regarded Cretan cooking course is run from Panormo; see p209 for details.

Sleeping & Eating

Villa Kynthia (☎ 28340 51102; www.kynthia.gr; d €97-129; ✷ ✷) This historic old mansion in the centre of the village has been lovingly restored and converted into charming B&B-style rooms and suites decorated with iron beds, antique furnishings and murals. One of the rooms has an elaborate frieze of the *Odyssey*. There is one family-size apartment. The pool and breakfast area is in a beautiful private garden courtyard.

Idyli (☎ 28340 20240; studio €70-100; ✷) This stone house has been restored and traditionally decorated with fine embroideries (it belongs to the family who run Hania's folklore museum). There are spacious studios with lofts sleeping up to four, kitchens, satellite TV and phone, making them suitable for families and people seeking longer stays.

Lucy's Pension (☎ 28340 51212; www.lucy.gr; d & studio €35-50) Well signposted in the centre of town, the owner Lucy has dated but well-maintained simple rooms with kitchenette. She also manages the Kastello apartments right on the waterfront, which are light-filled, spacious and have TV and small kitchens.

RETHYMNO

Konaki Studio-Apartments (☎ 28340 51026; www
.geocities.com/konakihotel; studios €60; 🖭) The garden
and pool of this small complex are nicer
than the rooms, but this friendly hotel is one
of the more pleasant options. It's up above
the beach on the northern side of town.

To Steki tou Sifaka (☎ 28340 51230; mayirefta
€4.50) This cosy taverna-cum-ouzeri is on a
paved street a block back from the waterfront. It has good home-style Cretan food.

Angira (☎ 28340 51022; grills €4.50-6) A giant
anchor on the eastern end of the harbour
points you to this respected seaside fish taverna, which serves fresh locally caught fish
and seafood, as well as the usual grills and
Cretan specialties.

Taverna Kastro (☎ 28340 51362; mezedes €2.70-6)
This faux castle not far from the bus stop
has a pleasant shady courtyard. There are
more than 30 appetisers available, including excellent zucchini fritters and creamy
mushrooms.

Getting There & Away

Buses from Rethymno to Iraklio (€1.70)
stop on the main road just outside of town.
There is a local bus from Rethymno every
20 minutes (€95).

BALI ΠΠΑΛΊ

pop 347

Bali, 38km east of Rethymno and 51km west
of Iraklio, has one of the most stunning
settings on the northern coast. No fewer
than five little coves are strung along the
indented shore, marked by hills, promont-
ories and narrow sandy beaches. But helter-
skelter development around the coast has
significantly marred the natural beauty of
this former fishing hamlet and the narrow
beaches are overcrowded and claustrophobic in the summer. Still, it's not a bad place
to rent a boat and get the full effect of the
dramatic landscape.

The name Bali has nothing to do with its
tropical namesake in Indonesia; it means
'honey' in Turkish, as excellent honey was
once collected and processed here. In antiquity the place was known as Astali, although
no traces of ancient Astali now remain.

Orientation & Information

Bali is a rather spread-out settlement and
it is a long and undulating walk from one
end to the other – 25 minutes or more – so

plan your accommodation and eating op
tions accordingly. The village is punctu
ated by a series of coves with hotels an
restaurants starting with Paradise Beach
followed by Kyma Beach and then Bal
Beach. The ensuing port has a small, bu
popular swimming area, but the last an
best beach is Evita Beach at the far norther
end. Walkers can take a short cut along
coastal path from the port, while riders an
drivers must make a circuitous approac
over the cliff tops.

There is an ATM near the Coast Guar
or you can change money at Racer Rent-a
Car (see p143) on the left as you enter tow
or in one of the travel agencies clustere
around the coves.

Posto Cafe (☎ 28340 94003; per hr €4) on th
port has Internet access.

Activities

There is a wide variety of water sports avail
able in Bali. **Hippocampos Dive Centre** (☎ 2834
94193; www.ippocampos.com; dives incl equipment fron
€42), near the port, offers beginners and ad
vanced dives. **Water Sports Lefteris** (☎ 2834
94102) on the port will rent you a pedal boa
(€5 an hour), a small canoe (€5 an hour), a
sailboat (€25 for two hours) or a jet ski (€3
for 15 minutes). Paragliding costs €38 for a
15-minute flight and there are also day-long
and sunset cruises.

Sleeping

There is little budget accommodation in
Bali, with most of it being designed fo
couples and families on longer holidays, o
taken over by package-holiday groups. Pre
booking is wise in high season.

Sunrise Apartments (☎ 28340 94267; d/apt €35/45
🖭) Right on Evita Beach, the rooms are very
clean, pleasant and spacious, with fridge and
basic cooking facilities. The owners will pick
up guests from Iraklio airport.

Bali Blue Bay (☎ 2810 20111; mooky@otenet.gr
d incl breakfast €45; 🖭 🖭) This sleek new hote
has great views over Bali from the room
and rooftop pool. The rooms are spaciou
and boast a tasteful, contemporary design
and are equipped with TV, fridge and hair
dryers.

Rose Apartments (☎ 28340 94440; fax 2834
94256; d/q €45/60; 🖭) On the left shortly afte
you enter Bali these tasteful studios have
kitchenette, umbrella-equipped balconie

nd ample parking. This is one of the bet-
er independent accommodation choices in
Bali for two or more people.

Apartments Ikonomakis (☎ 28340 94125; d/q
20/40;) This place is centrally located on
quiet street slightly inland from the port.
The building is looking a little run-down
and the bathrooms are basic, but the rooms
are comfortable and have kitchenettes.

Kyma Rooms (☎ 28340 94240; d €20) Attached
o the taverna of the same name, these very
asic rooms, with a fridge and fans, are
heap and right next to the beach.

ating

averna Karavostasi (☎ 28340 94267; Greek specials
4-6) Belonging to Sunrise Apartments, this
osy little eatery 30m back from Evita Beach
ffers, simple home cooking and snacks.
Okra with lamb is a popular dish.

Taverna Nest (☎ 28340 94289; grills €5-7) This
amily taverna just up from the port is not
on the waterfront, but dishes out home-style
ooking and excellent grills on a pleasant
ine-covered terrace. They have been going

strong since the 1980s and use their own
fresh produce and meat.

Kyma Restaurant (☎ 28340 94240; mains €4.50-6)
Right on Kyma Beach, this restaurant serves
good-value meals in a pleasant setting. The
chef recommends his oven-baked vegetables.

Panorama (☎ 28340 94217; mains €4.50-6) With
prime position overlooking the port, this
place is popular and specialises in fresh fish
and Cretan food.

Entertainment

One of the liveliest dance clubs in Bali is the
Highway Club is at the entrance to town.
It's an open-air space decorated as a tropical garden. On The Rocks, across from the
church, caters more to teenagers.

Getting There & Around

Buses from Rethymno to Iraklio (€5.90)
drop you at the main road, from where it is
a 2km walk to the port of Bali.

Racer Rent-a-Car (☎ 28340 94149; fax 28340
94249) has an office at the entrance to town
and one at the port.

RETHYMNO

Iraklio Ηρακλειο

he Iraklio region has Crete's most important and fascinating archaeological sites. The island's ich and unique cultural heritage comes alive when traipsing through the Minoan palaces of nossos, Phaestos, Agia Triada, Gortyna and Malia. The many treasures unearthed at these ites are in the exceptional collection of the Archaeological Museum in the city of Iraklio – he island's capital and busiest port, where most visitors to Crete land. The modern city of raklio is a little like the Athens of the south – though it, too, is undergoing a much-needed acelift, particularly around the waterfront.

The prefecture of Iraklio is a diverse region that embodies some of the best and worst of rete. The northern coast has unashamedly surrendered to package tourism, with the eastern esorts of Malia and Hersonisos summing up everything that is wrong with mass tourism. nd it's pretty much irreversible. Iraklio is also the heart of the island's wine industry, which becoming more sophisticated and visitor-friendly, while a new 18-hole golf course is the ioneer of a different type for tourism for the island.

The region also has its share of natural beauty, and wandering through the traditional nland villages and less-crowded beach communities can be refreshing and rewarding. In rhanes, you will see a prototype modern Cretan village, and from Zaros you can walk the egion's most significant gorge, Rouvas, and visit lovely monasteries in the mountains. In he quieter southern coast, the ex-hippy hangout of Matala is fairly developed, but Kastri nd Keratokambos provide a more tranquil holiday experience. A dramatic mountain drive eads to the isolated beach community of Lendas and the surrounding remote beaches.

IRAKLIO

HIGHLIGHTS

- Exploring the ruins of the Minoan civilisation at **Knossos** (p157), **Gortyna** (p164) and **Phaestos** (p165)
- Indulging in the lively nightlife and café scene of the island's capital, **Iraklio** (p147)
- Viewing the extraordinary collection of **Iraklio's Archaeological Museum** (p149)
- Unwinding on the lovely beaches of **Matala** (p169) and **Lendas** (p172) on the southern coast
- Enjoying the cool mountain air and monasteries of **Zaros** (p163)

IRAKLIO

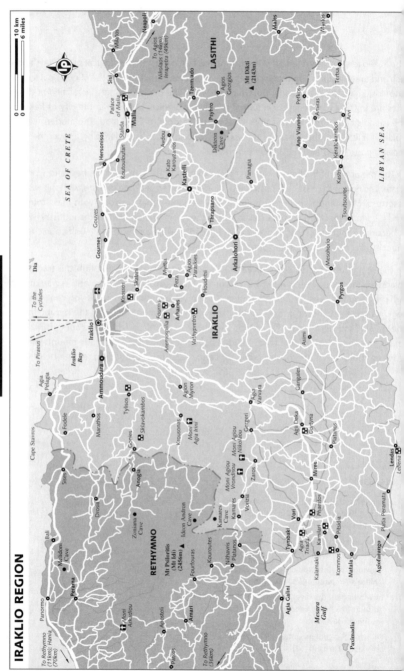

IRAKLIO REGION

0 — 10 km
0 — 6 miles

SEA OF CRETE

LIBYAN SEA

Mesara Gulf

Iraklio Bay

To Piraeus
To the Cyclades
Dia

To Rethymno (11km); Hania (70km)
To Rethymno (36km)

To Agios Nikolaos (14km); Ierapetra (49km)

RETHYMNO
IRAKLIO
LASITHI

Mt Psiloritis (Mt Idi) (2456m) ▲
Mt Dikti (2148m) ▲
Mt Dikti (2143m) ▲

Cape Stavros

Panormo
Bali
Melidoni Cave
Perama
Asotoli
Pakos
Amari
Moni Arkadiou
Fodele
Agia Pelagia
Marathos
Sises
Dissos
Zoniana Cave
Anogia
Gonies
Tylisos
Sklavokambos
Krousonas
Ideon Andron Cave
Fourfouras
Kouroutes
Kamares
Kamares Cave
Nathavris
Platanos
Agia Galini
Agios Myron
Moni Agia Irini
Moni Agiou Nikolaou
Moni Agiou Vrondisou
Vorizia
Zaros
Ammoudara
Iraklio
Knossos
Skalani
Fournis
Anemospilia
Arhanes
Vathypetro
Vathypetro
Myrtia
Peza
Agios Paraskies
Houdetsi
Agia Varvara
Gergeri
Agii Deka
Gortyna
Platanos
Mires
Vori
Phaestos
Pitsidia
Kamilari
Agia Triada
Tymbaki
Kalamaki
Kommos
Matala
Agiofarango
Platia Peramata
Lendas
Lebena
Paximadia
Asimi
Pyrgos
Mesohorio
Gangales
Arkalohori
Thrapsano
Panagia
Kastelli
Kato Karouzanos
Avdou
Koutouloufari
Stalida
Malia
Palace of Malia
Hersonisos
Gouves
Gournes
Sisi
Milatos
Neapoli
Males
Mylos
Tefeta
Amiras
Arvi
Peftos
Tzermiado
Agios Georgios
Psyho
Diktean Cave
Ano Viannos
Keratokambos
Kastri
Tsoutsouras

RAKLIO ΗΡΑΚΛΕΙΟ

οp 130,914

·aklio can be a shock to the senses when ou first arrive with a Greek island holiday ι mind. Crete's hectic, noisy and traffic-.dden capital is often perceived as a grim ecessity to be endured just long enough or an obligatory visit to the Archaeologi-al Museum and Knossos, before escaping o more inviting parts of the island. Much f the city is overdeveloped with concrete partment blocks, and it lacks the architec-ıral charms of Rethymno and Hania.

Yet Iraklio, Greece's fifth-largest city and nancial centre, does have a certain urban ophistication. It has undergone a signifi-ant makeover in recent years – partly as result of being chosen as an Olympic city iraklio hosted the soccer preliminaries uring the 2004 Athens Games) but mostly ecause of the city's (and country's) increas-ıg prosperity. Infrastructure works have ıcluded redevelopment of the waterfront, nproved roads and a city bypass to ease ·affic congestion, while much of the historic entre has been turned into pleasant pe-estrian strips. Many neighbourhoods have een rebuilt and there are enough euros to o around to support a thriving café and estaurant scene, and a lively nightlife.

The Archaeological Museum and the pal-ce at Knossos are a window into Minoan ulture, but Iraklio abounds in other remind-rs of its turbulent history. The 14th-century enetian walls and fortress underscore the nportance of Iraklio (then called Candia) o the Venetians, and many monuments ate from Venetian occupation, notably the Morosini Fountain, the Venetian Loggia and gios Markos Basilica.

HISTORY

·aklio is believed to have been settled since ıe Neolithic age. Little is known about the ıtervening years, but in AD 824 Iraklio /as conquered by the Saracens and became nown as Rabdh el Khandak (Castle of the)itch), after the moat that surrounded their ortified town. It was reputedly the slave-·ade capital of the eastern Mediterranean nd the launching pad for the region's no-orious pirates, who looted unwary ships nd sold the captive seamen into slavery.

Byzantine troops finally ousted the Arabs after a siege in AD 961 that lasted almost a year. The Byzantine leader Nikiforas Fokas made a lasting impression upon the Arabs by chopping off the heads of his prisoners and throwing them over the fortress walls.

The city became known as Handakas and remained the island's capital until Crete was sold to the Venetians in 1204. The Venetians also chose the city as the island's capital and named it Candia. The Venetians built magnificent public buildings and churches, and barricaded themselves inside the for-tress when necessary to protect themselves against a rebellious populace.

Under the Venetians, Candia became a centre for the arts and home to painters such as Damaskinos and El Greco. When the Turks captured Constantinople the walls of Candia's fortress were extended in anticipation of the growing Turkish men-ace. Although the Turks quickly overran the island in 1648, it took them 21 years to penetrate the walls of Candia.

Other European countries sent defenders and supplies from time to time, but it was mainly the strength of the walls that kept the Turks at bay. The Turks finally resorted to bribing a Venetian colonel to reveal the weak points in the wall and thus were able to cap-ture it in 1669. Casualties were high on both sides; the Venetian defenders lost 30,000 men and the Turks lost 118,000 men.

Under the Turks the city became known as Megalo Kastro (Big Castle) and a cloud

IRAKLIO

HOW DID IRAKLIO GET ITS NAME?

After King Minos' wife, Pasiphae, gave birth to the Minotaur, her lover (the bull) went wild and laid waste to the Cretan coun-tryside. He was out of control, tearing up crops and stamping down orchard walls. Fortunately, help was at hand in the form of iron-man Hercules, the man who killed a lion with his bare hands. His voyage to Crete to kill the bull was the seventh of his 12 mighty labours. Minos offered to help but Hercules would have none of it. As the mon-strous animal belched flames and fumes, Hercules captured it single-handedly and took it away. The ancient Cretans were so grateful that they named Minos' port city after their superman.

of darkness descended. Artistic life withered and most Cretans fled or were massacred.

In August 1898, a Turkish mob massacred hundreds of Cretans, 17 British soldiers and the British Consul. Within weeks, a squadron of British ships steamed into Iraklio's harbour and ended Turkish rule.

Hania became the capital of independent Crete at the end of Turkish rule in 1898, but Candia's central location soon saw it emerge as the commercial centre. It was renamed Iraklio and it resumed its position as an administrative centre in 1971.

The city suffered badly in WWII, when most of the old Venetian and Turkish town was destroyed by bombing.

ORIENTATION

Iraklio's two main squares are Plateia Venizelou and Plateia Eleftherias, near the harbour. Plateia Venizelou, recognisable by its famous landmark Morosini Fountain (better known as the Lion Fountain), is the heart of the city, with the city's major intersection (28 Augoustou/1821 and Dikeosynis/Kalokerinou) just south of the square.

The pedestrianised Dedalou, Korai and Perdikari streets are the heart of the city's café and dining scene.

Iraklio has three intercity bus stations (see p156). The ferry port is 500m to the east of the old port. Iraklio's airport is 3km to the east of the city centre.

INFORMATION
Bookshops
Newsstand (☎ 2810 220 135; Plateia Venizelos) Wide range of foreign press and magazines, and a selection of guidebooks, maps and books on Crete.
Planet International Bookshop (☎ 2810 281 558; cnr Hortatson & Kydonias) Stocks most of the books recommended in this guide.
Road Editions (☎ 2810 344 610; Handakos 29) A specialist travel bookshop with the best selection of maps.

Emergency
Tourist police (☎ 2810 210 171; Dikeosynis 10; ☉ 24hr)

Internet Access
Gallery Games (☎ 2810 282 804; www.gallerygames.net; Korai 14; per hr €1.50; ☉ 24hr) High-speed access, printers and PC games.
Sportc@fe (cnr 25 Avgoustou & Zotou; per hr €2; ☉ 24hr) Packed with PC gaming junkies, there is high-speed access but no printers.

Laundry
Most laundries charge €6 for wash and dry and offer dry cleaning.
Inter Laundry (☎ 2810 343 660; Mirabelou 25; ☉ 9am-9pm)
Laundry Perfect (☎ 2810 220 969; Idomeneos & Malikouti 32; ☉ 9am-9pm)

Left Luggage
Bus Station A Left-Luggage Office (☎ 2810 344 097; per day €1; ☉ 6.30am-7.30pm)
Heraklion Airport Luggage Service (☎ 2810 397 349; per day €3.50; ☉ 24hr) Near the local bus stop at the airport.
Iraklio Youth Hostel (per day €2) See p153 for more details.
Laundry Washsalon (Handakos 18; per day €1.50)

Medical Services
Apollonia Hospital (☎ 2810 229 713; Mousourou) Inside the old walls.
University Hospital (☎ 2810 392 111) At Voutes, 5km south of Iraklio, it's the city's best-equipped medical facility.

Money
Most of the city's banks are on 25 Avgoustou. American Express is represented by Adamis Travel Bureau (see below).
National Bank of Greece (25 Avgoustou 35) Has a 24-hour exchange machine.

Post
Central Post office (☎ 2810 234 468; Plateia Daskalogianni; ☉ 7.30am-8pm Mon-Fri, 7.30am-2pm Sat)
Mobile post office (El Greco Park; ☉ 8am-6pm Mon-Fri 8am-1.30pm Sat Jun-Aug) Just north of Plateia Venizelou.
OTE (☎ 2810 395 217; Minotaurou 10; ☉ 7.30am-11pm) Just west of El Greco Park.

Tourist Information
The official tourist office in Iraklio has closed, but good information is available online at www.heraklion-city.gr. There is also a useful KTEL **tourist office** (inside Bus Station A), where you will find details on local and regional tours, including the popular Samaria Gorge trek.

Travel Agencies
Adamis Travel Bureau (☎ 2810 346 202; 25 Avgoustou 23) A reputable travel agency.
Skoutelis Travel (☎ 2810 280 808; 25 Avgoustou 20; skoutel1@otenet) Makes airline and ferry bookings, and arranges accommodation and car hire.

IGHTS

rchaeological Museum of Iraklio

his outstanding **museum** (☎ 2810 226 092; Xan-
ioudidou 2; admission €6, incl Knossos €10; 🕑 12.30-7pm
ion, 8am-7pm Tue-Sun Apr-Oct; 8am-5pm Tue-Sun, noon-
5m Mon late-Oct–early Apr) is second in size and im-
ortance only to the National Archaeological
Museum in Athens. If you are seriously in-
erested in the Minoans you will want more
han one visit; even a fairly superficial perusal
f the contents requires half a day.

The exhibits, arranged in chronological
rder, include pottery, jewellery, figurines
nd sarcophagi, as well as some famous fres-
oes, mostly from Knossos and Agia Triada.
All testify to the remarkable imagination
nd advanced skills of the Minoans. Unfor-
unately, the exhibits are not very well ex-
lained. If they were, there would be no need
o part with €6.50 for a copy of the glossy
llustrated guide by the museum's director.

Room 1 is devoted to the Neolithic and
Early Minoan periods.

Room 2 has a collection from the Middle
Minoan period. Among the most fascinat-
ng exhibits are the tiny, glazed colour re-
iefs of Minoan houses from Knossos, called
he 'town mosaic'.

Room 3 covers the same period with finds
rom Phaestos, including the famous **Phaes-
os Disk** (see the boxed text on p165). The
ymbols inscribed on this 16cm diameter
disc have not been deciphered. The famous
Kamares pottery vases, named after the sacred
:ave of Kamares where the pottery was first
liscovered, are also on display. Case 40 con-
ains fragments of 'eggshell ware', so called
because of its fragility. The four large vases
n case 43 were part of a royal banquet set.
They are of exceptional quality and are some
of the finest examples of Kamares pottery.

Exhibits in Room 4 are from the Middle
Minoan period. Most striking is the 20cm
lack stone **Bull's Head**, which was a libation
vessel. The bull has a fine head of curls, from
which sprout horns of gold. The eyes of
painted crystal are extremely lifelike. Also in
:his room are relics from a shrine at Knossos,
ncluding two fine **snake goddess** figurines.

Room 5 contains pottery, bronze figurines
and seals, as well as vases imported from
Egypt and some Linear A and B tablets –
:he latter have been translated as household
or business accounts from the palace at
Knossos.

Room 6 is devoted to finds from Minoan cemeteries. Especially intriguing are
two small clay models of groups of figures
that were found in a *tholos* tomb. One depicts four male dancers in a circle, their
arms around each other's shoulders. The
dancers may have been participating in a
funeral ritual. The other model depicts two
groups of three figures in a room flanked
by two columns. Each group features two
large seated figures being offered libations
by a smaller figure. It is not known whether
the large figures represent gods or departed
mortals. On a more grisly level, there is a
display of the bones of a horse, which had
been sacrificed as part of Minoan worship.

The finds in Room 7 include the beautiful, fine gold bee pendant found at Malia
depicting two bees dropping honey into a
comb. There are also three celebrated vases
from Agia Triada. The **Harvester Vase**, of
which only the top part remains, depicts a
light-hearted scene of young farm workers
returning from olive picking. The **Boxer Vase**
shows Minoans indulging in two of their
favourite pastimes – wrestling and bull-
grappling. The **Chieftain Cup** depicts a more
cryptic scene: a chief holding a staff and
three men carrying animal skins.

Room 8 holds the finds from the palace
at Zakros. Don't miss the gorgeous crystal
vase that was found in over 300 pieces and
was painstakingly put back together again.
Other exhibits include a beautiful elongated
libation vessel decorated with shells and
other marine life.

Room 10 covers the Postpalatial period
(1580–1200 BC) when the Minoan civilisation was in decline and being overtaken by
the warlike Mycenaeans. Nevertheless, there
are still some fine exhibits, including a child
(headless) on a swing in case 143.

Room 13 is devoted to Minoan sarcophagi.
However, the most famous and spectacular
of these, the **sarcophagus from Agia Triada**, is upstairs in Room 14 (the Hall of Frescoes). This
stone coffin, painted with floral and abstract
designs and ritual scenes, is regarded as one
of the supreme examples of Minoan art.

The most famous of the Minoan frescoes
are also displayed in Room 14. Knossos-
sourced frescoes include the **Procession Fresco**,
the **Griffin Fresco** (from the Throne Room),
the **Dolphin Fresco** (from the Queen's Room)
and the amazing **Bull-Leaping Fresco**, which

IRAKLIO

IRAKLIO

A **B** **C** **D**

INFORMATION
Adamis Travel Bureau.....................1 C3
Alpha Bank....................................2 C3
American Express........................(see 1)
Apollonia Hospital..........................3 B5
EOS..4 D4
Gallery Games................................5 C4
Inter Laundry.................................6 D3
International Travel Service...............7 D4
Laundry Perfect.............................8 D3
Laundry Washshalon.......................9 B3
Mobile Post Office.........................10 C3
National Bank of Greece................11 C3
NewsStand..................................12 C4
OTE..13 B3
Planet International Bookshop........14 B3
Post Office..................................15 C4
Road Editions..............................16 B3
Skoutelis Travel............................17 C2
SportC@fé...................................18 C2

Summerland Travel........................19 D3
Tourist Office.............................(see 83)
Tourist Police...............................20 C4

SIGHTS & ACTIVITIES   (pp149–52)
Agios Dimitrios Church...................21 C3
Agios Markos Basilica....................22 C4
Agios Minas Cathedral...................23 B4
Archaeological Museum of Iraklio....24 D4
Battle of Crete Museum.................25 D3
Bembo Fountain...........................26 C5
Church of Agia Ekaterini (Icon
  Museum)...................................27 B4
Church of Agios Titos....................28 C3
Historical Museum of Crete............29 B2

Kazantzakis' Tomb........................30 B6
Koules Venetian Fortress...............31 D2
Morosini Fountain.........................32 C4
Municipal Art Gallery.....................33 C4
Municipal Garden..........................34 B6
Natural History Museum (new site)..35 A3
Ricoco..36 B4
Venetian Arsenal..........................37 D2
Venetian Loggia............................38 C3

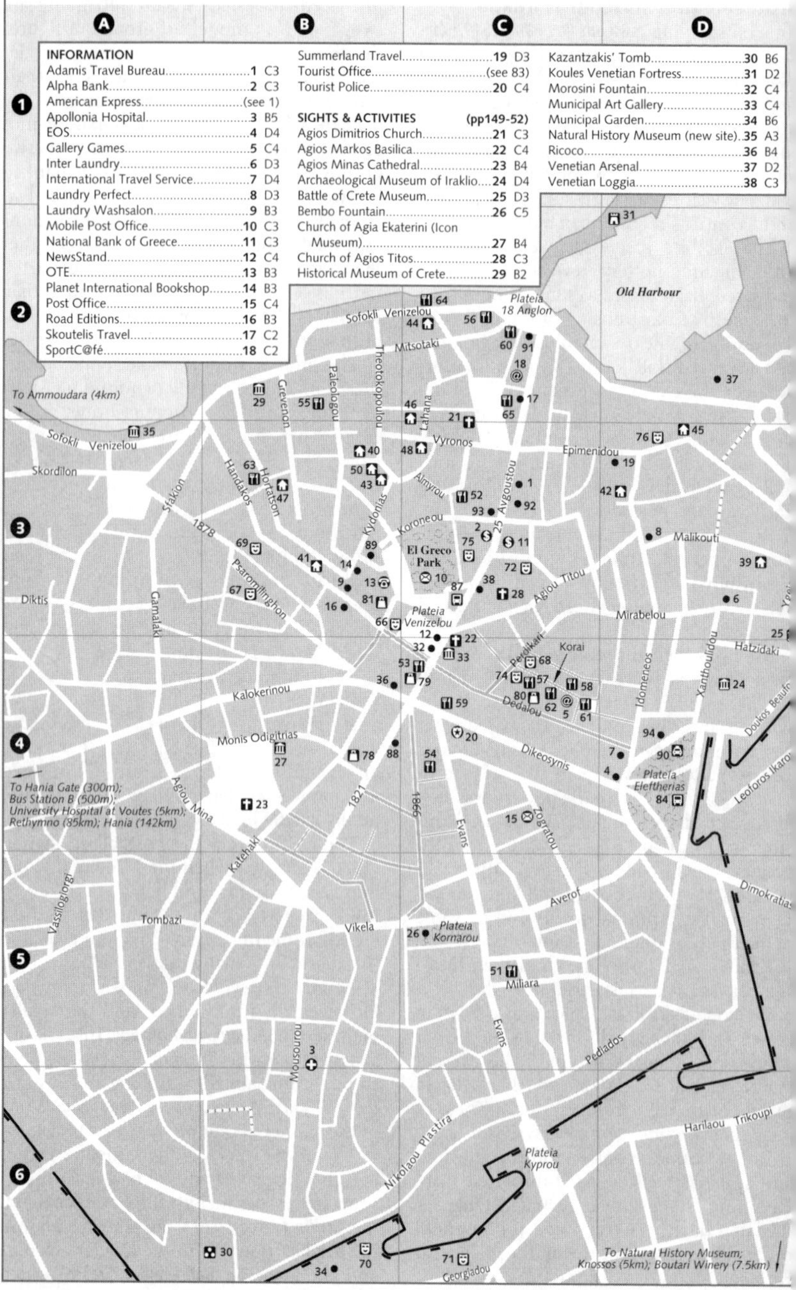

To Ammoudara (4km)

Old Harbour

To Hania Gate (300m);
Bus Station B (500m);
University Hospital at Voutes (5km);
Rethymno (35km); Hania (142km)

To Natural History Museum;
Knossos (5km); Boutari Winery (7.5km)

depicts a seemingly double-jointed acrobat somersaulting on the back of a charging bull. Other frescoes here include the two lovely **Frescoes of the Lilies** from Amnisos and fragments of frescoes from Agia Triada.

There are more frescoes in Rooms 15 and 16. Room 16 has a large wooden model of Knossos.

Historical Museum of Crete

A fascinating collection from Crete's more recent past is displayed at the **Historical Museum** (☎ 2810 283 219; Sofokli Venizelou; admission €3; 9am-4pm Mon-Fri, 9am-2pm Sat summer; 9am-3pm Mon-Sat winter). The ground floor covers the period from Byzantine to Turkish rule, displaying plans, charts, photographs, ceramics and maps. On the 1st floor is the only El Greco painting in Crete – *View of Mt Sinai and the Monastery of St Catherine* (1570). Other rooms contain fragments of 13th- and 14th-century frescoes, coins, jewellery, liturgical ornaments and vestments, and medieval pottery.

The 2nd floor has a reconstruction of the **library of author Nikos Kazantzakis** and displays letters, manuscripts and books. Another room is devoted to former prime minister Emmanouil Tsouderos, who was born in Rethymno. Some dramatic photographs of a ruined Iraklio are displayed in the **Battle of Crete** section. There is an outstanding **folklore collection** on the 3rd floor.

Natural History Museum of Crete

Established by the University of Crete, this leading **Natural History Museum** (☎ 2810 324 711; www.nhmc.uoc.gr; Paraliaki Leoforos; adult/child €4.50/free; 9am-7pm Mon-Fri, 10am-7pm Sat-Sun), was due to move to the restored stone, former electricity building on the harbour front in mid-2005. Apart from the broader evolution of humankind, it explores the flora and fauna of Crete, the island's ecosystem and habitats, and its caves, coastline and mountains. It also looks at the Minoan environment, including a reconstruction of a Minoan cottage and their daily activities.

Other Attractions

Iraklio burst out of its **city walls** long ago, but these massive fortifications, with seven bastions and four gates, are still very conspicuous, dwarfing the concrete structures of the 20th century. Venetians built the defences

IRAKLIO

between 1462 and 1562. You can follow the walls around the heart of the city for views of Iraklio's neighbourhoods, although it is not a particularly scenic city.

The 16th-century **Koules Venetian fortress** (Rocca al Mare; Iraklio Harbour; admission €2; 8.30am-3pm Tue-Sun), stands at the end of the Old Harbour's jetty. It stopped the Turks for 22 years and then became a Turkish prison for Cretan rebels. The exterior is most impressive with reliefs of the Lion of St Mark. The interior has 26 overly restored rooms and good views from the top. The rooms on the ground level are used as art galleries, while music and theatrical events are held in the upper level.

The vaulted arcades of the **Venetian Arsenal** are on the harbour front, opposite the fortress.

Several other notable vestiges from Venetian times survive in the city. Most famous is **Morosini Fountain** on Plateia Venizelou, which spurts water from four lions into eight ornate U-shaped marble troughs. The fountain, built in 1628, was commissioned by Francesco Morosini while he was governor of Crete. A marble statue of Poseidon with his trident used to stand at the centre, but was destroyed during the Turkish occupation. Opposite is the three-aisled 13th-century **Agios Markos Basilica**. It has been reconstructed many times and is now a public art gallery. A little north of here is the attractively reconstructed 17th-century **Venetian Loggia**. It was a Venetian version of a gentleman's club; the male aristocracy came here to drink and gossip. It is now the Town Hall.

The delightful **Bembo Fountain**, at the southern end of 1866, is shown on local maps as the Turkish Fountain, but it was actually built by the Venetians in the 16th century. It was constructed from a hotchpotch of building materials including an ancient statue. The ornate hexagonal edifice next to the fountain was a pump house added by the Turks, and now functions as a pleasant *kafeneio* (coffee house).

The former **Church of Agia Ekaterini** (2810 288 825; Monis Odigitrias; admission €2; 9am-6pm Mon-Fri), next to Agios Minas Cathedral, is now a museum housing an impressive collection of icons. Most notable are the six icons painted by Mihail Damaskinos, the mentor of El Greco.

The **Church of Agios Titos** (Agio Titou) was constructed after the liberation of the Crete in AD 961 and was converted to a Catholic church and then a mosque. It has been rebuilt twice after being destroyed by the big fire in 1554 and then the 1856 earthquake, and has been an Orthodox Church since 1925.

You can pay homage to Crete's most acclaimed contemporary writer, Nikos Kazantzakis (1883–1957; see p50), by visiting his **tomb** at the Martinengo Bastion (the largest and best-preserved bastion) in the southern part of town. The epitaph on his grave, 'I hope for nothing, I fear nothing, I am free', is taken from one of his works.

The **Battle of Crete Museum** (2810 346 554; cnr Doukos Beaufort & Hatzidaki; admission free; 8am-3pm) chronicles this historic battle through photographs, letters, uniforms and weapons.

IRAKLIO FOR CHILDREN

If the kids are museumed out and the heat is getting to them, the indoor playground **Ricoco** (2810 222 333; arcade off Plateia Venizelou; per child €4; 10am-10pm Mon-Sat, 4pm-10pm Sun) could be a godsend. It's upstairs in the arcade near the Lion Fountain. The **Natural History Museum of Crete** (p151) is another safe bet.

ACTIVITIES

The **Mountaineering and Skiing Club of Iraklio** (EOS; 2810 227 609; www.interkriti.org/orivatikos/oriva .html; Dikeosynis 53, Iraklio; 8.30pm-10.30pm) arranges mountain climbing, cross-country walking and skiing excursions across the island most weekends.

You can also sign up for a dive in Crete's clear warm waters. Try **Diver's Club** (2810 811 755; www.diversclub-crete.gr; Agia Pelagia) or **Cretas Diving Centre** (2821 093 616; Gefyra Klarissou 1).

TOURS

Iraklio's myriad travel agents run coach tours the length and breadth of Crete and provide specialist tours and bus excursions. Manolis Tsagarakis at the **International Travel Service** (2810 228 413; www.forthnet.gr/its; Dedalou 36) can organise a range of tours, including a trip to his 'traditional village' in Kato Karouzanos (see the boxed text on p175).

FESTIVALS & EVENTS

Iraklio's **Summer Arts Festival** presents international guest orchestras and dance troupes as well as local talent. The principal venue for performances is the huge open-air theatre **Nikos Kazantzakis Open Air Theatre** (☎ 2810 242 977; Jesus Bastion; box office ☺ 9am-2.30pm & 6.30-9.30pm), near the moat of the Venetian walls, and the nearby Manos Hatzidakis theatre. Events are also held at the Koules fortress. Log on to www.heraklion-city.gr for a programme.

SLEEPING

Iraklio's accommodation opportunities are weighted towards the needs of business travellers and are grouped in the centre of town. Many hotels were upgraded in the lead up to the 2004 Olympics. There are few domatia but not enough cheap hotels to cope with the number of budget travellers who arrive in the high season.

Budget

Mirabello Hotel (☎ 2810 285 052; www.mirabello hotel.gr; Theotokopoulou 20; s/d with shared bathroom €37/40, d with private bathroom €68; ☷) One of the most pleasant budget hotels in Iraklio is the relaxed Mirabello on a quiet street in the centre of town. The rooms are immaculate, although a little cramped, with TV and phones. Seven of the rooms share single-sex bathrooms.

Hotel Lena (☎ 2810 223 280; www.lena-hotel.gr; Lahana 10; s/d without bathroom €30/40, d with bathroom €50; ☷) Renovated extensively in 2003, Hotel Lena has 16 comfortable, airy rooms with phone, TV and double-glazed windows, but the bathrooms are still rather basic. Cheaper rooms without bathrooms are available.

Hellas Rent Rooms (☎ 2810 288 851; fax 2810 284 442; Handakos 24; dm/d/tr €10/28/40) Many travellers enjoy the lively atmosphere at this de facto youth hostel, which has a roof-top garden bar. Shared bathrooms are basic but clean and most rooms have balconies. Breakfast is available on the terrace.

Hotel Rea (☎ 2810 223 638; hotelrea@tellas.gr; Kalimeraki; s/d €25/30) Popular with a wide range of backpackers, Rhea has an easy, friendly atmosphere. Rooms all have fans and sinks, although bathrooms are shared. There's a small basic communal kitchen.

Iraklio Youth Hostel (☎ 2810 286 281; heraklioyouth hostel@yahoo.gr; Vyronos 5; dm/d/tr per person €10/12/12) This Greek Youth Hostel Organisation establishment is rather scruffy and run down, but it's the cheapest option for single travellers. The single-sex dorms are as basic as you can get. Luggage storage costs €2 per piece.

Camping Creta (☎ 2897 041 400; fax 2897 041 792; per tent/person €3.50/4.30) The nearest camp sites are at Gouves, 16km east of Iraklio. The camping ground is a flat, shadeless area, but there is a sand and pebble beach.

Mid-Range

Atrion Hotel (☎ 2810 246 000; www.atrion.gr; Hronaki 9; s/d €93/110; ☷) Fully refurbished in 2003, this is a now one of the city's more pleasant hotels. Rooms are tastefully decked out in neutral tones, with TV, fridge, hairdryers and data ports. The top rooms have sea views and small balconies.

Hotel Kastro (☎ 2810 284 185; www.kastro-hotel.gr; Theotokopoulou 22; s/d €90/110; ☷ ▣) A refurbished, modern, cheery B-Class hotel in the back streets, the Kastro is an excellent choice. The large rooms have fridges, TV, hairdryers, phones and ISDN Internet connectivity.

Hotel Kronos (☎ 2810 282 240; www.kronoshotel .gr; Sofokli Venizelou 2; d €55; ☷ ▣) This well-maintained older waterfront hotel has comfortable rooms with double-glazed windows and balconies, phone and TV, and many have fridges. It is one of the better-value C-class hotels in town. Ask for one of the rooms with sea views.

Hotel Irini (☎ 2810 226 561; www.hotelirini.com; Idomeneos 4; s/d incl breakfast €55/70; ☷) Close to the old harbour, Irini is a modern establishment with 59 large, airy rooms with TV, radio and telephone and plants and flowers on the balconies.

Top End

Hotel Lato (☎ 2810 228 103; www.lato.gr; Epimenidou 15; s/d €109/139; ☷) Overlooking the old and new harbours, the refurbished Lato is one of Iraklio's prime hotels. It is swish and modern and most rooms have spectacular views: the penthouse suite has the best view in the city and there is a great rooftop bar.

Atlantis Hotel (☎ 2810 229 103; www.grandhotel.gr; Ygias 2; s/d €105/145; ☷ ☲ ▣) The Atlantis' makeover has maintained its status as one of the city's best hotels. The rooms are comfortable, stylish and well equipped, and there is a health studio, sauna and small pool.

Megaron (☎ 2810 305 300; www.gdmmegaron.gr; Doukis Beaufort 9; s/d €225/255; ☷ ▣) This new arrival leaves every hotel in town for dead. The former derelict historic building on the harbour has been stunningly transformed with top design and fittings throughout. There is a fax in every room, Jacuzzis in the VIP suites and plasma-screen TVs. The rooftop restaurant and bar have fine harbour views and the glass-sided pool is unique.

EATING

Iraklio has restaurants to suit all tastes and pockets, from excellent fish tavernas to exotic international cuisine and formal-dining options. Note that the majority of restaurants are closed on Sunday.

Budget

Giakoumis Taverna (☎ 2810 280 277; Theodosaki 5-8; mayirefta €2.50-5; ☺ Mon-Sat) Theodosaki is lined with tavernas catering to the market on 1866 and this is one of the best. There's a full menu of Cretan specialities and turnover is heavy which means that the dishes are freshly cooked.

Loukoumades Cafe (☎ 2810 346 005; Dikeosynis 8; loukoumades per dozen €1.70; ☺ 5am-midnight) This is where to get the best *loukoumades* (honey-dipped fritters) in Iraklio.

Fyllo...Sofies (☎ 2810 284 774; Plateia Venizelou 33; bougatsa €1.90; ☺ 5am-late) Next to the Lion Fountain, this place does a roaring morning trade when both tourists off the early boats and the post-club crowd head straight for a delicious *bougatsa* (warm custard-filled pastry).

O Vrakas (☎ 6977 893 973; Plateia 18 Anglon; mains €2.90-3.50) This small street-side ouzeri grills fresh fish al fresco in front of diners. It's cheap and unassuming and the menu is limited, but still very popular with locals. Grilled octopus with ouzo is a good choice.

Mid-Range

Terzakis Ouzeri (☎ 2810 221 444; Marineli 17; mezedes €2.80-6.80) On a small square opposite the Agios Dimitrios church, this excellent ouzeri has a range of mezedes as well as *mayirefta* (casseroles) and grills. Try the sea urchin salad or, if you are really game to try a local specialty, ask if they have *ameletita* ('unmentionables'), meaning fried sheep testicles.

Peri Orexeos (☎ 2810 222 679; Korai 10; mains €6-8) This place offers excellent modern Greek food with creative takes like *kataïfi* with creamy chicken, as well as good Cretan cuisine. The setting is lovely, the prices very reasonable and there's also a wicked chocolate dessert.

Ippokambos Ouzeri (☎ 2810 280 240; Sofokli Venizelou 3; seafood mezes €4.20-7) Many locals come to this taverna at the edge of the tourist-driven waterfront dining strip. Take a peek inside at the fresh trays and pots of *mayirefta* such as baked cuttlefish, and enjoy eating at one of the sidewalk tables or on the promenade across the road.

I Avli tou Defkaliona (☎ 2810 244 215; Kalokerinou 8; meat dishes €4.20-13; ☺ dinner only) This taverna's wicker chairs, checked tablecloths and plastic grapevines put diners in a cheery mood that's intensified by delicious food. After the tourists leave at around 11pm, the locals pile in, the owner takes out his accordion and the festivities commence.

La Grande Trattoria (☎ 2810 300 225; Korai 6; pasta €6.50-12.50) In the heart of busy Korai, La Grande has decent upmarket Italian cuisine with a wide range of pastas if you feel like a break from Cretan food.

Embolo (☎ 2810 284 244; Miliara 7; mains €3.20-4.50) Run by former musician Giannis Stavrakakis from Anogia, Embolo dishes up fine Cretan food – excellent grills, *pittes* (pies) and large salads. Live music is played on Thursday, Friday and Saturday.

Ethrion (☎ 2810 289 542; Almyrou 2; mains €5-9; ☺ dinner only) For a more formal dining experience, the upmarket Ethrion serves a full menu of well-prepared Greek specialties. Linen tablecloths and a grand piano set a romantic tone for a meal on the plant-filled terrace.

Also recommended:

Ontas (☎ 2810 244 449) Ouzeri in a side street off Korai.
Taverna Kastella (☎ 2810 284 432; Sofokli Venizelou 3) On the waterfront.

Top End

Prassein Aloga (☎ 2810 283 429; cnr Handakos & Kydonias 21; mains €9.50-15) This little rustic-style café/restaurant and its associated delicatessen (opposite) have excellent innovative Mediterranean food from an ever-changing menu. It has dishes based on ancient Greek cuisine, such as pork medallions with dried fruit on wild rice.

Loukoulos (☎ 2810 224 435; Korai 5; mains €10-19) Loukoulos offers luscious Mediterranean specialties served on fine china and accompanied by soft classical music. You can either opt for the elegant interior or take your meal on the outdoor terrace under a lemon tree.

ENTERTAINMENT
When not being used by live performers in the summer (see p152), the Nikos Kazantzakis theatre operates as an **open-air cinema** (☎ 2810 242 977; Jesus Bastion; box office ☺ 9am-2.30pm & 6.30-9.30pm).

Iraklio has about half-a-dozen cinemas, but the most centrally located is the **Astoria Cinema** (☎ 2810 226 191; Plateia Eleftherias), which screens new-release movies in their original language, which is usually English.

Cafés & Bars
While the cafés around the Morosini Fountain are lively, the real action and place to be seen is on the pedestrian area of Korai and Perdikari, which is lined with stylish cafés and bars. The old buildings along Handakos contain relaxed bars and cafés with cosy interiors and enclosed patios more suitable for conversation than people-watching.

Pagopiion (☎ 2810 346 028; Plateia Agiou Titou; ☺ 10am-late) This is a former ice factory and the most original café/bar/restaurant on the island. The restaurant serves innovative but pricey dishes and salads and it becomes a lively bar after 11pm. It's gay-friendly.

Guernica (☎ 2810 282 988; Apokoronou Kritis 2; ☺ 10am-late) A great combination of traditional décor and contemporary music make this one of Iraklio's hippest bar/cafés. The rambling old building has a delightful terrace garden for the summer and a cosy fireplace in winter.

Veneto (☎ 2810 223 686; Epimenidou 9) This is probably the only café with a view of the harbour and fortress from its lovely terrace. It's in an historic building near Hotel Lato.

Take Five (☎ 2810 226 564; Akroleondos 7; ☺ 10am-late) An old favourite on the edge of El Greco Park, this place doesn't really get going until after sundown when the outside tables fill up with a diverse crowd. It's a gay-friendly place. The music and ambience are low-key, but the coffees are expensive.

Jasmin (☎ 2810 288 880; Handakos 45; ☺ noon-late) This friendly bar/café, with a pleasant back terrace, specialises in herbal teas and hot chocolates, but is also a bar in the evenings, playing rock and world music.

Ideon Antron (☎ 2810 242 041; Perdikari 1; ☺ 10am-late) On trendy Korai with its rows of postmodern kafeneia, this is a throwback to the past. The stone interior with its shiny wood bar creates a relaxed, inviting place.

Rebels (Cnr Korai & Perdikari) One of the pioneers in the neighbourhood, Rebels is still going strong.

Nightclubs
Iraklio has the smartest and most sophisticated nightlife on the island. The following venues open around midnight and close near dawn. The cover charge usually starts at about €6 and should include a drink.

Privilege (Doukos Beaufort 7) Iraklio's smart set packs this dancing club that can easily hold 1000 people. Like many of Crete's dancing clubs, there's international music (rock, techno etc) until about 2am when Greek music takes over.

Yacht Club (☎ 2810 343 500; Doukos Beaufort 9) Next door to Privilege, this club attracts a smartly dressed assortment of young locals and visitors. The clubs compete to attract the most chic from the chic crowd.

Leoforos Ikarou, just down from Plateia Eleftherias, serves up the wildest nightlife, with clubs presenting contemporary rock, techno and modern Greek dance music.

SHOPPING
Iraklio is where the money is, so it's a good place to pick up the latest fashion, replace a suitcase or shop for luxury goods. Dedalou is a pedestrian shopping street lined with mostly mainstream shops, but the market street, 1866, is also fun. This narrow street is packed on most days and stalls spill over with sponges, herbs, fruits, vegetables, utensils, T-shirts, nuts, honey, shoes and jewellery. For gold and silver jewellery, head to Kalokerinou or the busy commercial 25 Avgoustou where you'll find big Greek jewellers like **Fanourakis** (☎ 2810 282 708; Plateia N Foka).

Elli (☎ 2810 288 880; M Odigitiras 37) Local upcoming jeweller Elli Terzaki's small shop carries her unique designs, plus the Thallo range made from real flowers.

Folli Follie (☎ 2810 346 354; Daedalou 23) Greece's internationally successful handbag and jewellery chain.

Mastic Spa (☎ 2810 390 567; Kantanoleon 2) Has unique products made from Chois Island mastic, including foodstuffs and skin care.

Aerakis Music (☎ 2810 225 758; Daedalou 35; www .seistronmusic.gr) Offers arguably the best range of Cretan music, from old and rare recordings to the latest releases – many on Michalis Aerakis' own record label, Seistron Music.

IRAKLIO

GETTING THERE & AWAY
Air
Aegean Airlines (☎ 2810 344 324; fax 2810 344 330; Leof Dimokratias 11); airport office (☎ 2810 330 475)
Olympic Airlines (☎ 2810 244 824; 25 Avgoustou 27; ⏳ 8am-3.30pm Mon-Fri); airport office (☎ 2810 337 203)

DOMESTIC
Olympic Airlines offers at least six flights daily to Athens (€83) from Iraklio's Nikos Kazantzakis airport. It also has daily flights to Thessaloniki (€110) and Rhodes (€73).

Aegean Airlines has flights to Athens (€88, seven daily) and Thessaloniki (€110, two daily). Both airlines have regular special fare deals, although rarely in the summer peak season.

INTERNATIONAL
Iraklio has lots of charter flights from all over Europe; see p221 for more information. **Skoutelis Travel** (☎ 2810 280 808; 25 Avgoustou 20) is a good place to ask.

Boat
Minoan Lines (☎ 2104 145 700; www.minoan.gr) operate ferries every evening each way between Iraklio and Piraeus (seven hours). They depart from both Piraeus and Iraklio at 10pm. Fares are €29.50 for deck class and €49.50 for cabins. The Minoan Lines' high-speed boats, the F/B *Festos Palace* and F/B *Knossos Palace*, are much more modern and more comfortable than their ANEK rivals.

In summer, Minoan Lines runs extra six-hour services on weekends and some weekdays, departing Iraklio and Piraeus at 11am and arriving at 5pm (€28.50 deck class). This is by far the most convenient way to get to and from Iraklio.

Minoan also runs four ferries weekly to Thessaloniki (€31.50, 23 hours) via Santorini (€15, 3¾ hours), stopping at different islands each time, including Mykonos (€23, nine hours), Paros (€22.50, 7½ hours), Tinos (€24.50, 10¼ hours), Naxos (€20, seven hours), Syros (€21.50, 10 hours) and Skiathos (€36, 17¾ hours).

ANEK Lines (☎ 2810 244 912; www.anek.gr) has daily ferries to between Iraklio and Piraeus (€25.70, nine hours) at 8.30pm.

LANE Lines also has a ferry that leaves Iraklio for Sitia, Karpathos (€16.40, seven hours), Rhodes (€22.90, 10½ hours), and continues to Kasos, Halki, Kalymno, Kos, Samos, Chios, Mytilene and Alexandroupolis (total trip €39.50, 36½ hours).

Iraklio Port Authority (☎ 2810 244 912) has information about ferry schedules.

Bus
Iraklio has three intercity bus stations. Station A, which serves eastern Crete (including Knossos), is on the waterfront near the quay but there are plans to relocate it. Another bus station servicing Hania and Rethymno is opposite Station A. West of the city centre, Station B is just beyond Hania Gate, and serves Phaestos, Agia Galini and Matala.

There are buses every half-hour (hourly in winter) to Rethymno (€5.90, 1½ hours) and Hania (€10.50, 2½ hours) from the Rethymno/Hania bus station opposite Bus Station A. See the tables below for other destinations from **Bus Station A** (☎ 2810 245 020; www.ktel.org) and Bus Station B.

BUSES FROM BUS STATION A

Destination	Duration	Fare	Frequency
Agia Pelagia	45 min	€2.50	5 daily
Agios Nikolaos	1½ hr	€5	half-hourly
Arhanes	30 min	€1.30	hourly
Hersonisos/Malia	45 min	€2.20/2.70	half-hourly
Ierapetra	2½ hr	€7.50	7 daily
Knossos	20 min	€0.95	six hourly
Lasithi Plateau	2 hr	€5	2 daily
Milatos	1½ hr	€3.50	2 daily
Sitia	3½ hr	€10	5 daily

BUSES FROM BUS STATION B

Destination	Duration	Fare	Frequency
Agia Galini	2 hr	€5.50	9 daily
Anogia	1 hr	€2.60	6 daily
Matala	2½ hr	€5.50	9 daily
Phaestos	1½ hr	€4.50	8 daily

GETTING AROUND
Bus No 1 goes to and from the airport every 15 minutes between 6am and 1am. It leaves the city from near the Astoria Capsis Hotel on Plateia Eleftherias. A taxi to the airport costs around €8.

Long-Distance Taxis (☎ 2810 210 102/168/124) from Plateia Eleftherias, opposite the Astoria Capsis Hotel and Bus Station B, can take you to all parts of Crete. Sample fares include Agios Nikolaos (€40), Rethymno (€50) and Hania (€85).

The airport has a full range of car-rental companies including Hertz, National, Euro-dollar and Europcar, but you'll likely get the best deal from local car- and motorcycle-hire outlets, which are largely located on 25 Avgoustou. Try:

Loggeta Cars & Bikes (☎ 2810 289 462; Plateia Kallergon 6) Next to El Greco Park.

Motor Club (☎ 2810 222 408; Plateia 18 Anglon)

Sun Rise (☎ 2810 221 609; 25 Avgoustou 46)

AROUND IRAKLIO

KNOSSOS ΚΝΩΣΟΣ

Once the capital of Minoan Crete, **Knossos** (☎ 28102 31940; admission €6, incl Iraklio Archaeological Museum €10; ⏰ 8am-7pm Apr-Oct, 8am-5pm Nov-Mar) is now the island's major tourist attraction. Around 5km south of Iraklio, the road leading up to the famous site is an uninspiring gauntlet of souvenir shops and fruit-juice stands, but the palace is magnificent. The site is surrounded by green hills and shaded by pine trees, making it Crete's most evocative location.

The ruins of Knossos (k-nos-*os*) were uncovered in 1900 by the British archaeologist Sir Arthur Evans. Heinrich Schliemann, the legendary discoverer of ancient Troy, had his eye on the spot (a low, flat-topped mound), believing an ancient city was buried there, but he was unable to strike a deal with the local landowner. Arthur Evans was a well-travelled journalist, museum curator and classicist with an interest in ancient scripts when he came across some ancient stones engraved with what appeared to be hieroglyphic writing.

Learning that the stones came from Crete, Evans set sail in 1894. Still thinking that the low, flat-topped mound that interested Schliemann might contain the key to his hieroglyphics, Evans acquired a share of the site that, significantly, gave him exclusive rights to the excavation. He returned five years later and began digging with a group of Cretan workmen.

The flat-topped mound was called Kefala and the vanished palace that it contained emerged quickly. The first treasure to be unearthed was a fresco of a Minoan man followed by the discovery of the Throne Room. The archaeological world was stunned. Until he began his excavations no-one had suspected that a civilisation of this maturity and sophistication had existed in Europe at the time of the great pharaohs of Egypt. Some even speculated that it was the site of the lost city of Atlantis to which Plato referred to many centuries later.

Evans spent 25 years excavating the site, although his 'realistic' reconstruction methods were controversial – see the boxed text on p39 for details.

You will need to spend about four hours at Knossos to explore it thoroughly. There is no signage, so unless you have a travel guide, or

---

THE MYTH OF THE MINOTAUR

King Minos of Crete invoked the wrath of Poseidon when he failed to sacrifice a magnificent white bull sent to him for that purpose. Poseidon's revenge was to cause Pasiphae, King Minos' wife, to fall in love with the animal. In order to attract the bull, Pasiphae asked Daedalus, chief architect at Knossos and all-round handyman, to make her a hollow, wooden cow structure. When she concealed herself inside, the bull found her irresistible. The outcome of their bizarre association was the Minotaur: a hideous monster who was half-man and half-bull.

King Minos asked Daedalus to build a labyrinth in which to confine the Minotaur and demanded that Athens pay an annual tribute of seven youths and seven maidens. This was by way of compensation for the Athenians having killed Minos' son Androgeos at games in which he had participated and had been victorious. The hapless youths were fed to the Minotaur in order to satisfy the monster's huge appetite.

The Athenians became enraged by the tribute demanded by Minos. The Athenian hero, Theseus, vowed to kill the Minotaur and sailed off to Crete posing as one of the sacrificial youths. On arrival, he fell in love with Ariadne, the daughter of King Minos, and she promised to help him if he would take her away with him afterwards. She provided him with the ball of twine that he unwound on his way into the labyrinth and used to retrace his steps after slaying the monster. Theseus eventually fled Crete with his bride-to-be Ariadne.

hire a guide, you may not appreciate what you are looking at. To beat the crowds and avoid the heat, get there early and visit the Throne Room first before the tour buses arrive. The café at the site is expensive – you'd do better to bring a picnic along. Note that you can buy a combined ticket for €10 that also allows entry to the Archaeological Museum of Iraklio.

History

The first palace at Knossos was built around 1900 BC, but most of what you see dates from 1700 BC after the Old Palace was destroyed by an earthquake. It was then rebuilt to a grander and more sophisticated design. The palace was partially destroyed again sometime between 1500 BC and 1450 BC and inhabited for another 50 years before it was devastated once and for all by fire.

The New Palace was not erected helter-skelter but carefully designed to meet the needs of a complex society. There were domestic quarters for the king or queen, residences for officials and priests, homes for common folk, and burial grounds. Public reception rooms, shrines, workshops, treasuries and storerooms were built around a paved courtyard in a design so intricate that it may have been behind the legend of the labyrinth and the Minotaur.

It was once possible to enter the royal apartments, but in early 1997 it was decided to cordon this area off before it disappeared altogether under the continual pounding of feet. Extensive repairs are under way but it is unlikely to open to the public again.

Exploring the Site

The site's numerous rooms, corridors, dog-leg passages, staircases, and nooks and crannies preclude a detailed walk description of the palace. However, Knossos is not a site where you'll be perplexed by heaps of rubble. Thanks to Evans' reconstruction, the most significant parts of the complex are instantly recognisable (if not instantly found). While you wander you will come across many of Evans' reconstructed columns. Most are painted deep brown-red with gold-trimmed black capitals. These, like all Minoan columns, taper at the bottom.

Strategically placed copies of Minoan frescoes help infuse the site with the artistic spirit of these remarkable people. The

Minoan achievements in plumbing equal their achievements in painting; drains and pipes were carefully placed to avoid flooding, taking advantage of centrifugal force. It appears that at some points water ran uphill, demonstrating a mastery of the principle that water finds its own level. Also notice the placement of light wells and the relationship of rooms to passages, porches, light wells and verandas, which kept rooms cool in summer and warm in winter.

The usual entrance to the palace complex is across the Western Court and along the **Corridor of the Procession Fresco**. The fresco depicted a long line of people carrying gifts to present to the king; only fragments remain. A copy of one of these fragments, called the **Priest King Fresco**, can be seen to the south of the Central Court.

An alternative way to enter is to have a look at the Corridor of the Procession Fresco, then walk straight ahead to enter the site from the northern end. If you do this you will come to the **theatral area**, a series of steps whose function remains unknown. It could have been a theatre where spectators watched acrobatic and dance performances, or the place where people gathered to welcome important visitors arriving by the Royal Road.

The **Royal Road** leads off to the west. The road, Europe's first (Knossos has lots of firsts), was flanked by workshops and the houses of ordinary people. The **Lustral Basin** is also in this area. Evans speculated that this was where the Minoans performed a ritual cleansing with water before religious ceremonies.

Entering the **Central Court** from the north, you will pass the relief **Bull Fresco**, which depicts a charging bull. Relief frescoes were made by moulding wet plaster, and then painting it while still wet.

Also worth seeking out in the northern section of the palace are the **giant pithoi**. Pithoi were ceramic jars used for storing olive oil, wine and grain. Evans found over 100 of these huge jars at Knossos (some were 2m high). The ropes used to move them inspired the raised patterns that adorn the jars.

Once you have reached the Central Court, which in Minoan times was surrounded by the high walls of the palace, you can begin exploring the most important rooms of the complex.

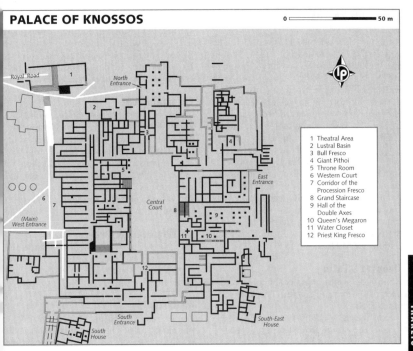

PALACE OF KNOSSOS

0 — 50 m

1 Theatral Area
2 Lustral Basin
3 Bull Fresco
4 Giant Pithoi
5 Throne Room
6 Western Court
7 Corridor of the Procession Fresco
8 Grand Staircase
9 Hall of the Double Axes
10 Queen's Megaron
11 Water Closet
12 Priest King Fresco

IRAKLIO

From the northern end of the west side of the palace, steps lead down to the **Throne Room**. This room is fenced off but you can still get a good view of it. The centrepiece, the simple, beautifully proportioned throne, is flanked by the **Griffin Fresco**. Griffins were mythical beasts regarded as sacred by the Minoans.

The room is thought to have been a shrine, and the throne the seat of a high priestess, rather than a king. Certainly, the room seems to have an aura of mysticism and reverence rather than pomp and ceremony. The Minoans did not worship their deities in great temples but in small shrines, and each palace had several.

On the 1st floor of this side of the palace is the section Evans called the **Piano Nobile**, for he believed the reception and state-rooms were here. A room at the northern end of this floor displays copies of some of the frescoes found at Knossos.

Returning to the Central Court, the impressive **grand staircase** leads from the middle of the eastern side of the palace to the royal apartments, which Evans called the **Domes-**tic Quarter. This section of the site is now cordoned off. Within the royal apartments is the **Hall of the Double Axes**. This was the king's megaron, a spacious double room in which the ruler both slept and carried out certain court duties. The room had a light well at one end and a balcony at the other to ensure air circulation.

The room takes its name from the double axe marks on its light well. These marks appear in many places at Knossos. The *labrys* (double axe) was a sacred symbol to the Minoans, and the origin of our word 'labyrinth'.

A passage leads from the Hall of the Double Axes to the **queen's megaron**. Above the door is a copy of the **Dolphin Fresco**, one of the most exquisite Minoan artworks. A blue floral design decorates the portal. Next to this room is the queen's bathroom, complete with terracotta bathtub and a **water closet**, touted as the first ever to work on the flush principle; water was poured down by hand.

Getting There & Away
Bus No 2 leaves Bus Station A in Iraklio every 10 minutes for Knossos.

AMMOUDARA ΑΜΜΟΥΔΆΡΑ
pop 1083

Ammoudara lies about 4km west of Iraklio and is the closest beach to the city and an alternative place to stay if you want to escape big-city Iraklio. Long, sandy and wide, the beach is relatively uncrowded but the area is nothing to get excited about. Haphazard development, dated apartment blocks, tourist shops and scores of medium-sized hotels spoil any ambience it might have had. At night, however, the discos and nightlife of Ammoudara lure tourists and Iraklio residents alike, and it's also a favoured spot for windsurfers: **Agapi Beach Water Sports** (☎ 2810 250502) can supply gear and advice. Although it may seem that the beach is completely barricaded by hotels, there is access next to the Agapi Beach and Candia Maris Hotel.

Sleeping & Eating

Ammoudara is dominated by large resort hotels but there are a few domatia scattered about.

Rent Rooms (☎ 28102 50265; s/d €25/30; P) Across the street from the tennis courts of the luxury Candia Maris Hotel, these rooms are simple, spacious and have kitchenettes and sea views from the balconies. The grounds are bare but there is parking out the back.

Hotel Armonia (☎ 28102 58770; www.hotelarmonia.com; d €35; 🖳 🏊) This hotel has small apartments off the main street and another newer block of rooms on the beach. There's a central pool and peacock enclosure. The bathrooms are a little basic but the rooms are good value.

The dining scene in Ammoudara is uninspiring, but of the restaurants on the main drag you could try Golden Wheat Chinese Restaurant for reasonably priced Chinese, La Bussola for Italian or the Petousis taverna for grills and Cretan fare.

Entertainment

There are several well-signposted clubs along and off the main road in Ammoudara, where major clubbing takes place in summer. The hot clubs change from year to year but the consensus on 'in' places at the time of research was Barracuda, Buddha Bar and Plus Soda, while Skol Pub is a popular rock bar with regular live music. They all open around 11pm and party til dawn.

Getting There & Away

The No 6 bus from Iraklio (outside the Capsis Astoria Hotel) stops in front of the Cretan Beach Hotel and the Agapi Beach Hotel in Ammoudara. By taxi it's €4.50.

AROLITHOS

On the road to Tylisos, 11km from Iraklio, the faux Cretan village of **Arolithos** (a-ro-li-thos) has recently added an **agricultural and folklife museum** (☎ 28108 21050; www.arolithosvillage.gr; adult/child €3/1.50; 🕑 9am-9pm summer; 9am-5pm Mon-Fri, 10am-6pm Sat winter). Built from scratch in the mid-80s, this family-run stone-built village has pottery, weaving and blacksmiths' workshops, a taverna, kafeneio, village shop with local handicrafts and a huge square that regularly hosts real Cretan weddings and baptisms. The three-level museum has a decent collection of household and agricultural items in themed displays showing all aspects

---

DETOUR: KROUSONAS

At the foothills of Mt Psiloritis, the women of the village of Krousonas have created a unique cottage industry making traditional Cretan pastry and local delicacies made from their grandmother's recipes. The successful venture is expanding to bigger purpose-built premises where 25 women will produce a mouth-watering range of sweet and savoury *kalitsounia* (pastries), almond biscuits, rusks, pasta, *baklava, galaktoboureko* (custard pastries) and other sweets. Their specialty is *kouloura* (ornate bread) for weddings and baptisms that can take two women eight hours to decorate. The cooperative is the biggest business in the village, catering for many weddings and social functions, and exporting all over Greece and as far as Germany.

After stocking up on Cretan treats you can visit the nearby **Moni Agia Irini**. This picturesque monastery dates from the last years of Venetian rule, but was destroyed by the Turks in 1822 and all the monks were killed. Rebuilt in 1940, today it's occupied by nuns.

Once you have been to the new **Boutari Winery** (☎ 28107 31617; www.boutari.gr; admission €3; 🕐 10am-6pm) anything else on the island seems positively primitive by comparison. Near Skalani, about 8km from Iraklio, this state-of-the-art winery is set on a hill in the middle of the Fantaxometoho estate and has a stunning tasting room and showroom overlooking the vineyard. Informative tours of the facility include a quirky futuristic video on Crete in the impressive cellar cinema where you watch the high-tech show wearing headphones (choice of four languages) and learn how to taste wine.

Nearby at Peza, **Minos winery** (☎ 28107 41595; www.minoswines.gr; video/tour €1/3; 🕐 9am-4pm Mon-Fri, 9am-3pm Sat) and the **Pezas Union of local producers** (☎ 28107 41945; Peza; admission free 🕐 9am-5pm Mon-Sat) also have tastings and videos, as well as mini-museums of the local wine industry. All sell wine direct to the public at cheaper than shop prices.

of rural life. There is also comfortable traditional-style **accommodation** (s/d €40/60).

On the way, from Iraklio you will pass the Koumbedes taverna, in a restored Ottoman building that was originally a mosque and then a Turkish Kafeneion. It has good food and pleasant views over the valley.

TYLISOS ΤΥΛΙΣΟΣ
The minor **Minoan site** (☎ 28108 31498; admission €2; 🕐 8.30am-3pm Tue-Sat) at the village of Tylisos (*til*-is-os), 13km south of Iraklio, is only for the insatiable enthusiast. Three villas dating from different periods have been excavated. Buses from Iraklio to Anogia go through Tylisos. They also go past another Minoan site at **Sklavokambos**, 8km closer to Anogia. The ruins date from 1500 BC and were probably the villa of a district governor.

MYRTIA
The municipality directly south of Iraklio is named after Crete's most famous writer, and his father's village of Myrtia, some 15km from Iraklio, is home to the **Nikos Kazantzakis Museum** (☎ 28107 42451; www.kazantzakis-museum.gr; adult/student & child €3/free; 🕐 9am-7pm Mar-Oct, 10am-

3pm Sun Nov-Feb). There is an excellent collection of memorabilia about the author and his works, including movie and theatre posters from his works from around the world (see also the boxed text on p50).

CENTRAL IRAKLIO

Although most travellers zip through the region between Iraklio and the south coast, several sights make it well worth a stop, but you need your own wheels to explore the region. Mt Psiloritis lies to the west in the Rethymno region; its eastern slopes taper down to a series of high plateaus and deep caves. The most famous cave is the **Ideon Andron Cave**, which was either the birthplace of Zeus or his playground as a child, depending on which legend you believe. There's not much to see in the cave and there are no paved roads, but if you have a motorcycle or a jeep, take the main road south from Anogia and follow the signs to the cave.

The main roads leading south from Iraklio pass through a series of bustling commercial centres and villages that see very few tourists. There are few hotels or domatia in this region. Arhanes, with a couple of interesting Minoan sites nearby and excellent tavernas, makes a worthwhile stop and Zaros is a good base to explore the surrounding region.

ARHANES ΑΡΧΑΝΕΣ
pop 4498
Arhanes, 16km south of Iraklio, is in the heart of Crete's main wine-producing district. The fertile basin of Arhanes has been settled since the Neolithic period. The ancient Minoans built a grand palace that was an administrative centre for the entire Arhanes basin, but it was destroyed along with the other great Minoan palaces. The town came back to life under the Mycenaeans, flourishing until the Dorian conquest in 1100 BC. Today Arhanes is a vibrant town with meticulously restored old houses and pleasant squares. It's considered a model of EU-funded rural town redevelopment and the new road from Iraklio, which makes it an easy commute, is bringing people back to the village.

Irakliots regularly visit to eat at Aharnes' fine tavernas and hang out in the cafés around the main square. There is small but excellent small archaeological museum and a few new accommodation options.

Orientation & Information

The village is divided into two. Ano (upper) Arhanes is home to the museum, while Kato (lower) Arhanes has the main square, post office and bus stop, which is across the street from a restored church. Uphill from the bus stop and a right fork is another small square. There are several banks in town.

Sights

Only scraps of the palace (signposted from the main road) remain. The **Archaeological Museum of Arhanes** (☎ 28107 52712; admission free; ⌚ 8.30am-3pm Wed-Mon) has several interesting finds from regional archaeological excavations. The exhibits include *larnakes* (coffins) and musical instruments from Fourni and an ornamental dagger from the Anemospilia temple (see opposite).

Sleeping & Eating

There are no cheap rooms in Arhanes.

Diahroniko Apartments (☎ 28107 51505; www .diahroniko-cafe.com; s/apt €50/60) On your right as you head into town, these new studios and apartments are run by the café of the same name.

Villa Arhanes (☎ 28103 90770; www.maris.gr) A more upmarket option in a restored 19th-century Cretan mansion where guests can also participate in rural work or other seasonal village activity.

All the tavernas in town have a good reputation, but **Lakaotos** (☎ 28107 52433) and **To Spitiko** (☎ 28107 51591) on the main square are regarded as the favourites.

Getting There & Away

There are buses hourly from Iraklio to Arhanes (€1.30, 30 minutes).

AROUND ARHANES

From the bus stop in Arhanes follow signs up a steep trail to the Minoan burial grounds at **Fourni**. The round stone 'beehive tombs' form the most extensive Minoan cemetery on the island and date from about 2500 BC. One of the tombs contained the remains of a Minoan noble woman whose jewellery is on display in the Archaeological Museum of Iraklio.

About 5km south of Arhanes, **Vathypetro Villa** (admission free; ⌚ 8.30am-3pm) is well signposted from the town. Dating from about 1600 BC, the villa was probably the home of a prosperous Minoan noble. The villa complex included some storerooms where archaeologists discovered wine and oil presses, a weaving loom and a kiln. Although the doors to the rooms with the wine press and oil press are locked, you can catch a glimpse of the tools through the barred windows. There isn't any public transport to the site, although several travel agencies in Iraklio include a visit to the villa as part of their tour itinerary.

Some 1.5km northwest of Ano Arhanes is the Minoan site of **Anemospilia** (Wind Cave). Discovered in 1979, this middle Minoan sanctuary is significant because it demonstrated that human sacrifice played at least some role in Minoan society. Unfortunately, the site is not open to the general public without special permission. See the boxed text on p41 for details of the sacrificial rites.

DETOUR: HOUDETSI

A few kilometres south of Arhanes, the otherwise unremarkable village of **Houdetsi** is now the home of much-lauded musician Ross Daly, one of the leading exponents of the Cretan lyra. With the help of the local municipality, Daly has transformed a derelict stone manor into the Labyrinth Musical Workshop and a **museum of musical instruments** (☎ 28107 41027; www.labyrinthmusic.gr; admission €3; ⌚ 10am-4pm Mar-Oct) displaying part of his extensive collection of mostly stringed instruments from around the world. More than 250 rare and priceless instruments are on display and an interactive audio system allows you to hear the sound of each one.

Each summer, leading international traditional musicians attend workshops and master classes and hold concerts in the lovely grounds outside the centre. Don't be surprised if you see Turks, Afghanis, Pakistanis, Bulgarians and Mongolians hanging out in Houdetsi. Daly, who is of Irish descent, is master of the modal nonharmonic music of Greece, the Balkans, Turkey, the Middle East, North Africa and North India, and has released more than 25 recordings (see p49).

ZAROS ΖΑΡΟΣ
pop 2215
If the name rings a bell, it's probably because 'Zaros' is the label on the litres of mineral water you've been guzzling. Around 46km south of Iraklio, **Zaros** is a refreshingly un-spoilt traditional village that's known for its spring water and bottling plant. Various excavations in the region indicate that the Minoans and the Romans settled here, lured by the abundant supply of fresh water. The spring water from Zaros also supplied the great Roman capital of Gortyna. Byzantine monasteries are nearly as abundant as the spring water. You can visit several of them and walk the stunning Rouvas gorge. Zaros makes an ideal base for walkers and is rela-tively close to the nearby beaches of Kom-mos and the area's archaeological sites.

Orientation & Information
The business end of Zaros is at the southern entrance of the town. The post office and a supermarket are across the street from the po-lice station. There's no OTE or Internet café. There's an ATM on the main street. Hotel Idi has details on treks to the monasteries and the Rouvas Gorge.

Sights & Activities
If you have your own wheels, the Byzantine monasteries and traditional villages tucked away in the hills are worth exploring. Take the road that leads west from Zaros and you will see a sign directing you to **Moni Agiou Nikolaou**, which is at the mouth of the verdant **Rouvas Gorge**. The monastery still houses several monks and the church con-tains some 14th-century paintings. A few kilometres later is the **Moni Agiou Andoniou Vrondisiou**, which is noteworthy for its 15th-century Venetian fountain. The monastery also has a church with excellent examples of early 14th-century frescoes from the Cretan School of Fresco Painting.

The drive to the monasteries and further on to the traditional mountain villages of **Vorizia** and **Kamares** is particularly scenic. From there, you can hike inland and up to Mt Psiloritis. You have a choice of head-ing westwards along the E4 trail down the mountain to Fourfouras or eastwards along the same trail down to the Nida Plateau. There is also a paved road to the village of Anogia (see also the boxed text on p131).

The Zaros **bottling plant** in the northern end of town will usually allow you to take a look at their packaging and bottling opera-tions. A short distance before the plant you will come to a lovely shady park, **Votomos**, with a small lake and a taverna, café and a children's playground, which makes a great picnic stop. From the lake, there is a walking path to the Moni Agiou Nikolaou monas-tery (900m) and the entry to Rouvas Gorge (2.5km), although it would be better to do it the other way around and end up at the lake for lunch.

Sleeping & Eating
Studios Keramos (☎/fax 28940 31352; s/d incl break-fast €30/3; ⚡) Close to the village centre, this homy hotel run by the friendly Katerina is decorated with Cretan crafts, weaving and family heirlooms. Many of the rooms and studios have antique beds and furniture, some with TV and kitchenette. Katerina is up early cooking up a scrumptious and copious traditional Cretan breakfast – don't miss it.

Hotel Idi (☎ 28940 31301; votomos@otenet.gr; s/d incl breakfast €33/47; ⚡ ⚡) One kilometre outside the village, Hotel Idi is surrounded by trees and greenery and makes for a restful rural escape. The rooms are pleasant and there is an old watermill and mini-museum. It is open all year and has tennis courts, a Jacuzzi and a sauna.

For larger groups, the fully equipped traditionally furnished **Anastasia guesthouse** (☎ 28940 31132; per person €20 or house €140) sleeps eight.

I Limni (☎ 28940 31338; trout per kg €22; ⏱ 9am-late) Right on the lake, this taverna is a peaceful oasis serving fresh grilled trout and Cretan specialties. The basket of starters that comes out with the bread adds a nice touch.

Votomos (☎ 28940 31666; trout per kg €25) Trout is the speciality at this superb fish restau-rant affiliated with the Hotel Idi. You'll see the trout gliding through a huge freshwater reserve so you know they're fresh.

Vengera (☎ 28940 31730) On the main street in the village, this charming *rakadiko* (raki restaurant) and taverna is run by Vivi and her mother Irini who cook traditional Cre-tan food.

Getting There & Away
There are two afternoon buses daily to Zaros from Iraklio (€3.40, one hour).

SOUTH-CENTRAL IRAKLIO

The main highway that runs from Tymbaki to Pyrgos divides the northern part of the Iraklio prefecture from the southern coastal resorts. Along the highway are busy commercial centres, such as Tymbaki, Mires, Agii Deka and Pyrgos that market the agricultural produce from the surrounding region. Although these towns hold little interest for tourists they do give a sense of the dynamism of the Cretan economy.

The south-central region of Crete is blessed with a trio of important archaeological sites – Phaestos, Agia Triada and Gortyna – and a cluster of minor sites spanning Cretan history from the Minoans to the Romans. Getting from one to the other ideally requires private transport or joining a comprehensive sites tour from Iraklio. Either way, allow some time to see the sites and consider basing yourself here for a day or two.

When you get tired of poking around ancient ruins, the south-coast beaches of Matala, Kommos, Kalamaki and Lendas beckon with long stretches of sandy beach. Further to the east are the quiet beach communities of Kastri and Keratokambos and the lovely mountain village of Ano Viannos.

GORTYNA ΓΟΡΤΥΝΑ

The archaeological site of **Gortyna** (☎ 28920 31144; admission €4; 🕑 8am-7pm, to 5pm in winter), 46km southwest of Iraklio, is the largest in Crete and one of the most fascinating. Also called Gortyn or Gortys, Gortyna (*gor*-tih-nah) doesn't have much from the Minoan period because it was little more than a subject town of powerful Phaestos until it began accumulating riches (mostly from piracy) under the Dorians. By the 5th century BC, however, it was as influential as Knossos. When the island was under threat from the Romans, the Gortynians cleverly made a pact with them and, when the Romans conquered the island in 67 BC, they made Gortyna the island's capital. The city blossomed under the Roman administrators who endowed it with lavish public buildings including a Praetorium, amphitheatre, public baths, a music school and temples. Except for the 7th-century-BC Temple of the Pythian Apollo and the 7th-century-AD Church of Agios Titos, most of what you see in Gortyna dates from the Roman period. Gortyna's centuries of splendour came to an end in AD 824 when the Saracens raided the island and destroyed the city.

The vastness of the site indicates how important Gortyna city was to the Romans. The city sprawls over a square kilometre of plains, foothills and the summit of Mt Agios Ioannis. As for most Roman cities, water was an important resource. The Romans needed water for their elaborate systems of fountains and public baths. At one time there must have been ducts and an aqueduct that brought water from the springs of Votomos lake, 15km away. There also must have been streets and a town square, but these have not been excavated.

Although Italian archaeologist Federico Halbherr first explored the site during the 1880s, excavations are continuing. There is a fenced area north of the main road with a large number of ruins outside the fenced area both north and south of the main road from Agii Deka.

Beginning south of the main road you'll first come to the **Temple of the Pythian Apollo**, which was the main sanctuary of pre-Roman Gortyna. Built in the 7th century BC, the temple was expanded in the 3rd century BC and converted into a Christian basilica in the 2nd century AD. Nearby is the **Praetorium** that was the palace of the Roman governor of Crete, an administrative building with a basilica and a private residence. Most of the ruins date from the 2nd century AD and were repaired in the 4th century. To the north is the 2nd-century **Nymphaeum**, a public bath supplied by an **aqueduct** bringing water from Zaros. It was originally adorned with statues of nymphs. South of the Nymphaeum is the **amphitheatre**, which dates from the late 2nd century AD.

The most impressive monument within the fenced area is the **Church of Agios Titos**, which is the finest early-Christian church in Crete. It was probably built on the site of an earlier church, but this construction dates from the 6th century. The stone cruciform church has two small apses and contains three levels, with the surviving apse providing a hint of its former magnificence. Nearby is the **Odeion**, a theatre built around the 1st century BC. Behind the Odeion is a plane tree that, according to legend, served as a love nest for Zeus and Europa.

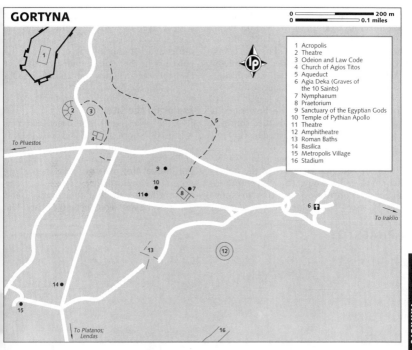

0 | 200 m
0 | 0.1 miles

1 Acropolis
2 Theatre
3 Odeion and Law Code
4 Church of Agios Titos
5 Aqueduct
6 Agia Deka (Graves of the 10 Saints)
7 Nymphaeum
8 Praetorium
9 Sanctuary of the Egyptian Gods
10 Temple of Pythian Apollo
11 Theatre
12 Amphitheatre
13 Roman Baths
14 Basilica
15 Metropolis Village
16 Stadium

To Phaestos

To Iraklio

To Platanos; Lendas

IRAKLIO

Beyond the Odeion is the star attraction – the stone tablets engraved with the 6th-century-BC **Laws of Gortyna**. The stone tablets containing the laws, 600 lines written in a Dorian dialect, were the earliest law code in the Greek world. Ancient Cretans were preoccupied with the same issues that drive people into court today – marriage, divorce, transfers of property, inheritance and adoption, as well as criminal offences. Dorian legal theories are interesting but the main value of these remarkable tablets is the insight they provide into the social organisation of pre-Roman Crete. It was an extremely hierarchical society, divided into slaves and several categories of free citizens, each of whom had strictly delineated rights and obligations.

It's a bit of a hike but it's worth visiting the **Acropolis** at the top of the hill in the northwest corner of the site. Following the road along the stream near the Odeion you will come to a gate beyond the theatre that marks the start of the path to the top. In addition to a bird's-eye view of the entire site, the acropolis contains impressive sections of the pre-Roman ramparts.

Buses to Phaestos from Iraklio also stop at Gortyna; see p167 for details.

PHAESTOS ΦΑΙΣΤΟΣ

The Minoan site of **Phaestos** (☎ 28920 42315; admission €4, incl Agia Triada €6; ☼ 8am-7pm Jun-Oct, 8am-5pm Nov-Apr), 63km from Iraklio, was the second-most-important palace-city in all of Minoan Crete. With amazing all-embracing views of the Mesara Plain and Mt Psiloritis, Phaestos (fes-*tos*), has the most awe-inspiring location of all the Minoan sites. The layout of the palace is similar to Knossos, with rooms arranged around a central court.

Pottery deposits indicate that the site was inhabited in the Neolithic era around 4000 BC when the first settlers established themselves on the slopes of Kastri Hill. The first palace was built around 2000 BC and then destroyed by the earthquake that levelled many Minoan palaces. The ruins were covered with a layer of lime and debris that formed the basis of a new palace that was begun around 1700 BC. It, too, was destroyed in the catastrophe that befell the island in 1450 BC. In the intervening centuries Phaestos was the political and administrative centre of the Mesara Plain. Ancient texts refer to the palace's importance and note that it minted its own coins. Although Phaestos continued to be inhabited in later centuries, it fell into decline as Gortyna rose in importance. Under the Dorians, Phaestos headed a league of cities that included Matala and Polyrrinia in western Crete. The leagues battled continuously and Phaestos was defeated by Gortyna in the 2nd century BC.

Excavation of the site began in 1900 by Professor Federico Halbherr of the Italian School of Archaeology, which is continuing the excavation work. In contrast to Knossos, Phaestos has yielded few frescoes; it

seems the palace walls were mostly covered with a layer of white gypsum. There has been no reconstruction of these ruins. The difficulty of visualising the structure of the palace is further compounded by the fact that the site includes remains of the Old Palace and the New Palace.

Exploring the Site

Past the ticket booth, the **Upper Court** that was used in both the Old and New Palaces contains the remains of buildings from the Hellenistic era. A stairway leads down to the **Theatral Area** that was once the staging ground for performances. The seats are at the northern end, and the southern end contains the **west façade of the Old Palace**. The

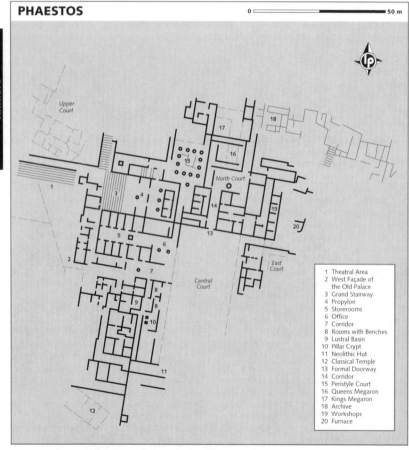

PHAESTOS

0 ⊏══════════════⊐ 50 m

1 Theatral Area
2 West Façade of the Old Palace
3 Grand Stairway
4 Propylon
5 Storerooms
6 Office
7 Corridor
8 Rooms with Benches
9 Lustral Basin
10 Pillar Crypt
11 Neolithic Hut
12 Classical Temple
13 Formal Doorway
14 Corridor
15 Peristyle Court
16 Queens Megaron
17 Kings Megaron
18 Archive
19 Workshops
20 Furnace

Upper Court

North Court

Central Court

East Court

IRAKLIO

THE PHAESTOS DISK

This 3600-year-old terracotta tablet, about 16cm in diameter, is an inscrutable relic from the Minoan archives. It was discovered at Phaestos in 1908 and has remained the object of much interpretational speculation ever since. The disk consists of a pictographic script made up of 241 'words' written in a continuous linear format from the outside of the disk to the inside (or the other way round). It has so far resisted all attempts at decipherment. The simplistic pictograms in most cases are easily identifiable – parts of the body, animal, tools etc – and bear only a passing similarity to the other scripts of Crete: Linear A and Linear B. Given that no other similar script has ever been discovered and that it is quite possible that the disk is an import from outside Crete, decipherment in the foreseeable future seems highly unlikely.

15m-wide **grand stairway** leads to the **Propylon**, which was a porch. Below the Propylon are the **storerooms** that still contain pithoi storage urns. The square hall next to the storerooms is thought to have been an **office**, where tablets containing Linear A script were found beneath the floor in 1955. South of the storeroom a **corridor** led to the west side of the **Central Court**. South of the corridor is a **lustral basin**, rooms with benches and a **pillar crypt** similar to that at Knossos. The Central Court is the centrepiece of the palace, affording spectacular views of the surrounding area. It is extremely well preserved and gives a good sense of the magnificence of the palace. Porticoes with columns and pillars once lined the long sides of the Central Court. Notice the **Neolithic hut** at the southwestern corner of the Central Court. The best-preserved parts of the palace complex are the reception rooms and private apartments to the north of the Central Court, where excavations continue. Enter through the **Formal Doorway** with half columns at either side, the lower parts of which are still *in situ*. The corridor leads to the north court; the **Peristyle Court**, which once had a paved veranda, is to the left of here. The royal apartments (**Queen's Megaron** and **King's Megaron**) are northeast of the Peristyle Court but they are currently fenced off. The celebrated Phaestos Disk (above) was found in a building to the north of the palace. It now resides in Iraklio's Archaeological Museum (p149).

Getting There & Away

Eight buses a day head to Phaestos from Iraklio's Bus Station B (€4.50, 1½ hours), and also stop at Gortyna. There are also buses from Agia Galini (€1.50 minutes, nine daily) and Matala (€1.30, 30 minutes, five daily).

VORI ΒΩΡΟΙ

pop 755

The pleasant unspoilt village of Vori, 4km east of Tymbaki, has an attractive main square surrounded by winding streets of whitewashed houses. The surprise attraction here is the outstanding private **Museum of Cretan Ethnology** (☎ 28920 91112; admission €3; 10am-6pm Apr-Oct, by appointment in winter ☎ 28920 91110), which provides a fascinating insight into traditional Cretan culture. The English-labelled exhibits follow themes such as rural life, war, customs, architecture, music, and the herbs, flora and fauna that form the basis of the Cretan diet. There some are some beautiful weavings, furniture, woodcarvings and musical instruments. The museum is well signposted from the main road.

There are a few tavernas around the lovely main square. Signposted about 400m up from the museum are the **Portokali Apartments** (☎ 28920 91128; studio €25;), four new excellent studios set in a lovely garden with barbecue facilities and lots of homey touches. They have bikes for guests.

AGIA TRIADA ΑΓΙΑ ΤΡΙΑΔΑ

The small Minoan site of **Agia Triada** (☎ 28920 91564; admission €3, incl Phaestos €6; 10am-4.30pm summer, 8.30am-3pm winter) is 3km west of Phaestos in an enchanting landscape surrounded by hills and orange groves. Like the site of Phaestos, it appears that Agia Triada has been occupied since the Neolithic era.

Masterpieces of Minoan art, such as the 'Harvester's Vase', the 'Boxer Vase' and the 'Chieftain's Cup', now in the Archaeological Museum of Iraklio, were found here but the palace was clearly not as important as the palace at Phaestos. Its principal building was smaller than the other royal palaces although it was built to a similar design. This, and the opulence of the objects found at the site, indicate that it was a royal residence, possibly a summer palace of Phaestos' rulers.

After the entrance, you will first pass the ruins of a **Minoan House** before reaching the **shrine** that dates from the early 14th century BC. It once contained a frescoed floor painted with octopuses and dolphins, which is now in the Archaeological Museum of Iraklio. Northwest of the shrine is a paved courtyard that excavators called the **Court of Shrines**. Notice the **magazines and workshops** in the southwest wing of the palace; the 'Chieftain's Cup' was found in one of these rooms. North of the workshops you will come to a **hall** and then the **inner chamber** that contains a raised slab that might have supported a bed, indicating that these were the residential quarters. The **archives room** once contained over 200 seal-stones and a wall painting of the wild cat of Crete, which is now in the Archaeological Museum of Iraklio. The **Rampa al Mare** ramp that runs beneath the north side of the palace is thought to have run down to the sea at one point. A path leads from the fenced site along the hillside to a Minoan **cemetery** that dates from around 2000 BC. There are two circular beehive tombs.

There is no public transport to Agia Triada and the site is about a 5km walk from any major village. The road to Agia Triada takes off to the right about 500m from Phaestos on the road to Matala.

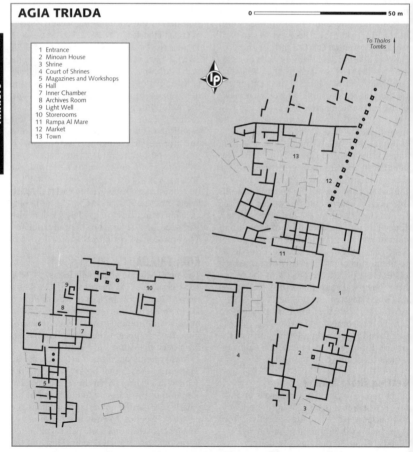

AGIA TRIADA

0 ‾‾‾‾‾‾ 50 m

1 Entrance
2 Minoan House
3 Shrine
4 Court of Shrines
5 Magazines and Workshops
6 Hall
7 Inner Chamber
8 Archives Room
9 Light Well
10 Storerooms
11 Rampa Al Mare
12 Market
13 Town

To Tholos Tombs

KOMMOS ΚΌΜΜΟΣ

The archaeological site of Kommos, 12km southwest of Mires along a beautiful beach, is still being excavated by American and Canadian archaeologists. Although the site is fenced off it's easy to get an idea of it from the outside. Kommos is believed to have been the port for Phaestos and contains a wealth of Minoan structures. It's even possible to spot the layout of the ancient town with its streets and courtyards, and the remains of workshops, dwellings and temples. Notice the Minoan road paved in limestone that leads from the southern section inland towards Phaestos; the ruts in the road from Minoan carts and a sewer on its northern side are still visible.

Kommos is about 3km north of Matala and makes for a pleasant walk.

MATALA ΜΑΤΑΛΑ
pop 100

Matala (*ma*-ta-la), on the coast 11km southwest of Phaestos, was once one of Crete's best-known hippie hang-outs. When you see the dozens of eerie caves speckling the rock slab on the edge of the beach, you'll see why '60s hippies found it, like, groovy man. The caves were originally Roman tombs cut out of the sandstone rock in the 1st century AD and have been employed as dwellings for many centuries. The soft rock allowed cave-dwellers to carve out windows, doors and beds.

The caves are all that remains of ancient Matala, which probably served as a port for the great Minoan centre of Phaestos. Matala enjoyed a burst of activity under the Romans that lasted from 67 BC until the Arab conquest in the 9th century. During those centuries Matala was the port for Gortyna. Excavations around Matala have revealed coins from Gortyna, along with vases and amphorae.

These days, Matala is a developed tourist resort that gets busy in the peak of summer but has lost its edge or any real 'scene', and is bleak and deserted in winter. The turtles like it, however. Matala and the area around it is a popular nesting ground for *Caretta caretta* sea turtles. The Sea Turtle Protection Society has a booth near the car park. The sandy beach below the caves is still beautiful and the resort is a convenient base to visit Phaestos and Agia Triada.

Orientation & Information

The bus stop is on the central square, one block back from the waterfront and there is parking before the town and beach. There is a mobile post office near the beach, and three ATMs in the village. There is no tourist office.

Monza Travel (☎ 28920 45757), on the right as you enter town, rents out rooms, apartments, cars and bikes, changes money and arranges for boat excursions.

You can check your email at **Zafiria Internet** (☎ 28920 45498; per hr €4; 🕙 10am-late).

Sights & Activities

Forget about museums, monuments and archaeological sites. Matala is about the beach and the **caves** (admission €2; 🕙 8am-7pm Jun-Sep), which are fenced off at night. The **beach** is great for swimming and has pine trees along the edge that cast some shade, plus ubiquitous umbrellas and sun lounges for rent.

For a less crowded experience, head to **Kokkini Ammos** (Red Beach). It's about a 30-minute scramble south over the rocks and attracts a smattering of nudists.

Sleeping

There are several pleasant options in Matala proper, including one handy camping ground. The street running inland to the left of the main drag is lined with budget accommodation, which makes it easy to haggle for the best deal. Hotels are also reasonably priced off-season.

Pension Andonios (☎ 28920 45123; fax 28920 45690; s/d/tr €25/30/35) This comfortable pension run by the genial Antonis has attractively furnished rooms, many with kitchenette, and the top rooms have balconies.

Fantastic Rooms to Rent (☎ 28920 45362; fax 28920 45292; d/tr €25/30, d with kitchen €30; 🖳) Here since the hippie heydays, this place has added a newer block at the back. The rooms are plain but comfortable, many with kitchenette, phone, kettle and fridge.

Silvia Rent Rooms (☎ 28920 45127; d/tr €25/30) On the same street as Fantastic Rooms you'll find Silvias. The nine rooms here are clean, simple and pleasant, with a fridge and balconies overlooking the cliffs. The bathrooms are a little dated and there's no air-con.

Hotel Zafiria (☎ 28920 45366; fax 28920 45725; d incl breakfast €40; 🖳 🅿 🖳) The sprawling Hotel

IRAKLIO

Zafiria takes up a whole block on Matala's main street. There is a spacious lobby bar and the comfortable rooms have balconies, sea views and telephones. A new pool has been added beneath the cliffs.

Matala Community Camping (☎ /fax 28920 45720; per tent/adult €2.90/4.10) This is a reasonable, shaded, although rather uneven, site just back from the beach.

Eating

Eating in Matala is hardly an experience in haute cuisine, but there are a few decent options among tourist joints scattered along the main drag.

Nikos (☎ 28920 45335; mains €4-7.50, fish per kg €27-41) This fish taverna garners most of its brownie points from its position on the cliffs above the beach next to the Roman cemetery, but is also well regarded.

Scala (☎ 28920 45489; seafood platter for 2 €10) Further along the cliffs from Nikos', this fish tavern also has prime position in a quiet spot overlooking the beach.

Gianni's Taverna (☎ 28920 45719; mains €4-7) Towards the end of the main street, Gianni's

Taverna is a no-frills place with good-value grills, including a mixed grill with salad and potatoes (€7).

Lions (☎ 28920 45108; specials €5.50-9) Overlooking the beach, Lions has been popular many years and the food is better than average. It is also a good place for a drink as it gets lively in the evening.

For self-caterers, there's a couple of minimarkets, a bakery and several other shops for supplies.

Getting There & Away

There are buses between Iraklio and Matala (€5.50, 2½ hours, nine daily), and between Matala and Phaestos (€1.30, 30 minutes, five daily).

AROUND MATALA

When Matala fills up in the summer or gets too much, many travellers head to **Pitsidia**, a little village 5km northeast of Matala. There's not much to do here except meet other travellers and take a horse-riding tour from **Melanouri Horse Farm** (☎ 28920 45040) through the surrounding region. All buses to Matala stop in Pitsidia; the bus stop is in the centre of the village in front of Hotel Aretousa.

Hotel Aretousa (☎ 28920 45555; s/d €21/29) This pleasant small hotel on the main road has lovely garden terrace out the front for breakfast. The rooms are clean, nicely decorated and have mosquito nets. The paintings of the wall are by the owner, Michalis.

Bodikos Rooms & Pizzeria (☎ 28920 45438; www.bodikos-matala.com; d/tr €25/30) Apart from the great wood-oven pizzas (€4 to €4.90), this place has large comfortable studios and rooms upstairs, as well as some family accommodation nearby.

Komos Beach camp site (☎ 28920 42332; per person/tent €3.50/2.50). This camping ground is at Komos Beach, about 4km before Matala on the road from Phaestos.

KAMILARI ΚΑΜΗΛΑΡΙ

pop 289

Built on three hills, Kamilari provides a complete escape into traditional Cretan village life, although most of the accommodation is on the outskirts of town. Its proximity to Kalamaki Beach makes it attractive to visitors, plus there's an important Minoan tomb just outside village. Since the

---

THE HIPPIE CONNECTION

Long before Mykonos was hip and Ios was hot, Matala was host to a colony of flower children and alternative lifestylers in the late 1960s and early 1970s who made Matala their very own pied-à-terre. The hippies turned the caves into a modern troglodyte city – moving ever higher up the cliff to avoid sporadic attempts by the local police to evict them. Singer Joni Mitchell was among a number of hippies who lived in the caves. In 'Carey' from her 1970's album *Blue* she sang: ...*but let's not talk about fare-thee-wells now, the night is a starry dome and they're playin' that scratchy rock and roll beneath the Matala moon.*

Drawn by the lure of free cave accommodation, a gorgeous beach, a smattering of low-key, cheap tavernas, free love and copious pot, Matala's hippies came in droves and hung around – wearing little more than headbands and guitars. Today, the caves are still there, but they are fenced off and most of the hippies have moved on. As one ex-hippie put it: 'Things ain't just cool no more...man!'

village is only 2.5km west of Phaestos, it's a good base to explore the beaches and archaeological sites of the southern coast.

Sights
The circular **Minoan Tomb** of Kamilari dates from 1900 BC and is extraordinarily well preserved with stone walls still standing 2m high. Archaeologists believe that outside the circular tomb there were five small rooms that were used for burial rites. Clay models depicting the funerary rituals were unearthed by excavators and are now in the Archaeological Museum of Iraklio. The road to the tomb is clearly indicated at the entrance to Kamilari. It is a good half-hour walk out to the tomb located in the middle of fields about 3km from the village.

Sleeping & Eating
There are plenty of rooms for rent sign-posted in the main square.

Apartments Ambeliotissa (☎ /fax 28920 42690; www.ambeliotissa.com; studio €25-47; ⚄) This place has furnished studios and apartments, all of which have air-con and heating for winter visitors. The pink and white stucco building has a stone fireplace, veranda and an outdoor barbecue. They also run Studios Pelekanos nearby.

Asterousia Apartments (☎ 28920 42832; www asterousia.com; s/d €27/32) The hammock out the front, a scattering of antiques and brightly painted open-plan rooms give this place a great ambience. There's a big old table on the veranda and a nice garden, making it a good base for longer stays and families.

Plaka Apartments (☎ 28920 42697; www.plaka .creta.com; d €30; ⚄) These lovely well-appointed apartments on a hill just outside the village have balconies with sea views and are decorated in cool blue and white shades. There is a garden with sun lounges in the back. Ask at Taverna Mylonas.

Taverna Mylonas (☎ 28920 42156; mains €5.50-6.50) This place has good home-cooked Cretan food in the centre of the village, and they have also added some Italian and Chinese-style dishes. There are great views of the surrounding mountains from the tables on the terrace.

Getting There & Away
There is one morning bus daily from Iraklio via Mires (€5, 1½ hours).

KALAMAKI ΚΑΛΑΜΆΚΙ
pop 75
The wide, sandy beach that stretches for many kilometres in either direction is Kalamaki's best feature and makes for a pleasant walk. Located 2.5km southwest of Kamilari, tourism is in its embryonic stage after the recent opening of a paved road all the way to the beach. Unfortunately, the beach is lined with a string of half-finished concrete structures that are slowly being turned into hotels. It's a quiet place to stay, however, and the swimming is good.

Orientation & Information
There is one main road leading into the village square, which is right behind the beach. There is no post office, tourist office or OTE, but **Monza Travel** (☎ /fax 28920 45692; ◷ 9am-2pm & 5-10pm) handles car and bike rentals, hotel reservations, air and boat tickets, and excursions around Crete.

Sleeping
Babis Studios (☎ 28920 45220; www.studio-babis.gr; d €30; ⚄) This complex right on the beach opened in 2004. The rooms are tastefully decorated and well appointed with TV and hairdryers. There are balconies overlooking the sea.

Kostas Hotel (☎ /fax 28920 45692; www.kreta -kalamaki.com; d €25-60; ⚄) These rooms above Monza Travel have fridges, TV and coffee-making equipment, and enjoy a communal roof garden that is great at night. Rooms of different sizes and configurations sleep up to six.

Pension Galini (☎ 28920 45042; fax 28920 23442; s/d €25/30; ⚄) About 100m away from the beach, this is one of the most attractive places to stay in the village. The spacious rooms boast balconies and are furnished in pine. Some also come with fully equipped kitchens. There's also a rooftop terrace with a view of the sea.

Eating
Yiannis (☎ 28920 45685; meze spread €6.50-10.50) It's easy to miss this tiny place, which was once on the beach but is now blocked by hotels. But Yiannis retains a loyal following for his excellent no-nonsense mezedes at reasonable prices. There are lots of vegetarian dishes and a complimentary glass of raki.

IRAKLIO

Taverna Avra (☎ 28920 45052; fish per kg €30) At the northern end of the beachfront, this is a good spot to sample fresh fish and Cretan home cooking, and also has daily oven-baked specials.

Also recommended is the **Delfinia** (☎ 28290 45697) fish taverna at the northern end of the beach.

Getting There & Away
There's one morning bus daily from Iraklio via Mires (€5, two hours).

LENDAS ΛΈΝΤΑΣ
pop 77
The major appeal of the small beach settlement at Lendas is its remoteness and laid-back feel. Lendas is reached via a long and winding road with a dramatic last few kilometres descending to the village, which clings to the cliff over the beach and has a pleasant view over the Libyan sea. The narrow pebbly beaches are pleasant enough, but there are some better beaches to explore nearby and some stunning rock formations. In recent times, Lendas has expanded as a tourist destination, but it still attracts mostly independent travellers, including regulars who have been coming for 20 years. It is never packed (although it does get busier in July and August when schools are out) and retains an appealing intimacy, plus a peacefulness that comes from not having any passing traffic. There is a lively beach scene, with a couple of beach bars.

Within walking distance there is an archaeological site and the Dytikos naturist beach where old hippies from Matala camp on the beach. Some people apparently live there year-round. It is a good place for long walks, tasty fish and relaxed holidays.

Orientation & Information
As you enter the village from the main road there's a left fork that takes you to the eastern car park and a right fork that takes you to the main 'square'. The bus stops outside the eastern car park and there are a couple of mini-markets for essential supplies. There is no post office, bank or OTE. The **Internet Café** (☎ 28290 95206; per hr €3) is near the beach.

To get to Dytikos beach follow the main road west for 1km or the path alongside the coastal cliffs.

Sights
The archaeological site of **Lebena** is right outside the village. Lebena was a health spa that the Romans visited for its therapeutic springs. Only two granite columns remain of a temple that dates from the 4th century BC. Next to the temple was a treasury with a mosaic floor that is still visible. Very little else is decipherable and the springs have been closed since the 1960s.

Sleeping & Eating
Studios Gaitani (☎ 28920 95341; www.studios-gaitani.gr studio €25-40; ⚡) It doesn't get more beachfront than this. These new studios and one large two-level apartment are a few steps down to the sand. They have kitchenettes, TV and fridge, and the larger ones can fit up to four.

Rooms & Taverna El Greco (☎ 28920 95322 s/d €35; ⚡) Some rooms here have balconies with sea views and there's an excellent taverna that overlooks a lovely lush garden and the sea. You can tuck into a wide selection of *mayirefta* and traditional Greek and international dishes. The local swordfish (€8.50) is recommended.

Rent Rooms Zorbas (☎ 28920 95228; €25; ⚡) The right fork from the main road takes you down to these rooms and adjoining restaurant on the cliffs over the beach. The rooms are pleasant and some have balconies with sea views.

Getting There & Away
There's a daily afternoon bus from Iraklio (€5, three hours).

ANO VIANNOS ΑΝΩ ΒΊΑΝΝΟΣ
pop 878
Ano Vianos, in the southeastern corner of Iraklio, is a quiet village built on the southern flanks of Mt Dikti. While there used to be a folklore museum in the village, it seems to have fallen by the wayside and the main sight is the village's tiny 14th-century **Church of Agia Pelagia** (admission free; ⏰ 9am-8pm summer). Follow the signs up to the top end of the village to find it. The interior walls, covered with luscious frescoes by Nikiforos Fokas, are in need of restoration but can still be appreciated.

You can stay and eat in Ano Viannos at **Taverna & Rooms Lefkes** (☎ 28950 22719; r €15) just downhill off the main road. While the

ooms under the taverna are dark and un-
nspiring, Maria's food is simple but good
with excellent salads, fresh eggs and local
Cretan dishes (€4 to €6) such as lamb baked
in a clay pot.

From Ano Viannos there are three buses
daily to Iraklio (€4.70, two hours) and Ierapetra (€3.05, one hour) via Myrtos.

KASTRI & KERATOKAMBOS
ΚΑΣΤΡΙ & ΚΕΡΑΤΟΚΑΜΠΟΣ
pop 353

At the twin mini-resorts and now contigu-
ous villages of Kastri and Keratokambos,
23 tortuous kilometres downhill, there's
a pleasant tree-lined beach and a number
of eating and sleeping choices. The tranquillity of this tiny resort is its chief asset.
Many Germans have moved in and bought
property here. If you like peace and quiet
and have a few books to read, this is your
kind of place.

Orientation & Information
There's no bank, post office, OTE or car-
rental agency, but there is a mini-market
and you can exchange money and rent cars
at Taverna Kriti.

Sleeping & Eating
Iloxenia Apartments (☎ 28950 51371; studio €32; ❄)
This is the best mid-range option. The lovely
two-to-three-person studios, wrapped in
a flower-filled garden, are equipped with
kitchenette, fridge and TV, and make for a
very pleasant base for a week or so.

Komis Studios (☎ 28950 51390; www.komisstudios.gr;
keratokambos; apt incl breakfast €94; ❄) These upmarket three-level apartments are ecologi-
cally sound and attractively decorated in
rustic style. They use wind and solar power
and the sewage is treated biologically. They
are well outfitted with telephone and TV,
and can accommodate two to four people.

Taverna Nikitas (☎ 28950 51477; mains €4-5) One
of a handful of tavernas along the beach in
Keratokambos, Nikitas offers consistently
high-quality and delicious grills, which are
surprisingly inexpensive. The goat in red
sauce is highly recommended, as is the local
wordfish.

To Livyko (☎ 28950 51290; grills €5-6) Makes
tasty grills from their own meat, along with
fresh fish and Cretan specials. The setting
is delightful.

Morning Star Taverna (☎ 28950 51209; Kastri;
mains €5-6) Succulent grills and fish dishes are
the go here, while the tasty artichoke stew is
a good choice for vegetarians.

Getting There & Away
There's no public transport available to
Keratokambos. The 8km road to Arvi in the
east is driveable in a conventional vehicle.

NORTHEASTERN COAST

Ever since the national road along the
northern coast opened in 1972, the coast
between Iraklio and Malia has seen a frenzy
of development. A concrete wall of hotels,
schnitzel outlets and tacky souvenir shops
lines every stretch of sandy beach. Even
if that appeals, there's not much here for
individual travellers since the hotels deal
almost exclusively with package-tour operators who block-book hotel rooms months
in advance. The prices for individual travellers are relatively steep, compared with
the discounts package-tourists receive, and
service is likely to be indifferent for those
without the clout of a tour operator behind
them. After a bad season in 2004, this may
well change as many tour operators strug-
gled to fill the rooms or went elsewhere.

The principle centres here are the overdeveloped tourist towns of Hersonisos and
Malia, and the less intimidating resort areas
at Gournes, Gouves and Stalida. Further
east, the villages of Sisi and Milatos are less
developed and attract more families. The
Minoan palace at Malia is the only significant site of cultural interest in the area.
There is a cave at Milatos and a massive
new aquarium was being built at a former
US air base at Gouves. Amid the low-brow
establishments, there are several high-end
resorts. Crete's first world-class 18-hole golf
course opened here in 2003.

HERSONISOS ΧΕΡΣΟΝΗΣΟΣ
pop 882

Hersonisos, 27km east of Iraklio, began its
days as a small fishing village on a hill, but
these days it is a brash, expansive mecca for
cheap package tourism with a long coastal
strip of neon-lit restaurants and look-alike
hotels. The beach is sandy, but it gets jam-
packed with lounge chairs and umbrellas.

Hersonisos is known for its action-packed nightclub scene and attracts party animals, along with neighbouring Malia. That said, there is always something to do in Hersonisos and there are plenty of excursions to all parts of the island.

Orientation & Information

The coastal road from Iraklio to Agios Nikolaos, which runs through the elongated village, is Eletheriou Venizelou. Most travel agencies, banks and services are located along here. The OTE office is north of Eletheriou Venizelou and the post office is in the centre of town on Digeni Akrita. There is also a beachfront road of tavernas, hotels and nightclubs. There is no tourist office but **Hermes Rent a Bike** (☎ 28970 32271) is a good source of information.

Uphill from the main road is the village of **Koutouloufari**, which is touristy but retains some semblance of traditional village atmosphere.

Sights & Activities

Towards the end of Limin Hersonisos there are signs to **Lychnostatis Museum** (☎ 28970 23660; www.lychnostatis.gr; admission €4.50; ☼ 9.30am-2pm Sun-Fri), a unique open-air museum dedicated to Cretan rural life and culture. Instead of selling out or building a hotel on the family land right next to the beach, the Markakis family have commendably created this sprawling museum. There are displays about all aspects of traditional rural life from weaving to raki making, a Cretan herb garden, as well as a small kafeneio. Instead of inscriptions there are clever *mandinades*, including the verses painted on the walls of the mill dedicated to his wife.

Crete Golf Club (☎ 28970 26000; www.crete-golf.g 18 holes €65) Crete's only 18-hole cours is not for hackers. It's a tough desert-styl course on the hills about 7km south o Hersonisos.

Sleeping & Eating

Most hotels only deal with groups, but th travel agents in town can usually recom mend places they have deals with. For decen accommodation and the chance of a quie night's sleep, head for Koutouloufari.

Elen Mari Apartments (☎ 28970 25525; apt €35 44) This is by far the best option. The full equipped studios are neat and well main tained and some have excellent views ove Hersonisos.

Emmanuel Taverna (☎ 28970 21022; Plateia Ele theriou Venizelou; specials €10) Run by a Greek Australian family, this homely taverna specialises in spit-roasted meats and dishe cooked in the wood oven. The owner rec ommends their specialty lamb in rose win with bay leaves (€10), or anything from th spit, which is fired up every night.

Rahati (☎ 28970 29303; Evropis 86; breakfast €4.75 After a hard night, take breakfast at thi neat, Dutch-run establishment. Munch o cakes and apples pies and wash it all dow with a strong coffee.

Fabrica (☎ 28970 23981; crepes €2.50-6.50) In th evening, head to this café/bar with a grea rooftop terrace with views below to Her sonisos. It's in an old stone building to th right past Sergiani.

Entertainment

Most people come to Hersonisos for th nightlife. As soon as the sun goes dowr the bars fill up, the discos crank up thei volume and the whole resort turns into one vast party. The nightspots, bars and discos wax and wane in popularity from one year to the next. Camelot, Status and Amnesia were *in* at the time of research but most places deliver a pounding blend of booze, rock and roll, retro, disco, techno, house and sometimes…garbage. Forget Greek entertainment. Hersonisos is for non-Greeks out for frantic fun.

Getting There & Away
There are buses to Hersonisos from Iraklio every 30 minutes (€2.20, 45 minutes).

MALIA ΜΑΛΙΑ
pop 3722
The township of Malia is a highly commercialised resort that developed during the 1970s because of its long sandy beach. Crowded and noisy, Malia is full of pubs, bars, tacky eateries, shops and amusement options that make is seem like one big fun park. The sheer scale of overdevelopment is confronting to the senses. The spread-out settlement is distinctly divided into two parts by the main through road: the rowdy, northern side (New Malia), where sunburnt British tourists roam around on quad bikes with their shirts off, and the quieter and southern side (Old Malia).

It's hardly worth making Malia your base, although it's within easy reach of the fascinating Minoan Palace of Malia. If you do stay then stick to the south side, but

---

---

overall Malia appears to have had its day – a couple of bad seasons have led to many places closing down, leaving a distinct air of decay.

Orientation & Information
New Malia is packed with hotels, restaurants, travel agencies and nightlife; south of the main road is Old Malia, or the 'village'. The **post office** (28 Oktovriou 2) is near the main road and the OTE is uphill about 500m and signposted from the main street. There are plenty of ATMs and places to change money on the main road. **Charlie's Travel** (☎ 28970 33834) can provide useful information and sells excursions. Check mail at **Internet Cafe Malia** (☎ 28970 29563; netmail@hrs .forthnet.gr; Dimokratias 78).

Sleeping & Eating
There is a distinct lack of decently priced places on the north side, which is full of hotels that are often block-booked by tour operators. Most travel companies can recommend accommodation and usually have arrangements with particular hotels and rooms. The old village of Malia has some quieter options.

For eating options, forget the northern side of Malia. There is simply nothing worth recommending.

Aquarius (☎ 28970 32117; John Kennedy 48; d €30) On the main road heading to Lasithi, this place has basic rooms with fridge but no air-con.

Espera (☎ 28970 31086; Old Malia; d/studio €25/40) Just off the main road near the Shell petrol station, Evangelia runs this quieter option. Rooms are basic, with a fridge and fans but no air-con.

You could try the colourful **San Giorgio Restaurant** (☎ 28970 32211) in Old Malia on the road to Lasithi for reasonable Cretan food.

Entertainment
Discos, bars and nightclubs are as ephemeral as the youthful tourists who patronise them. There are bars on every corner, selling every permutation of British and Irish beers. You can't miss them.

Getting There & Away
There are buses to Malia from Iraklio every 30 minutes (€2.70, one hour).

PALACE OF MALIA ΑΝΆΚΤΟΡΑ ΜΑΛΊΩΝ

The **Palace of Malia** (☎ 28970 31597; admission €4; ⏰ 8.30am-3pm Tue-Sun), 3km east of Malia, was built at about the same time as the two other great Minoan palaces at Phaestos and Knossos. The first palace was built here around 1900 BC and rebuilt after the earthquake of 1700 BC. What you see is the remains of the newer palace where many exquisite artefacts from Minoan society were found. Excavation began in 1915 by Greek archaeologists and is being continued by French archaeologists. Because the ground plan has been well preserved, it is an easy site to comprehend. Any bus going to or from Iraklio along the north coast can drop you at the site.

Exploring the Site

Access to the ruins is from the **West Court**. Head south through the **Magazines** and a the extreme southern end you'll come to the eight circular pits which archaeologist think were **grain silos**. To the east of the pit is the main entrance to the palace, which leads to the southern end of the **Central Court**. Moving northeast you'll come to the **Kernos Stone**, a disk with 24 holes around it edge. Archaeologists have yet to ascertain its function, but it probably had a religiou purpose. Adjacent to this is the **Grand Stair case**, which might have led to a shrine. To the north is the **Pillar Corridor** with intercon necting rooms and next to it is the **Pilla Crypt** with the Minoan double-axe symbo

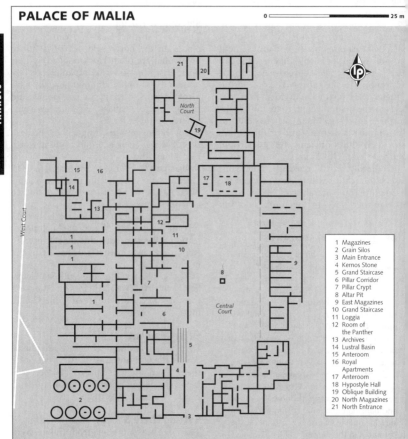

PALACE OF MALIA

0 ⸻ 25 m

North Court

West Court

Central Court

1 Magazines
2 Grain Silos
3 Main Entrance
4 Kernos Stone
5 Grand Staircase
6 Pillar Corridor
7 Pillar Crypt
8 Altar Pit
9 East Magazines
10 Grand Staircase
11 Loggia
12 Room of the Panther
13 Archives
14 Lustral Basin
15 Anteroom
16 Royal Apartments
17 Anteroom
18 Hypostyle Hall
19 Oblique Building
20 North Magazines
21 North Entrance

IRAKLIO

ngraved up on the pillars. The impressive **Central Court** is 48m long and 22m wide and contains remains of the Minoan columns. Notice the pit in the exact centre of the courtyard, which may have been an altar.

At the northern end of the western side of the court is the **Loggia**, which was probably used for ceremonial purposes. Next to the Loggia is the **Room of the Panther** in which 17th-century-BC stone axe shaped like a panther was found. Northwest are the **Royal Apartments** with a **Lustral Basin**. At the north end of the central court is the **Hypostyle Hall** with benches on the side indicating that it may have served as a kind of council chamber. Other rooms include the **archives room** in which tablets containing Linear A script were found. On your way out through the north entrance take note of the pithoi in the **North Court**.

Lasithi Λασιθι

CONTENTS

LASITHI

Crete's easternmost prefecture may receive far fewer visitors than the rest of the island, but the exclusive resorts around Elounda and Agios Nikolaos are the stronghold of Crete's high-end tourism. Elounda has become synonymous with luxury hotels – among them one of the world's top resorts – while the capital, Agios Nikolaos, is the region's contribution to the party scene.

At the centre of the north coast is the pleasant town of Sitia, with the impressive palm-lined beach of Vai in the far east. The fertile region of the Lasithi Plateau in the west provides excellent cycling opportunities through quiet rural villages to the Dikteon Cave where legend has it that Zeus was born.

The southern coast extends from the seaside village of Myrtos in the west to the commercial centre of Ierapetra and beyond to the lovely and relatively untouched beaches of Xerokambos and Kato Zakros. Archaeology buffs will enjoy exploring the Palace of Zakros, an evocative Minoan site in the east next to Kato Zakros Beach, while exciting new finds are likely to be unearthed near the current excavation site at Palekastro.

LASITHI

HIGHLIGHTS

- Cycling around the **Lasithi Plateau** (p188)
- Wandering among the fascinating ruins on **Spinalonga Island** (p187)
- Exploring the Minoan palace on the beach at **Kato Zakros** (p199)
- Relaxing on **Vai** (p196), Crete's only palm-lined beach
- Visiting the **Toplou monastery** (p196)

LASITHI

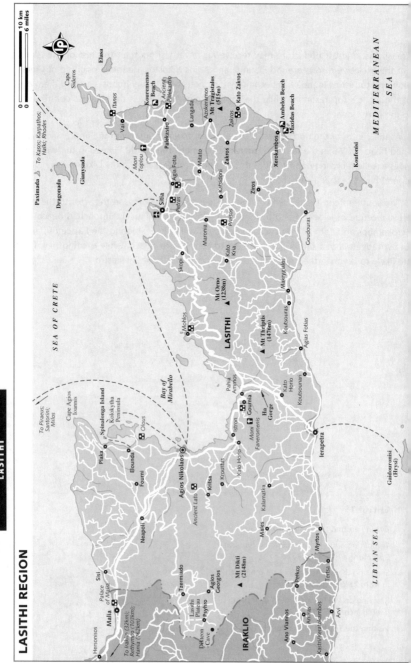

LASITHI REGION

NORTH COAST

AGIOS NIKOLAOS ΑΓΙΟΣ ΝΙΚΟΛΑΟΣ

op 10,080

Lasithi's capital, Agios Nikolaos (ah-yee-os nih-ko-laos), is an undeniably attractive, former fishing village set around a pleasant harbour and a small, picturesque lake connected to the sea.

In the early 1960s it became a chic hideaway for the likes of Jules Dassin and Walt Disney, but by the end of the decade package tourists were arriving in force and it became an overdeveloped tourist town.

During the day, you may wonder what all the fuss is about. While Agios Nikolaos is pleasant enough, there are no impressive beaches or hotels in town, and it lacks the historic atmosphere of Hania, Rethymno and even Iraklio. But Agios Nikolaos remains popular for its lively nightlife, drawing people from nearby resorts. When the cafés and restaurants around the lake and port light up, the ambience turns more vibrant and cosmopolitan. The crowd is generally older (over 30) and more subdued than in Malia and Hersonisos.

While there is superficially little to attract the independent traveller, there is reasonable accommodation, prices are not too horrendous and there is enough activity to cater for all tastes.

History

Agios Nikolaos emerged as a port for the city–state of Lato (see p191) in the early Hellenic years when it was known as Lato-py-Kamara. The harbour assumed importance in the Greco-Roman period after the Romans put an end to the piracy that had plagued the northern coast.

The town continued to flourish in the early Christian years and in the 8th or 9th century the small Byzantine Church of Agio Nikolaos was built.

When the Venetians bought Crete in the 13th century, the Castel Mirabello was built on a hill overlooking the sea and a settlement arose below. The castle was damaged in the earthquake of 1303 and was burned by pirates in 1537, before being rebuilt according to plans from the military architect Sammicheli. When the Venetians were forced to abandon the castle to the Turks

in 1645 they blew it up, leaving it in ruins. There's no trace of the Venetian occupation except the name they gave to the surrounding gulf – Mirabello or 'beautiful view'.

The town was resettled in the mid-19th century by fleeing rebels from Sfakia and was later named capital of the Lasithi region.

Orientation

The bus station is on the southern side of town about 500m from the town centre at Plateia Venizelou. The de facto town centre is around the Voulismeni Lake, 150m from Plateia Venizelou. Most banks, ATMs, travel agencies and shops are on Koundourou and the parallel pedestrianised 28 Oktovriou.

Information

Anna Karteri Bookshop (☎ 28410 22272; Koundourou 5) Well stocked with maps, books in English and other languages.

General Hospital (☎ 28410 66000; Knosou 3) On the west side of town.

Municipal Tourist Office (☎ 28410 22357; www.agios nikolaos.gr; 8am-9.30pm Apr-Nov) Right by the bridge; changes money and assists with accommodation.

National Bank of Greece (Nikolaou Plastira) Has a 24-hour exchange machine.

OTE (☎ 28410 95330; Sfakianaki 1; 8am-2pm)

Polyhoros Internet Cafe (☎ 28410 24876; 28 Oktovriou 13; per hr €4; 9am-2am)

Post Office (28 Oktovriou 9; 7.30am-2pm Mon-Fri)

Tourist Police (☎ 28410 91408; Erythrou Stavrou 47; 7.30am-2.30pm Mon-Fri)

Sights

The **Archaeological Museum** (☎ 28410 22943; Paleologou Konstantinou 74; admission €2; 8.30am-3pm Tue-Sun) has an extensive and well-displayed collection from eastern Crete. The exhibits are arranged in chronological order beginning with Neolithic finds from Mt Tragistalos, north of Kato Zakros, and early Minoan finds from Agia Fotia. The highlight is *The Goddess of Myrtos*, a clay jug from 2500 BC found near Myrtos.

The **folk museum** (☎ 28410 25093; Paleologou Konstantinou 4; admission €1; 1-3pm Sun-Fri), next to the municipal tourist office, has a well-displayed collection of traditional handicrafts and costumes.

The compact **Iris Museum** (☎ 28410 25899; 28 Oktovriou 21-23; admission €2; 9am-4pm Fri-Wed) has displays of dried herbs and the flora of Crete, and also sells local essential oils.

LASITHI

The town beaches of **Ammos** and **Kytroplatia Beach** are smallish and can get rather crowded. The sandy beach at **Almyros** about 1km south of town is the best of the lot and tends to be less crowded than the others. There's little shade but you can rent umbrellas. **Ammoudara Beach**, 1.5km further south along the road to Ierapetra, is a little better and supports a fairly busy restaurant and accommodation scene. Or you can keep going to towards Sitia to the pleasant **Istron Bay**.

Activities

Exception Biking (☎ 28410 89073; www.exception-biking.de) in Havania, north of Agios Nikolaos town, offers day-long cycling tours in the area and the Lasithi Plateau for around €35. They also have mountain-bike tours around Mt Dikti and Sarakina Gorge for around €45.

The **Roseta II** (☎ 28410 22156; oanak@agn.forthnet.gr) fishing boat takes ardent anglers on group fishing trips or private charters.

There is a **children's playground, swimming pool** and **mini golf** at the municipal beach on the south side of Agios Nikolaos.

Three diving centres in town offer boat dives and PADI-certification courses, as well as beginner courses:
Creta Underwater Centre (☎ 28410 22406) In the Mirabello Hotel.
Happy Divers (☎ 28410 82546) In front of the Coral Hotel.
Pelagos (☎ 28410 24376; www.divecrete.com) In the Minos Beach Hotel.

Tours

Travel agencies offer bus tours to Crete's top attractions. **Nostos Tours** (☎ 28410 22819; nostos@agn.forthnet.gr; Koundourou 30; ☻ 8am-9pm)

has boat trips to Spinalonga (€15), as well as guided tours of Phaestos, Zaros and Matal (€30), the Samaria Gorge (€35), and th Lasithi Plateau and Knossos (€32).

Festivals & Events

In July and August Agios Nikolaos host the **Lato Cultural Festival** at various venue around town. There are concerts by loca and international musicians, Cretan musi played on traditional instruments, foll dancing, *mandinades* (rhyming couplets contests, theatre, art exhibits, literary eve nings and swimming competitions. Ask a the tourist office for details. Agios Nikolao also celebrates **Marine Week**, during the las week of June in even-numbered years, with swimming, windsurfing and boat races, a well as a fireworks display.

Sleeping
BUDGET & MID-RANGE
Pergola Hotel (☎ 28410 28152; fax 28410 2556 Sarolidi 20; s/d €25/35; ☒) This family-run hote has a homy feel. Rooms are comfortabl and all have fridges, although TV, air-co and breakfast are extra. There is a pleasan veranda under a pergola to relax or hav breakfast. Front rooms have balconies an sea views.

Hotel Doxa (☎ 28410 24214; fax 28410 2461 Idomeneos 7; s/d incl breakfast €40/55; ☒) The plant filled lobby sets a homely tone for this hotel which has an attractive terrace for breakfas or drinks. Pleasant and clean rooms ar equipped with telephones, fridges, hairdry ers and TVs and some have views.

Apollon Hotel (☎ 28410 23023; fax 28410 28939 Kapetanaki 9; d incl breakfast €45; ☒ ☒) Convenien tly located near the centre of Agios Nikolao and Ammos Beach, this large modern hote offers rooms with balconies, telephones fridges and air-con. There is also a smal swimming pool and a games room with pool table.

Hotel Eva (☎ 28410 22587; Stratigou Koraka 20 r €20) A neat and quirky little place clos to the centre of the action, this has small ish, dated but reasonable rooms with basi bathrooms and ceiling fans.

Afrodite Rooms (☎ 28410 28058; Korytsas 27; d/t €20/30) These friendly rooms have mainl shared facilities as well as a tiny communa kitchen, and make for a reasonable budge option.

LAKE VOULISMENI

Lake Voulismeni is the subject of many stories in relation to its depth and origins. The locals have given it various names, including Xepatomeni (bottomless), Voulismeni (sunken) and Vromolimni (smelly). The lake isn't bottomless – it's 64m deep. The 'smelly' tag came about because the lake used to be stagnant and gave off quite a pong in summer. This was rectified in 1867 when a canal was built linking it to the sea.

AGIOS NIKOLAOS

LASITHI

TOP END

Miramare Hotel (☎ 28410 23875; fax 28410 24164; d incl half-board €134; ※ ☒ ℗) About 1km south of the town centre, Miramare Hotel has been attractively landscaped into a hillside. The skilfully decorated rooms are well outfitted and there are tennis courts, a fitness centre and lovely gardens.

Minos Beach Art Hotel (☎ 28410 22345; www .bluegr.com; s/VIP ste €127/568; ※ ☒) Aesthetics and design are at a premium and this veritable art gallery about 1km from Agios Nikolaos, full of paintings and sculptures. It's feng shui–approved, has cool white décor, and the VIP rooms are more than satisfactory. The presidential suite is a mere €2000 per night.

Other luxury resorts in the area include **St Nicholas Bay** (☎ 28410 25041; www.stnicolasbay.gr; ste €180-415; ※ ☒), which has a private yacht for guests, and **Minos Palace** (☎ 28410 23801; www .mamidakishotels.gr).

Coral Hotel (☎ 28410 28363; www.hermes-hotels .gr; Akti Koundourou 68; d €70; ※ ☒) Renovated in 2002, this handy and well-run B-class hotel on the northern waterfront is about as upmarket as places get in town. Rooms have satellite TV and fridges, and there is a pleasant roof garden and pool if you can't face the beach.

Eating

The lakeside restaurants, while visually tempting, tend to be the inevitably bland and often overpriced tourist 'Greek' food. Hit the back streets for the genuine article.

BUDGET & MID-RANGE

Taverna Itanos (☎ 28410 25340; Kyprou 1; mayirefta €4.50) This vast, friendly taverna with beamed ceilings and stucco walls has a few tables outside on the pavement. The food is traditional Cretan, with trays of excellent *mayirefta* (casseroles), based on family recipes, out the back. Try the lamb in filo with potato, feta, tomato and peas.

Sarri's (☎ 28410 28059; Kyprou 15; breakfast €3) Tucked away in the back streets, Sarri's is a good spot for breakfast, lunch and dinner on a shady terrace. Check the specials board which changes daily.

Aouas Taverna (☎ 28410 23231; Paleologou Konstantinou 44; mezedes €2-8) This is a family-run place where dishes include such oddities as herb pies and picked bulbs. The interior is plain but the enclosed garden is refreshing and the mezedes are wonderful.

Avli (☎ 28410 82479; Pringipos Georgiou 12; mezedes €3-8) Technically an ouzeri, Avli offers an outstanding selection of mezedes that make a meal in itself. Like many ouzeris, it's going upmarket and also offers good-value meals in a garden setting.

9 Muses (☎ 28410 24968; Akti Themistokleous 3; large pizzas €9.50) On the waterfront further east along the port from the main drag, this stylish newcomer serves excellent pizzas and pastas and gets lively at night.

Barko (☎ 28410 24610; Lasithiou 23; mezedes €4-8) Away from the tourist-oriented restaurants near the lake, this is a favourite with locals. Barko is classed as an *oinomayirio* ('wine cook house'). Dishes are mainly Cretanstyle meze and dining is in a cosy wood and stone interior.

TOP END

Migomis (☎ 28410 24353; N Plastira 20; mains €8-15) Overlooking Voulismeni Lake from the high southern side, Migomis is one of the better lakeside eating places. The cuisine is Greek international and the views and ambiance are stunning. The lamb chops in *mavrodaphne* (sweet dessert wine) sauce and rosemary, or chicken and spinach are recommended.

Pelagos (☎ 28410 25737; Katehaki 10; seafood dishes €7.50-15) For an excellent selection of fresh fish and seafood, this place, in a beautifully restored house, is generally considered the best (and priciest) restaurant in Agios Nikolaos. There is a lovely garden.

Entertainment

Nightlife is Agios Nikolaos' strongest point so you don't have to look far to amuse yourself at night. This is a town that slumbers during the day and comes alive at night mostly around the row of waterfront bars along Akti Koundourou and 'little Soho' or 25 Martiou. Just follow the crowds to find the 'in' place of the season.

Royale Bar (25 Martiou 20) A perennial favourite known for its excellent cocktails and relentlessly upbeat mood, it's no place for a quiet conversation but a good place to meet people.

Cafe du Lac (☎ 28410 26837; 28 Oktovriou 17) Above the restaurant of the same name, it has soothing views over Voulismeni Lake.

On Akti Koundourou, En Plo is a classy subdued bar/café that is usually less crowded than the other bars, with a leaning for jazz, Latin and reggae. The stylish Puerto has a lounge feel, great views from upstairs and a range of teas and chocolates, while trendy Rule attracts a younger crowd.

Rex 'Polycenter' (☎ 28410 83681; M Sfakianaki 35) is a 300-seat convention centre that doubles as a cinema.

Shopping

The bulk of shops in town offer mid-range ceramics, icons and beach gear.

Anemos (☎ 28410 23528; Koundourou 12) One of the stand-out jewellery shops in town, it has unique pieces by jewellers from around Greece, including well-regarded names such as Fanourakis.

Kerazoza (☎ 28410 22562; Koundourou 42) The name of this place means 'rainbow' in the Cretan dialect and refers to the shop's focus on make-believe and illusion. There are hand-made masks, marionettes and figurines derived from ancient Greek theatre, along with some good-quality sculptures, ceramics and jewellery produced by local artisans.

Getting There & Away

BOAT

LANE Lines (☎ 28410 26465; www.lane.gr) has ferries three times a week to Piraeus (€26.20, 12 hours), via Milos. On Thursday, there is a service to Piraeus via Santorini (€18) and Milos (€18.30). There is also a service from Piraeus via Milos to Agios Nikolaos, Sitia, Kassos, Karpathos, Halki and Rhodes.

Excursion boats also run to Spinalonga Island – see p186 for details.

BUS

Buses leave from Agios Nikolaos' **bus station** (☎ 28410 22234; Sofokli Venizelou) for the following destinations:

Destination	Duration	Fare	Frequency
Elounda	20 min	€1	20 daily
Ierapetra	1 hr	€2.50	every 2 hr
Iraklio	1½ hr	€5	half-hourly
Istron	30 min	€1	hourly
Kritsa	15 min	€1	hourly
Lasithi Plateau	3 hr	€3.50	2 daily
Sitia	1½ hr	€5.50	6 daily

Getting Around

You will find many car and motorcycle-hire outlets on the northern waterfront.

Scooterland (☎ 28410 82903; Akti Koundourou 10) has a huge range of scooters, motorcycles and cars. Prices begin at €18 a day for a scooter and go up to €50 a day for a Yamaha Dragstar 650. Cars range in price from €30 to €55.

ELOUNDA ΕΛΟΥΝΤΑ

pop 1655

There are magnificent mountain and sea views along the 11km road north from Agios Nikolaos to Elounda (el-*oon*-da). As you approach Elounda, the signs point to a cluster of luxury hotel complexes in the lovely coves along the coast. The first elite hotel was built here in the mid-1960s by a prominent Athenian, quickly establishing Elounda as the playground for Greece's glitterati and high flyers – soon after, the world's rich and famous followed suit. Elounda boasts some of the most exclusive resorts in Greece, which monopolise most of the nice beaches in the area.

Further along from the resorts, the once-quiet fishing village of Elounda bristles with tourists in summer, although it is calmer than its larger neighbour Agios Nikolaos. Busloads of day-trippers rock up on their way to Spinalonga Island. Elounda's attractive harbour is somewhat spoilt by the huge ugly neon signs on many restaurants. The pleasant but unremarkable sandy town beach, to the north of the port, can get very crowded. There's a sheltered lagoon-like stretch of water formed by the Kolokytha Peninsula.

Orientation & Information

The main square with a prominent clock tower and car park is next to the harbour. The bus stop is close to the square as are a couple of banks with **ATMs**. The post office is opposite the bus stop.

Babel Internet Cafe (☎ 28410 42336; Akti Vritomartidos) On the waterfront, north of the clock tower.

Eklektos (☎ 28410 42285) Sells maps and new and used English-language books.

Municipal Tourist Office (☎ 28410 42464; main square; ☺ 8am-11pm Jun-Oct) Helps with accommodation and information, and changes money.

Olous Travel (☎ 28410 41324) Handles air and boat tickets and finds accommodation.

Tours

Boats from Elounda Harbour offer trips to Spinalonga Island, all-day swimming and fishing trips, and four-hour cruises that include a visit to Spinalonga, swimming and a visit to the sunken city of Olous (see p187).

Sleeping

Unless you are lucky enough to be staying at one of the swanky resorts, it almost defeats the purpose of hanging out in Elounda. While there are some nice places around, Elounda is not particularly good value in peak season. Many hotels are booked out by tour operators. However, it's a much quieter and arguably more pleasant base than Agios Nikolaos for exploring the area.

BUDGET & MID-RANGE

Corali Studios (☎ 28410 41712; studio €50; 🛠) On the northern side, about 800m from the clock tower, these handy self-catering studios are set in lush lawns with a shaded patio. Next door and under the same management the spacious apartments at **Portobello Apartments** (☎ /fax 28410 41712; 2-4 bed apt €65; 🛠) are a good option for two or three people.

Delfinia Studios & Apartments (☎ 28410 41641; www.pediaditis.gr; studio/apt €43/56; 🛠 🛋) These pleasant studios are run by the same family as the bookshop on the main road. All rooms have balconies overlooking the sea and there is a range of options for larger groups and families.

Hotel Aristea (☎ 28410 41300; fax 28410 41302; s/d/tr incl breakfast €30/45/55; 🛠) In the town centre, this is an uninspiring but decent and clean option. Most rooms at least have a sea view, double-glazed windows, TV, fridge and hairdryers.

Grecotel Elounda Village (☎ 28410 41002; www .grecotel.gr; s/d from €125/167; 🛠 🛋 🅿) The first of Elounda's resort hotels on the main road from Agios Nikolaos, this complex boasts a splendid sprawling outdoor swimming pool, water-sports centre, tennis courts and lovely rooms and bungalows.

TOP END

Clustered to the south of Elounda there are some superb resorts. This is the stuff most people only dream about.

Elounda Beach (☎ 28410 41412; www.elounda beach.gr; 🛠 🛋) This trailblazer still justifiably ranks among the world's great luxury resorts. From 'simple' affairs with fresh flowers, bathrobes, twice-daily maid service and TVs in the bathrooms you can upgrade all the way to the royal suites with a private indoor swimming pool, personal fitness trainer, butler and cook (for a mere €15,000 per night). A simple double room will set you back around €400, or you can try a bungalow with a private outdoor swimming pool and platform on the sea for €1700. Next door, the **Elounda Bay Palace** (☎ 28410 41502; www.eloundabay .gr), run by the same management, is only marginally more affordable.

Blue Palace Resort & Spa (☎ 28410 65500; www .bluepalace.gr; without private pool €380; 🛠 🛋) About 3km north of Elounda, this huge new resort built of local stone has a lift to take you over the road to the beach and superb spa – the best on the island. The rooms are modern and super stylish, with decks overlooking Spinalonga Island. Many have private dipping pools if the lift seems too hard.

Eating

Marilena (☎ 28410 41322; mains €7.50-15) Opposite the playground on the beach, Marilena serves excellent mezedes, fish and lobster, as well as Cypriot dishes such as haloumi saganaki. There is a huge vine-covered courtyard out the back.

Nikos (☎ 28410 41439; fish/lobster per kg €30/41) While it lacks the ambience of the seafront eateries, no-frills Nikos on the main street is a good choice for fish and lobster because they generally catch their own. There are outdoor tables under a canopy across in the square. Service can be erratic but the food is good and very reasonably priced.

Vritomartis (☎ 28410 41325; mixed seafood for two €49) In the square right next to the harbour, Vritomartis bills itself as the oldest fish taverna in the village, and offers an impressive collection of fresh fish and mixed seafood platters.

Ferryman (☎ 28410 41230; local fish platter for two €44) Considered the best taverna in Elounda, the Ferryman claimed its moment of fame from being featured in the TV series *Who Pays the Ferryman*. Its specialty is fish, but a broader menu of Cretan specialties has been introduced by the charming Akis, who has taken over and spruced up the family taverna. The waterfront tables are lovely at night, the service is excellent and, while it is pricey, the consensus is that it's worth it.

Kalidon Restaurant (☎ 28410 41451; hot mezedes €4-15) On a floating pontoon that nearly overlooks the harbour, the rather touristy Kalidon provides a reasonable selection of fresh fish and Cretan dishes.

Entertainment
There are several bars and clubs at Elounda, but it's no Agios Nikolaos.

Katafygio (☎ 28410 42003) The most scenic bar in Elounda with tables along the water, it's in a former carob processing plant and the stone interior is impressive. We're not so sure about the weird shop dummies and photos of scantily dressed women though.

Alyggos Bar (☎ 28410 41569), on the main street, is popular with tourists and has an impressive display of soccer jumpers and games on TV, while **Babel** (☎ 28410 42336; Akti Vritomartidos) is another good place for a drink.

Getting There & Around
There are hourly buses from Agios Nikolaos to Elounda (€1, 20 minutes).

Elounda Travel (☎ 28410 41800; elounda@otenet.gr) in the town centre rents out cars, motorcycles and scooters.

KOLOKYTHA PENINSULA
ΧΕΡΣΟΝΗΣΟΣ ΚΟΛΟΚΥΘΑ
Just before Elounda (coming from Agios Nikolaos), a sign points right to **ancient Olous**, which was the port of Lato. The city stood on and around the narrow isthmus (now a causeway) that joined the southern end of the Kolokytha Peninsula to the mainland. Olous was a Minoan settlement that flourished from 3000 to 900 BC. Around 200 BC Olous entered into a treaty with the island of Rhodes as part of Rhodes' desire to control eastern Crete and put an end to the piracy that was ravaging the Aegean. Excavations indicate that Olous was an important trade centre with the eastern islands and minted its own currency. Little is known about Olous during the Greek, Roman and Byzantine eras, but it appears that Olous was destroyed by the Saracens in the 9th-century.

The isthmus sank as a result of the earthquakes that have repeatedly devastated Crete. In 1897 the occupying French army dug a canal across the isthmus connecting Spinalonga Bay to the open sea. Most of the ruins lie beneath the water, which makes it a popular place for snorkelling. The shallow water around here appears to be paradise for sea urchins and the area is known for the many birds that nest there. There is an early Christian mosaic near the causeway that was part of an early Christian basilica.

There is an excellent sandy **beach** 1km along a narrow but graded dirt road on the eastern side of the peninsula. The beach is sheltered, the water pristine and few people use it, other than visitors with small *caiques* (little boats).

PLAKA ΠΛΑΚΑ
A small fishing village 5km further north from Elounda, Plaka has a handful of good-value fish tavernas and basic rooms. Plaka has been somewhat dwarfed by the giant Blue Palace Resort that opened near the village, but there is a reasonable stretch of pebble **beach** to the north that is a good alternative to busy Elounda.

The **Spinalonga Taverna** (☎ 28410 41804; studio €30) run by a local fisherman and his family, will dish up a decent meal, rents out basic studios and can take you over to Spinalonga Island (€6).

SPINALONGA ISLAND ΝΗΣΟΣ ΣΠΙΝΑΛΟΓΚΑ
Spinalonga Island lies just north of the Kolokytha Peninsula and was strategically important from antiquity to the Venetian era. The island's massive **fortress** (admission €2; ☸ 10am-6pm) was built by the Venetians in 1579 to protect the bays of Elounda and Mirabello. It was considered impregnable and withstood Turkish sieges for longer than any other Cretan stronghold, but finally surrendered in 1715 some 40 years after the rest of Crete. The Turks used the island as a base for smuggling. Following the reunion of Crete with Greece, Spinalonga became a leper colony. The last member of the colony died in 1953 and the island has been uninhabited ever since.

There are regular excursion boats (€15, three daily) to the island from Agios Nikolaos and a boat every half-hour from Elounda (€8). Fishermen in Elounda and Plaka can also take you across.

The boats from Agios Nikolaos pass Bird Island and Kri-Kri Island, one of the last habitats of the kri-kri, Crete's wild goat. Both of these islands are designated wildlife sanctuaries and are uninhabited.

LASITHI

LASITHI PLATEAU
ΟΡΟΠΕΔΙΟ ΛΑΣΙΘΙΟΥ

Laid out like an immense patchwork quilt, the mountain-fringed Lasithi Plateau is a stunning site. At 900m above sea level, the plateau is a vast expanse of pear and apple orchards, almond trees and fields of potato crops, dotted by some 5000 windmills. These are not conventional stone windmills but slender metal constructions with white canvas sails, built by the Venetians to irrigate the land. There used to be up to 20,000 windmills but unfortunately not many of the original windmills are in use today.

The plateau's rich soil has been cultivated since Minoan times. The inaccessibility of the region made it a hotbed of insurrection during Venetian and Turkish rule. Following an uprising in the 13th century, the Venetians drove out the inhabitants of Lasithi and destroyed their orchards. The plateau lay abandoned for 200 years, preserving a rich forest and biotope, as a lack of drainage meant the plain flooded each spring with melted snow. Food shortages led the Venetians to cultivate the area and build the irrigation trenches and wells that still service the region.

There are 20 villages dotted around the periphery of the plateau. Tour buses regularly pass through the region, which relies heavily on tourism but is essentially an agricultural area with traditional rural villages that return to pastoral serenity when the tourists leave. It is worth an overnight stay to get a sense of rural Crete.

You can approach the plateau from several points, the main routes being from Iraklio via the Kastelli road or Malia, or the commercial town of Neapoli, with other turn-offs near Agios Nikolaos.

The perimeter of the plateau is a popular **bike route**, and on any given day you will be assailed by squadrons of helmet-clad cyclists pedalling their way around the relatively flat plateau landscape. Cycling to the plateau is another matter, since the approaches are long and steep. Enterprising cycle tour operators in Iraklio and Agios Nikolaos ferry bikes and cyclists to the plateau. This way cyclists can tour the 25km perimeter and then cruise home *downhill*.

TZERMIADO ΤΖΕΡΜΙΑΔΟ
pop 747

Tzermiado (dzer-mee-*ah*-do) is a sleepy town with dusty little streets lined with houses overgrown with vines and hanging plants. It's the largest and most important town on the Lasithi Plateau and has a fair amount of tourism from the tour buses going to the Dikteon Cave. A number of shops sell rugs and embroidered blouses, although they're not of a particularly high quality. Of better quality are Lasithi's superior potatoes, which are celebrated in a three-day festival at the end of August in Tzermiado.

There is only one main road running through town that takes you past the town square. The post office is on the town's main square and the bank, with an ATM, and the OTE are on the main street.

Sleeping & Eating

Hotel Kourites (☎ 28440 22194; s/d incl breakfast €25/40) On the left as you enter town from the east, this hotel has simple rooms with small balconies. There are additional rooms and apartments available in nearby buildings and you have free use of their bicycles.

Restaurant Kourites (Greek specials €4.50-7.30) This place serves filling and wholesome fare, and there are many dishes made in the wood oven – try the suckling pig.

Argoulias (☎ 28440 22754; d/tr incl breakfast €60/70) This small complex of 11 stone-built spacious apartments is built into the hillside, with panoramic views of the plateau. The rooms are traditionally decorated, while breakfast is made from fresh local produce.

Getting There & Away

From Agios Nikolaos there are two buses a day to Tzermiado (€3.50, two hours). From Iraklio there are two buses daily Monday to Friday to Tzermiado (€4.70, 1½ hours).

AGIOS GEORGIOS ΑΓΙΟΣ ΓΕΩΡΓΙΟΣ
pop 554

Agios Georgios (*agh*-ios ye-*or*-gios) is a tiny village on the southern side of the Lasithi Plateau and the most pleasant to stay in. If you have your own bicycle, you can base yourself here and explore the plateau at your leisure.

The village also boasts an excellent **folklore museum** (☎ 28440 31832; admission €2.50; ❧ 10am-4pm Apr-Oct) housed in the original home belonging to the Katsapakis family. The entry fee is also valid for the nearby **Eleftherios Museum**, primarily a photo collection dedicated to the former Greek statesman, and the little attached **church** with its Byzantine frescoes.

Sleeping & Eating

Hotel Maria (☎ 28440 31774; s/d €20/25) On the northern side of the village, the spacious rooms are nicely decorated with weavings and traditional furnishings (although larger people should note that the beds are very narrow). The rooms are run by Maria's daughters Hara and Kallia, while their affable mother does most of the cooking for the new Taverna Merastri in the plant-filled courtyard garden of the established **Taverna Rea** (☎ 28440 31209; specials €5-6) on the main street. Maria rustles up excellent grilled local meats (her husband is the butcher) and other staple Cretan fare based on fresh seasonal local produce. Their wine is on the house. They are also recently upgraded studios upstairs from the taverna.

Getting There & Away

Agios Georgios has two buses daily from Iraklio (€4.70, two hours) and one daily from Agios Nikolaos (€3.50, three hours).

PSYHRO ΨYΧΡΟ
pop 212

Psyhro (psi-*hro*) is the closest village to the Dikteon Cave. It has one main street with a few tavernas, and plenty of souvenir shops selling 'authentic' rugs and mats of non-Cretan origin. It is prettier and less dusty than Tzermiado and makes for a better rest stop. Buses to Psyhro drop you at the end of the town where it's about a kilometre walk uphill to the cave.

Sleeping & Eating

Zeus Hotel (☎ 28440 31284; s/d €25/30) This is a modern but rather featureless D-class hotel on the west side of the village near the start of the Dikteon Cave road.

Stavros (☎ 28440 31453; grills €5-8) With its neat folksy interior and street-side tables, Stavros serves a good range of traditional home-style Cretan dishes. Most of the meat and produce is from the family farm. Try the goat in lemon and rice sauce or the stuffed tomatoes.

Petros Taverna (☎ 28440 31600; grills €6) Former cave guardian Petros Zarvakis has opened a new taverna opposite the entrance to Dikteon Cave, serving Cretan food and grills. He also organises regular hikes up to Mt Dikti, camping out under the stars.

Getting There & Away

Public transportation around the Lasithi Plateau is tricky. From Agios Nikolaos there are daily buses that go through Tzermiado and Agios Georgios before terminating at Psyhro at the foot of the road leading to the Dikteon Cave. There is a morning bus from the Lasithi villages to Agios Nikolaos on the same days.

From Iraklio there are two buses daily Monday to Friday to Lasithi (€5, two hours) and three daily buses (except weekends) returning to Iraklio.

DIKTEON CAVE ΔΙΚΤΑΙΟΝ ΑΝΤΡΟΝ

Lasithi's major sight is the **Dikteon Cave** (☎ 6977 269684; adult/child €4/2; ☯ 8am-6.30pm), just outside the village of Psyhro. Here, according to legend, Rhea hid the newborn Zeus from Cronos, his offspring-gobbling father.

The cave, also known as the Psyhro Cave, covers 2200 sq metres and features both stalactites and stalagmites. It was excavated in 1900 by the British archaeologist David Hogarth, who found numerous votives indicating it was a place of cult worship. These finds are housed in the Archaeological Museum (p149) in Iraklio.

The cave began to be used for cult worship in the Middle Minoan period and continued, though less intensely, up to the 1st century AD. An altar for offerings and sacrifices was in the upper section. Stone tablets inscribed with Linear A script were found here along with religious bronze and clay figurines.

The upper cave is large and generally devoid of stalactites or stalagmites. A steep downward path brings you to the more interesting lower cave. In the back on the left is a smaller chamber where legend has it that Zeus was born. There is a larger hall on the right, which has small stone basins filled with water that Zeus allegedly drank from in one section and a spectacular stalagmite that came to be known as the Mantle of Zeus in the other. The entire cave is illuminated, although not particularly well, so watch your step.

LASITHI

THE MYTH OF ZEUS

Cronos was the leader of the seven Titans of mythical antiquity. Cronos married his sister Rhea, but wary of his mother Gaia's warning that he would be usurped by one of his own offspring, he swallowed every child Rhea bore him. When Rhea had her sixth child, Zeus, she smuggled him to Crete, and gave Cronos a stone in place of the child, which he duly swallowed. Rhea hid the baby Zeus in the Dikteon Cave in the care of three nymphs.

On reaching manhood, Zeus, determined to avenge his swallowed siblings, became Cronos' cupbearer and filled his cup with poison. Cronos drank from the cup, then disgorged first the stone and then his children Hestia, Demeter, Hera, Poseidon and Hades, all of whom were none the worse for their ordeal. Zeus, aided by his regurgitated brothers and sisters, deposed Cronos, and went to war against the Titans who refused to acknowledge him as chief god. Gaia told Zeus he would only be victorious with the help of the Cyclopes and the 100-handed giants, so he released them from Tartarus.

The Cyclopes gave Zeus a thunderbolt, and the three 100-handed giants threw rocks at the Titans, who eventually retreated. Zeus banished Cronos, as well as all of the Titans except Atlas (Cronos' deputy), to a far-off land. Atlas was ordered to hold up the sky.

Mt Olympus became 'home, sweet home' for Zeus and his family. Zeus soon took a fancy to his sister Hera. He tricked the unsuspecting Hera into holding him to her bosom by turning himself into a dishevelled cuckoo, then violated her. Hera reluctantly agreed to marry him and they had three children: Ares, Hephaestus and Hebe.

It is a steep 15-minute (800m) walk up to the cave entrance along a fairly rough track, or you can take a donkey ride (€10 return). There is a less obvious paved trail to the cave that starts from the left side of the car park, although it's not as shaded as the rougher track. Walk between the two restaurants and you will see people coming down from the paved track.

KRITSA ΚΡΙΤΣΑ
pop 1614

Kritsa (krit-sah) is a pretty mountain village of whitewashed houses terraced into the mountainside, offering sweeping views over the valley. Kritsa had a strong tradition of needlework and weaving, but the village appears to have become a more of a tourist attraction, with busloads of tourists swarming through the streets all summer.

The villagers exploit these invasions to the full. Weavings and embroidery are draped and hung on every available surface, and craft shops of every description line the main streets, along with some tacky souvenir shops that ruin the character of the village. The men gather in the *kafeneia* (coffee house) while the women hawk their merchandise in the shops or sit on stools outside the shops doing their needlework. Not much of the stuff on sale is handmade these days and the rug designs are not necessarily authentic. It's still possible to search out the traditional geometric designs of Crete and the odd finely handmade crocheted blankets and tablecloths but they are justifiably not cheap due to the labour-intensive work involved and the few women still able and prepared to do it.

Apart from the needlework, **Olive Wood** (☎ 28410 51585) is one of the few shops in town that has handmade local crafts.

In late August, Kritsa stages a traditional **Cretan wedding** replete with songs, dancing and traditional food for an admission price of about €9.

One narrow street runs through Kritsa but there are car parks at the top and bottom of the village. The post office is near the lower car park. There is an ATM halfway up the hill.

Sleeping & Eating

Rooms Argyro (☎ 28410 51174; s/d €25/35) This is the best place to stay. The 12 rooms are immaculate and there is a little shaded restaurant downstairs for breakfast and light meals. It's on your left as you enter the village.

Platanos (☎ 28410 51230; mains €4.50-6) A taverna/kafeneio that retains a traditional feel, Platanos has a lovely setting under a giant plane tree and vines. There's a standard menu of grills and *mayirefta* and it's well regarded by locals.

O Kastellos (☎ 28410 51254; mains €4.50-6) A cool,
restful place in the centre of Kritsa. Oven-
cooked veal and pasta is recommended.

Getting There & Away

There are hourly buses from Agios Nikolaos
to Kritsa (€1, 15 minutes).

AROUND KRITSA

The tiny triple-aisled **Church of Panagia Kera**
(☎ 28410 51525; admission €3; ☒ 8.30am-3pm) is on
the right 1km before Kritsa on the Agios
Nikolaos road and contains the most outstanding Byzantine frescoes on Crete. The
oldest part of the church is the central nave,
which is from the 13th century, but most of
the frescoes date from the early to mid-14th
century. The dome and nave are decorated
with four gospel scenes: the Presentation,
the Baptism, the Raising of Lazarus and
the Entry into Jerusalem. On the west wall
there's a portrayal of the Crucifixion and
grimly realistic depictions of the Punishment of the Damned. The vault of the south
aisle recounts the life of the Virgin and the
north aisle is an elaborately worked out
fresco of the Second Coming. Nearby is an
enticing depiction of Paradise next to the
Virgin and the Patriarchs – Abraham, Isaac
and Jacob. Judgement Day is portrayed on
the west end with the Archangel Michael
trumpeting the Second Coming.

ANCIENT LATO ΛΑΤΩ

The ancient city of **Lato** (admission €3; ☒ 8.30am-
3pm Tue-Sun), 4km north of Kritsa, is one of
Crete's few non-Minoan ancient sites. Lato
(la-to) was founded in the 7th century BC
by the Dorians and at its height was one of
the most powerful cities on Crete until it
was destroyed in 200 BC. It sprawls over
the slopes of two acropolises in a lonely
mountain setting, commanding stunning
views down to the Bay of Mirabello.

The city's name is derived from the goddess Leto whose union with Zeus produced
Artemis and Apollo, both of whom were
worshipped here.

The **city gate** is the entrance to the site
and leads to a long, stepped street. The wall
on the left contains two towers, which were
also residences. Follow the street to reach
the **agora**, built around the 4th century BC,
and which contained a cistern and a small
rectangular sanctuary. Excavations of the

temple have revealed a number of 6th-
century BC figurines. The circle of stones
behind the cistern was a threshing floor,
while the western side of the agora contains
a **stoa** with stone benches. There are remains
of a pebble mosaic nearby. A terrace above
the southeast corner of the agora contains
the remains of a **rectangular temple**, probably
built in the late-4th or early 3rd century BC.
The inscription at the base of the temple
statue is too damaged to be read. Between the
two towers on the northern end of the agora
there are steps leading to the **prytaneion**, the
administrative centre of the city–state. The
centre of the prytaneion contained a hearth
with a fire that burned day and night. On the
east side of the prytaneion is a colonnaded
court. Below the prytaneion is a semicircular
theatre that could seat about 350 people next
to an **exedra** (stage platform), which has a
bench around the walls.

There are no buses to Lato. The road to
the site is signposted to the right on the approach to Kritsa. It's a pleasant 30-minute
walk through olive groves along this road.

NORTHEAST COAST

MONI FANEROMENIS
ΜΟΝΉ ΦΑΝΕΡΩΜΈΝΗΣ
About 2km before Gournia, on the Agios
Nikolaos–Sitia road, a 5km road leads off
to the right to the late-Byzantine Moni Fan-
eromenis. If you have your own transport,
a visit to the monastery is worthwhile for
the stunning views down to the Gulf of Mirabello, although it is a steep, winding and
only partly asphalted road. Knock loudly if
the doors are not open. You will be shown
through the chapel with a 15th-century
fresco of the Panagia.

GOURNIA ΓΟΥΡΝΙΑ
The important Late Minoan site of **Gournia**
(☎ 28410 24943; admission €3; ☒ 8.30am-3pm Tue-Sun)
lies just off the coast road, 19km southeast
of Agios Nikolaos. The ruins, which date
from 1550 to 1450 BC, are made up of a
town overlooked by a small palace. Gournia's palace was far less ostentatious than
the ones at Knossos and Phaestos as it was
the residence of an overlord rather than a
king. The town is a network of streets and
stairways flanked by houses with walls up to

LASITHI

2m high. Domestic, agricultural and trade implements found on the site indicate that Gournia was a thriving little community.

South of the palace is a large rectangular **court**, which was connected to a network of paved stone streets. South of the palace is a large **stone slab** used for sacrificing bulls. The room to the west has a stone **kernos** (large earthen dish) ringed with 32 depressions and probably used for cult activity. North of the palace was a **Shrine of the Minoan Snake Goddess**, which proved to be a rich trove of objects from the Postpalatial Period. Notice the storage rooms, workrooms, and dwellings to the north and east of the site. The buildings were two-storey structures with the storage and workrooms in the basement and the living quarters on the first floors.

Gournia Moon Camping (☎ /fax 28420 93243; adult/tent €5.30/5; 🏊) is the closest camping ground to Agios Nikolaos. The well-organised site run by Brits has a cheap taverna, snack bar and mini-market. It's in a pretty location near a small rocky cove with a tiny beach and there are two pools with sun-beds. Buses to Sitia can drop you off outside.

Gournia is on the Sitia and Ierapetra bus routes from Agios Nikolaos (see p185) and buses can drop you at the site.

MOHLOS ΜΌΧΛΟΣ
pop 91

Mohlos (*moh*-los) is a pretty fishing village reached by a 5km winding road from the Sitia–Agios Nikolaos highway. In antiquity, it was joined to the homonymous island that now sits 200m offshore and was once a thriving Early Minoan community dating from the period 3000–2000 BC. Excavations still continue sporadically on both Mohlos Island and at Mohlos village. A short description of the archaeology of the area is presented on an information board overlooking the tiny harbour.

The village is an atmospheric place bedecked in hibiscus, bougainvillea and bitter laurel. It attracts mainly French and German independent travellers seeking peace and quiet. There is a small pebble-and-greysand beach where swimming is reasonable. Beware of strong currents further out in the small strait between the island and the village. Mohlos is an ideal traveller rest stop with a high chill-out factor. There are decent places to stay, plenty of good walks and many interesting villages to explore nearby. The tavernas at Mohlos enjoy a good reputation for fresh local fish and seafood, and attract many Cretans on weekends.

Orientation & Information

Mohlos is all contained within two or three blocks, all walkable within 10 minutes. There is no bank or post office, and few tourist facilities other than a couple of gift shops and two mini-markets.

Barbarossa Tours (☎ 28430 94723; barbarosso@otenet.gr) can arrange rooms, studios, excursions and boat and air tickets, as well as car rental. They also exchange money.

Activities

La Chlorophylle (☎ /fax 28430 94725) is run by Yiannis Petrakis and his Belgian botanist wife Ann Lebrun. She takes hikers on **nature walks** (€11-18) around Mohlos, while Yiannis offers guided jeep, motorbike and mountain-bike tours.

Sleeping & Eating

Hotel Sofia (☎ /fax 28430 94554; d/tr €28/32, apt €32-50; 🏊) The basic but clean and comfortable rooms above the Sofia taverna have TV and fridge, as well as spacious, fully equipped two-to four-person apartments 200m east of the harbour. Good for families and longer stays, many have balconies with great views. Try the excellent home cooking at the taverna – vegetarians will love the artichokes with peas or cauliflower in wine sauce.

Spyros Rooms (☎ /fax 28430 94204; d/tr €35/40; 🏊) These very pleasant, clean and modern rooms just behind the village have a fridge and air-con. See Spyros at the Kavouria restaurant to check in.

Kyma (☎ 28430 94177; solk@in.gr; studio €30) Fairly well signposted on the village's western side near a supermarket, the self-contained studios are spotless and good value.

To Bogazi (☎ 28430 94200; mezedes €1.50-5.80) Nearest to the island and with a sea view on two sides, To Bogazi serves over 30 inventive mezedes, including many vegetarian-friendly dishes. For a main course, try the cuttlefish and pan-tossed greens.

Ta Kochilia (☎ 28430 94432) Also on the seafront opposite the island, this place has superb views and is known for its fresh fish and simple, good food. Seafood lovers should try the sea urchin salad – dip your bread in it.

Getting There & Away

There is no public transport to Mohlos. Buses between Sitia and Agios Nikolaos will drop you off at the Mohlos turn-off. From there you'll need to hitch or walk the 6km to Mohlos village.

SITIA ΣΗΤΕΙΑ

pop 8238

Sitia (si-tee-a) has fortunately managed to escape the tourist frenzy that grips most of the north coast in summer. It's an attractive mid-sized coastal town with a pretty harbour-side promenade lined with tavernas and cafés that makes for a pleasant evening stroll.

In the bustling streets of the old town that wind their way uphill from the harbour you'll find the occasional example of old Venetian architecture mixed in with the new. The town's southern end is on a long, narrow stretch of sandy beach. While the place is tourist-friendly, it exists for the locals, who live from agriculture and commerce rather than tourism. Sitia attracts lots of French and Greek tourists, but even at the height of the season the town has a relatively laid-back feel that is refreshing compared with the commercialism of towns further west.

History

Archaeological excavations indicate that there were Neolithic settlements around Sitia and an important Minoan settlement at Petras, 2km southeast of the current town centre. The original settlement was destroyed and eventually abandoned after an earthquake in 1700 BC.

In the Greco–Roman era there was a town called Iteia in or around modern Sitia although its exact site has not yet been located. In Byzantine times Sitia became a bishopric, which was then eliminated by the Saracen conquest of Crete in the 9th century. Under the Venetians, Sitia became the most important port in eastern Crete. The town was racked by a disastrous earthquake in 1508 – a blow from which it never really recovered – and the Turkish blockade of Sitia in 1648 marked its death knell. The remaining inhabitants fled and the walls and buildings of the town were destroyed. It was not until the late-19th century when the Turks decided to make

Sitia an administrative centre that the town gradually came back to life. Crete's most famous poet, Vitsentzos Kornaros, was born in Sitia in 1614.

Orientation & Information

The town's main square is Plateia Iroon Plytehniou – recognisable by its palm trees and statue of a dying soldier.

The bus station is at the eastern end of Karamanli, which runs behind the bay. Ferries to/from Piraeus and the Dodecanese dock about 500m north of Plateia Agnostou.

Itanos Hotel (per hr €6; 9.30am-2.30pm) Has Internet access; see p195.

National Bank of Greece (Plateia El Venizelou) Has a 24-hour exchange machine, but there are lots of ATMs and places to change money in town.

OTE (☎ 28430 28299; Kapetan Sifinos; 7.30am-3pm)

Post office (Dimokritou; 7.30am-3pm)

Tourist office (☎ 28430 28300; Karamanli; 9.30am-2.30pm) Has town maps.

Tourist police (☎ 28430 24200; Therisou 31) In the police station.

Tzortzakis Travel (☎ 28430 25080; Kornarou 150) A good source of information.

Sights & Activities

The **Archaeological Museum** (☎ 28430 23917; Pisoke-falou; admission €2; 8.30am-3pm Tue-Sun) houses a well-displayed and important collection of local finds spanning Neolithic to Roman times, with emphasis on the Minoan civilization. One of the most significant exhibits is the *Palekastro Kouros* – a figure pieced together from fragments made of hippopotamus tusks and adorned with gold (see the boxed text on p197). The finds from the palace at Zakros include a wine press, bronze saw, jars, cult objects and pots that are clearly scorched from the great fire that destroyed the palace. Among the most valuable objects in the museum are the Linear A tablets which reflect the palace's administrative function.

Towering over the town is the fort or **kazarma** (from 'casa di arma') which was a garrison under the Venetians. They are the only remains of the wall that once protected the town. It is now used as an open-air theatre.

The **folklore museum** (☎ 28430 22861; Kapetan Sifinos 28; admission €1.50; 9.30am-2.30pm & 5-9pm Tue-Fri, 9.30am-2.30pm Sat) displays a fine collection of local weavings.

Festivals & Events

Sitia produces superior sultanas and the town holds a **Sultana Festival** in the last week of August, during which wine flows freely and Cretan dances are performed.

There is also the **Kornaria Festival** that runs from mid-July to the end of August in which concerts, folk dancing and theatre productions are staged in the *kazarma* and other venues. Posters around town announce the events, some of which are free.

Sleeping

Hotel Arhontiko (☎ 28430 28172; Kondylaki 16; d/studio €27/30) This small D-class guesthouse, uphill from the port, is in a beautifully maintained Neoclassical building and has a real old-world feel. It's spotless, with shared bathrooms and a lovely shady garden in the front.

Apostolis (☎ 28430 28172; Kazantzaki 27; d/tr €35/45 These upmarket domatia up from the waterfront have ceiling fans, and relatively modern bathrooms with handy touches such as shower curtains, and many have double beds. There's a communal balcony and fridge.

El Greco Hotel (☎ 28430 23133; elgreco@sit.forthne .gr; Arkadiou 13; s/d €32/45; ✻) For a modicum more comfort, the well-signposted El Greco has more character than the town's other C-class places. The Rooms are very clean and presentable, and all have a fridge and phone.

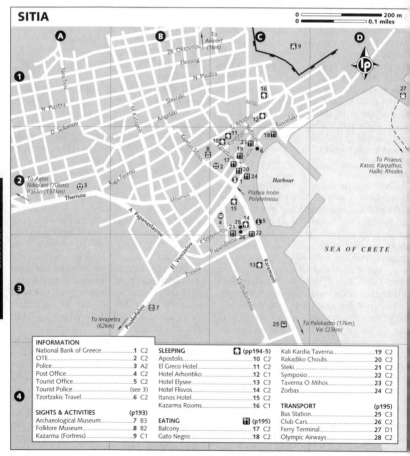

SITIA

0 ——————— 200 m
0 ——————— 0.1 miles

INFORMATION	
National Bank of Greece	1 C2
OTE	2 C2
Police	3 A2
Post Office	4 C2
Tourist Office	5 C2
Tourist Police	(see 3)
Tzortzakis Travel	6 C2

SIGHTS & ACTIVITIES	(p193)
Archaeological Museum	7 B3
Folklore Museum	8 B2
Kazarma (Fortress)	9 C1

SLEEPING	(pp194-5)
Apostolis	10 C2
El Greco Hotel	11 C2
Hotel Arhontiko	12 C1
Hotel Elysee	13 C3
Hotel Flisvos	14 C2
Itanos Hotel	15 C2
Kazarma Rooms	16 C1

EATING	(p195)
Balcony	17 C2
Gato Negro	18 C2

Kali Kardia Taverna	19 C2
Rakadiko Choulis	20 C2
Steki	21 C2
Symposio	22 C2
Taverna O Mihos	23 C2
Zorbas	24 C2

TRANSPORT	(p195)
Bus Station	25 C3
Club Cars	26 C2
Ferry Terminal	27 D1
Olympic Airways	28 C2

Kazarma Rooms (☎ 28430 23211; Ionias 10; d €30) Off-season these rooms are rented to students, but they are an attractive option as the rooms are well kept and have TV and ceilings fans. There's also a communal lounge and a well-equipped kitchen.

Hotel Flisvos (☎ 28430 27135; fax 28430 27136; Karamanli 4; s/d €45/60; ❄) Along the southern waterfront, Flisvos is a very attractive, new hotel that boasts excellent facilities. Rooms are spotless and have air-con, TV, fridge and phone.

Hotel Elysee (☎ 28430 22312; www.elysee-hotel.gr; Karamanli 14; s/d €48/58) Refurbished in 2002, this beachfront hotel has spacious airy rooms with TV, fridge and balconies overlooking the sea. The bathrooms are a little basic given the price and breakfast is extra.

Itanos Hotel (☎ 28430 22900; www.itanoshotel com; Karamanli 4; s/d incl breakfast €35/60; ❄ ▯) The B-class Itanos has a conspicuous location on the waterfront, as well as a popular terrace restaurant. The comfortable rooms come equipped with satellite TV, balconies, fridge and sound-proofing.

Eating

Taverna O Mihos (☎ 28430 22416; Kornarou 117; set menus €8.50-15.50) This taverna in a traditional stone house one block back from the waterfront has excellent charcoal-grilled meats and Cretan cooking. There are also tables on a terrace nearby on the beach.

Gato Negro (☎ 28430 25873; Galanaki 3; mains €6.20-9.80) At the northern end of the harbour next to the pier, this popular restaurant uses produce from the owner's farm to create excellent Cretan dishes. Sample the rabbit in red sauce, or *kalitsounia* (filled pastries) with wild greens and finish off the night with their excellent raki.

Balcony (☎ 28430 25084; Foundalidou 19; mains €8.90-12.60) The finest dining in Sitia is on the 1st floor of this charmingly decorated old building. The Balcony has an exceptional and creative menu of fusion cuisine, with interesting dishes such as rooster in wine with noodles, or veal and rigatoni with four cheeses.

Symposio (☎ 28430 25856; Karamanli 12; mains €5.50-10) Symposio utilises all-Cretan natural products such as organic olive oil from Moni Toplou. The food is top class, with the rabbit in rosemary and wine sauce highly recommended.

Also recommended are **Kali Kardia Taverna** (☎ 28430 22249; Foundalidou 22), **Steki** (☎ 28430 22857; Papandreou 13), with its pots of home-style cooking, and the classic **Rakadiko Choulis** (☎ 28430 28298; Venizelou 57) for meze and local raki, while Zorba's on the waterfront is famous for its lobster.

Getting There & Away

AIR

Sitia's **airport** (☎ 28430 24666) opened an expanded international-size runway in 2003, and a new international terminal was expected to open in 2005 allowing for direct international scheduled flights.

Olympic Airlines (☎ 28430 22270; 4 Septemvriou 3) has four daily flights to Athens (€65.50, 1¼ hours), one flight a week to Thessaloniki (€124.50, three hours) via Alexandroupolis (€78.5, 1¾ hours) and two flights a week to Preveza (€78.50, 1¾ hours).

BOAT

The *F/B Vitsentzos Kornaros* and *F/B Ierapetra* of **LANE Lines** (☎ 28430 25555; www.lane.gr) link Sitia with Piraeus (€25.30, 14½ hours), Kasos (€9, four hours), Karpathos (€15.50, six hours), Halki (€11.90, 5½ hours) and Rhodes (€23, 10 hours) three times weekly. Departure times change annually, so check locally for latest information.

BUS

There are seven buses a day to Ierapetra (€4.40, 1½ hours), five buses a day to Iraklio (€10, 3½ hours) via Agios Nikolaos (€5.50, 1½ hours), five to Vai (€2.10, one hour), and two to Kato Zakros via Palekastro and Zakros (€3.50, one hour). The buses to Vai and Kato Zakros run only between May and October; during the rest of the year, the Vai service terminates at Palekastro and the Kato Zakros service at Zakros.

Getting Around

TO/FROM THE AIRPORT

The airport (signposted) is 1km out of town, although the new terminal (due to open in 2005) will be a further 2km drive away. There is no airport bus; a taxi costs about €5.

CAR & MOTORCYCLE

Car- and motorcycle-hire outlets are mostly found on Papandreou and Itanou. Try **Club Cars** (☎ 28430 25104; Papandreou 8).

LASITHI

MONI TOPLOU ΜΟΝΗ ΤΟΠΛΟΥ

East of Sitia, the imposing **Moni Toplou** (☎ 28430 61226; admission €2.50; ⏲ 9am-1pm & 2-6pm Apr-Oct) looks more like a fortress than a monastery – a necessity imposed by the dangers it faced at the time of its construction. It is one of the most historically significant and well-run monasteries on Crete. The middle of the 15th century was marked by piracy, banditry and constant rebellions. The monks defended themselves with all the means at their disposal including a heavy gate, cannons (the name Toplou is Turkish for 'with a cannon') and small holes for pouring boiling oil onto the heads of their attackers. Nevertheless, it was sacked by pirates in 1498, looted by the Knights of Malta in 1530, pillaged by the Turks in 1646 and captured by the Turks in 1821.

Moni Toplou had always been active in the cause for Cretan independence and paid a price for it. Under the Turkish occupation, a secret school operated in the monastery, while its reputation for hiding rebels led to severe reprisals. During WWII, Abbot Silingakis was executed after sheltering resistance leaders operating an underground radio transmitter.

The monastery's star attraction is undoubtedly the icon *Lord Thou Art Great* by celebrated Cretan artist Ioannis Kornaros. Each of the 61 small scenes painted on the icon is beautifully worked out and each is inspired by a phrase from the Orthodox prayer that begins 'Lord, Thou Art Great'. The icon is in the northern aisle of the church, along with 14th-century frescoes and an antique icon stand from 1770.

An excellent **museum** tells the history of the monastery and has a fine collection of icons, engravings and books, as well as weapons and military souvenirs from the resistance.

There are three monks living at the monastery and abbot, Filotheos Spanoudakis, is one of the most dynamic on Crete, promoting organic farming through the local agricultural cooperative and cultivating the monastery's large landholdings. He was building an olive-oil bottling plant on the monastery grounds for the local community.

The well-stocked shop sells ecclesiastical souvenirs, hand-painted icons and books on Crete, plus the monastery's award-winning organic olive oil and wine.

The monastery is a 3km walk from the Sitia–Palekastro road. Buses can drop you off at the junction.

EAST COAST

VAI ΒΑΪ

The beach at Vai, on Crete's east coast 24km from Sitia, is famous for its unique palm forest. There are many stories about the origin of these palms, including the theory that they sprouted from date pits spread by Roman legionaries relaxing on their way back from conquering Egypt. While these palms are closely related to the date, they are a separate species found only on Crete.

In July and August, you'll need to arrive early to appreciate the setting, because the place is packed. There are more cars than palm trees, and the beach is covered in sunbeds and umbrellas (€6).

It's possible to escape the worst of the ballyhoo – jet skis and all – by clambering over a rocky outcrop southwards to a small secluded beach. Alternatively, there's a quiet beach over the hill to the north that is frequented by nudists.

Vai Watersports & Scuba Centre (☎ 28430 61070) is on the left side of the beach. Eat at the church-run **Restaurant-Cafeteria Vai** (☎ 28430 61129; mains €4-6). The restaurant is at the southern end of the beach and although it offers no great culinary treats, it's dependable and welcome after a hard day on the beach.

There are five buses a day to Vai from Sitia (€2.10, one hour) that stop at Palekastro. The car park charges €3 per vehicle, but there's free parking on the roadside 500m before Vai.

ITANOS ΙΤΑΝΟΣ

If you're after more secluded beaches, head north for another 3km to the ancient Minoan site of Itanos. Although inhabited from about 1500 BC, Itanos was clearly prosperous by the 7th century BC since it was an important trading post for exports to the Near East and Middle East. Its archrival was Praisos, near Ierapetra, and in 260 BC Itanos hosted a garrison of Egyptians to fortify its position against Praisos.

When Ierapetra destroyed Praisos in 155 BC, Itanos fought with Ierapetra as well and again received foreign help from Magnesia, a

Roman city. The town was destroyed somewhere towards the end of the Byzantine era and may have been re-inhabited by the Venetians. It's difficult to discern any recognisable building in Itanos, but there are remains of two early Christian basilicas and a Hellenistic wall. The site is well marked and next to swimming coves shaded by pine trees.

PALEKASTRO ΠΑΛΑΊΚΑΣΤΡΟ

pop 1084

Palekastro (pah-leh-kas-tro) is a modern farming town that is more of a stopover or useful base for exploring eastern Crete than as a destination in itself. It's situated in the midst of a rocky, barren landscape, but is within easy reach of the lovely Kouremenos Beach, Vai Beach, Moni Toplou and the nearby Minoan archaeological site. The town's economy is built on fishing and agriculture, with tourism limited to July and August. It's best to have your own transport.

Orientation & Information

The main street of Karamanli runs through the town and forks to the left and right in the town centre. The **tourist office** (☎ 28430 1546; 9am-10pm May-Oct), combined with the OTE, changes money and is also a good source of information on rooms and transport. There's an ATM next door and a postal agent near Itanos rooms. You can check email at **Argo Bookshop** (☎ 28430 29640; per 20 min €1.50; 9am-11pm Jun-Oct) around the corner from Hotel Hellas. The bus stop is in the centre of town.

Sleeping & Eating

Hotel Hellas (☎ 28430 61240; hellas_h@otenet.gr; s/d €30/40;) This is the best accommodation in town. Pleasant rooms have air-con, TV, telephone, new bathrooms and double-glazed windows. Downstairs at the Taverna Hellas, Marika cooks up reputedly the best lunch in town, with hearty home-style cooking. The *stifado* (stew) and eggplant imam are recommended.

Itanos Rooms (☎ 28430 61205; s/d €15/25) Overlooking the square, Itanos has simple clean rooms with fridge and fans. Some also have small balconies.

To Filistrini (☎ 28430 61117; mezedes €2-6) About 200m along the Vai road, this neat little ouzeri-cum-*mezedopoleio* (meze restaurant) dishes up tasty mezedes that go down well with a shot or 10 of raki.

Mythos (☎ 28430 61243; mezedes €4-4.50) Diagonally opposite Hellas, this pleasant and popular taverna has a big vegetarian meze selection and traditional *mayirefta*, fish and grills.

Getting There & Away

There are five buses a day from Sitia that stop at Palekastro on the way to Vai (€2.10, 30 minutes). The are also two buses daily from Sitia to Palekastro (€1.60, 45 minutes) that continue to Kato Zakros (€3.50).

AROUND PALEKASTRO

The closest beach to Palekastro is the lovely **Kouremenos**, a nearly deserted pebble beach with good shallow water swimming and excellent windsurfing. Two kilometres from

---

BURIED PALACE

About a kilometre from Palekastro town, there's a significant Minoan archaeological site believed to be part of a yet-to-be unearthed Minoan palace that is the second-largest Minoan city after Knossos. The **Ancient Palekastro** site is being excavated by the British School of Archaeology.

Excavations have so far produced important finds such as the Palekastro Kouros, on display in the Sitia Archaeological Museum (p193), along with mostly Bronze Age Kamares pottery, amphorae, soapstone serpentine lamps and pithoi. The Kouros, made of gold and ivory, is believed to be the first image of a Minoan god. Archaeologists believe this is site is one of two major temples on Crete referred to by Greek philosophers.

Although the site was excavated in the early 1900s, the 1960s and since 1988, these digs did not get to the heart of the site. With new technology used in oil exploration, archaeologists have confirmed that there is a huge structure under the olive groves nearby.

The site is open to visitors and makes for a pleasant walk. You can see the layout of the streets and there are signs indicating what was underneath the sections that were covered. A museum is in the planning to house the finds from the site.

Palekastro, **Hiona Beach**, is another quiet choice with some fine fish tavernas on the beach.

You can rent boards from **Kouremenos Windsurfing** (☎ 28430 61116, 6979 254967; www .freak-surf.com).

There are many pleasant small hotels and apartments scattered around the nearby beaches. The tourist information office in Palekastro can provide a full list.

Glaros Apartments (☎ 28430 61282; Kouremenos; d/q studio €55/65; ☒) Close to Kouremenos Beach, these tasteful self-contained studios are spacious and comfortable. There is also an attached restaurant.

Apartments Grandes (☎ 28430 61496; www.grandes .gr; q studio €65; ☒) This pretty place on Kouremenos Beach is surrounded by a flower garden and trees. It's well equipped, decorated with style and has a restaurant.

I Hiona (☎ 28430 61228; top fish per kg €42) Considered to be the best of the three tavernas on Hiona Beach, I Hiona is known for its super-fresh fish, although Kakavia taverna is renowned for its fish soup.

ZAKROS ΖΑΚΡΟΣ
pop 769
The village of Zakros (*zah*-kros), 45km southeast of Sitia, is the nearest permanent settlement to the east-coast Minoan site of Zakros, which is 7km away. The village is an important agricultural centre for the cultivation of olives, oranges, figs and a wide range of vegetables. While there is little incentive to linger in the village (there is only one hotel), it's a lively place where the kafeneia and ouzeris are always animated and there is rarely a tourist in sight. Zakros is also the starting point for the trail through the Zakros Gorge (see the boxed text on p200).

AROUND ZAKROS
A visit to Zakros Palace and Kato Zakros combines two of the best things about Crete – an intriguing archaeological site just 200m from a long and pleasant stretch of under-populated beach.

Zakros Palace
Although **Zakros Palace** (☎ 28430 26897; Kato Zakros; admission €3; ☼ 8am-7pm) was the last Minoan palace to have been discovered (1962), the excavations proved remarkably fruitful.

The exquisite rock-crystal vase and stone bull's head now in Iraklio's Archaeological Museum (see p149) were found at Zakros Palace, along with a treasure trove of Minoan antiquities. Ancient Zakros, the smallest of Crete's four palatial complexes was a major port in Minoan times, trading with Egypt, Syria, Anatolia and Cyprus. The ruins are not well preserved and water levels have risen over the years so that some parts of the palace complex are submerged.

If you enter the palace complex on the southern side you will first come to the **workshops** for the palace. The **King's apartment** and **Queen's apartment** are to the right of the entrance. Next to the King's apartment is the **Cistern Hall**, which once had a cistern in the centre surrounded by a colonnaded balustrade. Seven steps descended to the floor of the cistern, which may have been a swimming pool, an aquarium or a pool for a sacred boat. Nearby, the **Central Court** was the focal point of the whole palace. Notice the altar base in the northwestern corner of the court; there was also a **well** in the southeast corner of the court at the bottom of eight steps. When the site was excavated the well contained the preserved remains of olives that may have been offered to the deities.

Adjacent to the central court is the **Hall of Ceremonies** in which two rhytons were found. The room to the south is the **Banquet Hall**, so named for the quantity of wine vases found there. To the north of the central court is the **kitchen**. The column base probably supported the dining room above. To the west of the central court is another **light well** and to the left of the banquet hall is the **Lustral Basin**, which once contained a magnificent marble amphora. The Lustral Basin served as a washroom for those entering the nearby **Central Shrine**. You can still see a ledge and a niche in the south wall for the ceremonial idols.

Below the Lustral Basin is the **Treasury** that yielded nearly a hundred jars and rhytons. Next to the treasury is the **Archive Room** that once contained Linear A record tablets Although there were hundreds of tablets only those baked by the fire that destroyed the palace were preserved. Northeast of the archives room is the **bathroom** with a cesspit.

Kato Zakros Κατω Ζακροο
pop 24

Little more than a long stretch of pebbly beach shaded by pine trees and bordered by a string of tavernas, Kato Zakros (*kah-to zah*-kros) is just about the most tranquil place to stay on Crete's southeastern coast. Many people who come here have been doing so for years. The settlement is unlikely ever to expand thanks to restrictions imposed by the Culture Ministry's Archaeology and Antiquities department. There is little to do here but relax on the beach, snorkel, fish, sleep, poke around the archaeological site, walk the Zakros Gorge and deliberate on which taverna to have dinner.

SLEEPING

The domatia in Kato Zakros fill up fast in the high season, so it is best to book. If there are no rooms available you can camp at the southern end of the beach.

George's Villas (☎ /fax 28430 26833; d €30-50; ⬡) In a verdant, pine-tinged setting 800m along the old road to Zakros, these spotless, beautifully furnished rooms with terraces have ceiling fans and well-equipped kitchenettes.

Stella's Apartments (☎ /fax 28430 23739; studio €60) These charming studios are made from local stone and decorated with wooden furniture made by the owner. They are perfect for longer stays. The engaging owners can take guests on free treks and walks.

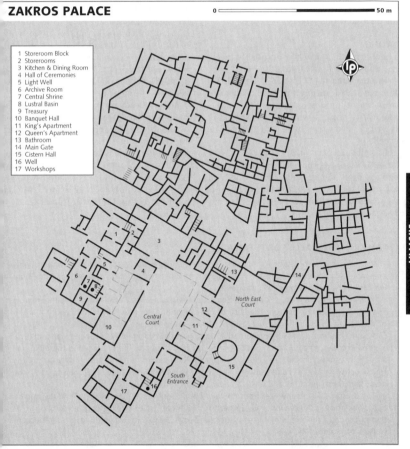

ZAKROS PALACE

0 ▭▭▭▭▭▭▭ 50 m

1 Storeroom Block
2 Storerooms
3 Kitchen & Dining Room
4 Hall of Ceremonies
5 Light Well
6 Archive Room
7 Central Shrine
8 Lustral Basin
9 Treasury
10 Banquet Hall
11 King's Apartment
12 Queen's Apartment
13 Bathroom
14 Main Gate
15 Cistern Hall
16 Well
17 Workshops

North East Court

Central Court

South Entrance

LASITHI

There are three good places all under the same management. **Athena Rooms** (☎ 28430 26893; d €35; ✂) is the better-quality choice; the rooms are very pleasant with heavy stone walls. Next door, **Rooms Coral** (☎ 28430 27064; d €35; 💻) has excellent, small but spotless rooms equipped with Internet connections. Both enjoy superb sea views from the communal balcony. **Poseidon Rooms** (☎ 28430 26893; akrogiali@sit.forthnet.gr; d €20, with bathroom €35), at the southern end of the waterfront, has small, dated but neat and clean rooms, and are a good budget choice. Some have shared bathrooms.

There is also the two-room Melina apartment in a restored old building, with a well-equipped kitchen, just behind Athena Rooms, plus cheaper rooms in the **Farangi Hotel** (☎ 28430 93144; d/apt €20/50), further up on the road to the village.

EATING

There are half-a-dozen good-quality tavernas and a grill house lining the beach.

Taverna Akrogiali (☎ 28430 26887; mains €4.50-9) Relaxed seaside dining and excellent service from the inimitable owner Nikos Perakis make this place a winner. The speciality is grilled swordfish steak and the raki is excellent.

Georgios Taverna Anesis (☎ 28430 26890; mayirefta €3.50-5) George specialises in home-cooked food and *mayirefta* dishes, as well a Cretan specials such as snails. Dining is right on the beach under the shade of tamarisk trees.

Restaurant Nikos Platanakis (☎ 28430 26887 meat dishes €7) This well-regarded taverna has a wide range of Greek staples such as rabbit stew, and other rarities including pheasant and partridge when in season. Nikos grilled meat and fish are also excellent.

GETTING THERE & AWAY

There are buses to Zakros from Sitia via Palekastro (one hour, €3.50, two daily). They leave Sitia at 11am and 2.30pm and return at 12.30pm and 4pm. From June to August, the buses continue to Kato Zakros.

XEROKAMBOS ΞΕΡΟΚΑΜΠΟΣ
pop 34

Xerokambos (kse-*ro*-kam-bos) is a quiet unassuming and spread-out agricultural village on the far southeastern flank of Crete Its isolation has so far meant that tourism is pretty much low-key and most certainly of the unpackaged kind. Its attraction lies in its isolation, a couple of splendid beaches a few scattered tavernas and a smattering of studio accommodation that is ideal for people wanting peace and quiet.

Ambelos Beach, on the northern side of the rocky headland that splits Xerokambos in two, is the smaller and more intimate beach and enjoys some shade. **Mazidas Beach**, on the southern side is larger, but has no shade whatsoever. Most accommodation and tavernas are on the more populated Ambelos side of Xerokambos. There is a well-stocked mini-market on the north side of Mazidas Beach.

WALKING THE 'VALLEY OF THE DEAD'

The spectacular Zakros Gorge – touted locally as the 'Valley of the Dead' – makes for a thoroughly enjoyable two-hour walk from Zakros village to Kato Zakros or, if time is pressing, for a one-hour walk from the halfway point to either end.

The signposted walk starts from just below Zakros village and winds it way through a narrow and (at times) soaring canyon. The base of the canyon is a riverbed (dry in summer) and a riot of vegetation and wild herbs, such as bitter laurel, oregano, sage and savoury.

About 3km from Zakros is an alternative starting point, indicated by a wooden sign and (usually) parked cars. The approach track dips steeply into the gorge before meeting the main trail after 10 minutes. Turn left for Zakros, or right for Kato Zakros. While not physically taxing, the trail is better tackled in stout footwear and in the early morning or late afternoon to avoid the heat. Take food and drink and make a relaxed picnic of the walk.

The canyon takes its moniker from the fact that ancient burial sites are located in the numerous caves dotting the canyon walls, rather than from hapless trekkers who failed to make it. At the eastern end the trail emerges close to the Zakros Palace site, while the azure sea beckons walkers for a refreshing swim.

Travellers usually approach Xerokambos from a long and winding road via Ziros, although there is an 8km dirt road linking Zakros with Xerokambos. This latter road is a bit rough in parts, but quite driveable with a conventional vehicle.

Sleeping & Eating

Akti Apartments (☎ 28430 26780; studio €35; 🔀) With balconies overlooking the beach, these comfortable studios are perfect for couples. They are nicely decorated and have kitchenettes. There's also a two-bedroom family apartment.

Akrogiali Taverna (☎ 28430 26777; mayirefta 3.50-4.50) The only beachside taverna in Xerokambos, Akrogiali is 50m from Ambelos Beach and near the Ambelos Beach Studios. The food ranges from grills and fish to their special home-cooked *mayirefta*.

Taverna Kostas (☎ 28430 26702; grills €4.50-6) Kosta and his German wife Vera run this lovely restaurant on the road to Zakros. Tables are on a shady terrace overlooking the sea and they specialise in local meats and fish. Beyond the restaurant are their apartments **Villa Petrino** (☎ 28420 26702; www.xerokambos.com; d €35; 🔀). These large fully equipped apartments overlooking the lovely garden are suitable for families. The top rooms also have great beach views.

Taverna Kastri (☎ 28420 26745; top fish per kg €35) This restaurant on Mazidas Beach serves up fish and seafood caught from its own caique, which makes it cheaper than most other places around. Try their enormous lobster-sized Cretan crayfish.

Getting There & Away

There are no buses to Xerokambos. To get there by car from Zakros take the Kato Zakros road, and on the outskirts of Zakros turn left at the signpost for Livyko View Restaurant. This 8km dirt road is driveable in a conventional vehicle. Otherwise there is a good paved road from Ziros.

SOUTH COAST

IERAPETRA ΙΕΡΑΠΕΤΡΑ
pop 11,678

Ierapetra (ee-yer-*a*-pet-rah) attracts relatively few package tourists and is a fairly unpretentious major town servicing the surrounding farming region. It is a pleasant place to stop for a few days. The town beach and surrounding beaches are good, the nightlife busy enough to keep you entertained and the scene is still Cretan enough to give you a less touristy experience of the island. The pleasant seafront is lined with cafés and tavernas. There is a Venetian fort on the harbour and the odd remnant of the Turkish quarter to explore.

From Ierapetra you can visit the offshore, low-lying, sandy island of Gaidouronisi (also known as Hrysi).

History

Ierapetra is Crete's most southerly major town. It was an important city for the Dorians and the last city to fall to the Romans, who made it a major port of call in their conquest of Egypt. Despite its antiquity, virtually nothing survives from the classical period.

The city languished under the Venetians, but they did build a small fortress at the western end of the harbour. In recent years agriculture has made the town wealthy enough to finance the restoration of the old town and the harbour-side.

Orientation & Information

There is no tourist office, but travel agents can help with tourist information and the website www.ierapetra.net is excellent. There are ATMs around the main square, a **post office** (☎ 28420 22271, Vintsenzou Kornarou 7) and an **OTE** (☎ 28420 22699, Koraka 25), and you can go online at **Net Internet Cafe** (☎ 28420 25900; Koundourou 16; per hr €3.60; ⏰ 9am-late).

Sights

Ierapetra's one-room **archaeological museum** (☎ 28420 28721; Adrianou 2; admission €2; ⏰ 8.30am-3pm Tue-Sun) is perfect for those with a short concentration span. It does have a good collection of headless classical statuary and a superb statue of the goddess of Demeter that dates from the 2nd century AD. Also notable is a *larnax*, or clay coffin, dating from around 1300 BC. The chest is decorated with 12 painted panels showing hunting scenes, an octopus and a chariot procession, among others. The 1899 building was a school during Ottoman times.

South along the waterfront from the central square is the 'Kales' **medieval fortress**

LASITHI

(admission free; 8.30am-3pm Tue-Sun), which was built in the early years of Venetian rule and strengthened by Francesco Morosini in 1626. It's in a pretty fragile state but you can visit it.

Inland from here is the labyrinthine **old quarter**, where you will see a **Turkish fountain**, the restored **Turkish mosque** with its minaret, and the old churches of **Agios Ioannis** and **Agios Georgios**. **Napoleon's house** is where the man himself is said to have stayed incognito with a local family when his ship anchored in Crete for one night in 1798 while on his way to Egypt. He apparently left a note the next day revealing his identity.

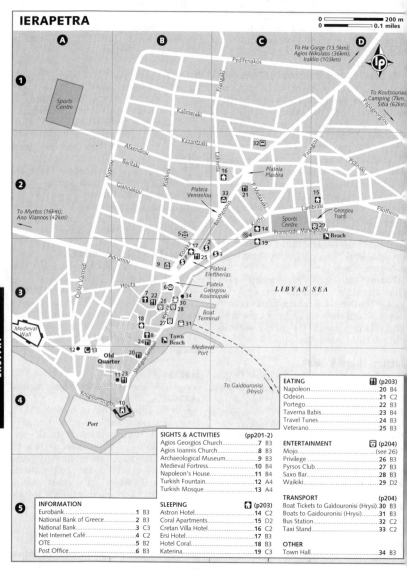

IERAPETRA

To Ha Gorge (13.5km);
Agios Nikolaos (36km);
Iraklio (103km)

To Koutsounari
Camping (7km;
Sitia (62km)

To Myrtos (16km);
Ano Viannos (42km)

LIBYAN SEA

To Gaidouronisi
(Hrysi)

The main **town beach** is near the harbour, while a second **beach** stretches east from the bottom of Patriarhou Metaxaki. Both have coarse, grey sand, but the main beach offers better shade.

Some 13.5km north of Ierapetra is the **Ha orge**, perhaps the most challenging gorge to traverse in all of Europe. More of an extreme climbing experience than a hike, the Ha Gorge is a narrow rent in the imposing mountains and is visible from the main Agios Nikolaos–Ierapetra road. Reputedly fully traversed by just 11 people, the gorge still regularly draws extreme climbers who attempt sections of this gut-wrenching and occasionally dangerous trek.

estivals & Events

Ierapetra's annual **Kyrvia Festival** runs from July through August and includes concerts, plays and art exhibits. Brochures are available in hotels and at the town hall. Some of the bands are free. There is also a **spring festival** between March and May.

Every Saturday there is a lively street **market** on Psilinaki St from 7am to 2pm.

leeping

Cretan Villa Hotel (☎ /fax 28420 28522; www.cretan villa.com; Lakerda 16; s/d €30/35; 🏠) This well-maintained 18th-century house is the most atmospheric place in town. The traditionally furnished rooms have a fridge and TV, and there is a peaceful courtyard. It's a five-minute walk from the bus station.

Ersi (☎ 28420 23208; Plateia Eleftherias 19; s/d €20/30; 🏠) Refurbished in 2004, this central hotel 50m from the beach is run by the same family as Coral Hotel, who also have the fully equipped **Coral Apartments** (Lambraki; d €30) on the other side of town for families or longer stays. The neat rooms have a fridge, TV and sea views.

Astron Hotel (☎ 28420 25114; htastron@otenet.gr; Kothri 56; d incl breakfast €68-75; 🏠) The top hotel in town is the B-class Astron at the beach end of Patriarhou Metaxaki. The comfortable rooms here are furnished with satellite TV and telephone; some have sea views.

Hotel Coral (☎ 28420 22846; Katzonovatsi 12; s/d €20/30) It can be a bit tricky to find this place, but it's a reasonable budget option. The rooms are a little dull, but well kept and clean. The hotel is two blocks inland close to the easily spotted church.

Katerina (☎ 28420 28345; fax 28420 28591; Marko-poulou 95; s/d €20/25; 🏠) On the seafront, Katerina has bland but comfortable rooms with phone, fridge and double-glazed windows. The bathrooms are a bit of a letdown. Most rooms have sea views.

Koutsounari Camping (☎ 28420 61213; www .camping-koutsounari.epimlas.gr; per tent/adult €3.50/4.90) About 7km east at Koutsounari, it has a restaurant, snack bar and mini-market. Ierapetra–Sitia buses pass the site.

Eating

Portego (☎ 28420 27733; Foniadaki 8; wood oven specials €2.50-8.50) This delightful restaurant serves excellent Cretan and Greek cuisine and has specials cooked in the wood-fired oven (so is their bread). Try the lamb in a clay pot with yogurt. It is housed in the historic 1900s house of local character Anna Bey, whose portrait is in the back room. It has a good wine list, a lovely courtyard for summer and there is a cool bar and kafeneio.

Odeion (Lasthenous 18; mezedes €3-4) This converted music school is believed to have been used as a torture chamber during the German occupation. These days its serves excellent mezedes in the basement to a generally younger crowd, while the 1st floor is a music bar. There is a pleasant garden in summer.

Veterano (☎ 28420 23175; Plateia Eleftherias) This *zaharoplasteio* (patisserie) is a popular hang out for breakfast and light meals during the day and has great sweets – try the excellent *galaktoboureko* (custard pastry).

Taverna Babis (☎ 28420 24048; Stratigou Samouil 68; mains €4-6.50) One of the better tavernas on the waterfront, Babis has an enormous range of mezedes dishes. Try the *kakavia* (fish soup) or the *staka* – a high-cal, warm cream cheese from curd.

Napoleon (☎ 28420 22410; Stratigou Samouil 26; mains €5-6.50) This is one of the oldest and most respected establishments. It's on the waterfront on the south side of town. There is fresh fish and Greek and Cretan specialties, but whatever you order is of a high quality.

Travel Tunes (☎ 28420 89021; Stratigou Samouil 18; www.travel-tunes.com; 🖳) A hammock hints at the laid-back feel of this newcomer run by a Dutch couple. The 'world café' theme is reflected in the music (and sandwiches) and there's a healthy buffet breakfast (€4 to €6.50). It is also an Internet café and there are stacks of travel books on Crete.

LASITHI

Entertainment

Kyrva is Ierapetra's main nightlife strip, while the Mojo and Privilege nightclubs are on Foniadaki. The popularity of the bars waxes and wanes yearly, but there are some standard hangouts. **Saxo Bar** (Kyrva 14) has mixed music, **Pyrsos Club** (Kyrva 22) is the flashiest nightspot on Kyrva, while the recently revamped **Waikiki** (☎ 28420 27731; Georgiou Tzardi 2) is the classiest bar in town, right on the beach at the eastern end of the promenade.

Getting There & Away

The **bus station** (☎ 28420 28237; Lasthenous) is on the eastern side of town, one street back from the beachfront. In summer, there are 10 buses a day from Ierapetra to Iraklio (€7.50, 2½ hours), via Agios Nikolaos (€2.50, one hour) and Gournia; seven to Sitia (€4.40, 1½ hours) via Koutsounari (for camp sites); six to Myrtos (€1.40, 30 minutes); and two a week to Ano Viannos (€3, one hour).

Taxis (☎ 28420 25512) can take you anywhere for a fixed fare. Fares are posted on Plateia Venizelou and destinations include Iraklio (€60), Agios Nikolaos (€25), Sitia (€40) and Myrtos (€11).

AROUND IERAPETRA

The good beaches to the east of Ierapetra tend to be crowded in peak season and you really need a car (or preferably a jeep or dirt bike) to explore the area and get to the off-the-track beaches. Much of this coastal drive is sadly spoiled by the plastic-covered hothouses that dominate the area. About 13km from Ierapetra is the lovely beach of **Agias Fotias**, although it's no longer the isolated beach that was popular with campers.

While the fine white sandy beach at the eastern end of **Makrigialos** is one of the best on the southeastern coast, the beach is scarred by tacky tourist shops and tavernas. The village, 24km from Ierapetra, has become an overdeveloped tourist town, but does have one stand-out place for foodies.

The excellent **Porfira taverna** (☎ 28430 52189) is owned by Leonidas Grammatika, considered one of the best chefs in Crete, renowned for creative takes on traditional Greek recipes.

Accommodation in Makrigialos is not cheap or particularly good value in July or August so it's probably best to cool off with a swim, then eat and run.

GAIDOURONISI (HRYSI)

Just off the coast of Ierapetra, you will find greater tranquillity at Gaidouronisi (Donkey Island) – universally marketed in Ierapetra as Hrysi or Hrissi (Golden Island) – where there are good, sandy beaches, three tavernas and a stand of Lebanon cedars, the only one in Europe. It can get a bit crowded when the tour boats are in, but you can always find a quiet spot of your own.

In summer, a number of **excursion boats** (€20) leave from the quay near the town centre for the islet every morning and return in the afternoon.

MYRTOS ΜΥΡΤΟΣ
pop 440

Myrtos (*myr*-tos), on the coast 17km west of Ierapetra, is a sparkling village of whitewashed houses with flower-filled balconies. It is a magnet for independent travellers, many of whom only come for a day or so, yet find themselves inextricably staying on for a couple of weeks. The village has a cosy, lived-in ambience where everyone seems to know each other. Myrto

---

ROUGHING IT

The tiny, primitive 300-year-old stone cottages at **Aspros Potamos** (☎ 28430 51694; www.asprospotamos .com; r €32-60) were traditionally used by village farmers during the winter. Twenty years ago, Aleka Halkia bought the ruins of the settlement and has slowly restored them in original style as guesthouses for people wanting to go back to nature and simple living. An award-winning eco-friendly photovoltaic system is used to heat water and power the bathroom light and fridge. The 11 cottages are lit with oil lamps and candles, and have stone floors, traditional furnishings and most have fireplaces for the winter. One is built right into the rock face. Aleka lives there year-round and runs them with her daughter Myrto, who has now moved to town for some mod cons. It's a few kilometres along the turn-off north to Pefki. It can be a little tricky to find by car, so call ahead and they'll meet you.

one of those few places left in Crete that
etains an element of authenticity yet pro-
ides the necessary creature comforts.

Myrtos is easily navigable as it is built on
grid system. To get to the waterfront from
he bus stop, head south and take the road
o the right for 150m. There is no post office,
ank or OTE, but **Aris Travel Agency** (☎ 28420
1017) on the main street has currency ex-
hange. Internet is available upstairs at **Edem
afe** (☎ 28420 51551; per hr €6; ☎ 1am-late), two
locks back from the waterfront.

leeping & Eating

ig Blue (☎ 28420 51094; www.forthnet.gr/big-blue;
studio/apt €35/60/75; 🔀) On the western edge
f town, Big Blue is one of the best places
o stay and is handy for the beach. You
ave a choice of more expensive, large airy
tudios with glorious beach and sea views,
r cheaper, cosy ground-floor rooms. They
ll have cooking facilities.

Hotel Myrtos (☎ 28420 51227; www.myrtoshotel
om; s/d incl breakfast €25/30; 🔀) This superior
C-class place in the middle of the main
treet has large, well-kept rooms with TV,
hone, mini-bar and balconies overlook-
ng the sea or mountains. It's 50m from
he beach and there's a restaurant.

Cretan Rooms (☎ 28420 51427; d €35) These
cosy, excellent traditional-styled rooms with
balconies, fridges and shared kitchens are
popular with independent travellers. Owner
Maria Daskalaki keeps them neat and clean.
They are prominently signposted from the
village.

Nikos House (☎ 28420 51116; d/apt €30/45) Two
blocks back from the waterfront in the thick
of things, these large and comfortable self-
contained apartments shelter beneath a large
mulberry tree and accommodate up to four
people.

Myrtos Taverna (☎ 28420 51227; mains €4-7) Always busy, it's popular with both locals and
tourists for its wide range of mezedes as well
as for its vegetarian dishes. The rabbit in red
wine sauce is recommended.

Taverna Akti (☎ 28420 51584; mains €5-6) At the
eastern end of the waterfront, Akti offers
pleasant seafood dining and better than average food. The best choices are usually the
daily specials.

Getting There & Away

There are six buses a day from Ierapetra to
Myrtos (€1.40, 30 minutes), while the Ano
Viannos–Ierapetra bus also passes through
Myrtos twice a week.

Directory

CONTENTS

ACCOMMODATION

There is a range of accommodation available in Crete to suit every taste and pocket size. All places to stay are subject to strict price controls set by the tourist police. By law, a notice must be displayed in every room that states the category of the room and the maximum price charged in each season. These official high season rates are generally quoted in this book, but there is often a lot of room for negotiation, especially out of high season and for longer stays. After a bad season in 2004, the prices may well drop from the peak rates quoted here.

Accommodation owners may add 10% surcharge for a stay of less than three nights, but this is not mandatory or common. A mandatory charge of 20% is levied if an extra bed is put into a room.

During July and August (especially in the middle of August) accommodation owners will usually charge the maximum price, but in spring and autumn, prices will drop by up to 20%, and perhaps even more in winter. These are the times to bring your bargaining skills into action.

PRACTICALITIES

- Use the metric system for weights and measures (see inside front cover for conversion formulas).

- Plug your electrical appliances into a two-pin adaptor before plugging into the electricity supply (220V AC, 50Hz).

- The main English-language newspapers in Greece are the weekly *Athens News* and the eight-page English-language section of the Greek daily *Kathimerini*, published with the *International Herald Tribune*.

- The English and German newspaper, *Cretasummer*, is published monthly during the summer in Rethymno. The monthly magazine, *Kreta*, is on sale in a variety of languages. Crete's e-zine **Stigmes** (www.stigmes.gr) is also worth a look.

- You can often pick up CNN and the BBC on free-to-air TV, and cable is available at many hotels. Radio signals are patchy, but you can try ERA's English broadcasts (107MHz on FM band and 665KHz on AM) for news in English (12.30pm and 9.30pm) or the BBC World Service throughout the day (6195kHZ, 15565kHZ, 17640kHZ and 12095kHZ).

- Greece uses the PAL video system, which is the same as Australia and New Zealand but incompatible with the North American and Japanese NTSC system.

Many domatia owners also charge extra or air-conditioning. This is only permissible if the price is lower than the maximum, which would include air-con.

Rip-offs rarely occur, but if you suspect you've been exploited by an accommodation owner, report it to either the tourist police or regular police and they'll act swiftly.

Many accommodation proprietors will want to keep your passport during your stay. However, this is not a compulsory requirement – they only need it to take down the details.

Camping

There are only about a dozen or so camping grounds in Crete. Most are privately run and very few are open outside the high season (April to October).

The **Panhellenic Camping Association** (☎ /fax 210 362 1560; www.panhellenic-camping-union.gr; Solonos 102, Athens) publishes an annual booklet listing all the camp sites and their facilities.

Camping fees are highest from 15 June to the end of August. Most camping grounds charge from €4 to €6 per adult and €1.80 to €2.50 for children aged four to 12. There's no charge for children aged under four. Tent sites cost from €3 per night for small tents, and from €4 per night for large tents. Caravan sites start at around €8.

Between May and mid-September it is warm enough to sleep out under the stars, although you will still need a lightweight sleeping bag to counter the pre-dawn chill. It's a good idea to have a foam pad to lie on and a waterproof cover to protect your sleeping bag.

Freelance (wild) camping is illegal, but the law is not always strictly enforced. It's wise to ask around before camping wild.

Domatia

Domatia are the Greek equivalent of the British B&B, minus the breakfast. Once upon a time domatia comprised little more than spare rooms in the family home that were rented out to travellers in summer, which made for very cheap holidays. Nowadays, many are purpose-built and some come complete with fully equipped kitchens, while older basic rooms have been upgraded along with the prices.

Standards of cleanliness are generally high. The décor runs the gamut from cool grey marble floors, coordinated pine furniture, pretty lace curtains and tasteful pictures on the walls, to floral mismatched sheets and so much kitsch you are almost afraid to move in case you break an ornament.

Domatia remain a popular option for budget travellers. Expect to pay from €15 to €30 for a single, and €20 to €50 for a double, depending on the class, whether bathrooms are shared or private, the season and how long you plan to stay.

Many domatia operate only between April and October.

Hostels

There are hostels in Iraklio, **Rethymno** (www.yh rethymno.com) and **Plakias** (www.yhplakias.com) run by the **Greek Youth Hostel Organisation** (☎ 210 751 9530; y-hostels@otenet.gr; Damareos 75, Athens 116 33).

Hostel rates vary from €7.50 to €15 and you don't have to be a member to stay in any of them.

Hotels

Hotels in Crete are divided into six categories: deluxe, A, B, C, D and E. Hotels are categorised according to the size of the room, whether or not they have a bar, and the ratio of bathrooms to beds, rather than standards of cleanliness, comfort of the beds and friendliness of staff – all elements which may be of greater relevance to guests.

As one would expect, deluxe, A- and B-class hotels have many amenities, private bathrooms and constant hot water. They usually, but not always, have air-conditioning. Even in expensive hotels the air-conditioning may only function part of the day or be turned off at night.

C-class hotels have a snack bar, rooms have private bathrooms, but hot water may only be available at certain times of the day.

D-class hotels may or may not have snack bars, most rooms will share bathrooms (but there may be some with private bathrooms) and they may have solar heated water, which means hot water is not guaranteed.

E-class hotels do not have a snack bar, bathrooms are shared and you may have to pay extra for hot water – if it exists at all.

Prices are controlled by the tourist police and the maximum rate that can be charged for a room must be displayed on a board behind the door of each room. The classification is not often much of a guide to price.

Rates in D- and E-class hotels are generally comparable with domatia. You can pay anywhere from €30 to €60 for a C-class single in high season and €45 to €75 for a double. Prices in B-class range from €45 to €75 for singles, and from €75 to €105 for doubles. A-class prices are not much higher.

Mountain Refuges
Mountain refuges are not plentiful on Crete but there are some lodges scattered around the Lefka Ori, Mt Psiloritis and Kallergi. A bunk bed will cost between €5 and €12.

Studios & Apartments
There is a growing trend in Crete to build self-catering studios or apartments for visitors. Studios are usually two-person affairs, while an apartment can take anywhere from two to five persons. These are excellent options for families and groups of friends. Facilities usually include a kitchenette, fridge and TV, and many include air-conditioning, heating for winter, a separate lounge area, separate bedrooms and occasionally washing facilities and microwaves. Costs for a studio in high season range from €35 to €50 while an apartment for four people in high season will cost between €50 and €80.

Traditional Houses & Settlements
Traditional settlements are old buildings of architectural merit that have been renovated and converted into tourist accommodation. The best in Crete are at Milia, Vamos and around Markigialos in the south. They're not cheap, but traditional features such as fireplaces and stone kitchens provide an unusual and appealing experience. A traditional house for four persons in Vamos will cost around €80 to €100, while a small stone cottage for two in Milia will cost around €50 to €56. Many historic houses and lovely stone cottages are also being restored and converted into fine accommodation.

ACTIVITIES
Crete's adventurous terrain lends itself to a host of activities for the more active traveller. For the full lowdown see the Crete Outdoors chapter (p57).

BUSINESS HOURS
Banks are open from 8am to 2.30pm Monday to Thursday, and 8am to 2pm Friday.

Post offices are open 7.30am to 2pm Monday to Friday. In the major cities the main post office stays open until 8pm, and open from 8am to 2pm on Saturday.

The opening hours of OTE (telephone offices vary. In smaller towns they are usually open 7.30am to 3pm daily, and in large towns from 6am until 8pm.

In summer, shops are open 9am to 2pm and 5.30pm to 8.30pm Tuesday, Thursday and Friday, and 8am to 3pm Monday, Wednesday and Saturday. They open 30 minutes later in winter, although these times are not always strictly adhered to. Many shops in tourist areas are open seven days a week. Periptera (street kiosks) open from early morning until late at night. They sell everything from bus tickets and cigarettes to condoms. Supermarkets generally open until 8pm.

Opening times of museums and archaeological sites vary, but most are closed on Monday.

CHILDREN
Crete is a safe and relatively easy place to travel with children. It's especially easy if you're staying by the beach or at a resort hotel. If you're travelling around, you will find there is a shortage of decent playgrounds and recreational facilities. However, there are air-conditioned indoor children's play centres for children in most major cities if you want a respite from the heat, and usually there's a café attached.

Don't be afraid to take children to ancient sites. Many parents are surprised by how much their children enjoy them. Young imaginations go into overdrive when let loose somewhere like the 'labyrinth' at Knossos.

Hotels and restaurants are usually very accommodating when it comes to meeting the needs of children, although highchairs are a rarity outside resorts. The service in restaurants is normally very quick, which is great when you've got hungry kids on your hands.

Fresh milk is readily available in large towns and tourist areas, but harder to find in small villages. Look in the supermarkets. Formula is available everywhere, as is condensed and heat-treated milk.

Mobility is an issue for parents with very small children. Strollers (pushchairs) aren't much use in Crete unless you're going to pend all your time in one of the few flat pots. They're hopeless on rough stone paths nd up steps, and a curse when getting on/ ff buses and ferries. Backpacks or front ouches are best.

Children under four travel free on ferries nd buses. They pay half fare up to the age f 10 (ferries) and 12 (buses); the full fare pplies otherwise. On domestic flights, you'll ay 10% of the fare to have a child under wo sitting on your knee. Kids aged two to 2 pay half fare.

The Greek publisher Malliaris-Paedia roduces a good series of books on Greek nyths, retold in English for young readers y Aristides Kesopoulos. The titles are *The Gods of Olympus and the Lesser Gods, The .abours of Hercules, Theseus and the Voy- age of the Argonauts, The Trojan War and he Wanderings of Odysseus* and *Heroes and Mythical Creatures*.

The Moon Over Crete, by Jyotsna Sreeni- rasen and Sim Gellman, is a modern-day tory based in Crete written for young girls ut with a mature message.

CLIMATE CHART
Crete has a typically Mediterranean climate with hot, dry summers and milder winters. You can swim off the island's southern coast from mid-April to November.

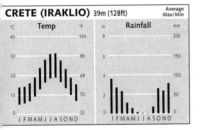

COURSES
The **University of Crete** (☎ 28310 77278; www.uch.gr; moderngreek@phl.uoc.gr) in Rethymno runs four- week summer courses in Modern Greek during July. Contact the university for full details.

UK-based **YOGA Plus** (☎ +44 1273-276175; www .yogaplus.co.uk) runs Astanga Vinyasa yoga workshops for one week or longer at its re- treat in Agios Pavlos (p139). The courses include accommodation, other activities and

wholesome food. The nearby **Triopetra Yoga Centre** (www.astanga.gr) also runs courses from beginners to advanced levels.

Workshops in Cretan cuisine are offered in Panormo and Axos in Rethymno prefec- ture. See p71 for details.

CUSTOMS
There are no longer duty-free restrictions within the European Union (EU). This does not mean, however, that customs checks have been dispensed with – random searches are still made for drugs. Upon entering the country from outside the EU, customs in- spection is usually cursory for foreign tour- ists. There may be spot checks, but you probably won't have to open your bags. You may bring the following into Greece duty free: 200 cigarettes or 50 cigars; 1L of spirits or 2L of wine; 50g of perfume; 250ml of eau de Cologne; one camera (still or video) and film; a pair of binoculars; a portable musi- cal instrument; a radio or tape recorder; a typewriter; sports equipment; and dogs and cats (with a veterinary certificate).

Importation of works of art and antiqui- ties is free, but they must be declared on entry, so that they can be re-exported. Im- port regulations for medicines are strict; if you are taking medication, make sure you get a statement from your doctor before you leave home. It is illegal, for instance, to take codeine into Greece without an accom- panying doctor's certificate. An unlimited amount of foreign currency and travellers cheques may be brought into Crete. If, how- ever, you intend to leave the country with foreign banknotes in excess of $1000, you must declare the sum upon entry.

It is strictly forbidden to export antiqui- ties (anything over 100 years old) without an export permit. This crime is second only to drug smuggling in the penalties imposed. It is an offence to remove even the smallest article from an archaeological site.

You can apply for an export permit at the Antique Dealers & Private Collections Section of the **Culture Ministry** (☎ 210 825 8684; Saripolou 6, Athens).

DANGERS & ANNOYANCES
Crime, especially theft, is low in Crete, but unfortunately it is on the increase. Keep track of your valuables on public transport and in markets. Do not leave luggage unattended

in cars. The vast majority of thefts from tourists are still committed by other tourists; the biggest danger of theft is probably in hostels and at camping grounds. If you are staying in a hotel room, and the windows and door do not lock securely, ask for your valuables to be locked in the hotel safe.

DISABLED TRAVELLERS

If mobility is a problem, visiting Crete will presents some serious challenges. The hard fact is that most hotels, ferries, museums and sites are not wheelchair accessible and the terrain of many areas is not suitable (although new hotels are disability-friendly).

If you are determined, then take heart in the knowledge that wheelchair-users do go to Crete for holidays. But the trip needs careful planning, so get as much information as you can before you go.

There is some useful English-language information on travelling in Greece on www .disabled.gr.

DISCOUNT CARDS
Senior Cards

Card-carrying EU pensioners can claim a range of benefits such as reduced admission charges at museums and ancient sites and discounts on trains.

Student & Youth Cards

The most widely recognised form of student ID is the **International Student Identity Card** (ISIC; www.isic.org). These cards are widely available from budget travel agencies (take along proof that you are a student). Holders qualify for half-price admission to some museums and ancient sites. There are no travel agencies authorised to issue ISICs in Crete, so arrange for one before leaving home. In Athens you can get one from the **International Student & Youth Travel Service** (ISYTS; ☎ 210 323 3767; 2nd fl, Nikis 11, Athens).

Some travel agencies in Greece offer discounts on organised tours to students. However, there are no student discounts for travel within Greece (although Olympic Airways gives a 25% discount on domestic flights that are part of an international flight).

If you are under 26 years of age but not a student, the **Federation of International Youth Travel Organisation** (FIYTO; www.fiyto.org) card gives similar discounts. Many budget travel agencies issue FIYTO cards.

COPIES

All important documents (passport data page and visa page, credit cards, travel insurance policy, air/bus/train tickets, driving licence etc) should be photocopied before you leave home. Leave one copy with someone at home and keep another with you, separate from the originals.

EMBASSIES & CONSULATES

Remember that you are bound by Greek laws. Your embassy will not be sympathetic if you end up in jail after committing a crime locally, even if such actions are legal in your own country.

In genuine emergencies you might get some assistance, but only if other channels have been exhausted. For example, if you need to get home urgently, a free ticket home is exceedingly unlikely – the embassy would expect you to have insurance. If you have all your money and documents stolen, it will assist with getting a new passport.

Greek Embassies & Consulates

Greek diplomatic missions abroad include
Australia (☎ 02-6273 3011; greekemb@greekembassy-au .org; 9 Turrana St, Yarralumla, ACT 2600)
Canada (☎ 613-238-6271; www.greekembassy.ca; 76-80 Maclaren St, Ottawa, Ontario K2P 0K6)
Japan (☎ 03-3403 0871/2; www.greekemb.jp; 3-16-30 Nishi Azabu, Minato-ku, Tokyo 304-5853)
New Zealand (☎ 04-473 7775; info@greece.org.nz; 5-7 Willeston St, Wellington)
South Africa (☎ 12-430 7351; embgrsaf@global.co.za; 1003 Church St, Hatfield, Pretoria 0028)
UK (☎ 020-7229 3850; www.greekembassy.org.uk; 1A Holland Park, London W11 3TP)
USA (☎ 202-939-1300; www.greekembassy.org; 2221 Massachusetts Ave NW, Washington, DC 20008)

Embassies & Consulates in Greece

The **UK embassy** (☎ 2810 224 012; Papalexandrou 16) in Iraklio is the only foreign embassy in Crete. The rest are in Athens and its suburbs.
Australia (☎ 210 870 4000; Level 6, Thon Building, cnr Kifissias & Alexandras, 11521)
Canada (☎ 210 727 3400; Gennadiou 4, 11521)
Cyprus (☎ 210 723 7883; Irodotou 16, 10675)
Ireland (☎ 210 723 2771; Leoforos Vasileos Konstantinou 7, 10674)
Japan (☎ 210 775 8101; Athens Tower, Leoforos Mesogion 2-4, 11527)

Netherlands (☎ 210 723 9701; Vasileos Konstantinou 5-7, 0674)

New Zealand (☎ 210 771 0112; Xenias 24, 11528)

South Africa (☎ 210 680 6645; Kifisias 60, Marousi, 15125)

USA (☎ 210 721 2951; Leoforos Vasilissis Sofias 91, 11521)

FESTIVALS & EVENTS

The Greek year is a succession of festivals and events, some of which are religious, some cultural, others an excuse for a good feast, and some a combination of all three. The following is by no means an exhaustive list, but it covers the most important events, both national and regional. If you're in the right place at the right time, you'll certainly be invited to join the revelry.

In summer, cultural festivals are staged across Crete. The most significant include the annual **Renaissance Festival** in Rethymno (p125), which features art exhibitions, plus dance, drama and films, and the **Kyrvia Festival** in Ierapetra (p203), which includes a range of musical, theatrical and artistic presentations.

Sitia's **Kornaria Festival** (p194) presents music, theatre, art exhibits and a beach volleyball competition. Iraklio's **Summer Arts Festival** (p155) runs from July to September and attracts international artists as well as local singers and dancers, while the **Lato Cultural Festival** in Agios Nikolaos (p182) features traditional and modern works performed by local and international orchestras and dance troupes.

January
Feast of Agios Vasilios (St Basil) The year kicks off with the New Year's Day festival. A church ceremony is followed by the exchanging of gifts, singing, dancing and feasting; the *vasilopitta* (New Year pie) is sliced and the person who gets the slice containing a coin will supposedly have a lucky year.

Epiphany (the Blessing of the Waters) On 6 January, Christ's baptism by St John is celebrated throughout Greece. Seas, lakes and rivers are blessed and crosses are thrown into the water. The brave soul who retrieves the cross is blessed for the year.

February/March
Shrove Monday (Clean Monday) On the Monday before Ash Wednesday (ie, the first day of Lent), people take to the hills throughout Greece to have picnics and fly kites.

March
Independence Day The anniversary of the hoisting of the Greek flag by Bishop Germanos at Moni Agias Lavras is celebrated on 25 March with parades and dancing. Germanos' act of revolt marked the start of the War of Independence. Independence Day coincides with the Feast of the Annunciation, so it is also a religious festival.

March/April
Easter This is taken much more seriously than any other religious holiday. On Palm Sunday (the Sunday before Orthodox Easter), worshippers return from church services with a cross woven of palm and myrtle. If you are in Crete at Easter you should endeavour to attend some of the Easter services, which include a candle-lit procession through the streets on Good Friday evening and ends with fireworks at midnight on Easter Saturday.

Feast of Agios Georgos (St George) The feast day of St George, Crete's patron saint and patron saint of shepherds, takes place on 23 April or the Tuesday following Easter (whichever comes first). The most elaborate celebration is in Asi Gonia where thousands of goats and sheep are gathered at the town church for shearing, milking and blessing. Fresh milk accompanies the ensuing feast.

Hohliovradia (Snail Night) Vamos celebrates the popular Cretan delicacy with a festival of cooked snails, washed down with wine and *tsikoudia* (a grape distilled spirit).

May
May Day On the first day of May there is a mass exodus from towns to the country. During picnics, wildflowers are gathered and made into wreaths to decorate houses.

Battle of Crete During the last week of May, the island commemorates the Battle of Crete with athletic competitions, folk dancing and ceremonial events in Hania, Rethymno, Iraklio and key battle memorials at Souda Bay, Stavronas and Preveli monastery. Representatives of Commonwealth countries attend the ceremonies each year.

June
Navy Week Celebrated in even-numbered years during the last week in June, it commemorates Crete's relationship with the sea. In Crete's harbour cities there is music and dancing on land and swimming and sailing competitions on the water.

Feast of St John the Baptist This feast day on 24 June is widely celebrated. Wreaths made on May Day are kept until this day, when they are burned on bonfires.

July
Feast of Agia Marina (St Marina) Celebrated on 17 July in many parts of the island, this feast day is a particularly important event in Agia Marina, outside of Hania.

DIRECTORY

Feast of Profitis Ilias Celebrated on 20 July at hill-top churches and monasteries dedicated to the prophet, especially in the Cyclades.

Wine Festival The Wine Festival of Rethymno is held in the municipal park with wine tastings and local cuisine.

Yakinthia Festival The mountain village of Anogia stages an annual cultural and musical extravaganza lasting one week. There are poetry recitals, talks, exhibitions and outdoor concerts featuring Cretan music. The festival takes place in the last week of July.

Renaissance Festival Rethymno's main festival is held during the July–September period, and features performances by Greece's leading theatre companies, as well as dance, music and acts from around Europe.

Summer Arts Festival International guest orchestras and dance troupes as well as local talent appear in Iraklio from July to September, with the main events held in an immense open-air theatre.

July/August

Kornaria Festival In Sitia, this festival runs from mid-July to the end of August, with concerts, folk dancing and theatre productions staged in the *kazarma* (fort) and other venues.

Lato Cultural Festival Agios Nikolaos hosts this festival that includes concerts by local and international musicians, Cretan music played on traditional instruments, folk dancing, *mandinades* (improvised rhyming couplets) contests, theatre, art exhibits and swimming competitions.

Kyrvia Festival Ierapetra's main festival includes concerts, plays and art exhibits.

August

Paleohora Music Festival Held on the first 10 days of August, song contests and concerts are staged every night.

Cultural Festival In Ano Viannos, there's a three-day Cultural Festival at the beginning of August with concerts, plays and art exhibits.

Wine Festival In Arhanes, 15 August is the merry conclusion of a five-day Wine Festival celebrating their excellent local wine.

Assumption Day Greeks celebrate Assumption Day (15 August) with family reunions. The whole population is on the move either side of the day, so it's a good time to avoid public transport.

Traditional Cretan wedding In late August, the village of Kritsa stages a traditional Cretan wedding complete with songs, dancing and traditional food for an admission of about €9.

Sultana Festival Sitia celebrates their superior sultana raisins with wine, music and dancing in the last week of the month.

Potato Festival Lasithi produces superior potatoes, a product which is celebrated in a three-day festival at the end of August in Tzermiado.

September

Genisis tis Panagias (the Virgin's Birthday) Celebrated on 8 September throughout Greece with various religious services and feasting.

October

Chestnut Festival The village of Elos stages a chestnut festival on the third Sunday of the month when everyone offered roasted chestnuts, chestnut sweets and *tsikoudia* (raki).

Ohi (No) Day Metaxas' refusal to allow Mussolini's troops free passage through Crete during WWII is commemorated on 28 October with a number of remembrance services, military parades, folk dancing and feasting.

November

One of the most important local holidays celebrated in Crete is the anniversary of the explosion at Moni Arkadiou, commemorated at the monastery from 7 to 9 November.

December

Christmas Day Although not as important as Easter, Christmas is still celebrated with religious services and feasting. Nowadays much Western influence is apparent, including Christmas trees, decorations and presents.

FOOD

For information on the staples of Greek food see p64. For large cities and towns, restaurant listings in this book are divided into budget (under €10), mid-range (€10 to €25) and top end (over €30) for two courses. Within each section, the restaurants are listed in order of author preference. Note that there is a separate cover charge added to the bill for each person, which in some high-end places can be as high as €2.

GAY & LESBIAN TRAVELLERS

While there is no legislation against homosexual activity in Greece, it is wise to be discreet and to avoid public displays of togetherness.

Unlike other islands such as Mykonos, Crete does not have a thriving gay scene. Since homosexuality is generally frowned upon and Crete has never been marketed as a gay destination to package tourists there is no overtly gay nightlife.

There are a number of venues in Iraklio that are gay-friendly, although not exclusively gay. Relaxed Paleohora is gay-friendly as are most nude beaches.

The *Spartacus International Gay Guide* published in Berlin by Bruno Gmunder, i widely regarded as the leading authority on the gay travel scene and has a wealth of information on gay venues around the Greek Islands.

Gayscape (www.gayscape.com) has a useful site with lots of links, or try www.gaygreece.gr for information about the Greek gay scene, although most of it is still in Greek, as is www.lesbian.gr.

HOLIDAYS

All banks and shops and most museums and ancient sites close on public holidays. Greek national public holidays observed in Crete are:

New Year's Day 1 January
Epiphany 6 January
First Sunday in Lent February
Greek Independence Day 25 March
Good Friday March/April
(Orthodox) Easter Sunday March/April
Spring Festival/Labour Day 1 May
Feast of the Assumption 15 August
Ohi Day 28 October
Christmas Day 25 December
St Stephen's Day 26 December

INSURANCE

A travel insurance-policy to cover theft, loss and medical problems is a wise move. Some policies specifically exclude dangerous activities, which can include scuba diving, motorcycling, even trekking.

You may prefer a policy that pays doctors or hospitals directly rather than you having to pay on the spot and claim later. If you have to claim later ensure you keep all documentation.

Check that the policy covers ambulances or an emergency flight home.

INTERNET ACCESS

Crete has a reasonable number of Internet cafés and each major town will have several places to surf and check your mail. Access costs range from €3 to €6 per hour. Many larger hotels also offer Internet access. Travellers with their own laptops or personal organisers can arrange Internet roaming with their local ISP, as there are reliable dial-up numbers in Crete. You can also buy Internet cards from *periptera* (kiosk) from €3 to €20, which give you eight to 200 hours' access.

If you need to access a specific account, rather than Web-based email such as Yahoo

or Hotmail, you'll need to carry three pieces of information with you: your incoming (POP or IMAP) mail server name, your account name and your password. Your ISP or network supervisor will be able to give you these. You should then be able to access your email from anywhere in the world.

Travellers from the UK must have an adaptor for the modem line as the phone jack in Greece is different.

LEGAL MATTERS

Greek drug laws are the strictest in Europe. Greek courts make no distinction between possession and pushing. Possession of even a small amount of marijuana is likely to land you in jail.

MAPS

Mapping is an important feature of this guide. Unless you are going to trek or drive, you probably won't need additional maps. Do not rely on the free maps handed out by tourist offices, which are often out of date and not particularly accurate. The maps below are widely available in bookshops and tourist shops in Crete.

The best maps are published by the Greek company **Road Editions** (☎ 210 364 0723; www.road.gr). Crete is covered by the company's 1:200,000 blue-covered *Crete* map (€6). There are also dedicated 1:100,000 *Eastern Crete* and *Western Crete* maps (€7.50). Even the smallest roads and villages are clearly marked, and the distance indicators are spot-on.

Emvelia Editions (☎ 210 771 7616, info@emvelia.gr) has a 1:185,000 map of *Crete* (€5.88) that is a little clearer to read. It has good maps of the major towns, as well as the five major archaeological sites. The German-published Harms Verlag 1:100,000 *Kreta Touristikkarte* come in two versions: the East *(Der Osten)* and the West *(Der Westen)* and cost a steep €10 each. These are probably the best maps for hikers and trekkers and depict the E4 Trekking Route (see p58) very clearly. The maps are available in Crete, or you can contact **Harms Verlag** (☎ 07275 8201; www.harms-ic-verlag.de) in Germany.

For serious walkers, the most detailed maps, **Petrakis Editions** (☎ 2810 282630; €5), are by Iraklio-based trekker Giorgos Petrakis, who has walked almost every inch of the island. He has produced trekking and road

DIRECTORY

maps for each of the four prefectures at a scale of 1:100,000. They include the E4 trail and all the mountainous routes of Crete, and are widely available in Crete.

MONEY

The unit of currency in Greece is the euro (€). Coins come in denominations of one, two, five, 10, 20, and 50 cents. Banknotes come in €5, €10, €20, €50, €100 and €500.

ATMs

ATMs are to be found in almost every town large enough to support a bank – and certainly in all the tourist areas. If you've got MasterCard or Visa/Access, there are plenty of places to withdraw money. Cirrus, Plus and Maestro users can make withdrawals in all major towns and tourist areas.

AFEMs (Automatic Foreign Exchange Machines) are common in major tourist areas. They take all the major European currencies, Australian and US dollars and Japanese yen.

Cash

Nothing beats cash for convenience, but if you lose any it's gone for good, and very few travel insurers will come to your rescue. Those that do normally limit the amount to about $300. It's best to carry no more cash than you need for the next few days. It's also a good idea to set aside a small amount of cash as an emergency stash.

Credit Cards

The great advantage of credit cards is that they allow you to pay for major items without carrying around great wads of cash. The main credit cards – MasterCard, Visa and Eurocard – are widely accepted in Crete. American Express and Diner's Club charge cards are widely accepted in tourist areas, but unheard of elsewhere.

The big hotels and some mid-range places accept credit cards, but budget hotels and domatia do not. Likewise, upmarket shops and restaurants accept plastic but village tavernas and small shops do not.

Moneychangers

Banks will exchange all major currencies in either cash, travellers cheques or Euro-cheques. A passport is required to change travellers cheques, but not always for cash.

Commission charged on the exchange of banknotes and travellers cheques varie not only from bank to bank but also from branch to branch. It's less for cash than fo travellers cheques. For travellers cheques, the commission at some banks is €2 for each cheque, regardless of the amount. Post of fices can exchange banknotes – but not trav ellers cheques – and charge less commission than banks. Travel agencies and hotels often change money and travellers cheques at bank rates, but commission charges are higher.

Tipping

In restaurants the service charge is included in the bill, but it is customary to leave a smal tip or at least round off the bill. Likewise fo taxis – a small amount is appreciated.

Bargaining is not widespread in Crete Prices in most shops are marked and non negotiable, however, it's worth haggling over the price of accommodation, especially if you intend to stay a few days. You may get short shrift in peak season, but prices can drop dramatically at other times. It can also be effective in souvenir shops and market stalls – walking away often gets results

Travellers Cheques

The main reason to carry travellers cheques rather than cash is the protection they offer against theft. They are, however, losing popularity as more and more travellers opt to withdraw from ATMs as they go along.

American Express, Visa and Thomas Cook cheques are all widely accepted and have efficient replacement policies. Maintaining a record of the cheque numbers and recording when you use them is vital for replacing lost cheques. Keep this record separate from the cheques themselves.

PHOTOGRAPHY & VIDEO
Film & Equipment

Major brands of film are widely available Because of the brilliant sunlight in summer you'll get better results using a polarising lens filter. As with elsewhere in the world developing film is a competitive business Most places charge from €0.11 to €0.13 print and up to €1.50 service charge.

Restrictions

Never photograph a military installation or anything else that has a sign forbidding photography. Flash photography is not allowed inside churches, and it's considered taboo to photograph the main altar. Cretans usually love having their photos taken, but always ask permission first. The same goes for video cameras.

POST

Tahydromia (post offices) are easily identifiable by means of the blue and yellow signs outside. Regular post boxes are also yellow. The red boxes are for express mail.

Postal Rates

The postal rate for postcards and airmail letters to destinations within the EU is €0.65 for up to 20g and €1 for up to 50g. To other destinations the rate is €0.65 for up to 20g and €1.60 for up to 100g. Post within Europe takes four to five days and to the USA, Australia and New Zealand, five to eight days. Some tourist shops also sell stamps, but with 10% surcharge.

Express mail costs €2.65 and should ensure delivery in three days within the EU – use the special red post boxes. Valuables should be sent by registered post, which costs an extra €1.

Sending Mail

It is usually advisable not to wrap a parcel before you post it – the post office may (but not always) wish to inspect the contents. In Iraklio, take your parcel to the central post office on Plateia Daskalogianni, and elsewhere to the parcel counter of a regular post office.

Receiving Mail

You can receive mail poste restante (general delivery) at any main post office. The service is free, but you must have your passport. Ask senders to write your family name in capital letters on the envelope and underline it, and to mark the envelope 'poste restante'. If letters you are expecting cannot be located, it's a good idea to ask the post office clerk to check under your first name as well.

After one month, uncollected mail is returned to the sender. If you are about to leave a town and expected mail hasn't arrived, ask the post office to forward it to your next destination, c/o poste restante.

Parcels are not delivered in Crete; they must be collected from the post office.

SHOPPING

Crete has a long tradition of artisanship that has become a giant industry. Blue ceramics, clay pottery, handmade leather goods, woven rugs, icons, embroidered linen and finely wrought gold jewellery fill shops in all the tourist centres. In addition to crafted objects there are also Cretan wild herbs, olive oil, wine, sweet fruit preserves, cheeses, olives and other edibles.

Most of the products available in the ubiquitous souvenir shops are mass-produced. Although they can still offer good value, it's worthwhile to seek out special shops that offer authentic Cretan goods. Of all the large towns, you'll find the best selection of crafts at Hania where in the streets behind the harbour inspired artisans produce the Crete's most artful leather, jewellery and rugs.

Rethymno has a few good craft places among the plethora of souvenir shops, while Iraklio has more high-end and mainstream shops for clothing, appliances and records.

Several villages in the interior are known for their crafts. Theoretically, you can get good buys on linen in Anogia and Kritsa while spending a pleasant afternoon tooling around the countryside. However, take note – many of the items on sale are these days mass-produced in Hong Kong or Indonesia. Check carefully about the origin of the item before buying. Weaving shops in Hania (p85) or lace ateliers in Gavalohori (p117) can usually be relied upon to provide the genuine article.

Antiques

It is illegal to buy, sell, possess or export any antiquity in Crete (see Customs, p209). However, there are antiques and 'antiques'; a lot of items only a century or two old are regarded as junk, rather than part of the national heritage. These items include handmade furniture and odds and ends from rural areas, ecclesiastical ornaments from churches and items brought back from far-flung lands.

Ceramics

You will see ceramic objects of every shape and size – functional and ornamental – for sale throughout Crete.

The shiny dark-blue glaze of Cretan ceramics is easily distinguishable from the lighter matt finish of other Greek ceramics. The glaze should be hard enough not to scratch under the blade of a knife; a glazed bottom is the best sign of machine-made pottery.

There are a lot of places selling plaster copies of statues, busts, grave stellae and so on.

Jewellery

You'll find more idiosyncratic pieces in silver than gold. Look for replicas of Minoan objects such as the Phaestos disk, which are well crafted and available only in Crete. Select shops carry a great range of creative designs from local jewellers and some of Greece's leading contemporary designers. You can see local artisans in action at their studios in Hania.

Knives

Cretans are rightly proud of their distinctive, hand-crafted knives with rams-horn handles and heat-forged, razor-sharp blades. You'll see them on sale in many tourist centres, but few of them are made the old-fashioned way and while they may look good, they don't always cut the mustard. See p85 and the boxed text on p86 for tips on where to find the genuine item and see them being made – the traditional way.

Leather Work

Most of the leather is hard rather than supple, but it's fairly priced nonetheless. Durable bags, wallets, shoes and boots are best bought on 'leather lane' in Hania (p85). In Rethymno there are a few shops renowned for excellent leather goods (see p128).

Weaving

You will see many woven rugs and wall hangings for sale all over Crete. While these may look good and even be of a reasonable quality, much of the product on sale is machine-made in Crete or worse still, in Asia. For really genuine articles that you can see being woven, look no further than Hania's Old Town (see p85).

Wicker Chairs

There was a time when all Cretan tavernas had these wonderfully whacky wicker chairs that were incredibly uncomfortable to sit on for long periods, were usually too small for big bottoms and generally expensive to maintain. Sadly, plastic fantastic is now taking over the taverna seating scene

and handmade, wicker chairs are seen and sat on less and less. One place in Kissamos Kastelli is still churning them out by hand and can be bought relatively inexpensively. Shipping them home is the hard bit.

SOLO TRAVELLERS

Crete is generally a safe, friendly and hospitable place and you will have no problem travelling alone. It is common to see solo travellers backpacking through the island and you will no doubt hook up with others if you are staying at hostels, which is the best option. If you are staying in hotels or domatia, being single can be a major disadvantage because of the cost, although most places will knock 20% off the double room rate.

In general, use common sense when travelling. Avoid dark streets and parks at night, particularly in the major cities, and ensure your valuables are safely stored.

TELEPHONE

The Greek telephone service is maintained by the partly privatised public corporation known as Organismos Tilepikinonion Elladas (OTE – pronounced o-tay). The system is modern and efficient. Public telephones take phonecards, which cost €3 for 100 units, €6 for 200 units or €18 for 500 units. The 100-unit cards are widely available at *periptera,* corner shops and tourist shops; the others can be bought at OTE offices.

All phones take international calls. The 'i' button brings up the operating instructions in English. Don't remove your card before you are told to do so or you could wipe out the remaining credit. Local calls cost one unit per minute.

It is possible to use various national card schemes, such as Telstra Australia's Telecard, to make international calls. You will still need a phonecard to dial the scheme's access number, which will cost you one unit and the time you spend on the phone is charged at local call rates.

Villages and remote islands without OTE offices almost always have at least one metered phone for international and long distance calls – usually in a shop, *kafenei* (coffee house) or taverna.

Reverse charge (collect) calls can be made from an OTE office. If you are using a private phone, dial the operator (domestic ☎ 151, international ☎ 161).

To call overseas direct from Crete, dial the Greek overseas access code (☎ 00), followed by the country code for the country you are calling, then the local area code (dropping the leading zero if there is one) and then the number.

Mobile Phones

If you have a compatible GSM mobile (cell) phone from a country with an overseas global roaming arrangement with Greece, you will be able to use your phone in Crete, although the charges can be hefty. You must activate global roaming through your provider before you leave.

Greece has three mobile phone service providers – Vodaphone, CosmOTE and TIM. Of the three, CosmOTE tends to have the best coverage in the more remote areas, so you could try re-tuning your phone to CosmOTE if you find your mobile coverage is patchy. All three companies offer pay-as-you-talk services, so you can buy a rechargeable SIM card and have your own Greek mobile number: a good idea if you plan to spend time in Greece. These pay-as-you-talk services now automatically revert to global roaming when you leave Greece and can be used to send and receive SMS messages.

Note that American and Canadian mobile phone users will not be able to use their handsets anywhere in Greece, unless they are dual-band.

TIME

Greece is two hours ahead of GMT/UTC and three hours ahead on daylight-saving time, which begins on the last Sunday in March when clocks are put forward one hour. Daylight saving ends on the last Sunday in September.

TOILETS

Almost all places in Crete have Western-style toilets, but very occasionally outside the big towns you might come across Asian-style squat toilets in older houses, *kafeneia* (coffee houses) and public toilets. Public toilets are rare, except at airports and bus and train stations. Cafés are the best option if you get caught short, but you may be expected to buy something for the privilege.

One peculiarity of the Greek plumbing system is that it can't handle toilet paper – apparently the pipes are too narrow or at least most places are paranoid about blockages. Toilet paper etc should be placed in the small bin provided.

TOURIST INFORMATION

Tourist information in Crete is generally no longer handled by the Greek National Tourism Organisation, known by the initials GNTO abroad and EOT (Ellinikos Organismos Tourismou) in Greece. Municipal tourist offices in some areas have taken over the role, leaving EOT to deal with administration like classifying hotels, setting prices and monitoring the industry.

Some municipal offices, like those in Agios Nikolaos and Rethymno, are friendly and have useful information, but others have little more than brochures and a few maps. Some have absolutely nothing to offer.

USEFUL PHONE NUMBERS

Directory inquiries	☎ 131;
from a mobile phone	☎ 11831
Greece country code	☎ 30
International access code	☎ 00
International directory inquiries	☎ 139
International reverse charge calls	☎ 139

Toll-free 24-hour Emergency Numbers

Ambulance	☎ 166
Fire Brigade	☎ 199
Forestry Fire Service	☎ 191
Police	☎ 100
Roadside Assistance (ELPA)	☎ 10400
Tourist Police	☎ 171

GNTO offices abroad can give general information about Greece.

Australia (☎ 02 9241 1663; 51 Pitt St, Sydney NSW 2000)
Canada (☎ 416-968 2220; 91 Scollard St, Toronto, Ontario M5R IG4)
Denmark (☎ 38 32 53 32; Vester Farimagsgade 1, DK-1606 Copenhagen)
Japan (☎ 03 350 55 911; Fukuda Building West, 5F 2-11-3 Akasaka, Minato-Ku, Tokyo 107)
Netherlands (☎ 020 6248786; Kerkstraat 61, Amsterdam NS 1017)
Sweden (☎ 08 679 6480; Birger Jarlsgatan 30, Box 5298 S, S-10246 Stockholm)
Switzerland (☎ 01 221 01 05; Löwenstrasse 25, CH 8001 Zurich)
UK (☎ 020-7499 4976; 4 Conduit St, London W1R 0DJ)
USA (☎ 212-421 5777; Olympic Tower, 645 5th Ave, New York, NY 10022)

Tourist Police

The **tourist police** (☎ 171) work in cooperation with the regular Cretan police and EOT. There's always at least one member of staff who speaks English. Hotels, restaurants, travel agencies, tourist shops, tourist guides, waiters, taxi drivers and bus drivers all come under their jurisdiction. If you think that you've been ripped off, report it to the tourist police and they will investigate. If you need to report a theft or loss of a passport, the tourist police will act as interpreters between you and the regular police. The tourist police also dispense maps and brochures, and provide information on transport.

TOURS

The vast majority (80%) of visitors to Crete opt for a package holiday. Flight and accommodation packages can be a remarkably good deal, costing far less than booking your air fare and hotel room separately. The best-value deals can often pop up at the last minute as operators struggle to fill charter flights and block-booked hotel rooms. Most of the offerings are for large resorts along the northern coast. For a less industrialised holiday experience, you can try one of the following companies:

Diktynna Travel (☎ 28210 41458, 28210 43930; www.diktynna-travel.gr; Sfakion 36, 731 34 Hania, Greece)
Pure Crete (☎ 020-8760 0879; www.pure-crete.com; 79 George Street, Croydon, Surrey CRO 1LD, UK)
Simply Crete (☎ 020-8541 2201; www.simplytravel.com; Kings Place, Wood St, Kingston upon Thames, Surrey KT1 1SG, UK).

VISAS

Countries whose citizens can stay in Greece for up to three months without a visa include Australia, Canada, all EU countries, Iceland, Israel, Japan, New Zealand, Norway, Switzerland and the USA. Others include Cyprus, Malta, the European principalities of Monaco and San Marino, and most South American countries. The list changes, so contact Greek embassies for the latest information. Those not on the list can expect to pay about €20 for a three-month visa (see www.greekembassy.org for more details).

Turkish-Occupied North Cyprus

Greece may be reluctant to grant entry to people whose passport indicates they have visited Turkish-occupied North Cyprus since 1983. This can be avoided if, upon entering North Cyprus, you ask officials to stamp a piece of paper (loose-leaf visa) rather than your passport. If you enter North Cyprus from the Greek Republic of Cyprus (only possible for a day visit), an entry stamp is not put into your passport.

Visa Extensions

If you want to stay in Greece for longer than three months, apply at a consulate abroad or at least 20 days in advance to the **Aliens Bureau** (☎ 210 510 2831; Leoforos Alexandras 173, Athens; ☻ 8am-1pm Mon-Fri). Take your passport and four passport photographs along. You may be asked for proof that you can support yourself financially, so keep all your bank exchange slips. These slips are not always automatically given – you may have to ask for them.

In Crete, apply to the main prefecture in Iraklio. You will be given a permit that will authorise you to stay in Greece for a period of up to six months. Most travellers get around this by visiting Bulgaria or Turkey briefly and then re-entering Greece.

WOMEN TRAVELLERS

Many women travel alone in Crete. The crime rate remains relatively low, and solo travel is probably safer than in most European countries. This does not mean that you should be lulled into complacency; bag snatching and rapes do occur, although violent offences are rare.

The biggest annoyance to foreign women travelling alone are the guys the Greeks have icknamed *kamaki*, although they appear o be a dying breed. The word means 'fishing rident' and refers to their favourite pastime, 'ishing' for foreign women. You used to find hem everywhere there were lots of tourists, ut they are the exception these days. They an be very persistent, but they are a hassle ather than a threat. The majority of Greek nen treat foreign women with respect, and re genuinely helpful.

WORK
Permits
U nationals don't need a work permit, but ney need a residency permit if they intend o stay longer than three months. Nationals f other countries are supposed to have a ork permit.

Bar & Hostel Work
'he best bar and hotel jobs can pay quite vell – so well that they are usually taken y young Greeks from the mainland. Language training has improved dramatically n recent years eliminating the need for nultilingual foreign workers. Resorts such s Hersonisos and Malia that cater to British travellers are the best bet for Brits looking for bar work.

Holiday Rep
As a package-tour destination par excellence, Crete provides terrific opportunities for those people interested in working as a representative for a package tour company. Package tour companies based in Britain begin looking for personnel around February to fill the summer season needs.

You need to have good presentation, an outgoing personality and, usually, some tertiary education. The pay is low but you can make tips and some outfits allow reps to earn a percentage of the packages they sell.

Summer Harvest
Seasonal harvest work seems to be monopolised by migrant workers from Albania, and is no longer a viable option for travellers.

Volunteer Work
The **Sea Turtle Protection Society of Crete** (☎ /fax 210 523 1342; www.archelon.gr; Solomou 57, Athens 10432) welcomes volunteers for its monitoring programmes on Crete.

Other Work
There are often jobs advertised in the classifieds of the English-language newspapers, or you can place an advertisement yourself.

Transport

TRANSPORT

GETTING THERE & AWAY

For many visitors, getting to Crete means first getting to mainland Greece, usually Athens. However, it is also possible to fly directly to Crete from all over Europe on scheduled and charter flights.

ENTERING THE COUNTRY

To enter Greece you need a valid passport or, for EU nationals, travel documents (ID cards). You must produce your passport or EU travel documents when you register in a hotel or pension in Crete. You will find that many accommodation proprietors will want to keep your passport during your stay. This is not a compulsory requirement;

THINGS CHANGE...

The information in this chapter is particularly vulnerable to change. Check directly with the airline or a travel agent to make sure you understand how a fare (and the ticket you may buy) works and be aware of the security requirements for international travel. Shop carefully. The details given in this chapter should be regarded as pointers and are not a substitute for your own careful, up-to-date research.

---

they need it only long enough to take down the details.

AIR

Most travellers arrive in Crete by air, which is the quickest way to get there. There are regular flights from Athens, where most international flights arrive. In summer there are direct charter flights between the UK, Europe and Iraklio, but very few direct scheduled flights; most change at Athens or Thessaloniki.

Airports & Airlines

If you are flying to Crete on a scheduled flight, chances are you'll arrive in Athens (or possibly Thessaloniki) and then take a domestic flight to your final destination.

Athens Eleftherios Venizelos International Airport (code ATH; ☎ 210 353 0000; www.aia.gr) is 27km east of Athens near the village of Spata.

Iraklio's **Nikos Kazantzakis International Airport** (code HER; ☎ 281 022 8401) is the point of entry for most travellers arriving on Crete. Built many years ago when tourism was just taking off in Crete, it is adequate, although can be strained at times with the massive influx of arrivals during the summer.

The **Hania airport** (code CHQ) is smaller and somewhat more isolated, at 14km from Hania's town centre. It is, however, convenient for travellers heading to the west of Crete.

The **Sitia airport** (code JSH) opened a new long runway in 2003 and a new international terminal is due to start operating in 2005, expanding access to this part of the island.

AIRLINES FLYING TO/FROM GREECE

Aegean Airlines (code A3; ☎ 210 998 8300; www.aegean air.com)

Air Canada (code AC; ☎ 210 617 5321; www.aircanada.ca)

Air France (code AF; ☎ 210 960 1100; www.airfrance.com)

British Airways (code BA; ☎ 210 890 6666; www.british airways.com)

Cyprus Airways (code CY; ☎ 210 372 2722; www.cyprus air.com.cy)

Delta Air Lines (code DL; ☎ 210 331 1660; www.delta .com)

Easyjet (code U2; ☎ 210 353 0300; www.easyjet.com)

Emirates (code EK; ☎ 210 933 3400; www.emirates.com)

Gulf Air (code GF; ☎ 210 322 0851; www.gulfairco.com)

Hellas Jet (code T4; ☎ 210 624 4244; www.hellas-jet.com)
KLM (code KL; ☎ 210 911 0000; www.klm.com)
Lufthansa (code LH; ☎ 210 617 5200; www.lufthansa.com)
Olympic Airlines (code OA; ☎ 210 966 6666; www.olympicairlines.com)
Singapore Airlines (code SQ; ☎ 210 372 8000; www.singaporeair.com)
Thai Airways (code TG; ☎ 210 969 2010; www.thaiair.com)
Transavia (code HV; ☎ 281 030 0878; www.transavia.nl)
United Airlines (code UA; ☎ 210 924 2645; www.ual.com)

Olympic Airlines is the country's much-maligned national carrier. It handles the vast majority of domestic flights and has offices wherever there are flights, as well as in other major towns. Olympic offers a 25% student discount on domestic flights, but only if the flight is part of an international journey.

Aegean Airlines has flights between Athens, Hania and Iraklio. Its aircraft are modern and well appointed, and the service is generally excellent. Aegean also accepts Internet bookings and issues e-tickets. There are flights from Crete to Thessaloniki and connections via Athens or Thessaloniki to Frankfurt, Düsseldorf, Munich, Stuttgart, Paris, Milan and Rome.

Forward planning on all airlines is advisable as domestic flights to Crete can be packed in the high season. See individual destination chapters for details of flights to a specific destination.

The information throughout this book is for flights during high season (from mid-June to late-September). Outside of these months, the number of flights to the islands drops considerably.

Tickets

If you are flying to Crete from outside Europe, your plane ticket will probably be the most expensive item in your travel budget, and buying it can be an intimidating business. Take time to research the options offered by different airlines and travel agents, and start early – some of the cheapest tickets must be bought months in advance, and popular flights tend to sell out quickly. Domestic flights are often cheaper if they are attached to an international ticket.

Surf the Internet for good ticket buys. A good place to start is www.travelocity.com or www.itn.net.

AIRPORT TAXES

The airport departure tax for international departures and domestic flights varies from airport to airport and there are other taxes, too – all of which are included in the total cost of the ticket.

Charter Flights

Cheap charter flights to Crete operate from across Europe between April and October. Charter tickets are for seats left vacant on flights that have been block-booked by package companies. Tickets are cheap but flights are often at ungodly hours and conditions may apply, such as 'compulsory' accommodation vouchers (although in practice this requirement may be overlooked nowadays). This is particularly so with the advent of cheap scheduled services with operators such as Easyjet, or rock-bottom discounts on night flights with mainline operators such as British Airways.

Charter flight tickets are valid for up to four weeks, and usually have a minimum-stay requirement of at least three days. The tickets can be so cheap that it can be worth buying a charter return even if you plan to stay for longer than four weeks.

Look for cheap charter deals in the travel section of major newspapers or on the Web.

Australia

Olympic Airlines no longer flies to Australia, but has a code-share arrangement for daily flights to Sydney with Gulf Air. Thai Airways and Singapore Airlines also have convenient connections to Athens two to three times a week. Emirates has five flights a week via Dubai and Larnaca (the last stop being a killer as you can't get off the plane) to Melbourne. Some flights are a 14-hour nonstop trip from Dubai to Melbourne.

Canada

Olympic Airlines has four flights weekly from Toronto to Athens via Montreal. There are no direct flights from Vancouver, but there are connecting flights via Toronto, Amsterdam, Frankfurt and London on Air Canada, KLM, Lufthansa and British Airways. British Airways also has two flights per week from Montreal to Athens via London.

TRANSPORT

Europe
Athens is linked to every major city in Europe by either Olympic Airlines or the flag carrier of each country.

CYPRUS
Cyprus Airways has four flights weekly direct from Larnaca to Iraklio and five to six flights daily to Athens. Cyprus Airways also flies from Paphos to Athens three times a week in summer (less frequently in winter). Olympic Airlines has four flights daily from Larnaca to Athens.

FRANCE
Air France and Olympic Airlines operate a minimum of four Paris–Athens flights daily between them. However, charter flights are usually much cheaper.

GERMANY
Aegean Airlines has several flights from Iraklio connecting to Stuttgart, Düsseldorf, Munich and Frankfurt. Iraklio is linked by Lufthansa to Frankfurt with a direct flight on Wednesday, Friday and Sunday.

GREECE
The following table will give you an idea of the high-season frequency and approximate range of direct flight costs between mainland Greece and Crete.

Origin	Destination	Frequency	Fare*
Athens	Hania	5 daily	€50-72
Athens	Iraklio	6 daily	€65-90
Athens	Sitia	4 weekly	€65.50
Thessaloniki	Hania	4 weekly	€78-100
Thessaloniki	Iraklio	1-7 daily	€78-110
Rhodes	Iraklio	1-7 daily	€75

*one way excluding tax

THE NETHERLANDS
KLM-associate Transavia has direct flights between Amsterdam and Iraklio five times per week.

New Zealand
There are no direct flights from any New Zealand city to Athens. However, there are connecting flights via Sydney, Melbourne, Bangkok and Singapore on Olympic Airlines, United Airlines, Thai Airways and Singapore Airlines.

The UK
Daily flights between London and Athens are operated by British Airways and Olympic Airlines. Olympic also runs five direct London–Thessaloniki flights a week – all leaving from Heathrow.

Easyjet has two Luton–Athens flights daily and one flight from Gatwick on its no frills service. It can be the cheapest carrier if you book well in advance.

HellasJet flies to Athens daily from London Heathrow, six times a week from Gatwick and twice a week from Manchester.

There are numerous charter flights to Crete from London, Birmingham, Bristol, Cardiff, Edinburgh, Glasgow, Luton, Manchester and Newcastle. Try www.charterflights.c .uk or www.justtheflight.co.uk.

The USA
The North Atlantic is the world's busiest long-haul air corridor, and the flight options to Europe (including Greece) are bewilderingly extensive. For a full list of routes, check out www.expedia.msn.com, www.itn.net or www.travelocity.com.

New York has the most direct flights to Athens, with good connections to Crete. Olympic Airlines has at least one flight day and Delta Airlines has a daily flight between New York and Athens.

There are no direct flights to Athens from the west coast. There are, however, connecting flights to Athens from many US cities either linking with Olympic Airlines in New York or flying with one of the European national airlines to their home country, and then on to Athens.

LAND
Overland travel between Western Europe and Greece is mainly undertaken by car and motorcycle these days. Most drivers and riders take their car or bike to one of the Italian ports such as Venice, Ancona, Bari or Brindisi and ship it across to Igoumenitsa or Patra. Passports are rarely required when crossing western European borders, the exception being the borders with Switzerland.

There are no bus services to Greece from western or northern Europe.

Car & Motorcycle
Crossing from Italy to Greece no longer requires border formalities and is preferred

y the great majority of drivers and riders heading to Greece. There are four main Italian ports serving Greece: Bari, Brindisi, Ancona and Trieste.

It is still possible to travel to Greece via Slovenia, Croatia, Yugoslavia and the Former Yugoslav Republic of Macedonia, but the savings are not huge and are far outweighed by the distance involved and the necessity to cross five borders.

It is feasible on weekends in summer to arrive in Patra by ferry in the morning and be on a high-speed ferry to Crete by lunchtime, arriving in Iraklio late the same day. Otherwise, you can just as easily take an overnight ferry to Crete on the same day you arrive in Greece.

Train

Unless you have an **InterRail** (www.interrail .net) or **Eurail** (www.eurail.com) pass or are aged under 26 and eligible for a discounted fare, travelling to Greece by train is prohibitively expensive. In order to get to Crete, you can take a train to Brindisi in Italy and use your rail pass for a free passage to Patra in Greece. From Patra you can take a train directly to Piraeus harbour, or to Kalamata for your onward ferry connection to Crete.

SEA

Crete is well served by ferries in the summer and has mainland connections from Piraeus, Thessaloniki, Rhodes, Kalamata and Gythio, plus a smattering of Cyclades islands and Kythira. From November to April, however, services are considerably curtailed. Ferries are generally large car ferries and range in quality from 'comfortable' to luxurious. See www.ferries.gr for routes and timetables.

Routes

Greece's ferry hub is Piraeus, the port of Athens. Ferries to Crete all depart from the western end of Piraeus' sprawling port. The departure points are convenient for the Larisis train station in Piraeus, but involve a 10-minute hike from either the metro station or the nearby Peloponnisou station. From central Piraeus allow a good 15 to 20 minutes' walking to reach the Crete quays. Ferries leave here for Iraklio, Rethymno, Hania, Agios Nikolaos and Kissamos-Kastelli. Check the destination board at the stern of the ferry for your own route.

Schedules

Ferry timetables change from year to year and season to season, and ferries are subject to delays and cancellations at short notice due to bad weather, strikes or mechanical problems. No timetable is infallible, but the comprehensive weekly list of departures from Piraeus put out by the EOT in Athens is as accurate as humanly possible. You can pick up the list from any EOT office, and the main ferry schedules are also published in the English-language edition of *Kathimerini* that comes with the *International Herald Tribune*. For the most up-to-date ferry information ask the local *limenarhio* (port police), whose offices are usually on or near the quayside. The website www.ferries.gr has a useful search program and links.

Throughout the year there is at least one ferry a day from Piraeus to Crete. In summer there may be three or four per day.

Travelling time can vary considerably, depending on the ship and the route it takes. Before buying your ticket, check how many stops the boat is going to make, and its estimated arrival time.

ISLAND HOPPING TO CRETE

From Piraeus there are only two options for hopping off at other islands along the way to Crete. ANEN Lines' F/B *Myrtidiotissa* does a long 'milk run' via two Peloponnese ports and the islands of Kythira and Antikythira, while LANE Lines makes a stop in Milos in the western Cyclades on its thrice-weekly run to eastern Crete ports. From Thessaloniki, you have a choice of stopping off at Skiathos, Syros, Naxos, Mykonos or Santorini on Minoan Lines' F/B *El Greco* on its thrice-weekly haul from one end of the Aegean to the other. Alternatively, you can head to any of these intermediate islands from Piraeus or elsewhere and pick up the Iraklio connection at your leisure. From Rhodes you have a choice of three islands to hop off at: Halki, Karpathos and Kasos, using LANE Lines' connections from the Dodecanese (twice or thrice weekly). GA Ferries' F/B *Rodianthi* has a weekly service from Iraklio to Santorini, Naxos, Paros and Piraeus.

TRANSPORT

Costs

Prices are fixed by the government, and are determined by the distance travelled rather than by the facilities of a particular boat. There can be big differences in the size, comfort and facilities of boats offering rival services, but the fares will be the same. You may find that differences in prices at ticket agencies are the result of some agents sacrificing part of the commission to qualify as a 'discount service'. The discount is seldom more than €1.

Classes

The large ferries nominally have two classes (first and second) but the demarcation lines between them are often blurred (see the boxed text below for details). You pay instead for either the quality of the cabin, or the choice between aircraft-type seats or deck passage.

Cabins range from double-berth outside cabins (1st class) to four-berth inside cabins (2nd class). Aircraft-type seats can be very comfortable (Minoan's high-speed boat to bearable (most older boats). Deck cla is hard and uncompromising and not usu ally custom-designed for deck-class sleep ers. Modern ferry boats tend to have bar exposed deck sections, but there are alway wind-protected areas where you can set u temporary camp.

Deck class remains a cheap way to trave while a 1st-class ticket can cost almost a much as flying on some routes. Childre under four travel free, while children be tween four and 10 pay half fare. Full fare apply for children over 10 years of age. Ur less you state otherwise when purchasing ticket, you will automatically be given dec class. See the boxed text below for som sample fares.

Tickets

Ferries can be prone to delays and cancella tions in bad weather, so it's best not to bu a ticket until it has been confirmed that th ferry is operating, unless you want a cabi

---

FERRY TRAVEL TO CRETE

It wasn't too long ago that ferry travel in Greece was a true ordeal. Deregulation of the formerly closed domestic ferry market, a gradual upgrade of fleets and the aftershock of the F/B *Express Samina* sinking in September 2000 have significantly improved the domestic and international ferry scene.

Ferry services to and from Crete still differ in quality and service. The high-speed boats of Minoan Lines linking Piraeus and Iraklio, and Blue Star's services to Hania are by far the most comfortable means to get to and from the island. Both day and night services make the run to Crete or Piraeus in a flat six hours on modern, monster ferries – notably the F/B *Festos Palace* and the almost identical F/B *Knossos Palace*. Minoan's competitors ANEK are a comfortable option, although they still use older, smaller boats. Two smaller, ageing ANEK boats – the F/B *Preveli* and the F/B *Arkadi* – make the overnight run between Rethymno and Piraeus and are a popular choice among backpackers wishing to make landfall in central Crete. Larger ANEK boats also link the western Crete port of Souda, which serves Hania.

The one-boat ANEN Lines of western Crete run a small ferry linking Piraeus and Gythio or Kalamata in the Peloponnese with Kissamos-Kastelli. It is a long haul to Kissamos (19 hours), so Iraklio may be a quicker option. To the east, LANE Lines links Piraeus with Agios Nikolaos and Sitia with a stop in Milos. Its two boats F/B *Vitsentzos Kornaros* and F/B *Ierapetra* are fairly old, but comfortable enough.

Origin	Destination	Frequency	Duration	Fare (one way)
Piraeus	Agios Nikolaos	3 weekly	12 hr	€26.20
Piraeus	Hania (Souda)	2-3 daily	6-9 hr	€16-23.50
Piraeus	Iraklio	daily	7 hr	€29.50
Piraeus	Kissamos-Kastelli	5 weekly	19 hr	€22
Piraeus	Rethymno	1 daily	9 hr	€24
Thessaloniki	Iraklio	4 weekly	23 hr	€31.50

TRANSPORT

r it's the August peak season. If you need
o reserve a car space, you may need to pay
n advance. If the service is cancelled, you
an transfer your ticket to the next available
ervice with that company.

Agencies selling tickets line the water-
ront of most ports, but there's rarely one
hat sells tickets for every boat, and often
n agency is reluctant to give information
bout a boat it doesn't sell tickets for. This
neans you will have to check the timeta-
les displayed outside each agency to find
ut which ferry is next to depart – or ask
he port police. Ticket booths open up be-
ide a ferry about an hour before it's due
o depart.

acht

'achting is probably *the* way to see the
ireek Islands, but Crete is a long way from
•ther islands and does not have a huge
achting industry.

The free EOT booklet *Sailing the Greek
eas*, although long overdue for an update,
ontains information about weather con-
itions, weather bulletins, entry and exit

regulations, entry and exit ports, and guidebooks for yachties. You can pick up a copy
of the booklet at any GNTO/EOT office
either abroad or in Greece.

The sailing season lasts from April until
October. The best time to go depends on
where you are going. The most popular
time is between July and September, which
ties in with the high season for tourism,
but the *meltemi* winds in the Aegean can
ground you regularly.

You can hire a bare boat (a yacht without
a crew) if two crew members have a sailing certificate; otherwise you need to hire
a skipper for an extra €105 per day. Prices
start at €2000 per week for a 36-footer,
which will sleep six to eight, to €8000 for
a 54-footer that sleeps up to 12. For information about yachting in Crete log on to
www.yachting.gr/crete/crete.html. Most of
the hire companies are based in and around
Athens, including:

Alpha Yachting (☎ 210 968 0486; mano@otenet.gr;
Posidonos 67, 166 74 Glyfada)
Vernicos Yachts (☎ 210 989 6000; www.vernicos.gr;
Posidonos 11, 141 21 Alimo)

GETTING AROUND

BICYCLE

Cycling is becoming more common on Crete, but the often-hilly terrain means you need strong leg muscles. You can hire bikes in most tourist places, but they are not as widely available as cars and motorbikes. Prices range from €5 to €16 per day, depending on the type and age of the bike. Bicycles are carried free on ferries. See www.cycling.gr for information on mountain-biking tours and rentals from adventure travel company Trekking Hellas.

BOAT
Ferry

There are smaller boats linking the towns along Crete's south coast, some of which are only accessible by sea.

In summer, there are daily boats from Paleohora to Hora Sfakion, via Agia Roumeli, Sougia and Loutro, that offer wonderful coastal views. Although the schedules change from year to year, there are usually two to three boats a day between Hora Sfakion and Agia Roumeli and one boat a day from Hora Sfakion to Paleohora. There are also three boats a week in the summer between Paleohora and Gavdos Island.

There are also tourist boats that take excursions to offshore islands, including Ierapetra to Gaidouronisi (Hrysi) Island, Agios Nikolaos to Spinalonga, and Kissamos-Kastelli to the Gramvousa Peninsula. While it may be possible to negotiate with fishermen for trips on their caiques, it is illegal for fishing boats to take passengers.

Taxi Boat

Most southern port cities have taxi boats – small speedboats – that operate like taxis, transporting people to places that are difficult to get to by land. Some owners charge a set price for each person, and others charge a flat rate for the boat, with the cost divided by the number of passengers. Either way, prices are usually quite expensive.

BUS

Crete is an easy place to travel around thanks to a comprehensive public transport system. A four-lane national highway follows the north coast from Hania in the west to Agios Nikolaos in the east, and is being extended further west to Kissamos-Kastelli. There are frequent buses linking all the major northern towns from Kissamos-Kastelli to Sitia. Less frequent buses operate between the north coast towns and resorts and places of interest on the south coast, via the mountain villages of the interior. Fares are fixed by the government, and are very reasonable by European standards.

Buses are operated by regional collectives known as **KTEL** (Kino Tamio Eispraxeon Leoforion; www.ktel.org). Every prefecture has its own KTEL. The website has schedules for all the island buses, or try www.crete-buses.gr and www.bus-service-crete-ktel.com. Alternatively you can pick up a handy leaflet with Crete bus schedules, maps and local KTEL numbers at major KTEL bus stops.

Larger towns usually have a central, covered bus station with seating, waiting room, toilets and a snack bar selling pies, cakes and coffee. In small towns and villages the 'bus station' may be no more than a bus stop outside a *kafeneio* (coffee house) or taverna, which doubles as a booking office. Most booking offices have timetables in both Greek and English. The timetables give both the departure and return times – useful if you are making a day trip.

Regular and reliable buses link the major northern towns from Kissamos-Kastelli to Sitia. These buses are generally in good shape and more are now air-conditioned. Buses do not have toilets on board and they don't have refreshments available, so make sure you are prepared on both counts. Smoking is prohibited on all buses in Greece; only the chain-smoking drivers dare to ignore the no smoking signs.

Most buses use the northern highway, but there are at least one or two buses each day that use the old roads. The trip is more scenic but takes much longer, so ask before you buy the ticket. In major towns it's best to buy your ticket at the station to ensure you get a seat, but if you board at a stop along the way you buy your ticket from the conductor. Seat numbers are often indicated on the back of each seat, not on the back of the seat in front, which can cause confusion. The bus stations in major towns keep long opening hours and are also a good source of information. See the destination chapters for timetable information.

AR & MOTORCYCLE

Crete is big enough to warrant having your own vehicle, which is the best way to see the island and visit smaller, more out-of-the-way places. Roads have improved enormously in recent years, but in the remoter areas (particularly the south) you'll still find unpaved roads that are only suitable for Jeeps. While it is now quite easy to bring your own vehicle from Europe, there are plenty of places to hire both cars and motorcycles.

If you plan to explore Crete by car or scooter, prepare to spend a lot of time poring over maps, as country roads are generally badly signposted. Road signs, when they exist, are usually marked in Greek and English (the English phonetic sign follows a few metres after the Greek) except in remote areas. Even when written in Latin letters, the spelling of place names can vary wildly from the names on your map or in this book. Invest in a good map, but even the best maps don't cover all the side roads.

Automobile Associations

The Greek automobile club **ELPA** (☎ 210 779 1615; www.elpa.gr; Athens Tower, Mesogion 2-4, Athens 115 27) offers reciprocal services to members of national automobile associations on production of a valid membership card. If your vehicle breaks down, dial ☎ 10400.

Bring Your Own Vehicle

Cars can be brought into Greece for six months without a carnet (a customs licence); only a green card (international third-party insurance) is required. Cars entering Italy are subject to no customs formalities. Your vehicle will be registered in your passport when you enter to prevent you leaving the country without it.

Crete is well served by car ferries, but they are fairly expensive. The price for a car from Piraeus to Crete is €70. Small motorbikes are free most of the time.

Driving Licence

Crete recognises all national driving licences, provided the licence has been held for at least one year. It also recognises an International Driving Permit, which should be obtained before you leave home. If you plan to rent a motorcycle in Crete it is a good idea to have a separate motorcycle licence, as a growing number of rental agencies are now asking for

them. European driver's licences that allow you to drive a bike under 50cc are accepted, but travellers from most other countries will need a motorbike licence that is consistent with the size of bike you are hiring.

Fuel

In general, petrol in Greece is expensive, and the further you get from a major city the more it costs. Prices vary from petrol station to petrol station. Unleaded petrol – available everywhere – averages around €0.85 per litre. Super is several cents more expensive. Diesel costs about €0.60 per litre.

Hire
CAR

Hiring a car in Crete is more expensive than in other European countries, but the prices have dropped recently due to increasing competition. Major international companies have offices in most towns, but you'll usually get a better deal if you rent from a local company. If you choose a company with offices across Crete, you can arrange to pick up the car at one end of the island and drop it off elsewhere if you don't want to backtrack.

From international outfits, high-season weekly rates with unlimited mileage start at about €350 for the smallest models, dropping to €260 in winter. The many local companies are normally much cheaper (closer to low-season rates for the big companies) and even more open to negotiation if business is slow. Their advertised rates are about 25% cheaper than those offered by the multinationals. Some rates include comprehensive insurance, while others may quote lower rates but require collision damage or theft waivers, otherwise you are liable for a hefty portion of the repair bill (much more for larger models). Some companies offer much cheaper pre-booked and prepaid rates.

You can't take a hire car onto a ferry unless you have written authorisation from the hire company. Most companies will only rent you a car if you have a credit card.

The minimum driving age in Greece is 18 years of age, but most car-hire firms require you to be at least 23 years old, although many will rent to 21 year olds as long as they have had their licence for more than a year.

See the Getting Around sections of relevant cities for details of car-rental outlets.

TRANSPORT

MOTORCYCLE

Caution should be exercised when travelling by motorcycle. Roads change without warning from smooth and paved to cracked and pothole-ridden. Watch your speed. Greece is not the best place to initiate yourself into the world of motorcycling: many tourists have accidents every year.

Mopeds and motorcycles are available for hire wherever there are tourists to rent them. Note that you may be asked for a motorbike licence if you are planning to hire one. Experienced motorcyclists will find that a lightweight Enduro motorcycle between 400cc and 600cc is ideal for negotiating Crete's roads. In many cases maintenance is minimal, so check the machine thoroughly before you hire it – especially the brakes: you'll need them! When you rent a moped, tell the shop where you'll be going to ensure that your vehicle has enough power to get you up Crete's steep interior hills.

Motorbikes provide a cheap way to travel around. Rates start from €7 to €15 per day for a moped or 50cc motorbike. For a 250cc motorbike it's €17 to €27 per day, depend-ing on the length of hire. Out of season these prices drop considerably, so use your bargaining skills. By October it is sometimes possible to hire a moped for as little as €8 per day. Most motorcycle hirers include third party insurance in the price, but it is wise to check this. This insurance will not include medical expenses.

Insurance

If you are planning to use a motorcycle or moped, check that your travel insurance covers you for injury resulting from a motorbike accident. Many insurance companies don't offer this cover, so check the fine print!

Road Rules

It is hardly surprising that Greece has one of the highest road-fatality rates in Europe; it's a good place to practise your defensive driving skills! Overtaking is the biggest cause of accidents. Slow-driving tourists in hire cars can often be a hazard to drivers accustomed to the faster Greek driving manner and may provoke impatient and dangerous overtaking manoeuvres.

ROAD DISTANCES (KM)

	Agia Galini	Agios Nikolaos	Anogia	Elafonisi	Hania	Hora Sfakion	Ierapetra	Iraklio	Kissamos-Kastelli	Kolymbari	Malia	Matala	Omalos	Paleohora	Plakias	Rethymno	Sitia	Spili	Tzermiado	Zakros
Agia Galini	---																			
Agios Nikolaos	144	---																		
Anogia	118	104	---																	
Elafonisi	224	314	218	---																
Hania	119	209	113	105	---															
Hora Sfakion	45	215	119	70	70	---														
Ierapetra	137	36	140	352	247	182	---													
Iraklio	75	69	35	247	148	148	105	---												
Kissamos-Kastelli	173	263	167	51	54	124	301	196	---											
Kolymbari	144	234	138	65	25	95	261	167	14	---										
Malia	112	32	72	284	179	185	68	37	233	204	---									
Matala	29	138	104	253	148	123		69	265	173	106	---								
Omalos	163	253	157	149	44	114	291	186	98	69	223	255	---							
Paleohora	206	296	200	64	87	157	335	229	51	65	266	298	131	---						
Plakias	50	198	94	200	95	44	187	123	149	120	161	79	139	183	---					
Rethymno	62	152	56	162	57	63	190	85	111	62	122	91	101	144	39	---				
Sitia	199	73	177	387	282	290	62	142	336	307	105	211	326	369	265	227	---			
Spili	26	182	86	192	87	68	163	215	141	112	252	55	131	174	24	30	257	---		
Tzermiado	130	49	90	302	202		85	55	251	222	44	124	241	284	178	139	122	270	---	
Zakros	235	106	211	421	316	322	98	176	370	341	138	229	360	405	285	259	36	289	155	---

Driving in the major cities is a nightmare f erratic one-way streets and irregularly nforced parking rules. Cars are not towed ut parking tickets can be expensive. Parkng for the disabled is a rarity.

In Greece, as throughout Continental Eupe, you drive on the right and overtake n the left. Major highways have four lanes, though some are still two-lane highways rith large hard shoulders. These hard shoulers are often used for driving in, especially rhen being overtaken. Be prepared to move ver if someone wants to pass you.

Seatbelts must be worn in the front and ack seats, and you must travel with a firstid kit, fire extinguisher and warning triangle. Carrying cans of petrol is banned. Outside uilt-up areas, traffic on a main road has ight of way at intersections. In towns, vehiles coming from the right have right of way. 1otorcyclists riding bikes of 50cc or more aust wear helmets.

Hefty fines are levied for speeding and ther traffic and parking offences. Speed mits for cars are 120km/h on highways, 0km/h on other major roads and 50km/h n built-up areas. Speed limits for motorcyles are 70km/h (up to 100cc) and 90km/h above 100cc).

The blood-alcohol limit is 0.05%. Drink riving will incur a fine of €150, while anyiing over 0.08% is a criminal offence.

Payment of traffic fines is not made on he spot – you will be told where to pay. Reciprocal legal agreements between EU ountries may well mean that an ignored arking fine will turn up in your mailbox at ome a few weeks later. If you are involved 1 an accident and no-one is hurt, the police vill not be required to write a report, but it s advisable to go to a nearby police station nd explain what happened. A police report s required for insurance purposes. If an ccident involves injury, a driver who does ot stop and does not inform the police aay face a prison sentence.

HITCHING

Hitching is never entirely safe in any counry, and we don't recommend it as it is potentially serious risk. People who do choose to hitch will be safer if they travel in pairs and they should let someone know where they are planning to go. Greece has a reputation for being a relatively safe place for women to hitch, but it is still unwise to do it alone and it's better for women to have a male companion. In Crete you don't hitch with your thumb up as in northern Europe, but with an outstretched hand, palm down to the road.

Getting out of major cities tends to be hard work; hitching is much easier in remote areas. On country roads, it is not unknown for someone to stop and ask if you want a lift even if you haven't asked for one.

LOCAL TRANSPORT
Bus

Local city buses operating from Iraklio, Rethymno and Hania largely service the suburbs and are not practical for getting around the cities themselves. They are cheap and reliable, however, if not terribly comfortable. Tickets are normally bought at *periptera* (kiosks), small shops or once you board the bus. Don't board a bus without a ticket.

Taxi

Taxis are widely available except in remote villages, and are relatively cheap by European standards. Large towns have taxi stands that post a list of prices to outlying destinations, which removes any anxiety about over-charging. Otherwise you pay what's on the meter. Flagfall is €0.73 followed by €0.18 per km (€0.40 per km outside town or between midnight and 5am). There's a €0.90 surcharge from a bus station or port. Each piece of luggage weighing more than 10kg carries a surcharge of €0.15, and there's a surcharge of €0.90 for radio taxis. Rural taxis often do not have meters, so you should always settle on a price before you get in.

Taxi drivers in Crete are, on the whole, friendly, helpful and honest. If you have a complaint about a taxi driver, take the cab number and report your complaint to the tourist police.

Health

CONTENTS

BEFORE YOU GO

Prevention is key to staying healthy while abroad. A little planning before departure, particularly for pre-existing illnesses, will save trouble later on. Bring medications in their original, clearly labelled, containers. A signed and dated letter from your physician describing your medical conditions and medications, including generic names, is a good idea. If carrying syringes or needles, be sure to have a physician's letter stating their medical necessity. If you're planning a long trip, make sure your teeth are OK and take your optical prescription with you.

INSURANCE

If you're an EU citizen, an E111 form, available from health centres (and post offices

---

WARNING

Codeine, which is commonly found in headache preparations, is banned in Greece; check labels carefully, or risk prosecution. There are strict regulations applying to the importation of medicines into Greece, so obtain a certificate from your doctor that outlines any medication you may have to carry into the country with you.

---

in the UK), covers you for most medical care but not emergency repatriation home or non-emergencies. Citizens from other countries should find out if there is a reciprocal arrangement for free medical care between their country and Greece. If you do need health insurance, make sure you get a policy that covers you for the worst possible scenario, such as an accident requiring an emergency flight home. Find out in advance if your insurance plan will make payments directly to providers or reimburse you later for overseas health expenditures.

RECOMMENDED VACCINATIONS

No jabs are required to travel to Greece but a yellow-fever vaccination certificate is required if you are coming from an infected area. The World Health Organization (WHO) recommends that all travellers should be covered for diphtheria, tetanus, measles, mumps, rubella and polio.

ONLINE RESOURCES

The WHO's publication *International Travel and Health* is revised annually and is available online at www.who.int/ith/. Other useful websites include www.mdtravelhealth.com (travel health recommendations for every country; updated daily), www.fitfortravel.scot.nhs.uk (general travel advice for the lay person), www.ageconcern.org.uk (advice on travel for the elderly) and www.mariestopes.org.uk (information on women's health and contraception).

IN TRANSIT

DEEP VEIN THROMBOSIS (DVT)

Blood clots may form in the legs during plane flights, chiefly because of prolonged immobility (the longer the flight, the greater the risk). The chief symptom of DVT is swelling or pain of the foot, ankle, or calf, usually but not always on just one side. When a blood clot travels to the lungs, it may cause chest pain and breathing difficulties. Travellers with any of these symptoms should immediately seek medical attention. To prevent the development of DVT on long flights ou should walk about the cabin, contract he leg muscles while sitting, drink plenty of luids and avoid alcohol and tobacco.

ET LAG

o avoid jet lag drink plenty of nonalcoholic luids and eat light meals. Upon arrival, get xposure to natural sunlight and readjust our schedule (for meals, sleep, etc) as soon s possible.

N CRETE

AVAILABILITY & COST OF HEALTH CARE

f you need an ambulance in Crete call ☎ 166. Crete's major cities of Iraklio, Hania nd Rethymno have modern, well-equipped ospitals. Pharmacies can dispense medi- ines that are available only on prescription n most European countries, so you can con- ult a pharmacist for minor ailments.

All this sounds fine but, although medical raining is of a high standard in Greece, the ealth service is badly underfunded. Hos- itals can be overcrowded, hygiene is not lways what it should be and relatives are xpected to bring in food for the patient – /hich could be a problem for a tourist. Conditions and treatment are better in pri- ate hospitals, which are expensive. All this neans that a good health-insurance policy s essential.

RAVELLER'S DIARRHOEA

f you develop diarrhoea, be sure to drink lenty of fluids, preferably in the form of n oral rehydration solution such as dio- alyte. If diarrhoea is bloody, persists for nore than 72 hours or is accompanied by ever, shaking, chills or severe abdominal ain you should seek medical attention.

NVIRONMENTAL HAZARDS
Bites, Stings & Insect-Borne Diseases

Vatch out for sea urchins around rocky eaches; if you get some of their needles mbedded in your skin, olive oil will help to oosen them. If they are not removed they /ill become infected. Be wary also of jelly- sh, particularly during the months of Sep- ember and October. Although they are not ethal in Greece, their stings can be painful.)ousing in vinegar will deactivate any sting-

ers that have not 'fired'. Calamine lotion, antihistamines and analgesics may reduce the reaction and relieve the pain. Much more painful than either of these, but thankfully much rarer, is an encounter with the weever fish. It buries itself in the sand of the tidal zone with only its spines protruding, and injects a painful and powerful toxin if trod- den on. Soaking your foot in very hot water (which breaks down the poison) should solve the problem. It can cause permanent local paralysis in the worst case.

Greece's only dangerous snake is the adder. To minimize the possibilities of being bit- ten, always wear boots, socks and long trou- sers when walking through undergrowth where snakes may be present. Don't put your hands into holes and crevices, and be careful when collecting firewood. Snake bites do not cause instantaneous death and an antivenin is widely available. Keep the victim calm and still, wrap the bitten limb tightly, as you would for a sprained ankle, and attach a splint to immobilize it. Seek medical help, if possible with the dead snake for identification. Don't attempt to catch the snake if there is a possibility of being bitten again. Tourniquets and suck- ing out the poison are now comprehen- sively discredited.

Always check all over your body if you have been walking through a potentially tick-infested area as they can cause skin infections and other more serious diseases such as lyme disease and typhus. If a tick is found attached, press down around the tick's head with tweezers, grab the head and gently pull upwards. Avoid pulling the rear of the body as this may squeeze the tick's gut contents into the skin, increasing the risk of infection and disease. Lyme disease begins with the spreading of a rash at the site of the bite, accompanied by fever, headache, extreme fatigue, aching joints and mus- cles and severe neck stiffness. If untreated, symptoms usually disappear but disorders of the nervous system, heart and joints can develop later. Treatment works best early in the illness – medical help should be sought. Typhus begins with a fever, chills, headache and muscle pains, followed a few days later by a body rash. There is often a large painful sore at the site of the bite and nearby lymph nodes are swollen and painful. There is no vaccine available.

HEALTH

Rabies is still found in Greece but only in isolated areas. Any bite, scratch or even lick from a warm-blooded, furry animal should scrubbed with soap and running water immediately and then cleaned with an alcohol solution. If there is any possibility that the animal is infected medical help should be sought immediately. Even if the animal is not rabid, all bites should be treated seriously as they can become infected or can result in tetanus.

Heatstroke

Heatstroke occurs following excessive fluid loss with inadequate replacement of fluids and salt. Symptoms include headache, dizziness and tiredness. Dehydration is already happening by the time you feel thirsty – aim to drink sufficient water to produce pale, diluted urine. To treat heatstroke drink water and/or fruit juice, and cool the body with cold water and fans.

Hypothermia

Hypothermia occurs when the body loses heat faster than it can produce it. As ever, proper preparation will reduce the risks of getting it. Even on a hot day in the mountains, the weather can change rapidly so carry waterproof garments, warm layers and a hat, and inform other people of your route. Hypothermia starts with shivering, loss of judgment and clumsiness. Unless rewarming occurs, the sufferer deteriorates into apathy, confusion and coma. Prevent any further heat loss by seeking shelter, putting on warm dry clothing, drinking something hot and sweet, and sharing body warmth.

TRAVELLING WITH CHILDREN

Make sure children are up to date with routine vaccinations and discuss possible travel vaccines well before departure as some vaccines are not suitable for children under year. Lonely Planet's *Travel with Children* includes travel health advice for younger children.

WOMEN'S HEALTH

Emotional stress, exhaustion and travelling through different time zones can all contribute to an upset in the menstrual pattern.

If using oral contraceptives, remember some antibiotics, diarrhoea and vomiting can stop the pill from working. Time zones, gastrointestinal upsets and antibiotics do not affect injectable contraception.

Travelling during pregnancy is usually possible but always consult your doctor before planning your trip. The most risky times for travel are during the first 12 weeks of pregnancy and after 30 weeks.

SEXUAL HEALTH

Condoms are readily available but emergency contraception may not be, so take the necessary precautions.

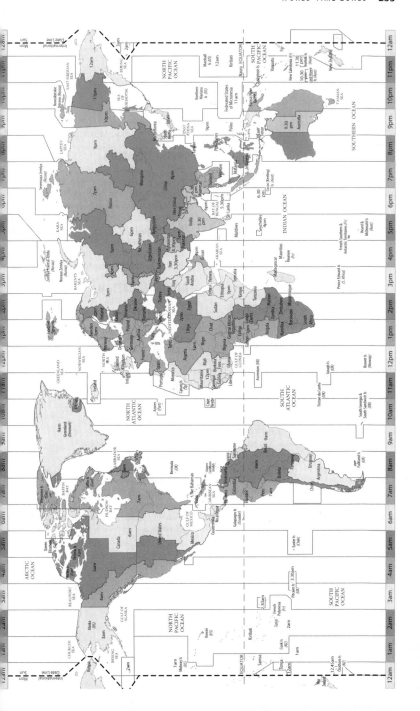

Language

The Greek language is probably the oldest European language, with an oral tradition of 4000 years and a written tradition of approximately 3000 years. Its evolution over the four millennia was characterised by its strength during the golden age of Athens and the Democracy (mid-5th century BC); its use as a lingua franca throughout the Middle Eastern world, spread by Alexander the Great and his successors as far as India during the Hellenistic period (330 BC to AD 100); its adaptation as the language of the new religion, Christianity; its use as the official language of the Eastern Roman Empire; and its eventual proclamation as the language of the Byzantine Empire (380–1453).

Greek maintained its status and prestige during the rise of the European Renaissance and was employed as the linguistic perspective for all contemporary sciences and terminologies during the period of Enlightenment. Today, Greek constitutes a large part of the vocabulary of any Indo-European language, and a large slice of the lexicon of any scientific repertoire.

The modern Greek language is a southern Greek dialect which is now used by most Greek speakers both in Greece and abroad. It is the result of an intralinguistic influence and synthesis of the ancient vocabulary combined with words from Greek regional dialects, namely Cretan, Cypriot and Macedonian.

Greek is spoken throughout Greece by a population of around 10 million, and by some five million Greeks who live abroad.

PRONUNCIATION

All Greek words of two or more syllable have an acute accent which indicates where the stress falls. For instance, άγαλμα (statue) is pronounced **aghalma**, and αγάπη (love) is pronounced **aghapi**. In the following transliterations, italic lettering indicate where stress falls. Note also that **dh** is pronounced as 'th' in 'then' and **gh** is a softer slightly guttural version of 'g'.

ACCOMMODATION

I'm looking for ...

psa·hno yi·a ...	Ψάχνω για ...
a room	
e·na dho·*ma*·ti·o	ένα δωμάτιο
a hotel	
e·na kse·no·dho·*chi*·o	ένα ξενοδοχείο
a youth hostel	
e·nan kse·*no*·na ne·*o*·ti·tas	έναν ξενώνα νεότητας

Where is a cheap hotel?

pou *i*·ne e·na fti·*no* xe·no·do·*hi*·o?
Πού είναι ένα φτηνό ξενοδοχείο;

What is the address?

pya *i*·ne i dhi·*ef*·thin·si?
Ποια είναι η διεύθυνση;

Could you write the address, please?

pa·ra·ka·*lo*, bo·*ri*·te na ghra·pse·te ti dhi·*ef*·thin·si?
Παρακαλώ, μπορείτε να γράψετε τη διεύθυνση;

Are there any rooms available?

i·*par*·chun e·*lef*·the·ra dho·*ma*·ti·a?
Υπάρχουν ελεύθερα δωμάτια;

I'd like to book ...

tha *i*·the·la na *kli*·so	Θα ήθελα να κλείσω ...
a bed	
e·na kre·*va*·ti	ένα κρεββάτι
a single room	
e·na mo·*no*·kli·o·no dho·*ma*·ti·o	ένα μονόκλινο δωμάτιο
a double room	
e·na *dhi*·kli·no dho·*ma*·ti·o	ένα δίκλινο δωμάτιο

THE GREEK ALPHABET & PRONUNCIATION

Greek	Pronunciation Guide		Example		
A α	a	as in 'father'	αγάπη	a-*gha*-pi	love
Β β	v	as in 'vine'	βήμα	*vi*-ma	step
Γ γ	gh	like a rough 'g'	γάτα	*gha*-ta	cat
	y	as in 'yes'	για	ya	for
Δ δ	dh	as in 'there'	δέμα	*dhe*-ma	parcel
Ε ε	e	as in 'egg'	ένας	*e*-nas	one (m)
Ζ ζ	z	as in 'zoo'	ζώο	*zo*-o	animal
Η η	i	as in 'feet'	ήταν	*i*-tan	was
Θ θ	th	as in 'throw'	θέμα	*the*-ma	theme
Ι ι	i	as in 'feet'	ίδιος	*i*-dhyos	same
Κ κ	k	as in 'kite'	καλά	ka-*la*	well
Λ λ	l	as in 'leg'	λάθος	*la*-thos	mistake
Μ μ	m	as in 'man'	μαμά	ma-*ma*	mother
Ν ν	n	as in 'net'	νερό	ne-*ro*	water
Ξ ξ	x	as in 'ox'	ξύδι	*ksi*-dhi	vinegar
Ο ο	o	as in 'hot'	όλα	*o*-la	all
Π π	p	as in 'pup'	πάω	*pa*-o	I go
Ρ ρ	r	as in 'road'	ρέμα	*re*-ma	stream
		a slightly trilled r	ρόδα	*ro*-dha	tyre
Σ σ, ς	s	as in 'sand'	σημάδι	si-*ma*-dhi	mark
Τ τ	t	as in 'tap'	τόπι	*to*-pi	ball
Υ υ	i	as in 'feet'	ύστερα	*is*-tera	after
Φ φ	f	as in 'find'	φύλλο	*fi*-lo	leaf
Χ χ	h	as the ch in Scottish loch, or like a rough h	χάνω	*ha*-no	I lose
			χέρι	*he*-ri	hand
Ψ ψ	ps	as in 'lapse'	ψωμί	pso-*mi*	bread
Ω ω	o	as in 'hot'	ώρα	*o*-ra	time

Combinations of Letters

The combinations of letters shown here are pronounced as follows:

Greek	Pronunciation Guide		Example		
ει	i	as in 'feet'	είδα	*i*-dha	I saw
οι	i	as in 'feet'	οικόπεδο	i-*ko*-pe-dho	land
αι	e	as in 'bet'	αίμα	*e*-ma	blood
ου	u	as in 'mood'	πού	pou	who/what
μπ	b	as in 'beer'	μπάλα	*ba*-la	ball
	mb	as in 'amber'	κάμπος	*kam*-bos	forest
ντ	d	as in 'dot'	ντουλάπα	dou-*la*-pa	wardrobe
	nd	as in 'bend'	πέντε	*pen*-de	five
γκ	g	as in 'God'	γκάζι	*ga*-zi	gas
γγ	ng	as in 'angle'	αγγελία	an-ge-*li*-a	announcement
γξ	ks	as in 'minks'	σφιγξ	sfinks	sphinx
τζ	dz	as in 'hands'	τζάκι	*dza*-ki	fireplace

The pairs of vowels shown above are pronounced separately if the first has an acute accent, or the second a dieresis, as in the examples below:

γαϊδουράκι	gai-dhou-*ra*-ki	little donkey
Κάιρο	*kai*-ro	Cairo

Some Greek consonant sounds have no English equivalent. The υ of the groups αυ, ευ and ηυ is generally pronounced 'v'. The Greek question mark is represented with the English equivalent of a semicolon ';'.

a room with a double bed
e·na dho·*ma*·ti·o me   ένα δωμάτιο με δυό
dhy·*o* kre·*va*·ti·a   κρεββάτια
a room with a bathroom
e·na dho·*ma*·ti·o me   ένα δωμάτιο με
ba·ni·o   μπάνιο

I'd like to share a dorm.
tha *i*·the·la na mi·*ra*·so e·na ki·*no* dho·*ma*·ti·o
me *al*·la *a*·to·ma
Θα ήθελα να μοιράσω ένα κοινό δωμάτιο
με άλλα άτομα

How much is it ...? *po*·so *ka*·ni ...?   Πόσο κάνει ...;
per night   ti ·vra·*dhya*   τη βραδυά
per person   to *a*·to·mo   το άτομο

May I see it?
bo·*ro* na to dho?   Μπορώ να το δω;
Where is the bathroom?
pou *i*·ne to·*ba*·ni·o?   Πού είναι το μπάνιο;
I'm/We're leaving today.
fev·gho/*fev*·ghou·me   Φεύγω/φεύγουμε
si·me·ra   σήμερα

CONVERSATION & ESSENTIALS
Hello.
ya·sas (polite)   Γειά σας.
ya·su (informal)   Γειά σου.
Goodbye.
an·*di*·o   Αντίο.
Yes.
ne   Ναι.
No.
o·hi   Οχι.
Please.
pa·ra·ka·*lo*   Παρακαλώ.
Thank you.
ef·ha·ri·*sto*   Ευχαριστώ.
That's fine/You're welcome.
pa·ra·ka·*lo*   Παρακαλώ.
Sorry. (excuse me, forgive me)
sigh·*no*·mi   Συγγνώμη.
What's your name?
pos sas *le*·ne?   Πώς σας λένε;
My name is ...
me *le*·ne ...   Με λένε ...
Where are you from?
a·*po* pou *i*·ste?   Από πού είστε;
I'm from ...
i·me a·*po* ...   Είμαι από ...
I (don't) like ...
(dhen) ma·*re*·si ...   (Δεν) μ' αρέσει ...
Just a minute.
mi·*so* lep·to   Μισό λεπτό.

DIRECTIONS
Where is ...?
pou *i*·ne ...?   Πού είναι...;
Straight ahead.
o·lo ef·*thi*·a   Ολο ευθεία.
Turn left.
strips·te a·ri·ste·ra   Στρίψτε αριστερά.
Turn right.
strips·te dhe·ksi·*a*   Στρίψτε δεξιά.
at the next corner
stin epo·me·ni gho·*ni*·a   στην επόμενη γωνία
at the traffic lights
sta *fo*·ta   στα φώτα

behind   *pi*·so   πίσω
in front of   bro·*sta*   μπροστά
far   ma·kri·*a*   μακριά
near (to)   kon·*da*   κοντά
opposite   a·*pe*·nan·di   απέναντι

acropolis   a·*kro*·po·li   ακρόπολη
beach   pa·ra·*li*·a   παραλία
bridge   *ye*fira   γέφυρα
castle   *ka*·stro   κάστρο
island   ni·*si*   νησί
main square   ken·dri·*ki*· pla·ti·a   κεντρική πλατεία
market   a·gho·*ra*   αγορά
museum   mu·*si*·o   μουσείο
old quarter   pa·li·a po·li   παλιά πόλη
ruins   ar·*he*·a   αρχαία
sea   *tha*·las·sa   θάλασσα
square   pla·*ti*·a   πλατεία
temple   na·*os*   ναός

HEALTH
I'm ill.   *i*·me a·ro·stos   Είμαι άρρωστος.
It hurts here.   po·*nai*· e·dho   πονάει εδώ.

TRANSLITERATION & VARIANT SPELLINGS: AN EXPLANATION

The issue of correctly transliterating Greek into the Latin alphabet is a vexed one, fraught with inconsistencies and pitfalls. The Greeks themselves are not very consistent in this respect, though things are gradually improving. The word 'Piraeus', for example, has been variously represented by the following transliterations: *Pireas*, *Piraievs* and *Pireefs*; and when appearing as a street name (eg Piraeus Street) you will also find *Pireos*!

This has been compounded by the linguistic minefield of diglossy, or the two forms of the Greek language. The purist form is called *Katharevousa* and the popular form is *Dimotiki* (Demotic). The Katharevousa form was never more than an artificiality and Dimotiki has always been spoken as the mainstream language, but this linguistic schizophrenia means there are often two Greek words for each English word. Thus, the word for 'baker' in everyday language is *fournos*, but the shop sign will more often than not say *artopoieion*. The baker's product will be known in the street as *psomi*, but in church as *artos*.

A further complication is the issue of anglicised vs hellenised forms of place names: Athina vs Athens, Patra vs Patras, Thiva vs Thebes, Evia vs Euboia – the list goes on and on! Toponymic diglossy (the existence of both an official and everyday name for a place) is responsible for Kerkyra/Corfu, Zante/Zakynthos, and Santorini/Thira. In this guide we usually provide modern Greek equivalents for town names, with one or two well known exceptions, eg Athens and Patras. For ancient sites, settlements or people from antiquity, we have tried to stick to the more familiar classical names; so we have Thucydides instead of Thoukididis, Mycenae instead of Mykines.

Problems in transliteration have particular implications for vowels, especially given that Greek has six ways of rendering the vowel sound 'ee', two ways of rendering the 'o' sound and two ways of rendering the 'e' sound. In most instances in this book, **y** has been used for the 'ee' sound when a Greek *upsilon* (υ, Υ) has been used, and **i** for Greek *ita* (η, Η) and *iota* (ι, Ι). In the case of the Greek vowel combinations that make the 'ee' sound, that is οι, ει and υι, an **i** has been used. For the two Greek 'e' sounds αι and ε, an **e** has been employed.

As far as consonants are concerned, the Greek letter *gamma* (γ, Γ) appears as **g** rather than **y** throughout this book. This means that *agios* (Greek for male saint) is used rather than *ayios*, and *agia* (female saint) rather than *ayia*. The letter *fi* (φ, Φ) can be transliterated as either **f** or **ph**. Here, a general rule of thumb is that classical names are spelt with a **ph** and modern names with an **f**. So Phaestos is used rather than Festos, and Folegandros is used rather than Pholegandros. The Greek *chi* (ξ, Ξ) has usually been represented as **h** in order to approximate the Greek pronunciation as closely as possible. Thus, we have Haralambos instead of Charalambos and Polytehniou instead of Polytechniou. Bear in mind that the **h** is to be pronounced as an aspirated 'h', much like the 'ch' in *loch*. The letter *kapa* (κ, Κ) has been used to represent that sound, except where well-known names from antiquity have adopted by convention the letter **c**, eg Polycrates, Acropolis.

Wherever reference to a street name is made, we have omitted the Greek word *odos*, but words for avenue (*leoforos*) and square (*plateia*) have been included.

I have ...		**penicillin**		
*e·*ho ...	Εχω ...	stin pe·ni·ki·*li*·ni	στην πενικιλλίνη
asthma		**bees**	
*asth·*ma	άσθμα	stis *me·*li·ses	στις μέλισσες
diabetes		**nuts**	
za·ha·ro·dhi·a·*vi*·ti	ζαχαροδιαβήτη	sta fi·*sti*·ki·a	στα φυστίκια
epilepsy			
e·pi·lip·*si*·a	επιληψία	**condoms**	pro·fi·la·kti·*ka*	προφυλακτικά
			(ka·*po*·tez)	(καπότες)
I'm allergic to ...		**contraceptive**	pro·fi·lak·ti·*ko*	προφυλακτικό
*i·*me a·ler·yi·*kos*/	Είμαι αλλεργικός/	**diarrhoea**	dhi·*a*·ri·a	διάρροια
a·ler·yi·*ki* ... (m/f)	αλλεργική ...	**medicine**	*farm·*a·ko	φάρμακο
antibiotics		**sunblock cream**	*kre·*ma i·*li*·u	κρέμα ηλίου
sta an·di·vi·o·ti·*ka*	στα αντιβιωτικά	**tampons**	tam·*bon*	ταμπόν
aspirin			
stin a·*spi*·ri·ni	στην ασπιρίνη		

LANGUAGE DIFFICULTIES

Do you speak English?
mi·*la*·te an·gli·*ka*?   Μιλάτε Αγγλικά;
Does anyone speak English?
mi·*lai* ka·*nis* an·gli·*ka*?   Μιλάει κανείς αγγλικά;
How do you say ... in Greek?
ps *le*·ghe·te ... sta   Πώς λέγεται ... στα
   el·li·ni·*ka*?   ελληνικά;
I understand.
ka·ta·la·*ve*·no   Καταλαβαίνω.
I don't understand.
dhen ka·ta·la·*ve*·no   Δεν καταλαβαίνω.
Please write it down.
ghrap·ste to, pa·ra·ka·*lo*   Γράψτε το, παρακαλώ.
Can you show me on the map?
bo·*ri*·te na mo·u to   Μπορείτε να μου το
   dhi·xe·te sto *har*·ti?   δείξετε στο χάρτη;

NUMBERS

0	mi·*dhen*	μηδέν
1	*e*·nas	ένας (m)
	mi·a	μία (f)
	e·na	ένα (n)
2	*dhi*·o	δύο
3	tris	τρεις (m&f)
	tri·a	τρία (n)
4	te·se·ris	τέσσερεις (m&f)
	te·se·ra	τέσσερα (n)
5	*pen*·de	πέντε
6	*e*·xi	έξη
7	ep·*ta*	επτά
8	oh·*to*	οχτώ
9	e·*ne*·a	εννέα
10	*dhe*·ka	δέκα
20	*ik*·o·si	είκοσι
30	tri·*an*·da	τριάντα
40	sa·*ran*·da	σαράντα
50	pe·*nin*·da	πενήντα
60	exin·da	εξήντα
70	ev·dho·*min*·da	εβδομήντα
80	oh·*dhon*·da	ογδόντα
90	ene*nin*da	ενενήντα
100	e·ka·*to*	εκατό
1000	*hi*·li·i	χίλιοι (m)
	hi·li·ez	χίλιες (f)
	hi·li·a	χίλια (n)
2000	dhi·o chi·*li*·a·dhez	δυό χιλιάδες

PAPERWORK

name
o·no·ma·te·*po*·ni·mo   ονοματεπώνυμο
nationality
i·pi·ko·o·ti·ta   υπηκοότητα
date of birth
i·me·ro·mi·*ni*·a yen·*ni*·se·os   ημερομηνία γεννήσεως

EMERGENCIES

Help!
vo·*i*·thya!   Βοήθεια!
There's been an accident.
ey·i·ne a·*ti*·hi·ma   Έγινε ατύχημα.
Go away!
fi·ye!   Φύγε!

Call ...!   fo·*nak*·ste ...!   Φωνάξτε ...!
   a doctor   *e*·na yi·a·*tro*   ένα γιατρό
   the police   tin a·sti·no·*mi*·a   την αστυνομία

place of birth
to·pos yen·*ni*·se·os   τόπος γεννήσεως
sex (gender)
fil·lon   φύλλον
passport
dhia·va·*ti*·ri·o   διαβατήριο
visa
vi·za   βίζα

QUESTION WORDS

Who/Which?
pi·*os*/pi·*a*/pi·*o*? (sg m/f/n)   Ποιος/Ποια/Ποιο;
pi·*i*/pi·*es*/pi·*a*? (pl m/f/n)   Ποιοι/Ποιες/Ποια;
Who's there?
pi·*os i*·ne e·*ki*?   Ποιος είναι εκεί;
Which street is this?
pi·*a* o·*dhos i*·ne af·*ti*?   Ποια οδός είναι αυτή;
What?
ti?   Τι;
What's this?
ti *i*·ne af·*to*?   Τι είναι αυτό;
Where?
pou?   Πού;
When?
po·te?   Πότε;
Why?
yi·a·*ti*?   Γιατί;
How?
pos?   Πώς;
How much?
po·so?   Πόσο;
How much does it cost?
po·so ka·ni?   Πόσο κάνει;

SHOPPING & SERVICES

I'd like to buy ...
the·lo n'a·gho·ra·so ...   Θέλω ν' αγοράσω ...
How much is it?
po·so ka·ni?   Πόσο κάνει;
I don't like it.
dhen mu a·*re*·si   Δεν μου αρέσει.

May I see it?
po·ro na to dho? | Μπορώ να το δω;
I'm just looking.
ap·los ki·ta·zo | Απλώς κοιτάζω.
It's cheap.
·ne fti·no | Είναι φτηνό.
It's too expensive.
·ne po·li a·kri·vo | Είναι πολύ ακριβό.
I'll take it.
tha to pa·ro | Θα το πάρω.

Do you accept ...? dhe·che·ste ...? | Δέχεστε ...;
  credit cards pi·sto·ti·ki kar·ta | πιστωτική κάρτα
  travellers tak·si·dhi·o·ti·kes | ταξιδιωτικές
  cheques e·pi·ta·ghes | επιταγές

more pe·ri·so·te·ro | περισσότερο
less li·gho·te·ro | λιγότερο
smaller mi·kro·te·ro | μικρότερο
bigger me·gha·li·te·ro | μεγαλύτερο

I'm looking for ... psach·no ya ... | Ψάχνω για ...
  a bank mya tra·pe·za | μια τράπεζα
  the church tin ek·kli·si·a | την εκκλησία
  the city centre to ken·dro tis po·lis | το κέντρο της πόλης
  the ... embassy tin ... pres·vi·a | την ... πρεσβεία
  the market ti· lai·ki· a·gho·ra | τη λαϊκή αγορά
  the museum to mu·si·o | το μουσείο
  the post office to ta·chi·dhro·mi·o | το ταχυδρομείο
  a public toilet mya dhi·mo·sia tu·a·let·ta | μια δημόσια τουαλέττα
  the telephone centre to ti·le·fo·ni·ko ken·dro | το τηλεφωνικό κέντρο
  the tourist office to tu·ri·st·iko ghra·fi·o | το τουριστικό γραφείο

TIME & DATES

What time is it? ti o·ra i·ne? | Τι ώρα είναι;
It's (2 o'clock). i·ne (dhi·o i· o·ra) | είναι (δύο η ώρα).
in the morning to pro·i | το πρωί
in the afternoon to a·po·yev·ma | το απόγευμα
in the evening to vra·dhi | το βράδυ
When? po·te? | Πότε;
today si·me·ra | σήμερα
tomorrow av·ri·o | αύριο
yesterday hthes | χθες

Monday dhef·te·ra | Δευτέρα
Tuesday tri·ti | Τρίτη
Wednesday te·tar·ti | Τετάρτη
Thursday pemp·ti | Πέμπτη
Friday pa·ras·ke·vi | Παρασκευή
Saturday sa·va·to | Σάββατο
Sunday kyri·a·ki | Κυριακή

January ia·nou·ar·i·os | Ιανουάριος
February fev·rou·ar·i·os | Φεβρουάριος
March mar·ti·os | Μάρτιος
April a·pri·li·os | Απρίλιος
May mai·os | Μάιος
June i·ou·ni·os | Ιούνιος
July i·ou·li·os | Ιούλιος
August av·ghous·tos | Αύγουστος
September sep·tem·vri·os | Σεπτέμβριος
October ok·to·vri·os | Οκτώβριος
November no·em·vri·os | Νοέμβριος
December dhe·kem·vri·os | Δεκέμβριος

TRANSPORT
Public Transport
What time does the ... leave/ arrive? ti o·ra fev·yi/ fta·ni to ...? | Τι ώρα φεύγει/ φτάνει το ...;
  boat pli·o | πλοίο
  (city) bus a·sti·ko | αστικό
  (intercity) bus le·o·fo·ri·o | λεωφορείο
  plane ae·ro·pla·no | αεροπλάνο
  train tre·no | τραίνο

I'd like (a) ... tha i·the·la (e·na) ... | Θα ήθελα (ένα) ...
  one way ticket a·plo isi·ti·ri·o | απλό εισιτήριο
  return ticket i·si·ti·ri·o me e·pi·stro·fi | εισιτήριο με επιστροφή
  1st class pro·ti· the·si | πρώτη θέση
  2nd class def·te·ri the·si | δεύτερη θέση

I want to go to ...
the·lo na pao sto/sti...
Θέλω να πάω στο/στη ...
The train has been cancelled/delayed.
to tre·no a·ki·rothi·ke/ka·thi·ste·ri·se
Το τραίνο ακυρώθηκε/καθυστέρησε

the first to pro·to | το πρώτο
the last to te·lef·te·o | το τελευταίο
platform number a·rithmos a·po·va·thras | αριθμός αποβάθρας
ticket office ek·dho·ti·ri·o i·si·ti·ri·on | εκδοτήριο εισιτηρίων
timetable dhro·mo·lo·gio | δρομολόγιο
train station si·dhi·ro·dhro·mi·kos stath·mos | σιδηροδρομικός σταθμός

Private Transport
I'd like to hire a ... tha i·the·la na ni·ki·a·so ... | Θα ήθελα να νοικιάσω ...

car	*e*·na af·ti·*ki*·ni·to	ένα αυτοκίντο
4WD	*e*·na *tes*·se·ra	ένα τέσσερα
	e·*pi tes*·se·ra	επί τέσσερα
(a jeep)	(*e*·na tzip)	(ένα τζιπ)
motorbike	*mya* mo·to·si·	μια μοτοσυ-
	klet·ta	κλέττα
bicycle	*e*·na po·*dhi*·la·to	ένα ποδήλατο

Is this the road to ...?
af·*tos i*·ne o *dhro*·mos ya ...?
Αυτός είναι ο δρόμος για ...;

Where's the next service station?
pu *i*·ne to e·*po*·me·no ven·zi·*na*·dhi·ko?
Πού είναι το επόμενο βενζινάδικο;

Please fill it up.
ye·*mi*·ste to pa·ra·ka·*lo*
Γεμίστε το, παρακαλώ.

I'd like (30) euros worth.
tha *i*·the·la (30) ev·*ro*
Θα ήθελα (30) ευρώ.

ROAD SIGNS

ΠΑΡΑΚΑΜΨΗ	Detour
ΑΠΑΓΟΡΕΥΕΤΕΑΙ Η ΕΙΣΟΔΟΣ	No Entry
ΑΠΑΓΟΡΕΥΕΤΑΙ Η ΠΡΟΣΠΕΡΑΣΗ	No Overtaking
ΑΠΑΓΟΡΕΥΕΤΑΙ ΗΣΤΑΘΜΕΥΣΗ	No Parking
ΕΙΣΟΔΟΣ	Entrance
ΜΗΝ ΠΑΡΚΑΡΕΤΕ ΕΔΩ	Keep Clear
(lit: don't park here)	
ΔΙΟΔΙΑ	Toll
ΚΙΝΔΥΝΟΣ	Danger
ΑΡΓΑ	Slow Down
ΕΞΟΔΟΣ	Exit

diesel	pet·*re*·le·o	πετρέλαιο
leaded petrol	*su*·per	σούπερ
unleaded petrol	a·*mo*·liv·dhi	αμόλυβδη

Can I park here?
bo·*ro* na par·*ka*·ro e·*dho*?
Μπορώ να παρκάρω εδώ;

Where do I pay?
pu pli·*ro*·no?
Πού πληρώνω;

The car/motorbike has broken down (at ...)
to af·to·*ki*·ni·to/mo·to·si·*klet*·ta *cha*·la·se sto ...
Το αυτοκίνητο/η μοτοσυκλέττα χάλασε στο ...

The car/motorbike won't start.
to af·to·*ki*·ni·to/mo·to·si·*klet*·ta dhen *per*·ni· bros
Το αυτοκίνητο/η μοτοσυκλέττα δεν παίρνει μπρος.

I have a flat tyre.
e·pa·tha *la*·sti·cho
Επαθα λάστιχο.

I've run out of petrol.
e·mi·na a·*po* ven·zi·ni
Εμεινα από βενζίνη.

I've had an accident.
e·pa·tha a·*ti*·chi·ma
Επαθα ατύχημα.

TRAVEL WITH CHILDREN

Is there a/an ...?	i·*par*·chi ...?	Υπάρχει ...;
I need a/an ...	chri·*a*·zo·me ...	Χρειάζομαι ...
a baby change	*me*·ros nal·*lak*·so	μέρος ν'αλλάξω
room	to mo·*ro*	το μωρό
car baby seat	*ka*·this·ma ya	κάθισμα για
	mo·*ro*	μωρό.
child-minding	*ba*·bi sit·ter	μπέιμπι σίττερ
service		
children's menu	me·*nu* ya pe·*dhya*	μενού για παιδιά
(disposable)	*pan*·nez Pam·pers	πάννες Pampers
nappies/diapers		
(English-	*ba*·bi sit·ter	μπέιμπι σίττερ
speaking)	pu mi·*la*	που μιλά
babysitter	an·ghl·*ika*	αγγλικά
highchair	pe·dhi·*ki* ka·*rek*·la	παιδική καρέκλα
potty	yo·*yo*	γιογιό
stroller	ka·rot·*sa*·ki	καροτσάκι

Do you mind if I breastfeed here?
bo·*ro* na thi·*la*·so e·*dho*?
Μπορώ να θηλάσω εδώ;

Are children allowed?
e·pi·*tre*·pon·de ta pe·*dhya*?
Επιρέπονται τα παιδιά;

Also available from Lonely Planet:
Greek Phrasebook

Glossary

Achaean civilisation – see *Mycenaean civilisation*

acropolis – highest point of an ancient city

agia (f), agios (m), agii (pl) – saint(s)

agora – commercial area of an ancient city; shopping precinct in modern Greece

amphora – large two-handled vase in which wine or oil was kept

architrave – part of the *entablature* that rests on the columns of a temple

arhontika – 17th- and 18th-century-AD mansions that belonged to arhons, the leading citizens of a town

baglamas – miniature *bouzouki* with a tinny sound

basilica – early Christian church

bouleuterion – council house

bouzouki – stringed lute-like instrument associated with *rembetika* music

bouzoukia – any nightclub where the *bouzouki* is played and low-grade folk songs are sung; see also *skyladika*

Byzantine Empire – characterised by the merging of Hellenistic culture and Christianity and named after Byzantium, the city on the Bosphorus that became the capital of the Roman Empire in AD 324; when the Roman Empire was formally divided in AD 395, Rome went into decline and the eastern capital, renamed Constantinople after Emperor Constantine I, flourished; the Byzantine Empire dissolved after the fall of Constantinople to the Turks in 1453

caïque – small, sturdy fishing boat

capital – top of a column

cella – room in a temple where the cult statue stood

choregos – wealthy citizen who financed choral and dramatic performances

classical Greece – period in which the Greek city–states reached the height of their wealth and power after the defeat of the Persians in the 5th century BC; ended with the decline of the city–states as a result of the Peloponnesian Wars, and the expansionist aspirations of Philip II, King of Macedon (r 359–336 BC) and his son, Alexander the Great (r 336–323 BC)

Corinthian – order of Greek architecture recognisable by columns with bell-shaped capitals with sculpted elaborate ornaments based on acanthus leaves

cornice – the upper part of the *entablature,* extending beyond the *frieze*

cyclopes – mythical one-eyed giants

dark age (1200–800 BC) – period in which Greece was under the rule of the *Dorians*

delfini – dolphin; common name for hydrofoil

dimarhio – town hall

Dimotiki – Demotic Greek language; the official spoken language of Greece

domatio (s), domatia (pl) – room; a cheap accommodation in most tourist areas

Dorians – Hellenic warriors who invaded Greece around 1200 BC, demolishing the city–states and destroying the Mycenaean civilisation; heralded Greece's *dark age*, when the artistic and cultural advancements of the Mycenaeans and Minoans were abandoned; the Dorians later developed into land-holding aristocrats, encouraging the resurgence of independent city–states led by wealthy aristocrats

Doric – order of Greek architecture characterised by a column that has no base, a fluted shaft and a relatively plain capital, when compared with the flourishes evident on *Ionic* and *Corinthian* capitals

ELPA – Elliniki Leshi Periigiseon & Aftokinitou; Greek motoring and touring club

ELTA – Ellinika Tahydromia; Greek post office

entablature – part of a temple between the tops of the columns and the roof

EOS – Ellinikos Orivatikos Syllogos; the association of Greek Mountaineering Clubs

EOT – Ellinikos Organismos Tourismou; Greek National Tourism Organisation

Epitaphios – structure depicting Christ on his bier, decorated for the Easter procession

estiatorio – restaurant

faïence – an ancient glazing technique that uses quartz instead of glass

Filiki Eteria – friendly society; a group of Greeks in exile; formed during Ottoman rule to organise an uprising against the Turks

fluted – of a column having vertical indentations on the shaft

FPA – foros prostithemenis axias; Value Added Tax, or VAT

frieze – part of the *entablature*, which is above the architrave

galaktopoleio (s), galaktopoleia (pl) – a shop that sells dairy products

Geometric period (1200–800 BC) – the period characterised by pottery decorated with geometric designs; sometimes referred to as Greece's *dark age*

Hellas, Ellas or Ellada – the Greek name for Greece

Hellenistic period – prosperous, influential period of Greek civilisation ushered in by Alexander the Great's empire-building and lasting until the Roman sacking of Corinth in 146 BC

hora – main town, usually on an island

iconostasis – altar screen embellished with icons
ikonostasia – miniature chapels
Ionic – order of Greek architecture characterised by a column with truncated flutes and capitals with ornaments resembling scrolls

kafeneio (s), kafeneia (pl) – traditionally a male-only coffee house where cards and backgammon are played
kalderimi – cobbled footpath
kastelli – castle
kastro – caste, fortress, bastion
katholikon – principal church of a monastic complex
kefi – an indefinable feeling of good spirit, without which no Greek can have a good time
kilimia – flat-woven rugs that were traditional dowry gifts
Koine – Greek language used in pre-Byzantine times; the language of the church liturgy
kore – female statue of the Archaic period; see also *kouros*
kouros – male statue of the Archaic period, characterised by a stiff body posture and enigmatic smile
kri-kri – endemic Cretan animal similar to a goat
KTEL – Kino Tamio Eispraxeon Leoforion; national bus cooperative, which runs all long-distance bus services

labrys – double-axe symbol of Minoan civilization
lammergeier – bearded vulture
leoforos – avenue
libation – in ancient Greece, wine or food which was offered to the gods
Linear A – Minoan script; so far undeciphered
Linear B – Mycenaean script; has been deciphered
lyra – small violin-like instrument, played on the knee; common in Cretan and Pontian music

malakas – literally 'wanker'; used as a familiar term of address, or as an insult, depending on context
mangas – 'wide boy' or 'dude'; originally a person of the underworld, now any streetwise person
mandinada (s), mandinades (pl) – traditional Cretan rhyming song/s, often with improvised lyrics
mayirefta – pre-made casseroles and bakes served at *tavernas* and other eateries
megaron – central room of a Mycenaean palace
meltemi – northeasterly wind that blows throughout much of Greece in the summer
metope – sculpted section of a Doric *frieze*
mezedopoleio – *mezes* restaurant
mezes (s), mezedes (pl) – appetiser/s
Minoan civilisation (3000–1200 BC) – Bronze Age culture of Crete named after the mythical King Minos and characterised by pottery and metalwork of great

beauty and artisanship; it has three periods: Protopalatial (3400–2100 BC), Neopalatial (2100–1580 BC) and Post-palatial (1580–1200 BC)
mitata – round stone shepherd's huts
moni – monastery or convent
Mycenaean civilisation (1900–1100 BC) – first great civilisation of the Greek mainland, characterised by power-ful independent city–states ruled by kings; also known as the *Achaean civilisation*

narthex – porch of a church
Nea Dimokratia – New Democracy; conservative political party
necropolis – literally 'city of the dead'; ancient cemetery
nomarhia – prefecture building
nomos – prefectures into which the regions and island groups of Greece are divided
nymphaeum – in ancient Greece, building containing a fountain and often dedicated to nymphs

odeion – ancient Greek indoor theatre
odos – street
OTE – Organismos Tilepikinonion Elladas; national telephone carrier
oud – a bulbous, stringed instrument with a sharply raked-back head
ouzeri – place that serves ouzo and light snacks

Panagia – Mother of God; name frequently used for churches
Pandokrator – painting or mosaic of Christ in the centre of the dome of a Byzantine church
pandopoleio – general store
paralia – waterfront
pediment – triangular section, often filled with sculpture above the columns, found at the front and back of a classical Greek temple
periptero (s), periptera (pl) – street kiosk
peristyle – columns surrounding a building, usually a temple or courtyard
pinakothiki – picture gallery
pithos (s), pithoi (pl) – large Minoan storage jar
plateia – square
propylon (s), propylaia (pl) – elaborately built main entrance to an ancient city or sanctuary; a propylon had one gateway and a propylaia more than one

raki – Crete's fiery spirit, distilled from grapes
rembetika – blues songs commonly associated with the underworld of the 1920s
rhyton – another name for a libation vessel
rizitika – traditional, patriotic songs of western Crete

sandouri – hammered dulcimer from Asia Minor
skyladika – literally 'dog songs'; popular, but not lyrically challenging, often sung in *bouzoukia* nightclubs

spileo – cave
stele (s), stelae (pl) – gravestone that stands upright
stoa – long colonnaded building, usually in an *agora*; used as a meeting place and shelter in ancient Greece

tahydromia – post offices
taverna – traditional restaurant that serves food and wine
temblon – votive screen

tholos – Mycenaean tomb shaped like a beehive
toumberleki – small lap drum played with the fingers
triglyph – sections of a Doric *frieze* between the *metopes*
trireme – ancient Greek galley with three rows of oars on each side
tsikoudia – a local version of a distilled spirit from grapes

volta – promenade; evening stroll
volute – spiral decoration on *Ionic* capitals

Behind the Scenes

THIS BOOK

This is the 3rd edition of *Crete*. The 1st edition was written in 2000 by Jeanne Oliver. Paul Hellander wrote the 2nd edition in 2002, and Victoria Kyriakopoulos thoroughly updated this 3rd edition. Many thanks to Graham Williams of Lonely Planet's London office, who contributed the Walks Around Loutro section in the Hania chapter.

THANKS from the Author

My heartfelt thanks to the many people who shared this journey, one way or another. I was overwhelmed by the kindness of many strangers who welcomed me along the way, proving that the renowned Cretan hospitality is not a myth.

Many thanks to those who helped me road test the book, shared their insight and love for Crete, tolerated my endless quizzing and shared some delicious meals, great conversations and copious quantities of raki: Maria Zygourakis, Eleni Giakoumaki and Grecotel, Dimitris Kalaitzidakis and Yiannis Papatzanis in Rethymno; Stelios Daskalakis, Iakovos Sourgoutsidis and Eleftheria Kourkounaki in Hania; Sonia Panagiotidou, Yiorgos Margarakis, Yiannis Xylouris and Yiorgos Petrakis in Iraklio; Theodoros Consolas and Yiorgos in Gavdos; Foni Patramani and family and the entire village of Episkopi; Nikos Perakis in Kato Zakros; Evangelia and Tom in Sitia; Grigoris Thomakakis in Avdou; Korina Miliaraki in Panormo; Antonios Bodikos in Matala; Kyriakos Kotaras at GATS travel; Dimitris, Nikoleta and Antonis in Agios Pavlos; and Voula Gogorosi, Philip Hunt, Voula Liaka, Apostolis Angelopoulos, Christina Pirovolakis, Giorgos Xylouris and Camilo Nollas.

Thanks also to Paul Hellander who worked on the previous edition, to archaeologist Alexander McGilivray, to Susie and John Rerakis in Melbourne, to Michala Green at Lonely Planet London for her patience, and to my family in Melbourne and Greece.

And special thanks to Chris Anastassiades for his friendship and support.

CREDITS

Crete 3 was commissioned in Lonely Planet's London office by Michala Green. Regional publishing manager Katrina Browning oversaw the development of this title with the assistance of Amanda Canning. Cartography was developed by Mark Griffiths and the project was managed by Glenn van der Knijff, with some last-minute help by Bridget Blair.

This book was edited by Pete Cruttenden and proofed by Nancy Ianni. Anthony Phelan coordinated the cartography, assisted by Jovan Djukanovic, while Indra Kilfoyle was responsible for the book's layout, with Kate McDonald and Adriana Mammarella overseeing its production. Thanks also to Annika Roojun who designed the cover and James Hardy for preparing the artwork.

THANKS from Lonely Planet

Many thanks to the following travellers who used the last edition and wrote to us with helpful hints, useful advice and interesting anecdotes.

B Hubert Bansemer, Sybille Birkhorst, Esthe & Aad Boevé **C** Brooke Cameron, Marie Coffey, Natalie Cohen **D** Mary & Miro Dancuk, Kate Dawson **E** Rit Elst, Walter Engelskirchen, Amanda Evans **F** Johan Forsberg **G** Jill & Ian Gibson, Wojciech Grabek, Sandra Grant, Ursula Groves **H** Christina Haigh, Paul Harris, Margaret Heuen, Ken Hunt **J** Lesley Jefferis, Laurie Jones, Rebecca Jones **K** Martin & Esther Kafer, Lou Kolberg, Jochen Kuehling **L** Marie-Andrée Laferrière, Miranda Lane, DC Long, Julian Lord, Tim Lucas **M** Deb Makewell, Paul Marijnissen, Neil McCabe, Catherine McClintock, Professor J H Medlock, Paddy Morton **O** FM Oddy, Rosemary O'Gorman **P** Alina Pantazidou, Eirini Pelekanaki, John Peppiatt, James Perrett, Clarisse Pizarro, Marilyn Powell **Q** Floor Quirijns **R** Petra Rothbart **S** Joseph Shaw, Lorna Slater, Russell Spencer, Toni Spiller, Robyn Spurdle, Peter Stephenson, Darren Stevens **T** Stephen Jesse Taylor **W** Judith Whitworth, Gareth Williams **Z** Michal Zaremba

ACKNOWLEDGMENTS

Globe on back cover © Mountain High Maps 1993 Digital Wisdom, Inc.

SEND US YOUR FEEDBACK

We love to hear from travellers – your comments keep us on our toes and help make our books better. Our well-travelled team reads every word on what you loved or loathed about this book. Although we cannot reply individually to postal submissions, we always guarantee that your feedback goes straight to the appropriate authors, in time for the next edition. Each person who sends us information is thanked in the next edition – and the most useful submissions are rewarded with a free book.

To send us your updates (and find out about Lonely Planet events, newsletters and travel news) visit our award-winning website: **www.lonelyplanet.com/feedback**.

Note: We may edit, reproduce and incorporate your comments in Lonely Planet products such as guidebooks, websites and digital products, so let us know if you don't want your comments reproduced or your name acknowledged. For a copy of our privacy policy visit www.lonelyplanet.com/privacy.

Index

INDEX

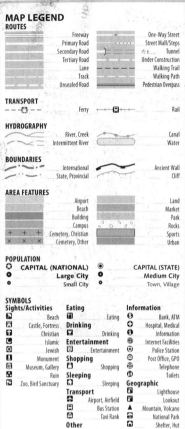

LONELY PLANET OFFICES

Australia
Head Office
Locked Bag 1, Footscray, Victoria 3011
☎ 03 8379 8000, fax 03 8379 8111
talk2us@lonelyplanet.com.au

USA
150 Linden St, Oakland, CA 94607
☎ 510 893 8555, toll free 800 275 8555
fax 510 893 8572, info@lonelyplanet.com

UK
72–82 Rosebery Ave,
Clerkenwell, London EC1R 4RW
☎ 020 7841 9000, fax 020 7841 9001
go@lonelyplanet.co.uk

Published by Lonely Planet Publications Pty Ltd
ABN 36 005 607 983

© Lonely Planet 2005

© photographers as indicated 2005

Cover photographs: Harbourside at Eloundra, Lasithi prefecture, Pe
Adams/Photolibrary.com (front); A doorway festooned with flowe
in Rethymno, Rethymno prefecture, Neil Setchfield/Lonely Plar
Images (back). Many of the images in this guide are available
licensing from Lonely Planet Images: www.lonelyplanetimages.com

Printed through Colorcraft Ltd, Hong Kong
Printed in China